Democracy in America

MODERN LIBRARY
COLLEGE EDITIONS

Advisor

R. JACKSON WILSON
Smith College

Democracy
IN AMERICA
By *ALEXIS DE TOCQUEVILLE*

THE HENRY REEVE TEXT
AS REVISED BY FRANCIS BOWEN
AND FURTHER CORRECTED BY
PHILLIPS BRADLEY

Abridged with an Introduction by
THOMAS BENDER
New York University

The Modern Library
New York

First Edition

98765

Library of Congress Cataloging in Publication Data

Tocqueville, Alexis Charles Henri Maurice Clérel de,
   1805–1859.
   Democracy in America.

   (Modern Library college editions)
   Translation of De la démocratie en Amérique.
   Bibliography: p.
   1. United States—Politics and government.
2. United States—Social conditions.   3. Democracy.
I. Bender, Thomas.   II. Title.
JK216.T7 1981   321.8′042′0973   80-24544
ISBN 0-394-32675-X

CONTENTS

[*Democracy in America* was originally published in French in four volumes; the first two were published together in 1835 and the second two in 1840. It has been customary to refer to the parts published in 1835 as Volume One and the parts published in 1840 as Volume Two. These two volumes have been brought together in one volume in this edition, but the combined Table of Contents preserves the traditional two-volume division.]

Contents of VOLUME I

Contents of VOLUME II

First Book

INFLUENCE OF DEMOCRACY ON THE ACTION OF INTELLECT IN THE UNITED STATES

CONTENTS

Second Book

INFLUENCE OF DEMOCRACY ON THE FEELINGS OF THE AMERICANS

Third Book

INFLUENCE OF DEMOCRACY ON MANNERS
PROPERLY SO CALLED

Fourth Book

INFLUENCE OF DEMOCRATIC IDEAS AND FEELINGS ON POLITICAL SOCIETY

INTRODUCTION

The book you are about to read has a particular history. It was written at a specific time for a specific audience and for a specific purpose. Yet it is also one of those books, those we call classics, that overflow such bounds to become timeless; that is to say, they speak to other times and places as well as to their own. My aim in this introduction is to place *Democracy in America* into its own context and to suggest as well why it will be read as long as democracy or the dream of democracy survives.

In 1831 Alexis de Tocqueville, a twenty-six-year-old Frenchman of aristocratic background, arrived in the United States with the intention, as he put it just before embarking, of "examining, in detail and as scientifically as possible, all the mechanisms of the vast American society which everyone talks of and no one knows." The book he wrote on his return to France in fact reached for far more. "I confess," he acknowledged in the introduction to *Democracy in America*, "that in America I saw more than America; I sought there the image of democracy itself."

Tocqueville came to America possessed by a single great idea, the progressive and inevitable leveling of social conditions in Western civilization. "The gradual development of the principle of equality," he wrote, "is a providential fact. It has all the chief characteristics of such a fact: it is universal, it is lasting, it constantly eludes all interference, and all events as well as all men contribute to its progress." The idea was not original with Tocqueville; he probably heard it developed in François Guizot's lectures on "The History of French Civilization," which he attended less than a year before he journeyed to America. Tocqueville's fame rests not on the idea itself but on his profound reflections on its implications. The immensity of the problem posed by this historical tendency was, as Tocqueville announced in his introduction, the grand theme for *Democracy in America:* "The whole book that is here offered to the public has been written under the influence of a kind of religious terror produced in the author's soul by the view of that irresistible revolution which has advanced for centuries in spite of every obstacle and which is still advancing in the midst of the ruin it has caused."*

The mood of lofty detachment that marks the pages of *Democracy in America* comes, in part, from Tocqueville's acceptance of this profoundly discomforting fact. He accepted equality as a modern condition that he could neither embrace nor reject. He recognized, as he feared conservatives in France did not, that the movement toward democracy had too much momentum to be stopped. Yet he did not counsel passivity or withdrawal before the challenge of equality and its political product, democracy. He insisted that its progress "is not yet so rapid that it cannot be guided." Tocqueville's self-appointed mission was to provide his countrymen with the political wisdom that would be required to direct the democracy that loomed inevitably on France's political horizon toward liberty rather than toward tyranny.

*This passage is badly translated in the widely accepted Henry Reeve text corrected by Francis Bowen here reprinted. This translation renders *d'une sort de terreur religieuse produite dans l'âme de l'auteur* as "a kind of religious awe produced in the author's mind." I have altered the translation because I think the Reeve-Bowen translation loses the full emotional impact of the statement as Tocqueville wrote it in French. I bother to make this point because Tocqueville referred to a personal feeling of terror only twice in his published work, here and in *The Old Regime and the Revolution* (1856) where he described his realization in reading the *cahiers* of 1789 that the sum of their demands amounted to the doom of every existing institution. For a man who lost family in the Terror of the French Revolution, these references to terror were not casual. Like the Revolution the egalitarian onslaught of the nineteenth century shook the aristocratic Tocqueville to the depths of his soul.

Although *Democracy in America* has often been cited by Americans as the most impressive example of the genre of foreign-travel literature on America, such a categorization misplaces Tocqueville and misuses his contribution to American culture studies. The quality that distinguishes *Democracy in America* from other travel accounts is not merely that Tocqueville was better than his fellow travelers to America, but rather that he sought to accomplish something far more ambitious. Describing America was secondary to his primary intention of instructing his countrymen about the philosophy of democracy in modern times. Such is Tocqueville's special contribution and the source of the rich texture that sets *Democracy in America* apart from other travel books. He belongs in more select company than that provided by travel writers, no matter how perceptive they might have been. He is more properly placed with political analysts in a tradition that includes Aristotle, Machiavelli, and, especially, his French predecessor Montesquieu.

The philosophical character of *Democracy in America* is apparent in the very structure of the book. The chapters in a travel book ordinarily follow the itinerary of the author; *Democracy in America,* in contrast, is made up of a sequence of intellectually cumulative philosophical propositions. Most travel books, moreover, are rich in vignettes, but *Democracy in America* is composed of general statements. Even in the notes he took and the letters he sent home from America, Tocqueville's philosophical rather than descriptive intentions are clearly evident. One finds Tocqueville using particular facts as the basis for reasoning his way to the formulation of general philosophical propositions. Or one finds him incorporating new information into formulations already in his mind. But astonishingly little actual description emerges from these many pages of letters and notes. Finally, the length of time it took Tocqueville to

compose the book provides additional insight into his
intentions. Travel books are usually written, for obvious
reasons, soon after a trip. But Tocqueville's project took ten
years to complete: the first part of *Democracy in America*
was published in France in 1835, the second in 1840.

The philosophical argument of *Democracy in America* is
at once strikingly simple and profoundly complex. Equality,
Tocqueville means to demonstrate, ramifies through every
aspect of culture. Political democracy is only one of its
consequences. Family life, literature, philosophical method,
trade, manners, and other dimensions of life are scrutinized
by Tocqueville in order to illuminate the meaning of
democracy. Always in these inquiries he is concerned with
discovering the effects of equality and democracy. But
though his aim is straightforward, his writing is seldom
direct. He circles around his theme, lecturing his French
readers while adding new propositions with each circular
pass, until he is able to say, like the Cartesian mathematician,
Q.E.D.

Tocqueville complicates the reader's task by failing to give
precise and fixed meanings to some of his key terms. Again
and again, he uses *democracy* and *equality* interchangeably,
even though in his notes he had reminded himself: "When I
understand [the new society] in the political sense, I say
démocratie. When I want to speak of the effects of equality, I
say *égalité*." Not only did he fail to obey this rule, he also
expanded his use of the two terms in several inconsistent
ways. The reader must be always alert when they appear.
When Tocqueville used the term *equality* he usually meant
equality of condition rather than equality of opportunity.
Yet when he acknowledged the existence of substantial
differences in the degree of wealth in America, he saved his
notion of equality by referring to equality of opportunity.
He wrote that if there were indeed men of wealth in America,
this wealth did not perpetuate itself. New men achieved

wealth, and old family wealth evaporated. When he contrasted democracy with aristocracy, he gave *equality* still another meaning—the absence of formal legal differences among members of society and equality of political and civil rights. Finally, and most confusing of all, at times he seemed to consider equality as an already realized fact, but at other times he referred to a degree of equality (for example, compared to Europe) or to equality as a condition still in the process of becoming, even in America.

Tocqueville's use of the word *democracy* is similarly nonspecific and confusing. He used the word to refer to political democracy, the fact of equality (whether social, economic, or political), and a general leveling trend in society. Sometimes he seems to be using *democracy* to refer to "the masses" or even to the "aberrations of the masses." Neither did he confine the term to democracy *in America*. Often his reference, especially in Volume Two, was to France or to democracy as a general abstraction or a future condition.

Yet *Democracy in America* remains an elegant and compelling book, truly a literary masterpiece. The book's great strength comes from the structure provided by Tocqueville's sustained contrast between aristocracy and democracy, particularly their different implications for cultural and political life. In this contrast we find an architecture for the book, an architecture so strong and clear that it easily carries Tocqueville's wide-ranging reflections. The grand architecture of *Democracy in America* and the repetition of particular formulations fit together to make the book a work of art as well as a philosophical argument.

Aristocracy and democracy, as used by Tocqueville, represent what sociologists would later call "ideal-types." An ideal-type is an abstraction or composite based on observed social fact but which lacks the details of any specific historical society. The great value of an ideal type is to enable the student of society to focus on the essential character of particular social forms. Such an approach is especially useful in comparative studies, as in Tocqueville's implicit comparison of France and America.

Tocqueville's contrast of aristocracy and democracy is twofold, historical and normative. On the one hand, he is specifying (sometimes explicitly, sometimes implicitly) the dimensions of change involved in the passage from one type of social order to another, from aristocracy to democracy. On the other hand, he is using the model of aristocracy as a baseline for an evaluation of the gains and losses, strengths and weaknesses of democracy.

As it emerges from Tocqueville's pages, the aristocratic era is characterized by permanent inequality. The social order is two-tiered. A small, privileged class—a territorially based aristocracy—constitutes the political nation. Hierarchy, tradition, and a pattern of reciprocal responsibilities between inferior and superior are the ruling principles of society. Men are born with status, participate in society on the basis of it, and expect to retain it. Permanent diversity characterizes the social landscape, and power is mediated through personal relations—between the king and aristocracy and between the aristocrat and "his people." This pattern of power, its personal and territorial character, means that an aristocratic society has many competing centers of power and this, Tocqueville assumed, guarantees liberty.

In a democracy, by contrast, all legal privileges vanish. The political body and the society are coextensive; everyone is a citizen with equal political rights. But Tocqueville's democracy involved more than formal political equality. He referred to a general leveling of wealth; the partition of great estates, which severed elite status from the land and weakened the power of families; and universal education. Most important for Tocqueville, however, is the "spirit" of equality, the way in which men regard their social status. In democracy the paternalism and dependence characteristic of aristocracy is replaced by a sense of equality in social intercourse. Although Tocqueville was alert enough to note that the rich in America did not invite the poor to their homes, he also observed that when rich and poor did meet, say in the street, they met as equals and shook hands. If aristocracy in Tocqueville's definition is marked by diversity and multiple centers of power, his great fear for democracy was that majority opinion might encourage a concentration of power in the central government that would produce a monotonous and deadening sameness in society.

Tocqueville's ideal types can be described in social terms, but it is striking how much he is concerned with collective psychology rather than with quantifiable social fact in his construction of ideal types. Tocqueville is not properly classified as a romantic writer, but compared with eighteenth-century writers, who concentrated on the external self of men in society, Tocqueville sought to grasp and explore the inner self—in this case the collective selves of men living under conditions of aristocracy and democracy. For example, Tocqueville is less interested in describing the social fact of privilege in aristocracy than in articulating the mentality associated with it. That mentality implied for Tocqueville less envy and desire for advancement than there is in democracy, a greater sense of security, and on the part of the aristocrats themselves a certain loftiness of spirit that, among other things, draws them to excellence in literature and the arts.

To understand why Tocqueville undertook to write *Democracy in America* and to gain insight into the concerns that gave the inquiry its basic orientation, one must consider the biography of the man and the history of France during the years when he conceived the project. Alexis Charles

Henri Clérel de Tocqueville was born in Paris on July 29, 1805, of a *petite noblesse* Norman family. Revolution terrified him, as well it might. His maternal grandfather, an aunt, and a great-grandfather had been guillotined during the French Revolution; his parents had been imprisoned. Although his father had taken the oath of allegiance to Napoleon and became mayor of Verneuil, it was not until the Bourbon Restoration in 1814 that wider opportunities in public life became available to him. Under the Bourbon government Tocqueville's father served as a prefect in several departments, eventually being promoted to the court at Versailles and being elevated to the peerage by Charles X. The family apparently flourished under the Bourbons, but the atmosphere in which young Tocqueville grew up was marked by a quality of sadness that derived from his family's experience in the Revolution; his mother particularly longed for the world destroyed by the Revolution.

The values and traditions Tocqueville received from his family were Catholic, conservative, and aristocratic. All would be challenged, and his personal quest was to find a way of living with modernity's tendency to undermine his inherited beliefs. His faith in Catholicism was shaken when, at the age of fifteen, he found and read in his father's library several agnostic and deist texts. He retained a belief in God, immortality, and Christian ethics, but he could no longer practice his faith. Although Tocqueville's political sensibility always remained essentially conservative, he nonetheless embraced liberalism because he cherished liberty above all other political ideals. The aristocratic values he inherited were challenged by the democratic movement that became the subject of his great book, but, as any reading of the book makes clear, at the core of his character he was an aristocrat.

For his first fifteen years, Tocqueville was educated at home, under the supervision of family friend and parish priest Abbé Lesueur. At fifteen he went to the Lycée at Metz; three years later he began the study of law in Paris. His formal education was conventional—Greek, Latin, rhetoric, history, and composition; he excelled only in rhetoric and composition. At the conclusion of his legal studies, he capped his education with travel in Italy. When he came of age in 1827, his father's influence secured him an appointment as a *judge auditeur* (apprentice magistrate, unpaid, with only consultative powers) at Versailles.

The young magistrate, conscientious though he was, did not particularly enjoy his work. Nor was he happy with what he could see of the condition of the government, which seemed to him to be without direction and without hope. In July 1830 the crisis he had anticipated came. Opposition to Charles X crystallized, the barricades went up in the streets, and after three days Charles X fled to England in exile. A bourgeois elite succeeded in establishing the head of the House of Orléans, Louis Philippe, on the throne. Ultra-conservatives, including Tocqueville's parents, remembering that the House of Orléans had betrayed the Bourbon monarchy during the Revolution, were appalled. But the young Tocqueville took an oath of allegiance to the new regime. He did not find this easy, but to him and many others an Orléans king seemed to be all France could hope for in 1830. "In acting thus I sought to fulfill the strict duty of a Frenchman," he later wrote in justification of his act. Yet he remained uneasy, and the government apparently continued to distrust him because of his family's strong Bourbon connections. This very uncomfortable position (which his friend and fellow traveler to America Gustave de Beaumont shared) caused him and Beaumont to think about ways of escaping Paris and the political conditions there. Hence a scheme to study American prisons. At just this time, prison reform was a much discussed topic in both France and the United States. Tocqueville and Beaumont saw a solution to their problem; in October 1830 they submitted to the government a request that they be allowed to form an official mission to study the new and widely publicized American prison reforms. The request was approved, though no government funds were appropriated and their respective families had to pay the costs of the trip.

The American trip—and a book about the new republic—held many attractions for Tocqueville. It was a graceful way to escape the discomfort he felt as a magistrate in the government of Louis Philippe, it enabled him to serve his country, and it offered him the opportunity to earn a reputation that would further his ambition of influencing political affairs in France. In 1830 the United States was an interesting and novel subject in France. And it was con- sidered important; politicians and intellectuals on all sides resorted to the American example in public debate. Becom- ing an expert on the United States would, Tocqueville recognized, "fix on [him] the attention of the parties" debating France's political future. Several questions at the center of this political debate in 1830 clearly helped to shape Tocqueville's inquiry. Men of affairs were concerned about the integration of the lower classes into the national political and cultural community without revolution; the relation of church and state, with liberals extremely anticlerical and conservative Catholics still refusing to accept the fact of the Revolution, one had to ask whether religion and repub- licanism were compatible; and Tocqueville was not alone in worrying about the fate of political liberty under democratic conditions.

Tocqueville and Beaumont arrived in New York City on May 11, 1831. Aboard ship, they had become friendly with Peter Schermerhorn and his family. The Schermerhorns were one of New York's wealthiest and most influential merchant families, and they introduced the two Frenchmen

into New York society. The hospitality of the Schermerhorns initiated a pattern that would characterize most of
Tocqueville's associations with Americans: he established
quick and congenial friendships with the elites of American
cities and towns, spent most of his time with them, and,
moreover, gathered most of his information from them.
Such Americans often had worries about democracy that
mirrored Tocqueville's preoccupations and prejudices. For
example, they worried about the character of democratic
leadership, fearing that lesser men than themselves were
elevated to office by the mass electorate; they worried about
the excesses of majority rule and about the effect of
democracy on science and literature—concerns Tocqueville
shared.

Tocqueville's American experience was limited—or to be
more precise, it was biased. Not only were his acquaintances
predominately from the upper classes, his itinerary was also
not fully representative of American geography (see pages
xlix–lvii). Six of his eight months in the United States were
spent in the Northeast; only slightly more than two weeks
were spent in the South. Most of his ideas had taken
recognizable form before he had seen more than a fraction of
the country. Within about two months of his arrival, most of
his time having been spent in New York, the essential
elements of his interpretation of American democracy were
already recorded in his notebooks and letters home. By the
time he got to New England, he was seeking evidence to fill
out the mental outline he had constructed. It was in New
England that Tocqueville found what he considered American
democracy in its purest form; New England town government was, he thought, at the heart of democratic practice
and education in America.

The United States impressed Tocqueville as a "middle-
class" society that seemed middling in every respect. If it
lacked splendor. it also lacked misery. If it boasted few

brilliant intellectual achievements, the general level of intelligence was impressive. A democratic nation, he concluded, "taken as a whole, will be less brilliant, less glorious, and perhaps less strong; but the majority of its citizens will enjoy a greater degree of prosperity, and the people will remain peaceable, not because they despair of a change for the better, but because they are conscious they are well off already." Such a stable, moral, prosperous example of democracy was heartening to a man who saw democracy as the future.

American religion particularly fascinated Tocqueville, not only because of his personal problem of religious belief but also because the relationship of church and state was a subject of lively discussion in France. Tocqueville was concerned about the unwillingness of many Catholics in France to accept the result of 1789 and the historical inevitability of democracy. America demonstrated, Tocqueville thought, that the liberal spirit in politics was not incompatible with the spirit of religion. But the key to such an accommodation, Tocqueville believed, was the American model of the separation of church and state. Through the example of democracy in America, Tocqueville gave his support to those in France who were arguing that the separation of church and state would strengthen rather than weaken religion.

Within a week of arriving in America Tocqueville noted, with an evident sense of relief, that the Americans "appear on the whole a religious people." But the religious spirit that Tocqueville found was not doctrinal or sectarian. What most impressed him was a generally accepted and religiously inspired system of moral values. What he discovered had been defined and given a name by Rousseau in the *Social Contract* (1762) and has recently been much discussed by sociologists: "civil religion." American society in this view was unified by a civil religion comprising notions of God, a life to come, the reward of virtue and punishment of vice, and religious toleration. This powerful current of civil religion flowed alongside the institutional church. In France the civil religion that emerged out of 1789 had a strong anticlerical thrust, but in America, Tocqueville emphasized, civil religion and the churches were mutually reenforcing. This he attributed to the separation of church and state.

For all his interest in religion, however, Tocqueville largely missed and completely misunderstood the place of revivalism in American religion. To him it was simply a form of "religious insanity" on the periphery of American life. In fact, it was central and nourished the patriotism, morality, and public activism that Tocqueville so much appreciated in America. He was no doubt misled not only by his own conservative sensibilities but also by his upper-class American acquaintances, particularly the New England Unitarians, whose views on the subject of American religion he tended to accept as authoritative. Tocqueville, then, was surely correct to see the profound importance of religion—and to recognize its character as a civil religion—but he erred in failing to grasp the significance of the revivalism sweeping America when he arrived.

At the heart of Tocqueville's reflections on democracy is a concern for the quality of public life or political activity. If he came to America armed with the grand idea of equality, he came also with a great passion for public life, and this profoundly affected his response to American democracy. Tocqueville was *l'homme politique*. Like Aristotle, who wrote in *Politics* that "man is a political animal," Tocqueville believed that anyone who did not assume a civic role was, as the ancient Greeks put it, either a barbarian or an idiot. An active citizenry was a prime political value for Tocqueville. When he arrived in a town or a city he responded to the level of political activity like a seismograph, and he judged societies by the level of political activity they nourished. The vitality he found in America fascinated and profoundly impressed him. In a notebook he reflected on the link between democracy and the active life in America. "The wonderful effect of republican governments," he observed, is to be found "in the way of life . . . It does not always and in all circumstances give the people a more skillful and faultless government; but it infuses throughout the body social an activity, a force and an energy which never exist without it, and which bring forth wonders. It is there that one must look for its advantages."

Many nineteenth-century European liberals were concerned about getting government out of the lives of individuals, but Tocqueville considered it equally important to get people into civic life and the political process. The United States, with its tradition of local self-government and its decentralized and generally weak administration, invited participation and called on the energies of its citizens. Even more impressive to Tocqueville was the manner in which an essentially anonymous public was drawn into political life. In an aristocracy political association was based on personal ties; in a democracy, he discovered, publicity (newspapers) and associations organized strangers for political purposes.

It is in the context of this concern for a vital public life that his famous observations on individualism must be understood. He gave the novel expression "individualism" to a condition he described as "a mature and calm feeling, which disposes each member of the community to sever himself from the mass of his fellows and to draw apart with his family and his friends, so that after he has thus formed a little circle of his own, he willingly leaves society at large to itself." This stricture is often misunderstood to mean that Americans, in Tocqueville's view, severed themselves from all social contacts, were isolated and atomized. His real objection is that individualism saps public life; men withdraw from public life into *gemeinschaftlich* networks of family and friends. It was Tocqueville's judgment, however, that in America this vice of democratic times was mitigated by the tradition of voluntary associations. "Americans," he observed, "have combated by free institutions the tendency of equality to keep men asunder, and they have subdued it." Voluntary associations and local government "perpetually bring men together and force them to help one another in spite of the propensities that sever them."

His equally famous warning about the tyranny of opinion also relates to his concern about participation and particularly leadership in public life. One even senses in his comments a very personal worry, a fear that men of independent thought like himself would be denied positions of leadership in a democratic society. "In America," he wrote, "the majority raises formidable barriers around the liberty of opinion; within these barriers an author may write what he pleases, but woe to him if he goes beyond them. Not that he is in danger of an auto-da-fé [public execution], but he is exposed to continued obloquy and persecution. His political career is closed forever." Such exclusion from political life was, in Tocqueville's opinion, "an existence worse than death."

In February 1832, Tocqueville returned to France to write the book that would, he hoped, bring him fame and political influence. He brought home a great number of reports and treatises from America, and with the assistance of a young man at the American Embassy in Paris, Tocqueville sought a wide range of documentary material to amplify and sharpen the impressions and formulations he had recorded in his notes and letters. After three years the first volume appeared; five years later Volume Two was published. During these years Tocqueville worked slowly and carefully, keeping one eye on his American notes and the other on the ways of the French politicians and intellectuals to whom his

xxviii DEMOCRACY IN AMERICA

book was directed. All the while he squeezed every fact recorded in his notes to extract from it the fullest philosophical import.

Soon after the publication of the first volume of *Democracy in America* Tocqueville was invited to visit Royer-Collard, a renowned Paris intellectual and a member of the *Académie Française*. In praising the book and its young author, Royer-Collard declared that "since Montesquieu there has been nothing like it." The association with Montesquieu was apt, and it must have pleased Tocqueville immensely because he had taken the author of *The Spirit of the Laws* (1748) as his master. Indeed, he had read Montesquieu daily while composing *Democracy in America.*

In approaching their respective tasks, Tocqueville and Montesquieu shared a somewhat similar outlook. Both were trained as lawyers, they assumed the value of comparative analysis, and they acknowledged the importance of the historical process through which present institutional arrangements took form. Both admired England and the English constitution, and both in turn came to be admired by English political theorists. Like Aristotle and Machiavelli before them, the two Frenchmen sought to discover and understand the basic types of human groupings and the laws, institutions, and values appropriate to them.

History for Tocqueville, as for Montesquieu, was an expansive mode of inquiry; it was not past politics in any simple sense. Although the interests of both were political, the object of their inquiries was society as a whole. They sought to penetrate the underlying structure of society—its principles and the configuration of its social groups. Their great concern was, how does the organization of society— the composition of its basic social units—affect political life? They were particularly anxious to understand the implications of social organization for the possibilities of liberty, the key political value for both of them. What Tocqueville accomplished, building on and surpassing Montesquieu, was to shift political inquiry from a narrow concern with the constitutional arrangements of the state to society itself.

However impressive the continuity of development that unites the work of Montesquieu and Tocqueville, the student of Tocqueville and of Tocqueville's America cannot but be struck by the manner in which Tocqueville's American experience caused him to stand Montesquieu on his head in respect to the important matter of republican virtue. Montesquieu believed, as had political analysts since Machiavelli, that a republic depended on civic virtue for stability and survival. In other words, a republic (and Montesquieu had in mind the small, ancient republics) required self-abnegation by its citizens. Tocqueville, as a close student of Montesquieu, came to America expecting to find civic virtue—citizens as virtuous, disinterested participants in public life—at the center of the American political experience. But after a month in Jacksonian America, a month spent largely in New York City, Tocqueville's ideas on this point had been reversed. In a letter to a friend in France, he stressed how different from the "ancient republics" things were in America. "What makes them a people?" he asked himself and his correspondent. *"L'intérêt.* That's the secret. Individual *intérêt* which sticks through them at each instant, *l'intérêt* which, moreover, comes out in the open and calls itself a social theory."

Later, in Volume Two of *Democracy in America,* Tocqueville devoted a chapter to the theme of "self-interest rightly understood." While Europeans "feign great abnegations which they no longer feel," Americans "are fond of explaining almost all of the actions of their lives by the principle of self-interest rightly understood." This principle, Tocqueville noted, "is not a lofty one, but it is clear and sure." And if it "produces no great acts of self-sacrifice," it nonetheless "suggests daily small acts of self-denial." The theory, as

Americans understand it, means "an enlightened regard for themselves constantly prompts them to assist one another." An American "knows when to sacrifice some of his private interest to save the rest; we want to save everything, and often we lose it all." None of this, Tocqueville explained, suffices to make a man virtuous, but "it disciplines a number of persons in habits of regularity, temperance, moderation, foresight, self-command; and if it does not lead men straight to virtue by the will, it gradually draws them in that direction by their habits."

In those parts of *Democracy in America* directed specifically to the United States (and most of them are in Volume One), Tocqueville consistently writes in an optimistic tone. But when he turns to democracy's prospects in France or to abstract discussions of modern democracy, this optimism fades. American democracy, he increasingly believed, was unique and exceptional because of the special circumstances of American history, culture, and geographical isolation. He stressed again and again that American political institutions could not serve as a ready-made model for France. They were the product of and peculiarly appropriate to a specific history and culture. Laws and constitutions, in Tocqueville's philosophy of history, were less important than experience and customs (and he defined the latter as the "moral and intellectual characteristics of men in society") in shaping the political character of a nation.

Among America's peculiar historical and cultural advantages he noted the Anglo-American tradition of local government, the conservative role of lawyers, the political character of juries, the absence of a great metropolis, and religion. The geographical isolation of American society meant that Americans did not have to fear a threatening neighbor; they could forego efficiency of administration in favor of broad participation that served as a school for democracy. France, so often a hinge in European politics and warfare, could not assume such a risk.

The differences between America and France, which increasingly impressed themselves on Tocqueville's mind as he wrote Volume Two, largely account for the oft noted differences between the two volumes. It is difficult but important to be precise about these differences. The differences are more than a matter of increasing pessimism and more than a difference in the subjects treated. It can be said, perhaps, that the first volume is primarily descriptive and only incidentally reflective; the second is primarily reflective and only incidentally descriptive. One can also suggest the dimensions of difference by noting that the concreteness of Volume One is lost in the abstraction of Volume Two. Or moving nearer to the substance of the volumes, one might recall that as late as November 1839 Tocqueville intended to use *equality* in place of *democracy* in the title of Volume Two. Does it clarify matters, then, to think of the first volume as a study of democracy and the second as a study of equality? Each of these speculations touches the problem but none enables us to grasp it fully. Both volumes are about democracy, but the meaning of democracy—and Tocqueville's fears about democracy—changed over the course of the decade he spent writing *Democracy in America.*

The portrait of democracy in America offered in Volume One is active; the democracy dominating Volume Two is passive, apathetic. To make the difference clearer, let us rephrase it in terms of Tocqueville's fears for democracy. The object of his fear in Volume One is the tyranny of the majority. This particular fear implies a mobilized citizenry. It was a matter of specific concern in America. Tocqueville's notes reveal, in fact, that he got the phrase "tyranny of the majority" from Jared Sparks of Boston in conversation, and he had obviously studied and learned from James Madison's observations on this point in *The Federalist Papers.* Finally,

one cannot miss the special pleasure Tocqueville takes in
citing Jefferson's similiar fear for America. That Jefferson,
who Tocqueville presents as "the most powerful advocate
democracy has ever had," shared Tocqueville's concern
served to validate it for the Frenchman.

In Volume Two one reads little of specifically American
problems or concerns about democracy. Now Tocqueville
fears political passivity, a form of oppression not described
in American terms and for which he says he can give no
name. Both *despotism* and *tyranny,* he says, are "inappropriate" to this entirely new thing threatening the world.
Since he cannot name it, he proceeds to define it in one of the
most powerful and passionate passages in the book:

The first thing that strikes the observation is an innumerable
multitude of men, all equal and alike, incessantly endeavoring to
procure the petty and paltry pleasures with which they glut their
lives. Each of them, living apart, is as a stranger to the fate of all the
rest; his children and his private friends constitute to him the whole
of mankind.... Above this race of men stands an immense and
tutelary power, which takes upon itself alone to secure their
gratifications, and to watch over their fate. That power is absolute,
minute, regular, provident, and mild. It would be like the authority
of a parent if, like that authority, its object was to prepare men for
manhood; but it seeks, on the contrary, to keep them in perpetual
childhood.... For their happiness such a government willingly
labors, but it chooses to be the sole agent and only arbiter of that
happiness; it provides for their security, foresees and supplies their
necessities, facilitates their pleasures, manages their principal
concerns, directs their industry, regulates the descent of property,
and subdivides their inheritances: what remains, but to spare them
all the care of thinking and all the trouble of living?... The
principle of equality has prepared men for these things; it has
predisposed men to endure them and often to look on them as
benefits.... The will of man is not shattered, but softened, bent,
and guided; men are seldom forced by it to act, but they are
constantly restrained from acting. Such a power does not destroy,

but it prevents existence; it does not tyrannize, but it compresses, enervates, extinguishes, and stupifies a people.

How Tocqueville moved from the rather benign and even occasionally enthusiastic approval of an energetic American democracy in Volume One to this frightening, even nightmarish, vision of modern democracy deserves our attention.

The referent of Tocqueville's work, the object that exemplified democracy for Tocqueville, shifted between the composition of the first and second volumes. In Volume One the connection between America and democracy is clear and consistent. Indeed, it was as much a book about America as about democracy. Much descriptive material not immediately relevant to his theme is included, apparently because readers in France curious about America would appreciate the information. And, recall, there was great interest in France during the early 1830s concerning America and American democracy. Volume Two is a book about equality and democracy; Tocqueville refers to America in no more than half the chapters. In Volume One he saw the democratic future through the prism of America; in Volume Two France was the prism. To the extent that America is considered in Volume Two, it is treated largely as a fortunate exception, a product of unusual traditions and circumstances not available to France and other democratic nations of the future.

When he finished the first draft of Volume Two in 1838, Tocqueville realized how his purposes had shifted over the course of his work. In a letter to Royer-Collard, he observed: "Now that I can see nearly the whole book I perceive that it is much more a question of the general effects of equality on *mores* than of the particular effects that it produces in America. Is that bad? Is my former reader so tied to what I already said of the United States that he will follow me only regretfully onto another terrain? In short, does he like America better than me?" This letter is enormously interesting and revealing. First, it clearly shows why the second volume is more abstract and so little interested in America. Perhaps even more fascinating is the light it throws on Tocqueville's own psychology and sense of success. Several years earlier, when French intellectuals hungered for reliable knowledge of American democracy, concentration on America promised attention and even fame. In 1838, however, when his travel notes were getting old and when France was more interested in the problem of democracy at home than in America, the man already acclaimed the Montesquieu of the nineteenth century no longer needed America.

Not only had America faded from the center of his attention, but developments in France and a fundamental insight about democracy and centralization drew him to an ever closer consideration of the dynamics of French history, including an essay on the "Political and Social Condition of France" (1836). While he was writing *Democracy in America,* Tocqueville saw disturbing evidence of withdrawal from politics in France. Even while he was writing Volume One he had noticed it, but he interpreted it then as a passing thing, easily explained in an era of political confusion. It hardly surprised him—and certainly implied little for a theory of democracy—that legitimists withdrew, as his father did, in protest of the Orléanist regime. By the late 1830s, however, he had concluded that this withdrawal was a fact of French democracy.

He was pushed to this conclusion, in part, by government policy. When he was writing the first volume, the government was proposing enhanced local self-government—the very decentralization that had seemed to give vitality to democracy in America—and in 1833 the government enacted a modest plan of administration decentralization. By 1835, however, this governmental thrust had come to an end. Instead the government proposed extended centralization in the interest of economic development. Worse yet, restrictions on the press were enacted at the same time. This was distressing to Tocqueville not only because it violated his liberal ideals but also because it was the press that he had described as the motor that gave movement to public life and associational activity in America. These developments deeply troubled Tocqueville, and his troubled reflections on these issues of withdrawal from public life, concentration of state power, and the enervation of voluntary associations in France more than his memories of America dominated Volume Two.

The second volume of *Democracy in America* also reflects Tocqueville's strikingly original and still important insight into the relationship of centralization to democracy. In Volume One decentralization of administration is treated as an important fact of American life, one that protects Americans against some of the possible dangers of democracy, particularly the tyranny of the majority. He does not, however, suggest any essential connection between democracy and centralization—or decentralization. Decentralization in America is the product of American history and circumstance, including the legacy of English local administration. By the time he began writing Volume Two, however, Tocqueville had come to see centralization as a part of the democratic phenomenon.

In the course of preparing an article on pauperism, he read the report of England's Royal Commission of Inquiry on the Poor Law. Seldom has a government document had such intellectual consequence. The document and the English legislation associated with it embodied a program of centralized administration in the interest of efficiency and uniformity. What struck Tocqueville, however, was the origin of the ideas informing the document. The men behind it were the philosophical radicals, men like his friend John Stuart Mill, men he rightly saw as the "democratic party" in

England. At this point, he achieved an entirely original insight: There is a connection between democracy (or equality) and centralization (or bureaucracy). His notes on the subject, recorded in 1835, bear quotation:

Centralization, a democratic instinct; instinct of a society which has succeeded in escaping from the individualistic system of the Middle Ages. Preparation for despotism. Why is centralization more suited to the habits of democracy? Great question to *dig into* in the third volume [the first half of what we now refer to as the second volume] of my work, if I can integrate it there. A *fundamental* question.

Heretofore bureaucracy had been associated with the administration of the absolutist state in Europe, but Tocqueville noted the essential compatibility of the uniformity, sameness, and insistence on universalized (as opposed to individualistic or particularistic) standards that equality seems to demand. This insight was not only incorporated into the second volume, but it later became one of the most provocative themes woven into his interpretation of eighteenth-century France in *The Old Regime and the Revolution*, in which he treated the rise of democracy and the rise of centralized administration in France as two aspects of the same historical process.

In time, Tocqueville was persuaded by Mill and other English friends that he had overreacted to the report, that in fact the Poor Law represented the English genius for mixed administration. In this later view the Poor Law was a sensible division of responsibility between central and local authorities. But although he came to alter his opinion of that particular piece of legislation, he had gained a new theoretical insight that remained at the center of his thought. Indeed, his discussions with Mill on the Poor Law and administration in general convinced Mill that administration was a central problem for political theory, and this understanding is reflected in Mill's great books *On Liberty* (1854) and *Considerations on Republican Government* (1861).

Tocqueville was one of many nineteenth-century intellectuals who sensed that the history of his time pointed toward equality. But no other prophet of equality devoted such agonizing attention to the problems equality might present for free men. Here it is useful to compare his work and philosophy of history with that of Karl Marx, only thirteen years younger than Tocqueville. Both men envisioned a future of equality, but apart from that differences are more important than similarities, and they reveal the distinctive qualities of the work of these major nineteenth-century social theorists.

The process of leveling described by Tocqueville was slow but inexorable, almost imperceptible. Marx's vision of history was quite different. History for him moved through self-conscious struggle and revolution. The achievement of equality itself, moreover, impressed Marx and Tocqueville quite differently. Marx assumed that equality once achieved was unproblematical and hardly worth the sort of sustained analysis that he devoted to the historical process of getting there. Tocqueville, by contrast, devoted little attention to explaining the process (it was "providential"), but he brooded over the condition of equality itself, especially, as we have seen, in Volume Two. As society moved toward equality, Marx foresaw little for the state to do, and he rarely discussed the future state; indeed, Engels, in a famous passage that undoubtedly reflected Marx's sentiments, predicted that the state would wither away. But Tocqueville worried that under democratic conditions the state threatened to expand beyond all reason and eclipse civil society.

In his inquiry into the "social condition" of equality, Tocqueville devoted astonishingly little attention to detailed analysis of the economy—its institutions, class relations, technology, and the like. There is nothing even remotely approaching the specific analysis one finds in *Capital* (1867, and later posthumous volumes). It is true that Tocqueville did include in *Democracy in America* a chapter warning that the growth of manufacturing in a democracy may bring it back to an aristocracy of the worst sort. He discussed the tendency for the division of labor to improve the work and degrade the worker, thus making a mockery of democracy. Unlike the old territorial aristocracy, he lamented, the manufacturers accepted no responsibility for their workers. "The manufacturing aristocracy of our age first impoverishes and debases the men who serve it and then abandons them to be supported by the charity of the public." His language is powerful, but the implications of industrial labor (or capital) hardly affect his general analysis. The evil of industrialism is a limited and confined phenomenon for Tocqueville; "it is a monstrous exception in the general aspect of society."

In the *Communist Manifesto* (1848) one finds strikingly similar and equally impassioned descriptive statements about the debasement of industrial workers. The industrial system, Marx wrote, has "degraded personal dignity to the level of exchange value." But for Marx the bipolar class division that is given such clarity under industrial capitalism is central rather than peripheral to historical understanding of the modern era. "The history of all human society . . . has been the history of class struggles," and in the nineteenth century, Marx asserted, "society is splitting into two great hostile camps, into two great and directly contraposed classes: bourgeoisie and proletariat."

The emotional responses of the two men toward the historical career of equality also reveal important differences that better enable us to grasp the character of Tocqueville's book. Tocqueville accepted the historical necessity he disliked; Marx thought a revolutionary movement could bring about the equality he desired. This difference is reflected in the literary style of these two compelling writers. Tocqueville's writing is cool and resigned; there is even a sad and mourning quality to it. Marx, by contrast, is embattled and utopian. Ironically, it is the utopian Marx who is consciously scientific in method; Tocqueville is explicitly intuitive, though not without rigor and system.

Unlike Marx, who had a fully ariticulated theory that gave shape to centuries of human history, Tocqueville rejected such systems. No doubt Tocqueville had Marx, the Saint-Simonians, and other prophets of Paris in mind when in his *Recollections,* written in the immediate aftermath of the revolution of 1848 but published posthumously, he affirmed the essential indeterminancy of historical understanding. "I detest those absolute systems," he wrote, "which represent all the events of history as depending upon great causes linked by the chain of fatality, and which, as it were, suppress men from the history of the human race. Antecedent facts, the nature of institutions, the caste of minds and the state of morals are the materials of which are composed those impromptus which astonish and alarm us." This profound sense of historical particularity and contingency runs deep in *Democracy in America,* and it largely explains the suppleness of a book spun out of the single idea of equality.

Democracy in America brought Tocqueville instant and permanent acclaim as a political philosopher. Sainte-Beuve's praise was typical of French reactions to the first volume:

There is not a chapter in the book which does not bespeak one of the best and most resolute minds, one of the most gifted in political observation in a field in which there have been few such brilliant and substantial contributions since the incomparable monument reared by Montesquieu.... M. de Tocqueville's book, if read completely, would furnish material for the student of all great questions in modern politics.

The second volume was less well received in France and elsewhere; when Tocqueville detached himself from the concreteness of American society, he lost some of his readers. Tocqueville had wondered in his letter to Royer-Collard whether this might happen. And when it did, he understood it. In another letter to a friend, he acknowledged that the book was "too abstract and raises too many questions to please the public."

When I wrote only upon the democratic society in the United States, I was understood directly. If I had written upon democratic society in France as it exists at the present day, that again would have been easily understood. But using ideas derived from American and French democracy only as data, I endeavored to paint the general features of democratic societies; no complete specimen of which can yet be said to exist.

Living a hundred and fifty years after Tocqueville visited America, we feel ourselves nearer, sometimes too near, to the conditions he described so abstractly in Volume Two, and through its lenses we better see premonitions of our modern condition in Jacksonian America. Unlike his contemporaries, we are drawn to Volume Two because it seems more profound and valuable for understanding our present circumstances. The very quality that Tocqueville saw as its drawback in 1840, his brilliant reach for a philosophical understanding of democracy itself, we now see as its source of greatness and timelessness.

Immediately after publication, Tocqueville's book also received acclaim in England and America, and it was translated for English and American editions. One might even say that it was most fully understood and most highly praised in England. The reputation of books often depends on the quality of their reviewers. Tocqueville had the good fortune of being reviewed in England by John Stuart Mill, that nation's most important liberal intellectual. "It has," Mill wrote of *Democracy in America,* "at once taken its rank among the most remarkable productions of our time; and is a book with which, both for its facts and its speculations, all who would understand, or who are called upon to exercise influence over their age, are bound to be familiar." And, like so many other commentators, Mill compared Tocqueville with his great French predecessor: "The author's mind, except that it is of a soberer character, seems to us to resemble Montesquieu most among the French writers." Mill's review was deeply appreciated by Tocqueville, who wrote to him that "of all my reviewers, you are perhaps, the only one who has thoroughly understood me.... The profession of an author would be too delightful if one met with many such readers!"

In America, the reception given *Democracy in America,* particularly Volume One, was favorable and appreciative. Americans were very sensitive about what previous Europeans had written about America. Often the reactions of Europeans had been in varying degrees critical, and this the American national ego would not brook. Often, too, it was evident that the European commentators did not really understand American social and political institutions; Tocqueville, by contrast, clearly understood them. *The United States Magazine and Democratic Review* praised *Democracy in America* as "decidedly the most remarkable and really valuable work that has yet appeared upon this country from the hand of a foreigner.... The difference between M. de Tocqueville and our common herd of travellers, is, that when he speaks of the principles of government he knows what he is talking of." Americans were less interested in Tocqueville as a political philosopher; they praised him for accurately describing America to those Europeans who did not understand the new nation. As a writer in the *Knickerbocker Magazine* pointed out, the United States "have hitherto been an enigma to all the world; our author has at last partly solved it." Nineteenth-century Americans also paid the Frenchman the compliment of including substantial selections from *Democracy in America* in American schoolbooks.

In France Tocqueville was properly honored for his book. After the publication of the second volume he was elected, at the age of thirty-six, to the *Académie Française,* the highest honor that can be bestowed on a French intellectual. The success of Tocqueville *l'homme politique* was more ambiguous. His purposes in writing *Democracy in America,* it will be recalled, included the opportunity to instruct France's political leaders and to achieve the reputation that would make a political role possible for himself. In 1839 he was elected to the Chamber of Deputies, where he served with only modest effectiveness until 1848. In that year of revolution he became a member of the Constituent Assembly and a member of the committee that drafted the constitution of the Second Republic. For a short time in 1849 he served as Minister of Foreign Affairs under the Second Republic. He took his political life seriously; indeed, he could not separate his role as an intellectual from his sense of obligation and desire for a role in public life. Yet history remembers him as a writer, not as a politician. And it is perhaps fitting that after the *coup d'etat* of Louis Napoleon in 1851, Tocqueville retired from politics and undertook what he envisioned as a three-volume study of the French Revolution. At the time of his death on April 16, 1859, only one volume, *The Old Regime and the Revolution* (1856), had been published. But this work, in its own way as magnificent as *Democracy in America,* again placed Tocqueville the writer in the public eye at the end of his life.

After his death, Tocqueville's reputation as a political philosopher remained high, but *Democracy in America* was cited less and less by historians. The first great professional historians in America, Frederick Jackson Turner and Charles A. Beard, seldom referred to Tocqueville in their work. In part this was because Turner and Beard emphasized conflict, whether based on sections or classes, and Tocqueville's portrait of America was a composite that deliberately avoided discussion of internal differentiation. The whole conservative sensibility that informs *Democracy in America* as well was at odds with the fundamental commitments of Turner and Beard.

During the 1940s and 1950s, however, American historians embraced Tocqueville. Intellectual historians relied on him as an analyst of the "national character" (a phrase used by Tocqueville). In an era of Cold War, Tocqueville's emphasis on American exceptionalism, consensus, and stability was attractive. And at a time when Americans felt threatened by Marxist ideology and by anticolonial revolutions in the Third World, they found confidence in Tocqueville's non-Marxian portrait of the nonrevolutionary American experience. Such major works of this period as Marvin Meyers's *Jacksonian Persuasion* (1957) and Louis Hartz's *The Liberal Tradition in America* (1955) were built explicitly on Tocqueville's book. Even those critical of America in the 1950s tended to prefer Tocqueville to Marx, and they took from Tocqueville his notions of tyranny of opinion, status anxiety, and mass society rather than using Marxian notions of class and power.

Why read Tocqueville today? His work is not the place to go for mere fact, for descriptive material alone. Tocqueville's achievement is interpretive, not descriptive. *Democracy in America* is both historically specific and timeless. He wrote at a time when the first impulses of what sociologists now call "modernization" were becoming apparent in

America, and we are today the product of that process. Tocqueville is less helpful in understanding the specifically economic aspects of this process than in widening our sense of the social, political, and cultural implications of it. He directs our attention to the ways in which this process transformed the relationships among the various units of society, particularly the relation of informal and formal groups, private life and public life.

It is unnecessary to say that in the following pages are innumerable insights of unmatched brilliance that illuminate the character of American culture and democracy. But it may be worth devoting a few lines to what seems to be missing or misjudged. Tocqueville's failure to grasp the significance of religious revivalism has already been noted, and it has been suggested that his discussion of the technological and economic changes that were transforming an agrarian economy into an urban and industrial one is inadequate. It is worth comparing Tocqueville's work in this respect with that of his fellow Frenchman Michel Chevalier, who was, significantly, an engineer by training. Reading Chevalier's *Lettres sur l'Amerique du Nord* (1833-35)* one recognizes the birth of a modern economy, a central historical fact largely absent from Tocqueville's account. Nor does Tocqueville seriously consider a major product of this economic transformation—the emergence of business associations or corporations. He is very much concerned about the concentration of power in the public realm, but he seemingly did not notice the threat of highly organized and centralized private power in democracy.

Several of Tocqueville's judgments must be at least questioned. He seems, for example, not to have fully appreciated the implications of the radically different cultures or ways of life emerging in the free and slave states.

*Translated as *Society, Manners and Politics in America*.

His confidence that the advantages of union (which he distinguished, incidentally, from the survival republicanism, about which he was even more optimistic) would overcome the danger of civil war proved misplaced. Or, to give a rather different example, his discussion of the sad fate of the American literary man failed to predict the flowering of transcendentalism just when *Democracy in America* was published. Ralph Waldo Emerson's *American Scholar* (1837) reveals an awareness of the problems of literary life in America that Tocqueville did not seem to grant Americans, and it proposes possibilities that Tocqueville did not anticipate. When Tocqueville described American political parties, he ignored or missed the role of patronage and party machinery in organizing a mass electorate and sustaining political power. State government is barely mentioned at all; he is clearly puzzled about just what state governments do. Yet he visited America during a period when state governments were making vast investments in internal improvements that would help transform the American economy.

But to enumerate these errors or omissions—and one could find others—is not so much to fault the book as to free the reader to approach Tocqueville with a critical eye. It does not honor a writer, even an acknowledged master, to read him without seeking to challenge him. Tocqueville becomes richer and more valuable rather than less so when studied critically and in conjunction with the modern scholarship that has so increased our knowledge of American democracy during the century and a half that has passed since Tocqueville visited America.

Tocqueville's work has earned a very special place in the library of the historian of American culture and the student of society. It represents a corpus of writing that should be visited and revisited by scholars seeking continual intellectual refreshment. *Democracy in America* is the locale of brilliant intuitive leaps and exemplifications of the breadth possible in social inquiry. Here is the model for those who wish to understand the relationships between society, culture, and politics. And here, particularly in Volume Two, are reflections on modernity and civic life that we ignore at our peril. Tocqueville's great fear, and, I trust, ours, is the enervation of public life in modern democracies—that is to say, any lessening of the capacity of citizens as strangers to collaborate in a political way.

Thomas Bender
New York City
October 1980

A NOTE ON THE TEXT

Abridging a classic is always a sensitive matter. Yet I have ventured to do so in this instance in order to make Tocqueville more manageable for students and more accessible to the wide audience he deserves. Tocqueville's work is best understood as a whole, and this fact has guided my decisions in abridging it. For the most part, I have cut sentences and paragraphs where he was wordy or repeated himself rather than cutting whole sections. In this way the original architecture and spirit of the work have been preserved.

To the extent that it is possible to put into a brief formula the rules guiding me, I would state it as follows: I have deleted repetitious material, digressions, and simple descriptions of American political institutions, which were intended for an early nineteenth-century French audience ignorant of them but which are widely understood by the modern reader. Deletions of this latter sort were especially substantial in Chapter V of Volume One. I have also deleted all footnotes and appendices. In all of this, of course, my decisions were most fundamentally influenced by my own sense of what is still provocative and valuable in Tocqueville for the student of American culture and democracy. My introductory essay will serve, I trust, as an adequate guide to my beliefs in this regard.

Finally, I should note two special cases that changed the original structure of the book. One chapter has been deleted and another chapter has been expanded to three chapters. Tocqueville's original Chapter VII in Volume One ("Political Jurisdiction in the United States"), a discussion of impeachment that is neither clearly argued nor important to his overall interpretation, has been omitted and the succeeding chapters renumbered. The titles for chapters XVIII and XIX in this edition have been drawn from subsection titles Tocqueville provided in Chapter XVII of Volume One. Because the subject of these sections is so different from the major topic of the original chapter, I felt that separating them out would help readers locate these important reflections on the future of the American democracy and union.

Tocqueville Itinerary,
May 11, 1831 – February 20, 1832

CANADA

Montreal
Sept. 2

Boston
Sept. 9–Oct. 3

Albany

Buffalo
July 18–19
and Aug. 17

New York
May 11–May 29
June 7–June 30
Oct. 8–Oct. 11
Feb. 7–Feb. 20, 1832

Green Bay
Aug. 9–10

Detroit
July 23
July 31
Aug. 14

Cincinnati
Dec. 1–4

Philadelphia
Oct. 12–Oct. 28
Nov. 6–Nov. 21

Washington, D.C.
Jan. 17–Feb. 3

Memphis
Dec. 17–25

Knoxville, Ga.
Jan. 8

New Orleans
Jan. 1–3

Areas not states as of 1831

TOCQUEVILLE'S AMERICAN ACQUAINTANCES*
April 1831–Jan. 1835

(The names of individuals who contributed most to his understanding of America are given in capitals.)

ON SHIPBOARD

Captain E. L. Keen
Mr. & Mrs. PETER SCHERMERHORN
J. J. Schermerhorn
P. A. Schermerhorn
C. N. Palmer (English traveller)
Miss (?) Edwards
Rev. William Creighton (N.Y.)
Mr. & Mrs. Samuel L. Breese
A. L. Montaut (Phila.)
Samuel P. Long (Portsmouth, N.H.)
Fortier (New Orleans)
Édouard Schérer (France)
Douant (St. Malo)
Dance (France)
L. F. Steiger & Family (Switzerland)
N. Hernandez (Havana)
A. Coutan(t) & family

NEW YORK CITY

NATHANIEL PRIME
RICHARD RIKER
ALBERT GALLATIN

---

*This list is taken in slightly modified form from George W. Pierson, *Tocqueville and Beaumont in America* (New York: Oxford University Press, 1938), pp. 781–85. Copyright George W. Pierson. Reprinted by permission of the author.

1

JAMES KENT
Schermerhorn family
Jones Family (related to Schermerhorns)
John R. Livingston, Jr. & family
Henry D. Sedgwick
James Gore King
John Duer
William Alexander Duer
William W. Campbell
Robert Emmet
James O. Morse
Rev. John Power
Enos T. Throop
Rev. Jonathan Mayhew Wainwright
Hugh Maxwell
Ogden Hoffman
Nicholas Fish
David Hosack
Philip Hone
Joseph Blunt
Miss Julia Fulton
Mrs. (?) Davis
N. C. Hart
John O. Woodruff (Blackwell's Island)
Walter Bowne
Durant St. André (French Consul)
Pessac (French Consul)

(also Palmer, Miss Edwards, Rev. Creighton & others from
 shipboard)

NEW YORK STATE

JOHN CANFIELD SPENCER & family
ELAM LYNDS
AZARIAH C. FLAGG

Enos T. Throop (Auburn)
C. C. Cambreleng (Albany)
Reuben Hyde Walworth (Albany)
Edward Cornelius Delavan (Albany)
Livingston family (near Yonkers)
Rev. James Richards (Auburn)
Rob. Wiltse (Sing Sing)
George W. Cartwright (Sing Sing)
Rev. (?) Prince (Sing Sing)
Mrs. & Miss MacHedge (?) (Sing Sing)
* * *, Sing Sing landlady
E. P. Livingston (Albany)
J. B. VanSchaick (Albany)
Isaiah Townsend (?) (Albany)
E. C. Genet (?) (Greenbush)
S. Warren (?) (Troy)
Rev. B. C. Smith (Auburn)
Clark, Auburn Prison clerk

(also Oneida fishwife, Oneida & Seneca Indians, etc.)

GREAT LAKES & CANADA

John Tanner (on Lake Erie)
Major John Biddle (Detroit)
Rev. Gabriel Richard (Detroit)
Mrs. Moderl (?) (Detroit)
Amasa Bagley (Pontiac)
Oliver Williams (Indian Trader)
Dr. Burns (Pontiac)
John & "Aunt Polly" Todd (Flint River)
G. D. (or E. S.) Williams (Saginaw)
Rev. James I. Mullon (on *Superior*)
G. T. Vigne (English traveller)
Miss Clemens (Englishwoman)
Miss Thompson (on *Superior*)

Misses Macomb (on *Superior*)
* * * (Lucius Smith?) Episcopal Minister
* * *, Presbyterian Minister
Samuel Abbott (Michilimackinac)
Mme Framboise (Michilimackinac)
Major Lamard (?) (Green Bay)
Dominique Mondelet (Montreal)
Charles J. E. Mondelet (Montreal)
Joseph-Vincent Quiblier (Montreal)
JOHN NEILSON
Jean Thomas Tascherau (Quebec)
(D. B.?) Viger (Quebec)
* * *, Quebec Merchant

(also Chippewa & Menominee Indians, fur traders,
    habitants)

MASSACHUSETTS

Sedgwick family (Stockbridge)
FRANCIS LIEBER
JARED SPARKS
JOSEPH COOLIDGE, JR.
FRANCIS CALLEY GRAY
EDWARD EVERETT
J. Q. ADAMS
Josiah Quincy
Rev. William Ellery Channing
Rev. Joseph Tuckerman
William Sullivan
Alexander Everett
Charles P. Curtis
Tappan brothers
Daniel Webster
David Sears
George Ticknor

H. G. Otis family
R. Fletcher
* * *, a judge
(?) Clay, Southern planter
Nathan Hale
LOUIS DWIGHT
E. M. P. Wells
Samuel A. Eliot
William Austin
Charles Lincoln, Jr.
Rev. Jared Curtis
Charles Wells
Sherman Leland
George Rogers (?)
Piquet (French Consul)

CONNECTICUT

Samuel H. Huntington
Robert C. Winthrop (of Mass.)
William C. Woodbridge (?)
Laurent Clerc
Prof. Gregorio Perdicaris
* * *, Hartford judge
Martin Welles
Rev. G. Barrett
Amos Pillsbury
Julia Brace

PENNSYLVANIA

JOSEPH McILVAINE
BENJAMIN W. RICHARDS
ROBERT WALSH
HENRY D. GILPIN
Ch. J. Ingersoll

Roberts Vaux
Peter S. Duponceau
Samuel R. Wood
George Washington Smith
J. J. Smith
James J. Barclay
Nicholas Biddle
James Brown
Charles S. Coxe
Samuel L. Southard (New Jersey)
John Vaughan
Joel Roberts Poinsett
E. S. Burd
Job R. Tyson
Rev. William H. DeLancey
George M. Dallas
John Sergeant
Thomas L. McKenney
William Short
M. Carey
Thomas Bradford
Dr. Franklin Bache
John Bacon
William H. Hood
* * *, House of Refuge Supt.
Dannery (French Consul)
Choiseul (French Consul)
John Patterson (Pittsburgh)

(also the prisoners of the Eastern State Penitentiary)

BALTIMORE

J. H. B. LATROBE
Ebenezer L. Finley
Charles Carroll of Carrollton

James Carrol(l?)
Dr. Richard S. Stewart
Richard W. Gill
George Howard
William Howard
Peter H. Cruse
Nicholas Brice (?)
Rev. * * * (St. Mary's Seminary)
George Henry Calvert
Z. H. Miller
Archibald (?) Stirling
John McEvoy
Mary Randolph (?)
Cte Jules de Menou
(?) Williamson

OHIO VALLEY AND SOUTH

TIMOTHY WALKER (Cincinnati)
John McLean (Cincinnati)
Salmon P. Chase (Cincinnati)
Bellamy Storer (Cincinnati)
Dr. Daniel Drake (Cincinnati)
D. Van Matre (Cincinnati)
(B. R.?) McIlvaine (Louisville)
Harris Family (Sandy Bridge)
* * *, Memphis family
Sam Houston
* * *, Capt. of *Louisville*
Étienne Mazureau (New Orleans)
Guillemin (French Consul)
A. B. Roman (New Orleans)
Josiah Stoddard Johnston (New Orleans)
* * *, Montgomery lawyer
JOEL ROBERTS POINSETT

(also miscellaneous settlers, travellers, Chickasaw and
   Choctaw Indians)

WASHINGTON

EDWARD LIVINGSTON
Nicholas P. Trist
Andrew Jackson
Joel Roberts Poinsett
Roger B. Taney
Louis McLane
John Marshall (?)
Daniel T. Patterson
Edward Everett
Serurier (French Minister)

(also many Senators and Representatives, etc.)

SELECTED BIBLIOGRAPHY

Drescher, Seymour. *Tocqueville and England.* Cambridge: Harvard University Press, 1964.

Goldstein, Doris. *Trial of Faith: Religion and Politics in Tocqueville's Thought.* New York: Elsevier, 1975.

Herr, Richard. *Tocqueville and the Old Regime.* Princeton: Princeton University Press, 1962.

Lively, Jack. *The Social and Political Thought of Alexis de Tocqueville.* Oxford: Clarendon Press, 1962.

Marshall, Lynn, and Seymour Drescher. "American Historians and Tocqueville's *Democracy.*" *Journal of American History,* 55 (December 1968), 512–32.

Mayer, J. P. *Alexis de Tocqueville: A Biographical Study in Political Science.* New York: Viking Press, 1940.

Pierson, George W. *Tocqueville and Beaumont in America.* New York: Oxford University Press, 1938.

Richter, Melvin. "Comparative Political Analysis in Montesquieu and Tocqueville." *Comparative Politics,* 1 (January 1969), 129–60.

Schleifer, James T. *The Making of Tocqueville's Democracy in America.* Chapel Hill: University of North Carolina Press, 1980.

Tocqueville, Alexis de. *Journey to America.* Translated by George Lawrence; edited by J. P. Mayer. Garden City, N.Y.: Anchor Books, 1971.

———. *The Old Regime and the French Revolution.* Translated by Stuart Gilbert. Garden City, N.Y.: Anchor Books, 1955.

———. *Recollections.* Translated by George Lawrence; edited by J. P. Mayer and A. P. Kerr. Garden City, N.Y.: Doubleday, 1970.

Author's Preface to the Twelfth Edition

HOWEVER SUDDEN AND MOMENTOUS the events which we have just beheld so swiftly accomplished, the author of this book has a right to say that they have not taken him by surprise. His work was written fifteen years ago, with a mind constantly occupied by a single thought—that the advent of democracy as a governing power in the world's affairs, universal and irresistible, was at hand. Let it be read over again and there will be found on every page a solemn warning that society changes its forms, humanity its condition, and that new destinies are impending. It was stated in the very Introduction to the work that "the gradual development of the principle of equality is a providential fact. It has all the chief characteristics of such a fact: it is universal, it is durable, it constantly eludes all human interference, and all events as well as all men contribute to its progress. Would it be wise to imagine that a social movement the causes of which lie so far back can be checked by the efforts of one generation? Can it be believed that the democracy which has overthrown the feudal system and vanquished kings will retreat before tradesmen and capitalists? Will it stop now that it is grown so strong and its adversaries so weak?"

He who wrote these lines in the presence of a monarchy which had been rather confirmed than shaken by the Revolution of 1830 may now fearlessly ask again the attention of the public to his work. And he may be permitted to add that the present state of affairs gives to his book an immediate interest and a practical utility that it had not when it was first published. Royalty was then in power; it has now been overthrown. The institutions of America, which were a subject only of curiosity to monarchical France, ought to be a subject of study for republican France.

It is not force alone, but good laws, that give stability to a new government. After the combatant comes the legislator; the one has pulled down, the other builds up; each has his office. Though it is no longer a question whether we shall have a monarchy or a republic in France, we are yet to learn whether we shall have a convulsed or a tranquil republic, whether it shall be regular or irregular, pacific or warlike, liberal or oppressive, a republic that menaces the sacred rights of property and family, or one that honors and protects them both. It is a fearful problem, the solution of which concerns not France alone, but the whole civilized world. If we save ourselves, we save at the same time all the nations which surround us. If we perish, we shall cause all of them to perish with us. According as democratic liberty or democratic tyranny is established here, the destiny of the world will be different; and it may be said that this day it depends upon us whether the republic shall be everywhere finally established or everywhere finally overthrown.

Now, this problem, which among us has but just been proposed for solution, was solved by America more than sixty years ago. The principle of the sovereignty of the people, which we enthroned in France but yesterday, has there held undivided sway for over sixty years. It is there reduced to practice in the most direct, the most unlimited, and the most absolute manner. For sixty years the people who have made it the common source of all their laws have increased continually in population, in territory, and in opulence; and—consider it well—it is found to have been, during that period, not only the most prosperous, but the most stable, of all the nations of the earth. While all the nations of Europe have been devastated by war or torn by civil discord, the American people alone in the civilized world have remained at peace. Almost all Europe was convulsed by revolutions; America has not had even a revolt. The republic there has not been the assailant, but the guardian, of all vested rights; the property of individuals has had better guarantees there than in any other country of the world; anarchy has there been as unknown as despotism.

Where else could we find greater causes of hope, or more instructive lessons? Let us look to America, not in order to make a servile copy of the institutions that she has established, but to gain a clearer view of the polity that will be the best for us; let us look there less to find examples than instruction; let us borrow from her the principles, rather than the details, of her laws. The laws of the French republic may be, and ought to be in many cases, different from those which govern the United States; but the principles on which the American constitutions rest, those principles of order, of the balance of powers, of true liberty, of deep and sincere respect for right, are indispensable to all republics; they ought to be common to all; and it may be said beforehand that wherever they are not found, the republic will soon have ceased to exist.

1848

Democracy in America

FIRST PART

Author's Introduction

Among the novel objects that attracted my attention during my stay in the United States, nothing struck me more forcibly than the general equality of condition among the people. I readily discovered the prodigious influence that this primary fact exercises on the whole course of society; it gives a peculiar direction to public opinion and a peculiar tenor to the laws; it imparts new maxims to the governing authorities and peculiar habits to the governed.

I soon perceived that the influence of this fact extends far beyond the political character and the laws of the country, and that it has no less effect on civil society than on the government; it creates opinions, gives birth to new sentiments, founds novel customs, and modifies whatever it does not produce. The more I advanced in the study of American society, the more I perceived that this equality of condition is the fundamental fact from which all others seem to be derived and the central point at which all my observations constantly terminated.

I then turned my thoughts to our own hemisphere, and thought that I discerned there something analogous to the spectacle which the New World presented to me. I observed that equality of condition, though it has not there reached the extreme limit which it seems to have attained in the United States, is constantly approaching it; and that the democracy which governs the American communities appears to be rapidly rising into power in Europe.

Hence I conceived the idea of the book that is now before the reader.

It is evident to all alike that a great democratic revolution is going on among us, but all do not look at it in the same light. To some it appears to be novel but accidental, and, as such, they hope it may still be checked; to others it seems irresistible, because it is the most uniform, the most ancient, and the most permanent tendency that is to be found in history.

I look back for a moment on the situation of France seven hundred years ago, when the territory was divided among a small number of families, who were the owners of the soil and the rulers of the inhabitants; the right of governing descended with the family inheritance from generation to generation; force was the only means by which man could act on man; and landed property was the sole source of power.

Soon, however, the political power of the clergy was founded and began to increase: the clergy opened their ranks to all classes, to the poor and the rich, the commoner and the noble; through the church, equality penetrated into the government, and he who as a serf must have vegetated in perpetual bondage took his place as a priest in the midst of nobles, and not infrequently above the heads of kings.

The different relations of men with one another became more complicated and numerous as society gradually became more stable and civilized. Hence the want of civil laws was felt; and the ministers of law soon rose from the obscurity of the tribunals and their dusty chambers to appear at the court of the monarch, by the side of the feudal barons clothed in their ermine and their mail.

While the kings were ruining themselves by their great enterprises, and the nobles exhausting their resources by private wars, the lower orders were enriching themselves by commerce. The influence of money began to be perceptible in state affairs. The transactions of business opened a new road to power, and the financier rose to a station of political influence in which he was at once flattered and despised.

Gradually enlightenment spread, a reawakening of taste for literature and the arts became evident; intellect and will contributed to success; knowledge became an attribute of government, intelligence a social force; the educated man took part in affairs of state.

The value attached to high birth declined just as fast as new avenues to power were discovered. In the eleventh century, nobility was beyond all price; in the thirteenth, it might be purchased. Nobility was first conferred by gift in 1270, and equality was thus introduced into the government by the aristocracy itself.

In the course of these seven hundred years it sometimes happened that the nobles, in order to resist the authority of the crown or to diminish the power of their rivals, granted some political power to the common people. Or, more frequently, the king permitted the lower orders to have a share in the government, with the intention of limiting the power of the aristocracy.

In France the kings have always been the most active and the most constant of levelers. When they were strong and ambitious, they spared no pains to raise the people to the level of the nobles; when they were temperate and feeble, they allowed the people to rise above themselves. Some assisted democracy by their talents, others by their vices. Louis XI and Louis XIV reduced all ranks beneath the throne to the same degree of subjection; and finally Louis XV descended, himself and all his court, into the dust.

As soon as land began to be held on any other than a feudal tenure, and personal property could in its turn confer influence and power, every discovery in the arts, every improvement in commerce of manufactures, created so many new elements of equality among men. Henceforward every new invention, every new want which it occasioned, and every new desire which craved satisfaction were steps towards a general leveling. The taste for luxury, the love of war, the rule of fashion, and the most superficial as well as the deepest passions of the human heart seemed to co-operate to enrich the poor and to impoverish the rich.

From the time when the exercise of the intellect became a source of strength and of wealth, we see that every addition to science, every fresh truth, and every new idea became a germ of power placed within the reach of the people. Poetry, eloquence, and memory, the graces of the mind, the fire of imagination, depth of thought, and all the gifts which Heaven scatters at a venture turned to the advantage of democracy; and even when they were in the possession of its adversaries, they still served its cause by throwing into bold relief the natural greatness of man. Its conquests spread, therefore, with those of civilization and knowledge; and literature became an arsenal open to all, where the poor and the weak daily resorted for arms.

In running over the pages of our history, we shall scarcely find a single great event of the last seven hundred years that has not promoted equality of condition.

The Crusades and the English wars decimated the nobles and divided their possessions: the municipal corporations introduced democratic liberty into the bosom of feudal monarchy; the invention of firearms equalized the vassal and the noble on the field of battle; the art of printing opened the same resources to the minds of all classes; the post brought knowledge alike to the door of the cottage and to the gate of the palace; and Protestantism proclaimed that all men are equally able to find the road to heaven. The discovery of America opened a thousand new paths to fortune and led obscure adventurers to wealth and power.

If, beginning with the eleventh century, we examine what has happened in France from one half-century to another, we shall not fail to perceive that at the end of each of these periods a twofold revolution has taken place in the state of society. The noble has gone down the social ladder, and the commoner has gone up; the one descends as the other rises. Every half-century brings them nearer to each other, and they will soon meet.

Nor is this peculiar to France. Wherever we look, we

perceive the same revolution going on throughout the Christian world.

The various occurrences of national existence have everywhere turned to the advantage of democracy: all men have aided it by their exertions, both those who have intentionally labored in its cause and those who have served it unwittingly; those who have fought for it and even those who have declared themselves its opponents have all been driven along in the same direction, have all labored to one end; some unknowingly and some despite themselves, all have been blind instruments in the hands of God.

The gradual development of the principle of equality is, therefore, a providential fact. It has all the chief characteristics of such a fact: it is universal, it is lasting, it constantly eludes all human interference, and all events as well as all men contribute to its progress.

Would it, then be wise to imagine that a social movement the causes of which lie so far back can be checked by the efforts of one generation? Can it be believed that the democracy which has overthrown the feudal system and vanquished kings will retreat before tradesmen and capitalists? Will it stop now that it has grown so strong and its adversaries so weak?

Whither, then, are we tending? No one can say, for terms of comparison already fail us. There is greater equality of condition in Christian countries at the present day than there has been at any previous time, in any part of the world, so that the magnitude of what already has been done prevents us from foreseeing what is yet to be accomplished.

The whole book that is here offered to the public has been written under the influence of a kind of religious terror produced in the author's soul by the view of that irresistible revolution which has advanced for centuries in spite of every obstacle and which is still advancing in the midst of the ruins it has caused.

It is not necessary that God himself should speak in order

that we may discover the unquestionable signs of his will. It is enough to ascertain what is the habitual course of nature and the constant tendency of events. I know, without special revelation, that the planets move in the orbits traced by the Creator's hand.

If the men of our time should be convinced, by attentive observation and sincere reflection, that the gradual and progressive development of social equality is at once the past and the future of their history, this discovery alone would confer upon the change the sacred character of a divine decree. To attempt to check democracy would be in that case to resist the will of God; and the nations would then be constrained to make the best of the social lot awarded to them by Providence.

The Christian nations of our day seem to me to present a most alarming spectacle; the movement which impels them is already so strong that it cannot be stopped, but it is not yet so rapid that it cannot be guided. Their fate is still in their own hands; but very soon they may lose control.

The first of the duties that are at this time imposed upon those who direct our affairs is to educate democracy, to reawaken, if possible, its religious beliefs; to purify its morals; to mold its actions; to substitute a knowledge of statecraft for its inexperience, and an awareness of its true interest for its blind instincts, to adapt its government to time and place, and to modify it according to men and to conditions. A new science of politics is needed for a new world.

This, however, is what we think of least; placed in the middle of a rapid stream, we obstinately fix our eyes on the ruins that may still be described upon the shore we have left, while the current hurries us away and drags us backward towards the abyss.

In no country in Europe has the great social revolution that I have just described made such rapid progress as in

France; but it has always advanced without guidance. The heads of the state have made no preparation for it, and it has advanced without their consent or without their knowledge. The most powerful, the most intelligent, and the most moral classes of the nation have never attempted to control it in order to guide it. Democracy has consequently been abandoned to its wild instincts, and it has grown up like those children who have no parental guidance, who receive their education in the public streets, and who are acquainted only with the vices and wretchedness of society. Its existence was seemingly unknown when suddenly it acquired supreme power. All then servilely submitted to its caprices; it was worshipped as the idol of strength; and when afterwards it was enfeebled by its own excesses, the legislator conceived the rash project of destroying it, instead of instructing it and correcting its vices. No attempt was made to fit it to govern, but all were bent on excluding it from the government.

The result has been that the democratic revolution has taken place in the body of society without that concomitant change in the laws, ideas, customs, and morals which was necessary to render such a revolution beneficial. Thus we have a democracy without anything to lessen its vices and bring out its natural advantages; and although we already perceive the evils it brings, we are ignorant of the benefits it may confer.

While the power of the crown, supported by the aristocracy, peaceably governed the nations of Europe, society, in the midst of its wretchedness, had several sources of happiness which can now scarcely be conceived or appreciated. The power of a few of his subjects was an insurmountable barrier to the tyranny of the prince; and the monarch, who felt the almost divine character which he enjoyed in the eyes of the multitude, derived a motive for the just use of his power from the respect which he inspired. The nobles, placed high as they were above the people, could take that calm and benevolent interest in their fate which the shepherd feels towards his flock; and without acknowledging the poor as their equals, they watched over the destiny of those whose welfare Providence had entrusted to their care. The people, never having conceived the idea of a social condition different from their own, and never expecting to become equal to their leaders, received benefits from them without discussing their rights. They became attached to them when they were clement and just and submitted to their exactions without resistance or servility, as to the inevitable visitations of the Deity. Custom and usage, moreover, had established certain limits to oppression and founded a sort of law in the very midst of violence.

As the noble never suspected that anyone would attempt to deprive him of the privileges which he believed to be legitimate, and as the serf looked upon his own inferiority as a consequence of the immutable order of nature, it is easy to imagine that some mutual exchange of goodwill took place between two classes so differently endowed by fate. Inequality and wretchedness were then to be found in society, but the souls of neither rank of men were degraded.

Men are not corrupted by the exercise of power or debased by the habit of obedience, but by the exercise of a power which they believe to be illegitimate, and by obedience to a rule which they consider to be usurped and oppressive.

On the one side were wealth, strength, and leisure, accompanied by the pursuit of luxury, the refinements of taste, the pleasures of wit, and the cultivation of the arts; on the other were labor, clownishness, and ignorance. But in the midst of this coarse and ignorant multitude it was not uncommon to meet with energetic passions, generous sentiments, profound religious convictions, and wild virtues.

The social state thus organized might boast of its stability, its power, and, above all, its glory.

But the scene is now changed. Gradually the distinctions of rank are done away with; the barriers that once severed mankind are falling; property is divided, power is shared by many, the light of intelligence spreads, and the capacities of all classes tend towards equality. Society becomes democratic, and the empire of democracy is slowly and peaceably introduced into institutions and customs.

I can conceive of a society in which all men would feel an equal love and respect for the laws of which they consider themselves the authors; in which the authority of the government would be respected as necessary, and not divine; and in which the loyalty of the subject to the chief magistrate would not be a passion, but a quiet and rational persuasion. With every individual in the possession of rights which he is sure to retain, a kind of manly confidence and reciprocal courtesy would arise between all classes, removed alike from pride and servility. The people, well acquainted with their own true interests, would understand that, in order to profit from the advantages of the state, it is necessary to satisfy its requirements. The voluntary association of the citizens might then take the place of the individual authority of the nobles, and the community would be protected from tyranny and license.

I admit that, in a democratic state thus constituted, society would not be stationary. But the impulses of the social body might there be regulated and made progressive. If there were less splendor than in an aristocracy, misery would also be less prevalent; the pleasures of enjoyment might be less excessive, but those of comfort would be more general; the sciences might be less perfectly cultivated, but ignorance would be less common; the ardor of the feelings would be constrained, and the habits of the nation softened; there would be more vices and fewer crimes.

In the absence of enthusiasm and ardent faith, great sacrifices may be obtained from the members of a commonwealth by an appeal to their understanding and their experience; each individual will feel the same necessity of union with his fellows to protect his own weakness; and as he knows that he can obtain their help only on condition of helping them, he will readily perceive that his personal interest is identified with the interests of the whole community. The nation, taken as a whole, will be less brilliant, less glorious, and perhaps less strong; but the majority of the citizens will enjoy a greater degree of prosperity, and the people will remain peaceable, not because they despair of a change for the better, but because they are conscious that they are well off already.

If all the consequences of this state of things were not good or useful, society would at least have appropriated all such as were useful and good; and having once and forever renounced the social advantages of aristocracy, mankind would enter into possession of all the benefits that democracy can offer.

But here it may be asked what we have adopted in the place of those institutions, those ideas, and those customs of our forefathers which we have abandoned.

The spell of royalty is broken, but it has not been succeeded by the majesty of the laws. The people have learned to despise all authority, but they still fear it; and fear now extorts more than was formerly paid from reverence and love.

I perceive that we have destroyed those individual powers which were able, single-handed, to cope with tyranny; but it is the government alone that has inherited all the privileges of which families, guilds, and individuals have been deprived; to the power of a small number of persons, which if it was sometimes oppressive was often conservative, has succeeded the weakness of the whole community.

The division of property has lessened the distance which separated the rich from the poor; but it would seem that, the nearer they draw to each other, the greater is their mutual hatred and the more vehement the envy and the dread with which they resist each other's claims to power; the idea of right does not exist for either party, and force affords to both the only argument for the present and the only guarantee for the future.

The poor man retains the prejudices of his forefathers without their faith, and their ignorance without their virtues; he has adopted the doctrine of self-interest as the rule of his actions without understanding the science that puts it to use; and his selfishness is no less blind than was formerly his devotion to others.

If society is tranquil, it is not because it is conscious of its strength and its well-being, but because it fears its weakness and its infirmities; a single effort may cost it its life. Everybody feels the evil, but no one has courage or energy enough to seek the cure. The desires, the repinings, the sorrows, and the joys of the present time lead to nothing visible or permanent, like the passions of old men, which terminate in impotence.

We have, then, abandoned whatever advantages the old state of things afforded, without receiving any compensation from our present condition; we have destroyed an aristocracy, and we seem inclined to survey its ruins with complacency and to accept them.

The phenomena which the intellectual world presents are not less deplorable. The democracy of France, hampered in its course or abandoned to its lawless passions, has overthrown whatever crossed its path and has shaken all that it has not destroyed. Its empire has not been gradually introduced or peaceably established, but it has constantly advanced in the midst of the disorders and the agitations of a conflict. In the heat of the struggle each partisan is hurried beyond the natural limits of his opinions by the doctrines and the excesses of his opponents, until he loses sight of the end of his exertions, and holds forth in a way which does not correspond to his real sentiments or secret instincts. Hence arises the strange confusion that we are compelled to witness.

I can recall nothing in history more worthy of sorrow and pity than the scenes which are passing before our eyes. It is as if the natural bond that unites the opinions of man to his tastes, and his actions to his principles, was now broken; the harmony that has always been observed between the feelings and the ideas of mankind appears to be dissolved and all the laws of moral analogy to be abolished.

Zealous Christians are still found among us, whose minds are nurtured on the thoughts that pertain to a future life, and who readily espouse the cause of human liberty as the source of all moral greatness. Christianity, which has declared that all men are equal in the sight of God, will not refuse to acknowledge that all citizens are equal in the eye of the law. But, by a strange coincidence of events, religion has been for a time entangled with those institutions which democracy destroys; and it is not infrequently brought to reject the equality which it loves, and to curse as a foe that cause of liberty whose efforts it might hallow by its alliance.

By the side of these religious men I discern others whose thoughts are turned to earth rather than to heaven. These are the partisans of liberty, not only as the source of the noblest virtues, but more especially as the root of all solid advantages; and they sincerely desire to secure its authority, and to impart its blessings to mankind. It is natural that they should hasten to invoke the assistance of religion, for they must know that liberty cannot be established without morality, nor morality without faith. But they have seen religion in the ranks of their adversaries, and they inquire no further; some of them attack it openly, and the rest are afraid to defend it.

In former ages slavery was advocated by the venal and slavish-minded, while the independent and the warm-hearted were struggling without hope to save the liberties of mankind. But men of high and generous character are now to be met with, whose opinions are directly at variance with their inclinations, and who praise that servility and meanness which they have themselves never known. Others, on the contrary, speak of liberty as if they were able to feel its sanctity and its majesty, and loudly claim for humanity those rights which they have always refused to acknowledge.

There are virtuous and peaceful individuals whose pure morality, quiet habits, opulence, and talents fit them to be the leaders of their fellow men. Their love of country is sincere, and they are ready to make the greatest sacrifices for its welfare. But civilization often finds them among its opponents, they confound its abuses with its benefits, and the idea of evil is inseparable in their minds from that of novelty.

Near these I find others whose object is to materialize mankind, to hit upon what is expedient without heeding what is just, to acquire knowledge without faith, and prosperity apart from virtue; claiming to be the champions of modern civilization, they place themselves arrogantly at its head, usurping a place which is abandoned to them, and of which they are wholly unworthy.

Where are we, then?

The religionists are the enemies of liberty, and the friends of liberty attack religion; the high-minded and the noble advocate bondage, and the meanest and most servile preach independence; honest and enlightened citizens are opposed to all progress, while men without patriotism and without principle put themselves forward as the apostles of civilization and intelligence.

Has such been the fate of the centuries which have preceded our own? and has man always inhabited a world like the present, where all things are not in their proper relationships, where virtue is without genius, and genius without honor; where the love of order is confused with a taste for oppression, and the holy cult of freedom with a contempt of law; where the light thrown by conscience on human actions is dim, and where nothing seems to be any longer forbidden or allowed, honorable or shameful, false or true?

I cannot believe that the Creator made man to leave him in an endless struggle with the intellectual wretchedness that surrounds us. God destines a calmer and a more certain future to the communities of Europe. I am ignorant of his designs, but I shall not cease to believe in them because I cannot fathom them, and I had rather mistrust my own capacity than his justice.

There is one country in the world where the great social revolution that I am speaking of seems to have nearly reached its natural limits. It has been effected with ease and simplicity; say rather that this country is reaping the fruits of the democratic revolution which we are undergoing, without having had the revolution itself.

The emigrants who colonized the shores of America in the beginning of the seventeenth century somehow separated the democratic principle from all the principles that it had to contend with in the old communities of Europe, and transplanted it alone to the New World. It has there been able to spread in perfect freedom and peaceably to determine the character of the laws by influencing the manners of the country.

It appears to me beyond a doubt that, sooner or later, we shall arrive, like the Americans, at an almost complete equality of condition. But I do not conclude from this that we shall ever be necessarily led to draw the same political consequences which the Americans have derived from a similar social organization. I am far from supposing that they have chosen the only form of government which a democracy may adopt; but as the generating cause of laws and manners in the two countries is the same, it is of immense interest for us to know what it has produced in each of them.

It is not, then, merely to satisfy a curiosity, however legitimate, that I have examined America; my wish has been to find there instruction by which we may ourselves profit. Whoever should imagine that I have intended to write a panegyric would be strangely mistaken, and on reading this book he will perceive that such was not my design; nor has it been my object to advocate any form of government in particular, for I am of the opinion that absolute perfection is rarely to be found in any system of laws. I have not even pretended to judge whether the social revolution, which I believe to be irresistible, is advantageous or prejudicial to mankind. I have acknowledged this revolution as a fact already accomplished, or on the eve of its accomplishment; and I have selected the nation, from among those which have undergone it, in which its development has been the most peaceful and the most complete, in order to discern its natural consequences and to find out, if possible, the means of rendering it profitable to mankind. I confess that in America I saw more than America; I sought there the image of democracy itself, with its inclinations, its character, its prejudices, and its passions, in order to learn what we have to fear or to hope from its progress.

In the first part of this work I have attempted to show the distinction that democracy, dedicated to its inclinations and tendencies and abandoned almost without restraint to its instincts, gave to the laws the course it impressed on the government, and in general the control which it exercised over affairs of state. I have sought to discover the evils and the advantages which it brings. I have examined the safeguards used by the Americans to direct it, as well as those that they have not adopted, and I have undertaken to point out the factors which enable it to govern society.

My object was to portray, in a second part, the influence which the equality of conditions and democratic government in America exercised on civil society, on habits, ideas, and customs; but I grew less enthusiastic about carrying out this plan. Before I could have completed the task which I set for myself, my work would have become purposeless. Someone else would before long set forth to the public the principal traits of the American character and, delicately cloaking a serious picture, lend to the truth a charm which I should not have been able to equal.

I do not know whether I have succeeded in making known what I saw in America, but I am certain that such has been my sincere desire, and that I have never, knowingly, molded facts to ideas, instead of ideas to facts.

Whenever a point could be established by the aid of written documents, I have had recourse to the original text, and to the most authentic and reputable works. I have cited my authorities in the notes, and anyone may verify them. Whenever opinions, political customs, or remarks on the manners of the country were concerned, I have endeavored to consult the most informed men I met with. If the point in question was important or doubtful, I was not satisfied with one witness, but I formed my opinion on the evidence of several witnesses. Here the reader must necessarily rely upon my word. I could frequently have cited names which either are known to him or deserve to be so in support of my assertions; but I have carefully abstained from this practice. A stranger frequently hears important truths at the fireside of his host, which the latter would perhaps conceal from the ear of friendship; he consoles himself with his guest for the silence to which he is restricted, and the shortness of the traveler's stay takes away all fear of an indiscretion. I carefully noted every conversation of this nature as soon as it occurred, but these notes will never leave my writing-case. I had rather injure the success of my statements than add my name to the list of those stangers who repay generous hospitality they have received by subsequent chagrin and annoyance.

I am aware that, notwithstanding my care, nothing will be easier than to criticize this book should anyone care to do so.

Those readers who may examine it closely will discover, I think, in the whole work a dominant thought that binds, so to speak, its several parts together. But the diversity of the subjects I have had to treat is exceedingly great, and it will not be difficult to oppose an isolated fact to the body of facts which I cite, or an isolated idea to the body of ideas I put forth. I hope to be read in the spirit which has guided my labors, and that my book may be judged by the general impression it leaves, as I have formed my own judgment not on any single consideration, but upon the mass of evidence.

It must not be forgotten that the author who wishes to be understood is obliged to carry all his ideas to their utmost theoretical conclusions, and often to the verge of what is false or impracticable; for if it be necessary sometimes to depart in action from the rules of logic, such is not the case in discourse, and a man finds it almost as difficult to be inconsistent in his language as to be consistent in his conduct.

I conclude by pointing out myself what many readers will consider the principal defect of the work. This book is written to favor no particular views, and in composing it I have entertained no design of serving or attacking any party. I have not undertaken to see differently from others, but to look further, and while they are busied for the morrow only, I have turned my thoughts to the whole future.

Chapter I

EXTERIOR FORM OF NORTH AMERICA

North America presents in its external form certain general features which it is easy to distinguish at the first glance.

A sort of methodical order seems to have regulated the separation of land and water, mountains and valleys. A simple but grand arrangement is discoverable amid the confusion of objects and the prodigious variety of scenes.

This continent is almost equally divided into two vast regions. One is bounded on the north by the Arctic Pole, and on the east and west by the two great oceans. It stretches towards the south, forming a triangle, whose irregular sides meet at length above the great lakes of Canada. The second region begins where the other terminates, and includes all the remainder of the continent. The one slopes gently towards the Pole, the other towards the Equator.

. . .

When Europeans first landed on the shores of the West Indies, and afterwards on the coast of South America, they thought themselves transported into those fabulous regions of which poets had sung. The sea sparkled with phosphoric light, and the extraordinary transparency of its waters disclosed to the view of the navigator all the depths of the ocean. Here and there appeared little islands perfumed with odoriferous plants, and resembling baskets of flowers floating on the tranquil surface of the ocean. Every object that met the sight in this enchanting region seemed prepared to satisfy the wants or contribute to the pleasures of man. Almost all the trees were loaded with nourishing fruits, and those which were useless as food delighted the eye by the brilliance and variety of their colors. In groves of fragrant lemon trees, wild figs, flowering myrtles, acacias, and oleanders, which were hung with festoons of various climbing plants, covered with flowers, a multitude of birds unknown in Europe displayed their bright plumage, glittering with purple and azure, and mingled their warbling with the harmony of a world teeming with life and motion.

Underneath this brilliant exterior death was concealed. But this fact was not then known, and the air of these climates had an indefinably enervating influence, which made man cling to the present, heedless of the future.

North America appeared under a very different aspect: there everything was grave, serious, and solemn; it seemed created to be the domain of intelligence, as the South was that of sensual delight. A turbulent and foggy ocean washed its shores. It was girt round by a belt of granitic rocks or by wide tracts of sand. The foliage of its woods was dark and gloomy, for they were composed of firs, larches, evergreen oaks, wild olive trees, and laurels.

Beyond this outer belt lay the thick shades of the central forests, where the largest trees which are produced in the two hemispheres grow side by side. The plane, the catalpa, the sugar maple, and the Virginian poplar mingled their branches with those of the oak, the beech, and the lime.

In these, as in the forests of the Old World, destruction was perpetually going on. The ruins of vegetation were heaped upon one another; but there was no laboring hand to remove them, and their decay was not rapid enough to make room for the continual work of reproduction. Climbing plants, grasses, and other herbs forced their way through the mass of dying trees; they crept along their bending trunks, found nourishment in their dusty cavities, and a passage beneath the lifeless bark. Thus decay gave its assistance to life, and their respective productions were mingled together. The depths of these forests were gloomy and obscure, and a thousand rivulets, undirected in their course by human industry, preserved in them a constant moisture. It was rare to meet with flowers, wild fruits, or birds beneath their shades. The fall of a tree overthrown by age, the rushing torrent of a cataract, the lowing of the buffalo, and the howling of the wind were the only sounds that broke the silence of nature.

.   .   .

Although the vast country that I have been describing was inhabited by many indigenous tribes, it may justly be said, at the time of its discovery by Europeans, to have formed one great desert. The Indians occupied without possessing it. It is by agricultural labor that man appropriates the soil, and the early inhabitants of North America lived by the produce of the chase. Their implacable prejudices, their uncontrolled passions, their vices, and still more, perhaps, their savage virtues, consigned them to inevitable destruction. The ruin of these tribes began from the day when Europeans landed on their shores; it has proceeded ever since, and we are now witnessing its completion. They seem to have been placed by Providence amid the riches of the New World only to enjoy them for a season; they were there merely to wait till others came. Those coasts, so admirably adapted for commerce and industry; those wide and deep rivers; that inexhaustible valley of the Mississippi; the whole continent, in short, seemed prepared to be the abode of a great nation yet unborn.

In that land the great experiment of the attempt to construct society upon a new basis was to be made by civilized man; and it was there, for the first time, that theories hitherto unknown, or deemed impracticable, were to exhibit a spectacle for which the world had not been prepared by the history of the past.

Chapter II

ORIGIN OF THE ANGLO-AMERICANS, AND IMPORTANCE OF THIS ORIGIN IN RELATION TO THEIR FUTURE CONDITION

. . .

America is the only country in which it has been possible to witness the natural and tranquil growth of society, and where the influence exercised on the future condition of states by their origin is clearly distinguishable.

At the period when the peoples of Europe landed in the New World, their national characteristics were already completely formed; each of them had a physiognomy of its own; and as they had already attained that stage of civilization at which men are led to study themselves, they have transmitted to us a faithful picture of their opinions, their manners, and their laws. The men of the sixteenth century are almost as well known to us as our contemporaries. America, consequently, exhibits in the broad light of day the phenomena which the ignorance or rudeness of earlier ages conceals from our researches. The men of our day seem destined to see further than their predecessors into human events; they are close enough to the founding of the American settlements to know in detail their elements, and far enough away from that time already to be able to judge what these beginnings have produced. Providence has given us a torch which our forefathers did not possess, and has allowed us to discern fundamental causes in the history of

23

the world which the obscurity of the past concealed from them.

If we carefully examine the social and political state of America, after having studied its history, we shall remain perfectly convinced that not an opinion, not a custom, not a law, I may even say not an event is upon record which the origin of that people will not explain. The readers of this book will find in the present chapter the germ of all that is to follow and the key to almost the whole work.

The emigrants who came at different periods to occupy the territory now covered by the American Union differed from each other in many respects; their aim was not the same, and they governed themselves on different principles.

These men had, however, certain features in common, and they were all placed in an analogous situation. The tie of language is, perhaps, the strongest and the most durable that can unite mankind. All the emigrants spoke the same language; they were all children of the same people. Born in a country which had been agitated for centuries by the struggles of faction, and in which all parties had been obliged in their turn to place themselves under the protection of the laws, their political education had been perfected in this rude school; and they were more conversant with the notions of right and the principles of true freedom than the greater part of their European contemporaries. At the period of the first emigrations the township system, that fruitful germ of free institutions, was deeply rooted in the habits of the English; and with it the doctrine of the sovereignty of the people had been introduced into the very bosom of the monarchy of the house of Tudor.

The religious quarrels which have agitated the Christian world were then rife. England had plunged into the new order of things with headlong vehemence. The character of its inhabitants, which had always been sedate and reflective, became argumentative and austere. General information had been increased by intellectual contests, and the mind had received in them a deeper cultivation. While religion was the topic of discussion, the morals of the people became more pure. All these national features are more or less discoverable in the physiognomy of those Englishmen who came to seek a new home on the opposite shores of the Atlantic.

Another observation, moreover, to which we shall have occasion to return later, is applicable not only to the English, but to the French, the Spaniards, and all the Europeans who successively established themselves in the New World. All these European colonies contained the elements, if not the development, of a complete democracy. Two causes led to this result. It may be said that on leaving the mother country the emigrants had, in general, no notion of superiority one over another. The happy and the powerful do not go into exile, and there are no surer guarantees of equality among men than poverty and misfortune. It happened, however, on several occasions, that persons of rank were driven to America by political and religious quarrels. Laws were made to establish a gradation of ranks; but it was soon found that the soil of America was opposed to a territorial aristocracy. It was realized that in order to clear this land, nothing less than the constant and self-interested efforts of the owner himself was essential; the ground prepared, it became evident that its produce was not sufficient to enrich at the same time both an owner and a farmer. The land was then naturally broken up into small portions, which the proprietor cultivated for himself. Land is the basis of an aristocracy, which clings to the soil that supports it; for it is not by privileges alone, nor by birth, but by landed property handed down from generation to generation that an aristocracy is constituted. A nation may present immense fortunes and extreme wretchedness; but unless those fortunes are territorial, there is no true aristocracy, but simply the class of the rich and that of the poor.

All the British colonies had striking similarities at the time of their origin. All of them, from their beginning, seemed destined to witness the growth, not of the aristocratic liberty of their mother country, but of that freedom of the middle and lower orders of which the history of the world had as yet furnished no complete example.

In this general uniformity, however, several marked divergences could be observed, which it is necessary to point out. Two branches may be distinguished in the great Anglo-American family, which have hitherto grown up without entirely commingling; the one in the South, the other in the North.

Virginia received the first English colony; the immigrants took possession of it in 1607. The idea that mines of gold and silver are the sources of national wealth was at that time singularly prevalent in Europe; a fatal delusion, which has done more to impoverish the European nations who adopted it, and has cost more lives in America, than the united influence of war and bad laws. The men sent to Virginia were seekers of gold, adventurers without resources and without character, whose turbulent and restless spirit endangered the infant colony and rendered its progress uncertain. Artisans and agriculturists arrived afterwards; and, although they were a more moral and orderly race of men, they were hardly in any respect above the level of the inferior classes in England. No lofty views, no spiritual conception, presided over the foundation of these new settlements. The colony was scarcely established when slavery was introduced; this was the capital fact which was to exercise an immense influence on the character, the laws, and the whole future of the South. Slavery, as I shall afterwards show, dishonors labor; it introduces idleness into society, and with idleness, ignorance and pride, luxury and distress. It enervates the powers of the mind and benumbs the activity of man. The influence of slavery, united to the English character, explains the manners and the social condition of the Southern states.

On this same English foundation there developed in the North very different characteristics. Here I may be allowed to enter into some details.

In the English colonies of the North, more generally known as the New England states, the two or three main ideas that now constitute the basis of the social theory of the United States were first combined. The principles of New England spread at first to the neighboring states; they then passed successively to the more distant ones; and at last, if I may so speak, they *interpenetrated* the whole confederation. They now extend their influence beyond its limits, over the whole American world. The civilization of New England has been like a beacon lit upon a hill, which, after it has diffused its warmth immediatley around it, also tinges the distant horizon with its glow.

The foundation of New England was a novel spectacle, and all the circumstances attending it were singular and original. Nearly all colonies have been first inhabited either by men without education and without resources, driven by their poverty and their misconduct from the land which gave them birth, or by speculators and adventurers greedy of gain. Some settlements cannot even boast so honorable an origin; Santo Domingo was founded by buccaneers; and at the present day the criminal courts of England supply the population of Australia.

The settlers who established themselves on the shores of New England all belonged to the more independent classes of their native country. Their union on the soil of America at once presented the singular phenomenon of a society containing neither lords nor common people, and we may almost say neither rich nor poor. These men possessed, in proportion to their number, a greater mass of intelligence than is to be found in any European nation of our own time. All, perhaps without a single exception, had received a good education, and many of them were known in Europe for their talents and their acquirements. The other colonies had been founded by adventurers without families; the immigrants of New England brought with them the best elements of order and morality; they landed on the desert coast accompanied by their wives and children. But what especially distinguished them from all others was the aim of their undertaking. They had not been obliged by necessity to leave their country; the social position they abandoned was one to be regretted, and their means of subsistence were certain. Nor did they cross the Atlantic to improve their situation or to increase their wealth; it was a purely intellectual craving that called them from the comforts of their former homes; and in facing the inevitable sufferings of exile their object was the triumph of an idea.

The immigrants, or, as they deservedly styled themselves, the Pilgrims, belonged to that English sect the austerity of whose principles had acquired for them the name of Puritans. Puritanism was not merely a religious doctrine, but corresponded in many points with the most absolute democratic and republican theories. It was this tendency that had aroused its most dangerous adversaries. Persecuted by the government of the mother country, and disgusted by the habits of a society which the rigor of their own principles condemned, the Puritans went forth to seek some rude and unfrequented part of the world where they could live according to their own opinions and worship God in freedom.

It must not be imagined that the piety of the Puritans was merely speculative, or that it took no cognizance of the course of worldly affairs. Puritanism, as I have already remarked, was almost as much a political theory as a religious doctrine. No sooner had the immigrants landed on the barren coast than it was their first care to constitute a society, by subscribing the following Act [Mayflower Compact]:

"IN THE NAME OF GOD. AMEN. We, whose names are underwitten, the loyal subjects of our dread Sovereign Lord King James, &c. &c., Having undertaken for the glory of God, and advancement of the Christian Faith, and the honour of our King and country, a voyage to plant the first colony in the northern parts of Virginia; Do by these presents solemnly and mutually, in the presence of God and one another, covenant and combine ourselves together into a civil body politick, for our better ordering and preservation, and furtherance of the ends aforesaid: and by virtue hereof do enact, constitute, and frame such just and equal laws, ordinances, acts, constitutions, and offices, from time to time, as shall be thought most meet and convenient for the general good of the Colony; unto which we promise all due submission and obedience," etc.

This happened in 1620, and from that time forwards the emigration went on. The religious and political passion which ravaged the British Empire during the whole reign of Charles I drove fresh crowds of sectarians every year to the shores of America. In England the stronghold of Puritanism continued to be in the middle classes; and it was from the middle classes that most of the emigrants came. The population of New England increased rapidly; and while the hierarchy of rank despotically classed the inhabitants of the mother country, the colony approximated more and more the novel spectacle of a community homogeneous in all its parts. A democracy more perfect than antiquity had dared to dream of started in full size and panoply from the midst of an ancient feudal society.

The English government was not dissatisfied with a large emigration which removed the elements of fresh discord and further revolutions. On the contrary, it did everything to encourage it and seemed to have no anxiety about the destiny of those who sought a shelter from the rigor of their laws on the soil of America. It appeared as if New England was a region given up to the dreams of fancy and the unrestrained experiments of innovators.

The English colonies (and this is one of the main causes of their prosperity) have always enjoyed more internal freedom and more political independence than the colonies of other nations; and this principle of liberty was nowhere more extensively applied than in the New England states.

It was generally allowed at that period that the territories of the New World belonged to that European nation which had been the first to discover them. Nearly the whole coast of North America thus became a British possession towards the end of the sixteenth century. The means used by the English government to people these new domains were of several kinds: the king sometimes appointed a governor of his own choice, who ruled a portion of the New World in the name and under the immediate orders of the crown; this is the colonial system adopted by the other countries of Europe. Sometimes grants of certain tracts were made by the crown to an individual or to a company, in which case all the civil and political power fell into the hands of one or more persons, who, under the inspection and control of the crown, sold the lands and governed the inhabitants. Lastly, a third system consisted in allowing a certain number of emigrants to form themselves into a political society under the protection of the mother country and to govern themselves in whatever was not contrary to her laws. This mode of colonization so favorable to liberty, was adopted only in New England.

In 1628 a charter of this kind was granted by Charles I to the emigrants who went to form the colony of Massachusetts. But, in general, charters were not given to the colonies of New England till their existence had become an established fact. Plymouth, Providence, New Haven, Connecticut, and Rhode Island were founded without the help and almost without the knowledge of the mother country. The new settlers did not derive their powers from the head of the empire, although they did not deny its supremacy; they constituted themselves into a society, and it was not till thirty or forty years afterwards, under Charles II, that their existence was legally recognized by a royal charter.

This frequently renders it difficult, in studying the earliest historical and legislative records of New England, to detect the link that connected the emigrants with the land of their forefathers. They continually exercised the rights of sovereignty; they named their magistrates, concluded peace or declared war, made police regulations, and enacted laws, as if their allegiance was due only to God. Nothing can be more curious and at the same time more instructive than the legislation of that period; it is there that the solution of the great social problem which the United States now presents to the world is to be found.

Among these documents we shall notice as especially characteristic the code of laws promulgated by the little state of Connecticut in 1650.

The legislators of Connecticut begin with the penal laws, and, strange to say, they borrow their provisions from the text of Holy Writ.

"Whosoever shall worship any other God than the Lord," says the preamble of the Code, "shall surely be put to death." This is followed by ten or twelve enactments of the same kind, copied verbatim from the books of Exodus, Leviticus, and Deuteronomy. Blasphemy, sorcery, adultery, and rape were punished with death; an outrage offered by a son to his parents was to be expiated by the same penalty. The legislation of a rude and half-civilized people was thus applied to an enlightened and moral community. The consequence was, that the punishment of death was never more frequently prescribed by statute, and never more rarely enforced.

The chief care of the legislators in this body of penal laws was the maintenance of orderly conduct and good morals in the community; thus they constantly invaded the domain of conscience, and there was scarcely a sin which was not subject to magisterial censure. The reader is aware of the rigor with which these laws punished rape and adultery; intercourse between unmarried persons was likewise severely repressed. The judge was empowered to inflict either a pecuniary penalty, a whipping, or marriage on the misdemeanants, and if the records of the old courts of New Haven may be believed, prosecutions of this kind were not infrequent. We find a sentence, bearing the date of May 1, 1660, inflicting a fine and reprimand on a young woman who was accused of using improper language and of allowing herself to be kissed. The Code of 1650 abounds in preventive measures. It punishes idleness and drunkenness with severity. Innkeepers were forbidden to furnish more than a certain quantity of liquor to each consumer; and simple lying, whenever it may be injurious, is checked by a fine or a flogging. In other places the legislator, entirely forgetting the great principles of religious toleration that he had himself demanded in Europe, makes attendance on divine service compulsory, and goes so far as to visit with severe punishment, and even with death, Christians who chose to worship God according to a ritual differing from his own. Sometimes, indeed, the zeal for regulation induces him to descend to the most frivolous particulars: thus a law is to be found in the same code which prohibits the use of tobacco. It must not be forgotten that these fantastic and oppressive laws were not imposed by authority, but that they were freely voted by all the persons interested in them, and that the customs of the community were even more austere and puritanical than the laws. In 1649 a solemn association was formed in Boston to check the worldly luxury of long hair.

These errors are no doubt discreditable to human reason; they attest the inferiority of our nature, which is incapable of laying firm hold upon what is true and just and is often reduced to the alternative of two excesses. In strict connection with this penal legislation, which bears such striking marks of a narrow, sectarian spirit and of those religious passions which had been warmed by persecution and were still fermenting among the people, a body of political laws is to be found which, though written two hundred years ago, is still in advance of the liberties of our age.

The general principles which are the groundwork of modern constitutions, principles which, in the seventeenth century, were imperfectly known in Europe, and not completely triumphant even in Great Britain, were all recognized and established by the laws of New England: the intervention of the people in public affairs, the free voting of taxes, the responsibility of the agents of power, personal liberty, and trial by jury were all positively established without discussion.

These fruitful principles were there applied and developed to an extent such as no nation in Europe has yet ventured to attempt.

In Connecticut the electoral body consisted, from its origin, of the whole number of citizens; and this is readily to be understood. In this young community there was an almost perfect equality of fortune, and a still greater uniformity of opinions. In Connecticut at this period all the executive officials were elected, including the governor of the state. The citizens above the age of sixteen were obliged to bear ams; they formed a national militia, which appointed its own officers, and was to hold itself at all times in readiness to march for the defense of the country.

In the laws of Connecticut, as well as in all those of New England, we find the germ and gradual development of that township independence which is the life and mainspring of American liberty at the present day. The political existence of the majority of the nations of Europe commenced in the superior ranks of society and was gradually and imperfectly communicated to the different members of the social body. In America, on the contrary, it may be said that the township was organized before the county, the county before the state, the state before the union.

In New England, townships were completely and definitely constituted as early as 1650. The independence of the township was the nucleus round which the local interests, passions, rights, and duties collected and clung. It gave scope to the activity of a real political life, thoroughly democratic and republican. The colonies still recognized the supremacy of the mother country; monarchy was still the law of the state; but the republic was already established in every township.

The towns named their own magistrates of every kind, assessed themselves, and levied their own taxes. In the New England town the law of representation was not adopted; but the affairs of the community were discussed, as at Athens, in the marketplace, by a general assembly of the citizens.

In studying the laws that were promulgated at this early era of the American republics, it is impossible not to be struck by the legislator's knowledge of government and advanced theories. The ideas there formed of the duties of society towards its members are evidently much loftier and more comprehensive than those of European legislators at that time; obligations were there imposed upon it which it elsewhere slighted. In the states of New England, from the first, the condition of the poor was provided for; strict measures were taken for the maintenance of roads, and surveyors were appointed to attend to them; records were established in every town, in which the results of public deliberations and the births, deaths, and marriages of the citizens were entered; clerks were directed to keep these records; officers were appointed to administer the properties having no claimants, and others to determine the boundaries of inherited lands, and still others whose principal functions were to maintain public order in the community. The law enters into a thousand various details to anticipate and satisfy a crowd of social wants that are even now very inadequately felt in France.

But it is by the mandates relating to public education that the original character of American civilization is at once placed in the clearest light. "Whereas," says the law, "Satan, the enemy of mankind, finds his strongest weapons in the ignorance of men, and whereas it is important that the wisdom of our fathers shall not remain buried in their tombs, and whereas the education of children is one of the prime concerns of the state, with the aid of the Lord...." Here follow clauses establishing schools in every township and obliging the inhabitants, under pain of heavy fines, to support them. Schools of a superior kind were founded in the same manner in the more populous districts. The municipal authorities were bound to enforce the sending of children to school by their parents; they were empowered to inflict fines upon all who refused compliance; and in cases of continued resistance, society assumed the place of the parent, took possession of the child, and deprived the father of those natural rights which he used to so bad a purpose. The reader will undoubtedly have remarked the preamble of these enactments: in America religion is the road to knowledge, and the observance of the divine laws leads man to civil freedom.

I have said enough to put the character of Anglo-American civilization in its true light. It is the result (and this should be constantly kept in mind) of two distinct elements, which in other places have been in frequent disagreement, but which the Americans have succeeded in incorporating to some extent one with the other and combining admirably. I allude to the *spirit of religion* and the *spirit of liberty*.

The settlers of New England were at the same time ardent sectarians and daring innovators. Narrow as the limits of some of their religious opinions were, they were free from all political prejudices.

Hence arose two tendencies, distinct but not opposite, which are everywhere discernible in the manners as well as the laws of the country.

Men sacrifice for a religious opinion their friends, their family, and their country; one can consider them devoted to the pursuit of intellectual goals which they came to purchase at so high a price. One sees them, however, seeking with almost equal eagerness material wealth and moral satisfaction; heaven in the world beyond, and well-being and liberty in this one.

Under their hand, political principles, laws, and human institutions seem malleable, capable of being shaped and combined at will. As they go forward, the barriers which imprisoned society and behind which they were born are lowered; old opinions, which for centuries had been controlling the world, vanish; a course almost without limits, a field without horizon, is revealed: the human spirit rushes forward and traverses them in every direction. But having reached the limits of the political world, the human spirit stops of itself; in fear it relinquishes the need of exploration; it even abstains from lifting the veil of the sanctuary; it bows with respect before truths which it accepts without discussion.

Thus in the moral world everything is classified, systematized, foreseen, and decided beforehand; in the political world everything is agitated, disputed, and uncertain. In the one is a passive though a voluntary obedience; in the other, an independence scornful of experience, and jealous of all authority. These two tendencies, apparently so discrepant, are far from conflicting; they advance together and support each other.

Religion perceives that civil liberty affords a noble exercise to the faculties of man and that the political world is a field prepared by the Creator for the efforts of mind. Free and powerful in its own sphere, satisfied with the place reserved for it, religion never more surely establishes its empire than when it reigns in the hearts of men unsupported by aught beside its native strength.

Liberty regards religion as its companion in all its battles and its triumphs, as the cradle of its infancy and the divine source of its claims. It considers religion as the safeguard of morality, and morality as the best security of law and the surest pledge of the duration of freedom.

Chapter III

SOCIAL CONDITION OF THE ANGLO-AMERICANS

Social condition is commonly the result of circumstances, sometimes of laws, oftener still of these two causes united; but when once established, it may justly be considered as itself the source of almost all the laws, the usages, and the ideas which regulate the conduct of nations; whatever it does not produce, it modifies.

If we would become acquainted with the legislation and the manners of a nation, therefore, we must begin by the study of its social condition.

Many important observations suggest themselves upon the social condition of the Anglo-Americans; but there is one that takes precedence of all the rest. The social condition of the Americans is eminently democratic; this was its character at the foundation of the colonies, and it is still more strongly marked at the present day.

I have stated in the preceding chapter that great equality existed among the immigrants who settled on the shores of New England. Even the germs of aristocracy were never planted in that part of the Union. The only influence which obtained there was that of intellect; the people became accustomed to revere certain names as representatives of knowledge and virtue. Some of their fellow citizens acquired a power over the others that might truly have been called aristocratic if it had been capable of transmission from father to son.

This was the state of things to the east of the Hudson: to the southwest of that river, and as far as the Floridas, the case was different. In most of the states situated to the southwest of the Hudson some great English proprietors had settled who had imported with them aristocratic principles and the English law of inheritance. I have explained the reasons why it was impossible ever to establish a powerful aristocracy in America; these reasons existed with less force to the southwest of the Hudson. In the South one man, aided by slaves, could cultivate a great extent of country; it was therefore common to see rich landed proprietors. But their influence was not altogether aristocratic, as that term is understood in Europe, since they possessed no privileges; and the cultivation of their estates being carried on by slaves, they had no tenants depending on them, and consequently no patronage. Still, the great proprietors south of the Hudson constituted a superior class, having ideas and tastes of its own and forming the center of political action. This kind of aristocracy sympathized with the body of the people, whose passions and interests it easily embraced; but it was too weak and too shortlived to excite either love or hatred. This was the class which headed the insurrection in the South and furnished the best leaders of the American Revolution.

At this period society was shaken to its center. The people, in whose name the struggle had taken place, conceived the desire of exercising the authority that it had acquired; its democratic tendencies were awakened; and having thrown off the yoke of the mother country, it aspired to independence of every kind. The influence of individuals gradually ceased to be felt, and custom and law united to produce the same result.

But the law of inheritance was the last step to equality. I am surprised that ancient and modern jurists have not attributed to this law a greater influence on human affairs. It is true that these laws belong to civil affairs; but they ought, nevertheless, to be placed at the head of all political institutions; for they exercise an incredible influence upon the social state of a people, while political laws show only what this state already is. They have, moreover, a sure and uniform manner of operating upon society, affecting, as it were, generations yet unborn.

. . .

Among nations whose law of descent is founded upon the right of primogeniture, landed estates often pass from generation to generation without undergoing division; the consequence of this is that family feeling is to a certain degree incorporated with the estate. The family represents the estate, the estate the family, whose name, together with its origin, its glory, its power, and its virtues, is thus perpetuated in an imperishable memorial of the past and as a sure pledge of the future.

When the equal partition of property is established by law, the intimate connection is destroyed between family feeling and the preservation of the paternal estate; the property ceases to represent the family; for, as it must inevitably be divided after one or two generations, it has evidently a constant tendency to diminish and must in the end be completely dispersed. The sons of the great landed proprietor, if they are few in number, or if fortune befriends them, may indeed entertain the hope of being as wealthy as their father, but not of possessing the same property that he did; their riches must be composed of other elements than his. Now, as soon as you divest the landowner of that interest in the preservation of his estate which he derives from association, from tradition, and from family pride, you may be certain that, sooner or later, he will dispose of it; for there is a strong pecuniary interest in favor of selling, as floating capital produces higher interest than real property and is more readily available to gratify the passions of the moment.

Great landed estates which have once been divided never come together again; for the small proprietor draws from his land a better revenue, in proportion, than the large owner from his; and of course he sells it at a higher rate. The reasons of economy, therefore, which have led the rich man to sell vast estates will prevent him all the more from buying little ones in order to form a large one.

What is called family pride is often founded upon an illusion of self-love. A man wishes to perpetuate and immortalize himself, as it were, in his great-grandchildren. Where family pride ceases to act, individual selfishness comes into play. When the idea of family becomes vague, indeterminate, and uncertain, a man thinks of his present convenience; he provides for the establishment of his next succeeding generation and no more. Either a man gives up the idea of perpetuating his family, or at any rate he seeks to accomplish it by other means than by a landed estate.

Thus, not only does the law of partible inheritance render it difficult for families to preserve their ancestral domains entire, but it deprives them of the inclination to attempt it and compels them in some measure to co-operate with the law in their own extinction. The law of equal distribution proceeds by two methods: by acting upon things, it acts upon persons; by influencing persons, it affects things. By both these means the law succeeds in striking at the root of landed property, and dispersing rapidly both families and fortunes.

. . .

In the United States it has nearly completed its work of destruction, and there we can best study its results. The English laws concerning the transmission of property were abolished in almost all the states at the time of the Revolution. The law of entail was so modified as not materially to interrupt the free circulation of property. The first generation having passed away, estates began to be parceled out; and the change became more and more rapid with the progress of time. And now, after a lapse of a little more than sixty years, the aspect of society is totally altered; the families of the great landed proprietors are almost all commingled with the general mass. In the state of New York, which formerly contained many of these, there are but two who still keep their heads above the stream; and they must shortly disappear. The sons of these opulent citizens have become merchants, lawyers, or physicians. Most of them have lapsed into obscurity. The last trace of hereditary ranks and distinctions is destroyed; the law of partition has reduced all to one level.

I do not mean that there is any lack of wealthy individuals in the United States; I know of no country, indeed, where the love of money has taken stronger hold on the affections of men and where a profounder contempt is expressed for the theory of the permanent equality of property. But wealth circulates with inconceivable rapidity, and experience shows that it is rare to find two succeeding generations in the full enjoyment of it.

This picture, which may, perhaps, be thought to be overcharged, still gives a very imperfect idea of what is taking place in the new states of the West and Southwest. At the end of the last century a few bold adventurers began to penetrate into the valley of the Mississippi, and the mass of the population very soon began to move in that direction: communities unheard of till then suddenly appeared in the desert. States whose names were not in existence a few years before, claimed their place in the American Union; and in the Western settlements we may behold democracy arrived at its utmost limits. In these states, founded offhand and as it were by chance, the inhabitants are but of yesterday. Scarcely known to one another, the nearest neighbors are ignorant of each other's history. In this part of the American continent, therefore, the population has escaped the influence not only of great names and great wealth, but even of the natural aristocracy of knowledge and virtue. None is there able to wield that respectable power which men willingly grant to the remembrance of a life spent in doing good before their eyes. The new states of the West are already inhabited, but society has no existence among them.

It is not only the fortunes of men that are equal in America; even their acquirements partake in some degree of the same uniformity. I do not believe that there is a country in the world where, in proportion to the population, there are so few ignorant and at the same time so few learned individuals. Primary instruction is within the reach of everybody; superior instruction is scarcely to be obtained by any. This is not surprising; it is, in fact, the necessary consequence of what I have advanced above. Almost all the Americans are in easy circumstances and can therefore obtain the first elements of human knowledge.

In America there are but few wealthy persons; nearly all Americans have to take a profession. Now, every profession requires an apprenticeship. The Americans can devote to general education only the early years of life. At fifteen they enter upon their calling, and thus their education generally ends at the age when our begins. If it is continued beyond that point, it aims only towards a particular specialized and profitable purpose; one studies science as one takes up a business; and one takes up only those applications whose immediate practicality is recognized.

In America most of the rich men were formerly poor; most of those who now enjoy leisure were absorbed in business during their youth; the consequence of this is that when they might have had a taste for study, they had no time for it, and when the time is at their disposal, they have no longer the inclination.

There is no class, then, in America, in which the taste for

intellectual pleasures is transmitted with hereditary fortune and leisure and by which the labors of the intellect are held in honor. Accordingly, there is an equal want of the desire and the power of application to these objects.

A middling standard is fixed in America for human knowledge. All approach as near to it as they can; some as they rise, others as they descend. Of course, a multitude of persons are to be found who entertain the same number of ideas on religion, history, science, political economy, legislation, and government. The gifts of intellect proceed directly from God, and man cannot prevent their unequal distribution. But it is at least a consequence of what I have just said that although the capacities of men are different, as the Creator intended they should be, the means that Americans find for putting them to use are equal.

. . .

America, then, exhibits in her social state an extraordinary phenomenon. Men are there seen on a greater equality in point of fortune and intellect, or, in other words, more equal in their strength, than in any other country of the world, or in any age of which history has preserved the remembrance.

The political consequences of such a social condition as this are easily deducible.

It is impossible to believe that equality will not eventually find its way into the political world, as it does everywhere else. To conceive of men remaining forever unequal upon a single point, yet equal on all others, is impossible; they must come in the end to be equal upon all.

Now, I know of only two methods of establishing equality in the political world; rights must be given to every citizen, or none at all to anyone. For nations which are arrived at the same stage of social existence as the Anglo-Americans, it is, therefore, very difficult to discover a medium between the sovereignty of all and the absolute power of one man: and it would be vain to deny that the social condition which I have been describing is just as liable to one of these consequences as to the other.

There is, in fact, a manly and lawful passion for equality that incites men to wish all to be powerful and honored. This passion tends to elevate the humble to the rank of the great; but there exists also in the human heart a depraved taste for equality, which impels the weak to attempt to lower the powerful to their own level and reduces men to prefer equality in slavery to inequality with freedom. Not that those nations whose social condition is democratic naturally despise liberty; on the contrary, they have an instinctive love of it. But liberty is not the chief and constant object of their desires; equality is their idol: they make rapid and sudden efforts to obtain liberty and, if they miss their aim, resign themselves to their disappointment; but nothing can satisfy them without equality, and they would rather perish than lose it.

On the other hand, in a state where the citizens are all practically equal, it becomes difficult for them to preserve their independence against the aggressions of power. No one among them being strong enough to engage in the struggle alone with advantage, nothing but a general combination can protect their liberty. Now, such a union is not always possible.

From the same social position, then, nations may derive one or the other of two great political results; these results are extremely different from each other, but they both proceed from the same cause.

The Anglo-Americans are the first nation who, having been exposed to this formidable alternative, have been happy enough to escape the dominion of absolute power. They have been allowed by their circumstances, their origin, their intelligence, and especially by their morals to establish and maintain the sovereignty of the people.

Chapter IV

THE PRINCIPLE OF THE SOVEREIGNTY
OF THE PEOPLE OF AMERICA

Whenever the political laws of the United States are to be discussed, it is with the doctrine of the sovereignty of the people that we must begin.

The principle of the sovereignty of the people, which is always to be found, more or less, at the bottom of almost all human institutions, generally remains there concealed from view. It is obeyed without being recognized, or if for a moment it is brought to light, it is hastily cast back into the gloom of the sanctuary.

. . .

In America the principle of the sovereignty of the people is neither barren nor concealed, as it is with some other nations; it is recognized by the customs and proclaimed by the laws; it spreads freely, and arrives without impediment at its most remote consequences. If there is a country in the world where the doctrine of the sovereignty of the people can be fairly appreciated, where it can be studied in its application to the affairs of society, and where its dangers and its advantages may be judged, that country is assuredly America.

. . .

Chapter V

NECESSITY OF EXAMINING THE CONDITION OF THE STATES BEFORE THAT OF THE UNION AT LARGE

In the following chapter the form of government established in America on the principle of the sovereignty of the people will be examined; what are its means of action, its hindrances, its advantages, and its dangers. The first difficulty that presents itself arises from the complex nature of the Constitution of the United States, which consists of two distinct social structures, connected, and, as it were, encased one within the other; two governments, completely separate and almost independent, the one fulfilling the ordinary duties and responding to the daily and indefinite calls of a community, the other circumscribed within certain limits and only exercising an exceptional authority over the general interests of the country. In short, there are twenty-four small sovereign nations, whose agglomeration constitutes the body of the Union. To examine the Union before we have studied the states, would be to adopt a method filled with obstacles. The form of the Federal government of the United States was the last to be adopted; and it is in fact nothing more than a summary of those republican principles which were current in the whole community before it existed, and independently of its existence. Moreover, the Federal government, as I have just observed, is the exception; the government of the states is the rule. The author who should attempt to exhibit the picture as a whole before he had explained its details would necessarily fall into obscurity and repetition.

The great political principles which now govern American society undoubtedly took their origin and their growth in the state. We must know the state, then, in order to gain a clue to the rest. The states that now compose the American Union all present the same features, as regards the external aspect of their institutions. Their political or administrative life is centered in three focuses of action, which may be compared to the different nervous centers that give motion to the human body. The township is the first in order, then the county, and lastly the state.

It is not without intention that I begin this subject with the township. The village or township is the only association which is so perfectly natural that, wherever a number of men are collected, it seems to constitute itself.

The town or tithing, then, exists in all nations, whatever their laws and customs may be: it is man who makes monarchies and establishes republics, but the township seems to come directly from the hand of God. But although the existence of the township is coeval with that of man, its freedom is an infrequent and fragile thing. A nation can always establish great political assemblies, because it habitually contains a certain number of individuals fitted by their talents, if not by their habits, for the direction of affairs. The township, on the contrary, is composed of coarser materials, which are less easily fashioned by the legislator. The difficulty of establishing its independence rather augments than diminishes with the increasing intelligence of the people. A highly civilized community can hardly tolerate a local independence, is disgusted at its numerous blunders, and is apt to despair of success before the experiment is completed. Again, the immunities of townships, which have been obtained with so much difficulty, are least of all protected against the encroachments of the supreme power. They are unable to struggle, single-handed, against a strong and enterprising government, and they cannot defend themselves with success unless they are identified with the customs of the nation and supported by public opinion. Thus until the independence of townships is amalgamated with the manners of a people, it is easily destroyed; and it is only after a long existence in the laws that it can be thus amalgamated. Municipal freedom is not the fruit of human efforts; it is rarely created by others, but is, as it were, secretly self-produced in the midst of a semi-barbarous state of society. The constant action of the laws and the national habits, peculiar circumstances, and, above all, time, may consolidate it; but there is certainly no nation on the continent of Europe that has experienced its advantages. Yet municipal institutions constitute the strength of free nations. Town meetings are to liberty what primary schools are to science; they bring it within the people's reach, they teach men how to use and how to enjoy it. A nation may establish a free government, but without municipal institutions it cannot have the spirit of liberty. Transient passions, the interests of an hour, or the chance of circumstances may create the external forms of independence, but the despotic tendency which has been driven into the interior of the social system will sooner or later reappear on the surface.

To make the reader understand the general principles on which the political organization of the counties and townships in the United States rests, I have thought it expedient to choose one of the states of New England as an example, to examine in detail the mechanism of its constitution, and then to cast a general glance over the rest of the country.

The township and the country are not organized in the same manner in every part of the Union; it is easy to perceive, however, that nearly the same principles have guided the formation of both of them throughout the Union. I am inclined to believe that these principles have been carried further and have produced greater results in New

England than elsewhere. Consequently they stand out there in higher relief and offer greater facilities to the observations of a stranger.

The township institutions of New England form a complete and regular whole; they are old; they have the support of the laws and the still stronger support of the manners of the community, over which they exercise a prodigious influence. For all these reasons they deserve our special attention.

The township of New England holds a middle place between the *commune* and the *canton* of France. Its average population is from two to three thousand, so that it is not so large, on the one hand, that the interests of its inhabitants would be likely to conflict, and not so small, on the other, but that men capable of conducting its affairs may always be found among its citizens.

In the township, as well as everywhere else, the people are the source of power; but nowhere do they exercise their power more immediately. In America the people form a master who must be obeyed to the utmost limits of possibility.

In New England the majority act by representatives in conducting the general business of the state. It is necessary that it should be so. But in the townships, where the legislative and administrative action of the government is nearer to the governed, the system of representation is not adopted. There is no municipal council; but the body of voters, after having chosen its magistrates, directs them in everything that exceeds the simple and ordinary execution of the laws of the state.

This state of things is so contrary to our ideas, and so different from our customs that I must furnish some examples to make it intelligible.

The general laws of the state impose certain duties on the selectmen, which they may fulfill without the authority of their townsmen, but which they can neglect only on their own responsibility. The state law requires them, for instance, to draw up a list of voters in their townships; and if they omit this duty, they are guilty of a misdemeanor. In all the affairs that are voted in a town meeting, however, the selectmen carry into effect the popular mandate, as in France the *maire* executes the degree of the municipal council. They usually act upon their own responsibility and merely put in practice principles that have been previously recognized by the majority. But if they wish to make any change in the existing state of things or to undertake any new enterprise, they must refer to the source of their power. If, for instance, a school is to be established, the selectmen call a meeting of the voters on a certain day at an appointed place. They explain the urgency of the case; they make known the means of satisfying it, the probable expense, and the site that seems to be most favorable. The meeting is consulted on these several points: it adopts the principle, marks out the site, votes the tax, and confides the execution of its resolution to the selectmen.

The selectmen alone have the right of calling a town meeting; but they may be required to do so. If ten citizens wish to submit a new project to the assent of the town, they may demand a town meeting; the selectmen are obliged to comply and have only the right of presiding at the meeting. These political forms, these social customs, doubtless seem strange to us in France. I do not here undertake to judge them or to make known the secret causes by which they are produced and maintained. I only describe them.

. . .

In this part of the Union political life had its origin in the townships; and it may almost be said that each of them originally formed an independent nation. When the kings of England afterwards asserted their supremacy, they were content to assume the central power of the state. They left the townships where they were before; and although they are now subject to the state, they were not at first, or were hardly so. They did not receive their powers from the central authority, but, on the contrary, they gave up a portion of their independence to the state. This is an important distinction and one that the reader must constantly recollect. The townships are generally subordinate to the state only in those interests which I shall term *social,* as they are common to all the others. They are independent in all that concerns themselves alone; and among the inhabitants of New England I believe that not a man is to be found who would acknowledge that the state has any right to interfere in their town affairs. The towns of New England buy and sell, sue and are sued, augment or diminish their budgets, and no administrative authority ever thinks of offering any opposition.

. . .

In France the state collector receives the local imposts; in America the town collector receives the taxes of the state. Thus the French government lends its agents to the *commune;* in America the township lends its agents to the government. This fact alone shows how widely the two nations differ.

In America not only do municipal bodies exist, but they are kept alive and supported by town spirit. The township of New England possesses two advantages which strongly excite the interest of mankind: namely, independence and authority. Its sphere is limited, indeed; but within that sphere its action is unrestrained. This independence alone gives it a real importance, which its extent and population would not ensure.

It is to be remembered, too, that the affections of men generally turn towards power. Patriotism is not durable in a conquered nation. The New Englander is attached to his township not so much because he was born in it, but because it is a free and strong community, of which he is a member, and which deserves the care spent in managing it. In Europe the absence of local public spirit is a frequent subject of regret to those who are in power; everyone agrees that there is no surer guarantee of order and tranquillity, and yet nothing is more difficult to create. If the municipal bodies were made powerful and independent, it is feared that they would become too strong and expose the state to anarchy. Yet without power and independence a town may contain good subjects, but it can have no active citizens. Another important fact is that the township of New England is so constituted as to excite the warmest of human affections without arousing the ambitious passions of the heart of man. The officers of the county are not elected, and their authority is very limited. Even the state is only a second-rate community whose tranquil and obscure administration offers no inducement sufficient to draw men away from the home of their interests into the turmoil of public affairs. The Federal government confers power and honor on the men who conduct it, but these individuals can never be very numerous. The high station of the Presidency can only be reached at an advanced period of life; and the other Federal functionaries of a high class are generally men who have been favored by good luck or have been distinguished in some other career. Such cannot be the permanent aim of the ambitious. But the township, at the center of the ordinary relations of life, serves as a field for the desire of public esteem, the want of exciting interest, and the taste for authority and popularity; and the passions that commonly embroil society change their character when they find a vent so near the domestic hearth and the family circle.

In the American townships power has been distributed with admirable skill, for the purpose of interesting the greatest possible number of persons in the common weal. Independently of the voters, who are from time to time called into action, the power is divided among innumerable functionaries and officers, who all, in their several spheres, represent the powerful community in whose name they act. The local administration thus affords an unfailing source of profit and interest to a vast number of individuals.

The American system, which divides the local authority among so many citizens, does not scruple to multiply the functions of the town officers. For in the United States it is believed, and with truth, that patriotism is a kind of devotion which is strengthened by ritual observance. In this manner the activity of the township is continually perceptible; it is daily manifested in the fulfillment of a duty or the exercise of a right; and a constant though gentle motion is thus kept up in society, which animates without disturbing it. The American attaches himself to his little community for the same reason that the mountaineer clings to his hills, because the characteristic features of his country are there more distinctly marked; it has a more striking physiognomy.

. . . .

The native of New England is attached to his township because it is independent and free: his co-operation in its affairs ensures his attachment to its interests; the well-being it affords him secures his affection; and its welfare is the aim of his ambition and of his future exertions. He takes a part in every occurrence in the place; he practices the art of government in the small sphere within his reach; he accustoms himself to those forms without which liberty can only advance by revolutions; he imbibes their spirit; he acquires a taste for order, comprehends the balance of powers, and collects clear practical notions on the nature of his duties and the extent of his rights.

The division of the counties in America has considerable analogy with that of the *arrondissements* of France. The limits of both are arbitrarily laid down, and the various districts which they contain have no necessary connection, no common tradition or natural sympathy, no community of existence; their object is simply to facilitate the administration.

.   .   .

Nothing is more striking to a European traveler in the United States than the absence of what we term the government, or the administration. Written laws exist in America, and one sees the daily execution of them; but although everything moves regularly, the mover can nowhere be discovered. The hand that directs the social machine is invisible. Nevertheless, as all persons must have recourse to certain grammatical forms, which are the foundation of human language, in order to express their thoughts, so all communities are obliged to secure their existence by submitting to a certain amount of authority, without which they fall into anarchy. This authority may be distributed in several ways, but it must always exist somewhere.

There are two methods of diminishing the force of authority in a nation. The first is to weaken the supreme power in its very principle, by forbidding or preventing society from acting in its own defense under certain circumstances. To weaken authority in this manner is the European way of establishing freedom.

The second manner of diminishing the influence of authority does not consist in stripping society of some of its rights, nor in paralyzing its efforts, but in distributing the exercise of its powers among various hands and in multiplying functionaries, to each of whom is given the degree of power necessary for him to perform his duty. There may be nations whom this distribution of social powers might lead to anarchy, but in itself it is not anarchical. The authority thus divided is, indeed, rendered less irresistible and less perilous, but it is not destroyed.

The Revolution of the United States was the result of a mature and reflecting preference for freedom, and not of a vague or ill-defined craving for independence. It contracted no alliance with the turbulent passions of anarchy, but its course was marked, on the contrary, by a love of order and law.

It was never assumed in the United States that the citizen of a free country has a right to do whatever he pleases; on the contrary, more social obligations were there imposed upon him than anywhere else. No idea was ever entertained of attacking the principle or contesting the rights of society; but the exercise of its authority was divided, in order that the office might be powerful and the officer insignificant, and that the community should be at once regulated and free. In no country in the world does the law hold so absolute a language as in America; and in no country is the right of applying it vested in so many hands. The administrative power in the United States presents nothing either centralized or hierarchical in its constitution; this accounts for its passing unperceived. The power exists, but its representative is nowhere to be seen.

I have already mentioned that the independent townships of New England were not under guardianship, but took care of their own private interests; and the municipal magistrates are the persons who either execute the laws of the state or see that they are executed. Besides the general laws the state sometimes passes general police regulations; but more commonly the townships and town officers, conjointly with the justices of the peace, regulate the minor details of social life, according to the necessities of the different localities, and promulgate such orders as concern the health of the community and the peace as well as morality of the citizens. Lastly, these town magistrates provide, of their own accord and without any impulse from without, for those unforeseen emergencies which frequently occur in society.

It results from what I have said that in the state of Massachusetts the administrative authority is almost entirely restricted to the township, and that it is there distributed among a great number of individuals.

. . .

I have already said that, after examining the constitution of the township and the county of New England in detail, I should take a general view of the remainder of the Union. Townships and town arrangements exist in every state, but in no other part of the Union is a township to be met with precisely similar to those of New England. The farther we go towards the South, the less active does the business of the township or parish become; it has fewer magistrates, duties, and rights; the population exercises a less immediate influence on affairs; town meetings are less frequent, and the subjects of debate less numerous. The power of the elected magistrate is augmented and that of the voter diminished, while the public spirit of the local communities is less excited and less influential. These differences may be perceived to a certain extent in the state of New York; they are very evident in Pennsylvania; but they become less striking as we advance to the Northwest. The majority of the immigrants who settle in the Northwestern states are natives of New England, and they carry the administrative habits of their mother country with them into the country which they adopt. A township in Ohio is not unlike a township in Massachusetts.

We have seen that in Massachusetts the mainspring of

public administration lies in the township. It forms the common center of the interests and affections of the citizens. But this ceases to be the case as we descend to the states in which knowledge is less generally diffused, and where the township consequently offers fewer guarantees of a wise and active administrative. As we leave New England, therefore, we find that the importance of the town is gradually transferred to the county, which becomes the center of administration and the intermediate power between the government and the citizen. In Massachusetts the business of the county is conducted by the court of sessions, which is composed of a quorum appointed by the governor and his council; but the county has no representative assembly, and its expenditure is voted by the state legislature. In the great state of New York, on the contrary, and in those of Ohio and Pennsylvania, the inhabitants of each county choose a certain number of representatives, who constitute the assembly of the county. The county assembly has the right of taxing the inhabitants to a certain extent; and it is in this respect a real legislative body. At the same time it exercises an executive power in the county, frequently directs the administration of the townships, and restricts their authority within much narrower bounds than in Massachusetts.

Such are the principal differences which the systems of county and town administration present in the Federal states. Were it my intention to examine the subject in detail, I should have to point out still further differences in the executive details of the several communities. But I have said enough to show the general principles on which the administration in the United States rests. These principles are differently applied; their consequences are more or less numerous in various localities, but they are always substantially the same. The laws differ and their outward features change, but the same spirit animates them. If the township and the county are not everywhere organized in the same manner, it is at least true that in the United States the county and the township are always based upon the same principle: namely that everyone is the best judge of what concerns himself alone, and the most proper person to supply his own wants. The township and the county are therefore bound to take care of their special interests; the state governs, but does not execute the laws. Exceptions to this principle may be met with, but not a contrary principle.

. . .

I have described the townships and the administration; it now remains for me to speak of the state and the government. This is ground I may pass over rapidly without fear of being misunderstood, for all I have to say is to be found in the various written constitutions, copies of which are easily to be procured. These constitutions rest upon a simple and rational theory; most of their forms have been adopted by all constitutional nations, and have become familiar to us.

. . .

"Centralization" is a word in general and daily use, without any precise meaning being attached to it. Nevertheless, there exist two distinct kinds of centralization, which it is necessary to discriminate with accuracy.

Certain interests are common to all parts of a nation, such as the enactment of its general laws and the maintenance of its foreign relations. Other interests are peculiar to certain parts of the nation, such, for instance, as the business of the several townships. When the power that directs the former or general interests is concentrated in one place or in the same persons, it constitutes a centralized government. To concentrate in like manner in one place the direction of the latter or local interests, constitutes what may be termed a centralized administration.

Upon some points these two kinds of centralization

coincide, but by classifying the objects which fall more particularly within the province of each, they may easily be distinguished.

It is evident that a centralized government acquires immense power when united to centralized administration. Thus combined, it accustoms men to set their own will habitually and completely aside; to submit, not only for once, or upon one point, but in every respect, and at all times. Not only, therefore, does this union of power subdue them compulsorily, but it affects their ordinary habits; it isolates them and then influences each separately.

These two kinds of centralization assist and attract each other, but they must not be supposed to be inseparable. It is impossible to imagine a more completely centralized government than that which existed in France under Louis XIV; when the same individual was the author and the interpreter of the laws, and the representative of France at home and abroad, he was justified in asserting that he constituted the state. Nevertheless, the administration was was much less centralized under Louis XIV than it is at the present day.

In England the centralization of the government is carried to great perfection; the state has the compact vigor of one man, and its will puts immense masses in motion and turns its whole power where it pleases. But England, which has done such great things for the last fifty years, has never centralized its administration. Indeed, I cannot conceive that a nation can live and prosper without a powerful centralization of government. But I am of the opinion that a centralized administration is fit only to enervate the nations in which it exists, by incessantly diminishing their local spirit. Although such an administration can bring together at a given moment, on a given point, all the disposable resources of a people, it injures the renewal of those resources. It may ensure a victory in the hour of strife, but it gradually relaxes the sinews of strength. It may help admirably the transient greatness of a man, but not the durable prosperity of a nation.

Observe that whenever it is said that a state cannot act because it is not centralized, it is the centralization of the government that is spoken of. It is frequently asserted, and I assent to the proposition, that the German Empire has never been able to bring all its powers into action. But the reason is that the state has never been able to enforce obedience to its general laws; the several members of that great body always claimed the right, or found the means, of refusing their co-operation to the representatives of the common authority, even in the affairs that concerned the mass of the people; in other words, there was no centralization of government. The same remark is applicable to the Middle Ages; the cause of all the miseries of feudal society was that the control, not only of administration, but of government, was divided among a thousand hands and broken up in a thousand different ways. The want of a centralized government prevented the nations of Europe from advancing with energy in any straightforward course.

I have shown that in the United States there is no centralized administration and no hierarchy of public functionaries. Local authority has been carried farther than any European nation could endure without great inconvenience, and it has even produced some disadvantageous consequences in America. But in the United States the centralization of the government is perfect; and it would be easy to prove that the national power is more concentrated there than it has ever been in the old nations of Europe. Not only is there but one legislative body in each state, not only does there exist but one source of political authority, but numerous assemblies in districts or counties have not, in general, been multiplied lest they should be tempted to leave their administrative duties and interfere with the government. In America the legislature of each state is supreme;

nothing can impede its authority, neither privileges, nor local immunities, nor personal influence, nor even the empire of reason, since it represents that majority which claims to be the sole organ of reason. Its own determination is therefore the only limit to its action. In juxtaposition with it, and under its immediate control, is the representative of the executive power, whose duty it is to constrain the refractory to submit by superior force. The only symptom of weakness lies in certain details of the action of the government. The American republics have no standing armies to intimidate a discontented minority; but as no minority has as yet been reduced to declare open war, the necessity of an army has not been felt. The state usually employs the officers of the township or the county to deal with the citizens. Thus, for instance, in New England the town assessor fixes the rate of taxes; the town collector receives them; the town treasurer transmits the amount to the public treasury; and the disputes that may arise are brought before the ordinary courts of justice. This method of collecting taxes is slow as well as inconvenient, and it would prove a perpetual hindrance to a government whose pecuniary demands were large. It is desirable that, in whatever materially affects its existence, the government should be served by officers of its own, appointed by itself, removable at its pleasure, and accustomed to rapid methods of proceeding. But it will always be easy for the central government, organized as it is in America, to introduce more energetic and efficacious modes of action according to its wants.

The want of a centralized government will not, then, as has often been asserted, prove the destruction of the republics of the New World; far from the American governments being not sufficiently centralized, I shall prove hereafter that they are too much so. The legislative bodies daily encroach upon the authority of the government, and their tendency, like that of the French Convention, is to appropriate it entirely to themselves. The social power thus centralized is constantly changing hands, because it is subordinate to the power of the people. It often forgets the maxims of wisdom and foresight in the consciousness of its strength. Hence arises its danger. Its vigor, and not its impotence, will probably be the cause of its ultimate destruction.

The system of decentralized administration produces several different effects in America. The Americans seem to me to have overstepped the limits of sound policy in isolating the administration of the government; for order, even in secondary affairs, is a matter of national importance. As the state has no administrative functionaries of its own, stationed on different points of its territory, to whom it can give a common impulse, the consequence is that it rarely attempts to issue any general police regulations. The want of these regulations is severely felt and is frequently observed by Europeans. The appearance of disorder which prevails on the surface leads one at first to imagine that society is in a state of anarchy; nor does one perceive one's mistake till one has gone deeper into the subject. Certain undertakings are of importance to the whole state; but they cannot be put in execution, because there is no state administration to direct them. Abandoned to the exertions of the towns or counties, under the care of elected and temporary agents, they lead to no result, or at least to no durable benefit.

The partisans of centralization in Europe are wont to maintain that the government can administer the affairs of each locality better than the citizens can do it for themselves. This may be true when the central power is enlightened and the local authorities are ignorant; when it is alert and they are slow; when it is accustomed to act and they to obey. Indeed, it is evident that this double tendency must augment with the increase of centralization, and that the readiness of the one and the incapacity of the others must become more and more prominent. But I deny that it is so when the people are as enlightened, as awake to their interests, and as accustomed to reflect on them as the Americans are. I am persuaded, on the contrary, that in this case the collective strength of the citizens will always conduce more efficaciously to the public welfare than the authority of the government. I know it is difficult to point out with certainty the means of arousing a sleeping population and of giving it passions and knowledge which it does not possess; it is, I am well aware, an arduous task to persuade men to busy themselves about their own affairs. It would frequently be easier to interest them in the punctilios of court etiquette than in the repairs of their common dwelling. But whenever a central administration affects completely to supersede the persons most interested, I believe that it is either misled or desirous to mislead. However enlightened and skillful a central power may be, it cannot of itself embrace all the details of the life of a great nation. Such vigilance exceeds the powers of man. And when it attempts unaided to create and set in motion so many complicated springs, it must submit to a very perfect result or exhaust itself in bootless efforts.

Centralization easily succeeds, indeed, in subjecting the external actions of men to a certain uniformity, which we come at last to love for its own sake, independently of the objects to which it is applied, like those devotees who worship the statue and forget the deity it represents. Centralization imparts without difficulty an admirable regularity to the routine of business; provides skillfully for the details of the social police; represses small disorders and petty misdemeanors; maintains society in a *status quo* alike secure from improvement and decline; and perpetuates a drowsy regularity in the conduct of affairs which the heads of the administration are wont to call good order and public tranquillity; in short, it excels in prevention, but not in action. Its force deserts it when society is to be profoundly moved, or accelerated in its course; and if once the cooperation of private citizens is necessary to the furtherance of its measures, the secret of its impotence is disclosed. Even while the centralized power, in its despair, invokes the assistance of the citizens, it says to them: "You shall act just as I please, as much as I please, and in the direction which I please. You are to take charge of the details without aspiring to guide the system; you are to work in darkness; and afterwards you may judge my work by its results." These are not the conditions on which the alliance of the human will is to be obtained; it must be free in its gait and responsible for its acts, or (such is the constitution of man) the citizen had rather remain a passive spectator than a dependent actor in schemes with which he is unacquainted.

It is undeniable that the want of those uniform regulations which control the conduct of every inhabitant of France is not infrequently felt in the United States. Gross instances of social indifference and neglect are to be met with; and from time to time disgraceful blemishes are seen, in complete contrast with the surrounding civilization. Useful undertakings which cannot succeed without perpetual attention and rigorous exactitude are frequently abandoned; for in America, as well as in other countries, the people proceed by sudden impulses and momentary exertions. The European, accustomed to find a functionary always at hand to interfere with all he undertakes, reconciles himself with difficulty to the complex mechanism of the administration of the townships. In general it may be affirmed that the lesser details of the police, which render life easy and comfortable, are neglected in America, but that the essential guarantees of man in society are as strong there as elsewhere. In America the power that conducts the administration is far less regular, less enlightened, and less skillful, but a hundredfold greater than in Europe. In no country in the world do the citizens make such exertions for the common weal. I know of no people who have established schools so numerous and efficacious, places of public worship better suited to the wants of the inhabitants, or roads kept in better repair. Uniformity or permanence of design, the minute arrangement of details, and the perfection of adminstrative system must not be sought for in the United States; what we find there is the presence of a power which, if it is somewhat wild, is at least robust, and an existence checkered with accidents, indeed, but full of animation and effort.

Granting, for an instant, that the villages and counties of the United States would be more usefully governed by a central authority which they had never seen than by functionaries taken from among them; admitting, for the sake of argument, that there would be more security in America, and the resources of society would be better employed there, if the whole administration centered in a single arm—still the *political* advantages which the Americans derive from their decentralized system would induce me to prefer it to the contrary plan. It profits me but little, after all, that a vigilant authority always protects the tranquillity of my pleasures and constantly averts all dangers from my path, without my care or concern, if this same authority is the absolute master of my liberty and my life, and if it so monopolizes movement and life that when it languishes everything languishes around it, that when it sleeps everything must sleep, and that when it dies the state itself must perish.

There are countries in Europe where the native considers himself as a kind of settler, indifferent to the fate of the spot which he inhabits. The greatest changes are effected there without his concurrence, and (unless chance may have apprised him of the event) without his knowledge; nay, more, the condition of his village, the police of his street, the repairs of the church or the parsonage, do not concern him;

for he looks upon all these things as unconnected with himself and as the property of a powerful stranger whom he calls the government. He has only a life interest in these possessions, without the spririt of ownership or any ideas of improvement. This want of interest in his own affairs goes so far that if his own safety or that of his children is at last endangered, instead of trying to avert the peril, he will fold his arms and wait till the whole nation comes to his aid. This man who has so completely sacrificed his own free will does not, more than any other person, love obedience; he cowers, it is true, before the pettiest officer, but he braves the law with the spirit of a conquered foe as soon as its superior force is withdrawn; he perpetually oscillates between servitude and license.

When a nation has arrived at this state, it must either change its customs and its laws, or perish; for the source of public virtues is dried up; and though it may contain subjects, it has no citizens. Such communities are a natural prey to foreign conquests; and if they do not wholly disappear from the scene, it is only because they are surrounded by other nations similar or inferior to themselves; it is because they still have an indefinable instinct of patriotism; and an involuntary pride in the name of their country, or a vague reminiscence of its bygone fame, suffices to give them an impulse of self-preservation.

. . .

Laws cannot rekindle an extinguished faith, but men may be interested by the laws in the fate of their country. It depends upon the laws to awaken and direct the vague impulse of patriotism, which never abandons the human heart; and if it be connected with the thoughts, the passions, and the daily habits of life, it may be consolidated into a durable and rational sentiment. Let it not be said that it is too late to make the experiment; for nations do not grow old as men do, and every fresh generation is a new people ready for the care of the legislator.

It is not the *administrative,* but the *political* effects of decentralization that I most admire in America. In the United States the interests of the country are everywhere kept in view; they are an object of solicitude to the people of the whole Union, and every citizen is as warmly attached to them as if they were his own. He takes pride in the glory of his nation; he boasts of its success, to which he conceives himself to have contributed; and he rejoices in the general prosperity by which he profits. The feeling he entertains towards the state is analogous to that which unites him to his family, and it is by a kind of selfishness that he interests himself in the welfare of his country.

To the European, a public officer represents a superior force; to an American, he represents a right. In America, then, it may be said that no one renders obedience to man, but to justice and to law. If the opinion that the citizen entertains of himself is exaggerated, it is at least salutary; he unhesitatingly confides in his own powers, which appear to him to be all-sufficient. When a private individual meditates an undertaking, however directly connected it may be with the welfare of society, he never thinks of soliciting the co-operation of the government; but he publishes his plan, offers to execute it, courts the assistance of other individuals, and struggles manfully against all obstacles. Undoubtedly he is often less successful than the state might have been in his position; but in the end the sum of these private undertakings far exceeds all that the government could have done.

As the administrative authority is within the reach of the citizens, whom in some degree it represents, it excites neither their jealousy nor hatred; as its resources are limited, everyone feels that he must not rely solely on its aid. Thus when the administration thinks fit to act within its own limits, it is not abandoned to itself, as in Europe; the duties of private citizens are not supposed to have lapsed because the state has come into action, but everyone is ready, on the contrary, to guide and support it. This action of individuals, joined to that of the public authorities, frequently accomplishes what the most energetic centralized administration would be unable to do.

It would be easy to adduce several facts in proof of what I advance, but I had rather give only one, with which I am best acquainted. In America the means that the authorities have at their disposal for the discovery of crimes and the arrest of criminals are few. A state police does not exist, and passports are unknown. The criminal police of the United States cannot be compared with that of France; the magistrates and public agents are not numerous; they do not always initiate the measures for arresting the guilty; and the examinations of prisoners are rapid and oral. Yet I believe that in no country does crime more rarely elude punishment. The reason is that everyone conceives himself to be interested in furnishing evidence of the crime and in seizing the delinquent. During my stay in the United States I witnessed the spontaneous formation of committees in a county for the pursuit and prosecution of a man who had committed a great crime. In Europe a criminal is an unhappy man who is struggling for his life against the agents of power, while the people are merely a spectator of the conflict; in America he is looked upon as an enemy of the human race, and the whole of mankind is against him.

I believe that provincial institutions are useful to all nations, but nowhere do they appear to me to be more necessary than among a democratic people. In an aristocracy order can always be maintained in the midst of liberty; and as the rulers have a great deal to lose, order is to them a matter of great interest. In like manner an aristocracy protects the people from the excesses of despotism, because it always possesses an organized power ready to resist a despot. But a democracy without provincial institutions has no security against these evils. How can a populace unaccustomed to freedom in small concerns learn to use it temperately in great affairs? What resistance can be offered to tyranny in a country where each individual is weak and where the citizens are not united by any common interest? Those who dread the license of the mob and those who fear absolute power ought alike to desire the gradual development of provincial liberties.

I am also convinced that democratic nations are most likely to fall beneath the yoke of a centralized administration, for several reasons, among which is the following:

The constant tendency of these nations is to concentrate all the strength of the government in the hands of the only power that directly represents the people; because beyond the people nothing is to be perceived but a mass of equal individuals. But when the same power already has all the attributes of government, it can scarcely refrain from penetrating into the details of the administration, and an opportunity of doing so is sure to present itself in the long run, as was the case in France. In the French Revolution there were two impulses in opposite directions, which must never be confounded; the one was favorable to liberty, the other to despotism. Under the ancient monarchy the king was the sole author of the laws; and below the power of the sovereign certain vestiges of provincial institutions, half destroyed, were still distinguishable. These provincial institutions were incoherent, ill arranged, and frequently absurd; in the hands of the aristocracy they had sometimes been converted into instruments of oppression. The Revolution declared itself the enemy at once of royalty and of provincial institutions; it confounded in indiscriminate hatred all that had preceded it, despotic power and the checks to its abuses; and its tendency was at once to republicanize and to centralize. This double character of the French Revolution is a fact which has been adroitly handled by the friends of absolute power. Can they be accused of laboring in the cause of despotism when they are defending that centralized administration which was one of the great innovations of the Revolution? In this manner popularity may be united with hostility to the rights of the people, and the secret slave of tyranny may be the professed lover of freedom.

I have visited the two nations in which the system of provincial liberty has been most perfectly established, and I have listened to the opinions of different parties in those countries. In America I met with men who secretly aspired to destroy the democratic institutions of the Union; in England I found others who openly attacked the aristocracy; but I found no one who did not regard provincial independence as a great good. In both countries I heard a thousand different causes assigned for the evils of the state, but the local system was never mentioned among them. I heard citizens attribute the power and prosperity of their country to a multitude of reasons, but they *all* placed the advantages of local institutions in the foremost rank.

Am I to suppose that when men who are naturally so divided on religious opinions and on political theories agree on one point (and that one which they can best judge, as it is one of which they have daily experience) they are all in error? The only nations which deny the utility of provincial liberties are those which have fewest of them; in other words, only those censure the institution who do not know it.

Chapter VI

JUDICIAL POWER IN THE UNITED STATES, AND ITS INFLUENCE ON POLITICAL SOCIETY

I have thought it right to devote a separate chapter to the judicial authorities of the United States, lest their great political importance should be lessened in the reader's eyes by merely incidental mention of them. Confederations have existed in other countries besides America; I have seen republics elsewhere than upon the shores of the New World alone: the representative system of government has been adopted in several states of Europe; but I am not aware that any nation of the globe has hitherto organized a judicial power in the same manner as the Americans. The judicial organization of the United States is the institution which a stranger has the greatest difficulty in understanding. He hears the authority of a judge invoked in the political occurrences of every day, and he naturally concludes that in the United States the judges are important political functionaries; nevertheless, when he examines the nature of the tribunals, they offer at the first glance nothing that is contrary to the usual habits and privileges of those bodies; and the magistrates seem to him to interfere in public affairs only by chance, but by a chance that recurs every day.

When the Parliament of Paris remonstrated, or refused to register an edict, or when it summoned a functionary accused of malversation to its bar, its political influence as a judicial body was clearly visible; but nothing of the kind is to be seen in the United States. The Americans have retained all the ordinary characteristics of judicial authority and have carefully restricted its action to the ordinary circle of its functions.

The first characteristic of judicial power in all nations is the duty of arbitration. But rights must be contested in order to warrant the interference of a tribunal; and an action must be brought before the decision of a judge can be had. As long, therefore, as a law is uncontested, the judicial authority is not called upon to discuss it, and it may exist without being perceived. When a judge in a given case attacks a law relating to that case, he extends the circle of his customary duties, without, however, stepping beyond it, since he is in some measure obliged to decide upon the law in order to decide the case. But if he pronounces upon a law without proceeding from a case, he clearly steps beyond his sphere and invades that of the legislative authority.

The second characteristic of judicial power is that it pronounces on special cases, and not upon general principles. If a judge, in deciding a particular point, destroys a general principle by passing a judgment which tends to reject all the inferences from that principle, and consequently to annul it, he remains within the ordinary limits of his functions. But if he directly attacks a general principle without having a particular case in view, he leaves the circle in which all nations have agreed to confine his authority; he assumes a more important and perhaps a more useful influence than that of the magistrate, but he ceases to represent the judicial power.

The third characteristic of the judicial power is that it can act only when it is called upon, or when, in legal phrase, it has taken cognizance of an affair. This characteristic is less general than the other two; but, notwithstanding the exceptions, I think it may be regarded as essential. The judicial power is, by its nature, devoid of action; it must be put in motion in order to produce a result. When it is called upon to repress a crime, it punishes the criminal; when a wrong is to be redressed, it is ready to redress it; when an act requires interpretation, it is prepared to interpret it; but it does not pursue criminals, hunt out wrongs, or examine evidence of its own accord. A judicial functionary who should take the initiative and usurp the censureship of the laws would in some measure do violence to the passive nature of his authority.

The Americans have retained these three distinguishing characteristics of the judicial power: an American judge can pronounce a decision only when litigation has arisen, he is conversant only with special cases, and he cannot act until the cause has been duly brought before the court. His position is therefore exactly the same as that of the magistrates of other nations; and yet he is invested with immense political power. How does this come about? If the sphere of his authority and his means of action are the same as those of other judges, whence does he derive a power which they do not possess? The cause of this difference lies in the simple fact that the Americans have acknowledged the right of judges to found their decisions on the *Constitution* rather than on the *laws*. In other words, they have permitted them not to apply such laws as may appear to them to be unconstitutional.

. . .

In the United States the Constitution governs the legislator as much as the private citizen: as it is the first of laws, it cannot be modified by a law; and it is therefore just that the tribunals should obey the Constitution in preference to any law. This condition belongs to the very essence of the judicature; for to select that legal obligation by which he is most strictly bound is in some sort the natural right of every magistrate.

Whenever a law that the judge holds to be unconstitutional is invoked in a tribunal of the United States, he may refuse to admit it as a rule; this power is the only one peculiar to the American magistrate, but it gives rise to immense political influence. In truth, few laws can escape the searching analysis of the judicial power for any length of time, for there are few that are not prejudicial to some private interest or other, and none that may not be brought before a court of justice by the choice of parties or by the necessity of the case. But as soon as a judge has refused to apply any given law in a case, that law immediately loses a portion of its moral force. Those to whom it is prejudicial learn that means exist of overcoming its authority, and similar suits are multiplied until it becomes powerless. The alternative, then, is, that the people must alter the Constitution or the legislature must repeal the law. The political power which the Americans have entrusted to their courts of justice is therefore immense, but the evils of this power are considerably diminished by the impossibility of attacking the laws except through the courts of justice. If the judge had been empowered to contest the law on the ground of theoretical generalities, if he were able to take the initiative and to censure the legislator, he would play a prominent political part; and as the champion or the antagonist of a party, he would have brought the hostile passions of the nation into the confict. But when a judge contests a law in an obscure debate on some particular case, the importance of his attack is concealed from public notice; his decision bears upon the interest of an individual, and the law is slighted only incidentally. Moreover, although it is censured, it is not abolished; its moral force may be diminished, but its authority is not taken away; and its final destruction can be accomplished only by the reiterated attacks of judicial functionaries. It will be seen, also, that by leaving it to private interest to censure the law, and by intimately uniting the trial of the law with the trial of an individual, legislation is protected from wanton assaults and from the daily aggressions of party spirit. The errors of the legislator are exposed only to meet a real want; and it is always a positive and appreciable fact that must serve as the basis of a prosecution.

I am inclined to believe this practice of the American courts to be at once most favorable to liberty and to public order. If the judge could attack the legislator only openly and directly, he would sometimes be afraid to oppose him; and at other times party spirit might encourage him to brave it at every turn. The laws would consequently be attacked when the power from which they emanated was weak, and obeyed when it was strong; that is to say, when it would be useful to respect them, they would often be contested; and when it would be easy to convert them into an instrument of oppression, they would be respected. But the American judge is brought into the political arena independently of his own will. He judges the law only because he is obliged to judge a case. The political question that he is called upon to resolve is connected with the interests of the parties, and he cannot refuse to decide it without a denial of justice. He performs his functions as a citizen by fulfilling the precise duties which belong to his profession as a magistrate. It is true that, upon this system, the judicial censorship of the courts of justice over the legislature cannot extend to all laws indiscriminately, inasmuch as some of them can never give rise to that precise species of contest which is termed a lawsuit; and even when such a contest is possible, it may happen that no one cares to bring it before a court of justice. The Americans have often felt this inconvenience; but they have left the remedy incomplete, lest they should give it an efficacy that might in some cases prove dangerous. Within these limits the power vested in the American courts of justice of pronouncing a statute to be unconstitutional forms one of the most powerful barriers that have ever been devised against the tyranny of political assemblies.

Chapter VII

THE FEDERAL CONSTITUTION

. . .

In small states, the watchfulness of society penetrates everywhere, and a desire for improvement pervades the smallest details; the ambition of the people being necessarily checked by its weakness, all the efforts and resources of the citizens are turned to the internal well-being of the community and are not likely to be wasted upon an empty pursuit of glory. The powers of every individual being generally limited, his desires are proportionally small. Mediocrity of fortune makes the various conditions of life nearly equal, and the manners of the inhabitants are orderly and simple. Thus, all things considered, and allowance being made for the various degrees of morality and enlightenment, we shall generally find more persons in easy circumstances, more contentment and tranquillity, in small nations than in large ones.

When tyranny is established in the bosom of a small state, it is more galling than elsewhere, because, acting in a narrower circle, everything in that circle is affected by it. It supplies the place of those great designs which it cannot entertain, by a violent or exasperating interference in a multitude of minute details; and it leaves the political world, to which it properly belongs, to meddle with the arrangements of private life. Tastes as well as actions are to be regulated; and the families of the citizens, as well as the state, are to be governed. This invasion of rights occurs but seldom, however, freedom being in truth the natural state of small communities. The temptations that the government offers to ambition are too weak and the resources of private individuals are too slender for the sovereign power easily to fall into the grasp of a single man; and should such an event occur, the subjects of the state can easily unite and overthrow the tyrant and the tyranny at once by a common effort.

Small nations have therefore always been the cradle of political liberty; and the fact that many of them have lost their liberty by becoming larger shows that their freedom was more a consequence of their small size than of the character of the people.

The history of the world affords no instance of a great nation retaining the form of republican government for a long series of years, and this has led to the conclusion that such a thing is impracticable. For my own part, I think it imprudent for men who are every day deceived in relation to the actual and the present, and often taken by surprise in the circumstances with which they are most familiar, to attempt to limit what is possible and to judge the future. But it may be said with confidence, that a great republic will always be exposed to more perils than a small one.

All the passions that are most fatal to republican institutions increase with an increasing territory, while the virtues that favor them do not augment in the same proportion. The ambition of private citizens increases with the power of the state; the strength of parties with the importance of the ends they have in view; but the love of country, which ought to check these destructive agencies, is not stronger in a large than in a small republic. It might, indeed, be easily proved that it is less powerful and less developed. Great wealth and extreme poverty, capital cities of large size, a lax morality, selfishness, and antagonism of interests are the dangers which almost invariably arise from the magnitude of states. Several of these evils scarcely injure a monarchy, and some of them even contribute to its strength and duration. In monarchical states the government has its peculiar strength; it may use, but it does not depend on, the community; and the more numerous the people, the stronger is the prince. But the only security that a republican government possesses against these evils lies in the support of the majority. This support is not, however, proportionably greater in a large republic than in a small one; and thus, while the means of attack perpetually increase, in both number and influence, the power of resistance remains the same; or it may rather be said to diminish, since the inclinations and interests of the people are more diversified by the increase of the population, and the difficulty of forming a compact majority is constantly augmented. It has been observed, moreover, that the intensity of human passions is heightened not only by the importance of the end which they propose to attain, but by the multitude of individuals who are animated by them at the same time. Everyone has had occasion to remark that his emotions in the midst of a sympathizing crowd are far greater than those which he would have felt in solitude. In great republics, political passions become irresistible, not only because they aim at gigantic objects, but because they are felt and shared by millions of men at the same time.

It may therefore be asserted as a general proposition that nothing is more opposed to the well-being and the freedom of men than vast empires. Nevertheless, it is important to acknowledge the peculiar advantages of great states. For the very reason that the desire for power is more intense in these communities than among ordinary men, the love of glory is also more developed in the hearts of certain citizens, who regard the applause of a great people as a reward worthy of their exertions and an elevating encouragement to man. If we would learn why great nations contribute more powerfully to the increase of knowledge and the advance of civilization than small states, we shall discover an adequate cause in the more rapid and energetic circulation of ideas and in those great cities which are the intellectual centers where all the rays of human genius are reflected and combined. To this it may be added that most important discoveries demand a use of national power which the government of a small state is unable to make: in great nations the government has more enlarged ideas, and is more completely disengaged from the routine of precedent and the selfishness of local feeling; its designs are conceived with more talent and executed with more boldness.

In time of peace the well-being of small nations is undoubtedly more general and complete; but they are apt to suffer more acutely from the calamities of war than those great empires whose distant frontiers may long avert the presence of the danger from the mass of the people, who are therefore more frequently afflicted than ruined by the contest.

But in this matter, as in many others, the decisive argument is the necessity of the case. If none but small nations existed, I do not doubt that mankind would be more happy and more free; but the existence of great nations is unavoidable.

Political strength thus becomes a condition of national prosperity. It profits a state but little to be affluent and free if it is perpetually exposed to be pillaged or subjugated; its manufacturers and commerce are of small advantage if another nation has the empire of the seas and gives the law in all the markets of the globe. Small nations are often miserable, not because they are small, but because they are weak; and great empires prosper less because they are great than because they are strong. Physical strength is therefore one of the first conditions of the happiness and even of the existence of nations. Hence it occurs that, unless very peculiar circumstances intervene, small nations are always united to large empires in the end, either by force or by their own consent. I do not know a more deplorable condition than that of a people unable to defend itself or to provide for its own wants.

The federal system was created with the intention of combining the different advantages which result from the magnitude and the littleness of nations; and a glance at the United States of America discovers the advantages which they have derived from its adoption.

In great centralized nations the legislator is obliged to give a character of uniformity to the laws, which does not always suit the diversity of customs and of districts; as he takes no cognizance of special cases, he can only proceed upon general principles; and the population are obliged to conform to the requirements of the laws, since legislation cannot adapt itself to the exigencies and the customs of the population, which is a great cause of trouble and misery. This disadvantage does not exist in confederations; Congress regulates the principal measures of the national government, and all the details of the administration are reserved to the provincial legislatures. One can hardly imagine how much this division of sovereignty contributes to the well-being of each of the states that compose the Union. In these small communities, which are never agitated by the desire of aggrandizement or the care of self-defense, all public authority and private energy are turned towards internal improvements. The central government of each state, which is in immediate relationship with the citizens, is daily apprised of the wants that arise in society; and new projects are proposed every year, which are discussed at town meetings or by the legislature, and which are transmitted by the press to stimulate the zeal and to excite the interest of the citizens. This spirit of improvement is constantly alive in the American republics, without compromising their tranquillity; the ambition of power yields to the less refined and less dangerous desire for well-being. It is generally believed in America that the existence and the permanence of the republican form of government in the New World depend upon the existence and the duration of the federal system; and it is not unusual to attribute a large share of the misfortunes that have befallen the new states of South America to the injudicious erection of great republics nstead of a divided and confederate sovereignty.

It is incontestably true that the tastes and the habits of republican government in the United States were first created in the townships and the provincial assemblies. In a small state, like that of Connecticut, for instance, where cutting a canal or laying down a road is a great political question, where the state has no army to pay and no wars to carry on, and where much wealth or much honor cannot be given to the rulers, no form of government can be more natural or more appropriate than a republic. But it is this same republican spirit, it is these manners and customs of a free people, which have been created and nurtured in the different states, that must be afterwards applied to the country at large. The public spirit of the Union is, so to speak, nothing more than an aggregate or summary of the patriotic zeal of the separate provinces. Every citizen of the United States transfers, so to speak, his attachment to his little republic into the common store of American patriotism. In defending the Union he defends the increasing prosperity of his own state or county, the right of conducting its affairs, and the hope of causing measures of improvement to be adopted in it which may be favorable to his own interests; and these are motives that are wont to stir men more than the general interests of the country and the glory of the nation.

On the other hand, if the temper and the manners of the inhabitants especially fitted them to promote the welfare of a great republic, the federal system renders their task less difficult. The confederation of all the American states presents none of the ordinary inconveniences resulting from large associations of men. The Union is a great republic in extent, but the paucity of objects for which its government acts assimilates it to a small state. Its acts are important, but they are rare. As the sovereignty of the Union is limited and incomplete, its exercise is not dangerous to liberty; for it does not excite those insatiable desires for fame and power which have proved so fatal to great republics. As there is no common center to the country, great capital cities, colossal wealth, abject poverty, and sudden revolutions are alike unknown; and political passion, instead of spreading over the land like a fire on the prairies, spends its strength against the interests and the individual passions of every state.

Nevertheless, tangible objects and ideas circulate throughout the Union as freely as in a country inhabited by one people. Nothing checks the spirit of enterprise. The government invites the aid of all who have talents or knowledge to serve it. Inside of the frontiers of the Union profound peace prevails, as within the heart of some great empire; abroad it ranks with the most powerful nations of the earth: two thousand miles of coast are open to the commerce of the world; and as it holds the keys of a new world, its flag is respected in the most remote seas. The Union is happy and free as a small people, and glorious and strong as a great nation.

.   .   .

No one can be more inclined than I am to appreciate the advantages of the federal system, which I hold to be one of the combinations most favorable to the prosperity and freedom of man. I envy the lot of those nations which have been able to adopt it; but I cannot believe that any confederate people could maintain a long or an equal contest with a nation of similar strength in which the government is centralized. A people which, in the presence of the great military monarchies of Europe, should divide its sovereignty into fractional parts would, in my opinion, by that very act abdicate its power, and perhaps its existence and its name. But such is the admirable position of the New World that man has no other enemy than himself, and that, in order to be happy and to be free, he has only to determine that he will be so.

Chapter VIII

Thus far I have examined the institutions of the United States; I have passed their legislation in review and have described the present forms of political society in that country. But above these institutions and beyond all these characteristic forms, there is a sovereign power, that of the people, which may destroy or modify them at its pleasure. It remains to be shown in what manner this power, superior to the laws, acts; what are its instincts and its passions, what the secret springs that retard, accelerate, or direct its irresistible course, what the effects of its unbounded authority, and what the destiny that is reserved for it.

HOW IT CAN BE STRICTLY SAID
THAT THE PEOPLE GOVERN
IN THE UNITED STATES

In America the people appoint the legislative and the executive power and furnish the jurors who punish all infractions of the laws. The institutions are democratic, not only in their principle, but in all their consequences; and the people elect their representatives *directly,* and for the most part *annually,* in order to ensure their dependence. The people are therefore the real directing power; and although the form of government is representative, it is evident that the opinions, the prejudices, the interests, and even the passions of the people are hindered by no permanent obstacles from exercising a perpetual influence on the daily conduct of affairs. In the United States the majority governs in the name of the people, as is the case in all countries in which the people are supreme. This majority is principally composed of peaceable citizens, who, either by inclination or by interest, sincerely wish the welfare of their country. But they are surrounded by the incessant agitation of parties, who attempt to gain their co-operation and support.

Chapter IX

PARTIES IN THE UNITED STATES

. . .

The political parties that I style great are those which cling to principles rather than to their consequences; to general and not to special cases; to ideas and not to men. These parties are usually distinguished by nobler features, more generous passions, more genuine convictions, and a more bold and open conduct than the others. In them private interest, which always plays the chief part in political passions, is more studiously veiled under the pretext of the public good; and it may even be sometimes concealed from the eyes of the very persons whom it excites and impels.

Minor parties, on the other hand, are generally deficient in political good faith. As they are not sustained or dignified by lofty purposes, they ostensibly display the selfishness of their character in their actions. They glow with a factitious zeal; their language is vehement, but their conduct is timid and irresolute. The means which they employ are as wretched as the end at which they aim. Hence it happens that when a calm state succeeds a violent revolution, great men seem suddenly to disappear and the powers of the human mind to lie concealed. Society is convulsed by great parties, it is only agitated by minor ones; it is torn by the former, by the latter it is degraded; and if the first sometimes save it by a salutary perturbation, the last invariably disturb it to no good end.

America has had great parties, but has them no longer; and if her happiness is thereby considerably increased, her morality has suffered. When the War of Independence was terminated and the foundations of the new government were to be laid down, the nation was divided between two opinions—two opinions which are as old as the world and which are perpetually to be met with, under different forms and various names, in all free communities, the one tending to limit, the other to extend indefinitely, the power of the people. The conflict between these two opinions never assumed that degree of violence in America which it has frequently displayed elsewhere. Both parties of the Americans were agreed upon the most essential points; and neither of them had to destroy an old constitution or to overthrow the structure of society in order to triumph. In neither of them, consequently, were a great number of private interests affected by success or defeat: but moral principles of a high order, such as the love of equality and of independence, were concerned in the struggle, and these sufficed to kindle violent passions.

The party that desired to limit the power of the people, endeavored to apply its doctrines more especially to the Constitution of the Union, whence it derived its name of *Federal*. The other party, which affected to be exclusively attached to the cause of liberty, took that of *Republican*. America is the land of democracy, and the Federalists, therefore, were always in a minority; but they reckoned on their side almost all the great men whom the War of Independence had produced, and their moral power was very considerable. Their cause, moreover, was favored by circumstances. The ruin of the first Confederation had impressed the people with a dread of anarchy, and the Federalists profited by this transient disposition of the multitude. For ten or twelve years, they were at the head of affairs, and they were able to apply some, though not all, of their principles; for the hostile current was becoming from day to day too violent to be checked. In 1801 the Republicans got possession of the government: Thomas Jefferson was elected President; and he increased the influence of their party by the weight of his great name, the brilliance of his talents, and his immense popularity.

. . .

Great political parties, then, are not to be met with in the United States at the present time. Parties, indeed, may be found which threaten the future of the Union; but there is none which seems to contest the present form of government or the present course of society. The parties by which the Union is menaced do not rest upon principles, but upon material interests. These interests constitute, in the different provinces of so vast an empire, rival nations rather than parties. Thus, upon a recent occasion the North contended for the system of commercial prohibition, and the South took up arms in favor of free trade, simply because the North is a manufacturing and the South an agricultural community; and the restrictive system that was profitable to the one was prejudicial to the other.

In the absence of great parties the United States swarms with lesser controversies, and public opinion is divided into a thousand minute shades of difference upon questions of detail. The pains that are taken to create parties are inconceivable, and at the present day it is no easy task. In the United States there is no religious animosity, because all religion is respected and no sect is predominant; there is no jealousy of rank, because the people are everything and none can contest their authority; lastly, there is no public misery to serve as a means of agitation, because the physical position of the country opens so wide a field to industry that man only needs to be let alone to be able to accomplish prodigies. Nevertheless, ambitious men will succeed in creating parties, since it is difficult to eject a person from authority upon the mere ground that this place is coveted by others. All the skill of the actors in the political world lies in the art of creating parties. A political aspirant in the United States begins by discerning his own interest, and discovering those other interests which may be collected around and amalgamated with it. He then contrives to find out some doctrine or principle that may suit the purposes of this new association, which he adopts in order to bring forward his party and secure its popularity: just as the imprimatur of the king was in former days printed upon the title page of a volume and was thus incorporated with a book to which it in no wise belonged. This being done, the new party is ushered into the political world.

To a stranger all the domestic controversies of the Americans at first appear to be incomprehensible or puerile, and he is at a loss whether to pity a people who take such arrant trifles in good earnest or to envy that happiness which enables a community to discuss them. But when he comes to study the secret propensities that govern the factions of America, he easily perceives that the greater part of them are more or less connected with one or the other of those two great divisions which have always existed in free communities. The deeper we penetrate into the inmost thought of these parties, the more we perceive that the object of the one is to limit and that of the other to extend the authority of the people. I do not assert that the ostensible purpose or even that the secret aim of American parties is to promote the rule of aristocracy or democracy in the country; but I affirm that aristocratic or democratic passions may easily be detected at the bottom of all parties, and that, although they escape a superficial observation, they are the main point and soul of every faction in the United States.

To quote a recent example, when President Jackson attacked the Bank of the United States, the country was excited, and parties were formed; the well-informed classes rallied round the bank, the common people round the

President. But it must not be imagined that the people had formed a rational opinion upon a question which offers so many difficulties to the most experienced statesmen. By no means. The bank is a great establishment, which has an independent existence; and the people, accustomed to make and unmake whatsoever they please, are startled to meet with this obstacle to their authority. In the midst of the perpetual fluctuation of society, the community is irritated by so permanent an institution and is led to attack it, in order to see whether it can be shaken, like everything else.

It sometimes happens in a people among whom various opinions prevail that the balance of parties is lost and one of them obtains an irresistible preponderance, overpowers all obstacles, annihilates its opponents, and appropriates all the resources of society to its own use. The vanquished despair of success, hide their heads, and are silent. The nation seems to be governed by a single principle, universal stillness prevails, and the prevailing party assumes the credit of having restored peace and unanimity to the country. But under this apparent unanimity still exist profound differences of opinion, and real opposition.

This is what occurred in America; when the democratic party got the upper hand, it took exclusive possession of the conduct of affairs, and from that time the laws and the customs of society have been adapted to its caprices. At the present day the more affluent classes of society have no influence in political affairs; and wealth, far from conferring a right, is rather a cause of unpopularity than a means of attaining power. The rich abandon the lists, through unwillingness to contend, and frequently to contend in vain, against the poorer classes of their fellow citizens. As they cannot occupy in public a position equivalent to what they hold in private life, they abandon the former and give themselves up to the latter; and they constitute a private society in the state which has its own tastes and pleasures.

They submit to this state of things as an irremediable evil, but they are careful not to show that they are galled by its continuance; one often hears them laud the advantages of a republican government and democratic institutions when they are in public. Next to hating their enemies, men are most inclined to flatter them.

Chapter X

LIBERTY OF THE PRESS IN
THE UNITED STATES

The influence of the liberty of the press does not affect
political opinions alone, but extends to all the opinions of
men and modifies customs as well as laws. In another part of
this work I shall attempt to determine the degree of influence
that the liberty of the press has exercised upon civil society in
the United States and to point out the direction which it has
given to the ideas as well as the tone which it has imparted to
the character and the feelings of the Anglo-Americans. At
present I propose only to examine the effects produced by
the liberty of the press in the political world.

. . .

In countries where the doctrine of the sovereignty of the
people ostensibly prevails, the censorship of the press is not
only dangerous, but absurd. When the right of every citizen
to a share in the government of society is acknowledged,
everyone must be presumed to be able to choose between the
various opinions of his contemporaries and to appreciate
the different facts from which inferences may be drawn. The
sovereignty of the people and the liberty of the press may
therefore be regarded as correlative, just as the censorship of
the press and universal suffrage are two things which are
irreconcilably opposed and which cannot long be retained
among the institutions of the same people. Not a single
individual of the millions who inhabit the United States has

as yet dared to propose any restrictions on the liberty of the press.

. . .

America is perhaps, at this moment, the country of the whole world that contains the fewest germs of révolution; but the press is not less destructive in its principles there than in France, and it displays the same violence without the same reasons for indignation. In America as in France it constitutes a singular power, so strangely composed of mingled good and evil that liberty could not live without it, and public order can hardly be maintained against it. Its power is certainly much greater in France than in the United States, though nothing is more rare in the latter country than to hear of a prosecution being instituted against it. The reason for this is perfectly simple: the Americans, having once admitted the doctrine of the sovereignty of the people, apply it with perfect sincerity. It was never their intention out of elements which are changing every day to create institutions that should last forever; and there is consequently nothing criminal in an attack upon the existing laws, provided a violent infraction of them is not intended. They are also of the opinion that courts of justice are powerless to check the abuses of the press, and that, as the subtlety of human language perpetually eludes judicial analysis, offenses of this nature somehow escape the hand which attempts to seize them. They hold that to act with efficacy upon the press it would be necessary to find a tribunal not only devoted to the existing order of things, but capable of surmounting the influence of public opinion; a tribunal which should conduct its proceedings without publicity, which should pronounce its decrees without assigning its motives, and punish the intentions even more than the language of a writer. Whoever should be able to create and maintain a tribunal of this kind would waste his time in prosecuting the liberty of the press; for he would be the absolute master of the whole community and would be as free to rid himself of the authors as of their writings. In this question, therefore, there is no medium between servitude and license; in order to enjoy the inestimable benefits that the liberty of the press ensures, it is necessary to submit to the inevitable evils that it creates. To expect to acquire the former and to escape the latter is to cherish one of those illusions which commonly mislead nations in their times of sickness when, tired with faction and exhausted by effort, they attempt to make hostile opinions and contrary principles coexist upon the same soil.

The small influence of the American journals is attributable to several reasons, among which are the following:

The liberty of writing, like all other liberty, is most formidable when it is a novelty, for a people who have never been accustomed to hear state affairs discussed before them place implicit confidence in the first tribune who presents himself. The Anglo-Americans have enjoyed this liberty ever since the foundation of the colonies; moreover, the press cannot create human passions, however skillfully it may kindle them where they exist. In America political life is active, varied, even agitated, but is rarely affected by those deep passions which are excited only when material interests are impaired; and in the United States these interests are prosperous. A glance at a French and an American newspaper is sufficient to show the difference that exists in this respect between the two nations. In France the space allotted to commerical advertisements is very limited, and the news intelligence is not considerable, but the essential part of the journal is the discussion of the politics of the day. In America three quarters of the enormous sheet are filled with advertisements, and the remainder is frequently occupied by political intelligence or trivial anecdotes; it is only from time to time that one finds a corner devoted to passionate discussions like those which the journalists of France every day give to their readers.

It has been demonstrated by observation, and discovered by the sure instinct even of the pettiest despots, that the influence of a power is increased in proportion as its direction is centralized. In France the press combines a twofold centralization; almost all its power is centered in the same spot and, so to speak, in the same hands, for its organs are far from numerous.

. . .

Neither of these kinds of centralization exists in America. The United States has no metropolis; the intelligence and the power of the people are disseminated through all the parts of this vast country, and instead of radiating from a common point they cross each other in every direction; the Americans have nowhere established any central direction of opinion, any more than of the conduct of affairs. This difference arises from local circumstances and not from human power; but it is owing to the laws of the Union that there are no licenses to be granted to printers, no securities demanded from editors, as in France, and no stamp duty, as in France and England. The consequence is that nothing is easier than to set up a newspaper, as a small number of subscribers suffices to defray the expenses.

Hence the number of periodical and semi-periodical publications in the United States is almost incredibly large. The most enlightened Americans attribute the little influence of the press to this excessive dissemination of its power; and it is an axiom of political science in that country that the only way to neutralize the effect of the public journals is to multiply their number. I cannot see how a truth which is so self-evident should not already have been more generally admitted in Europe.

. . .

In America there is scarcely a hamlet that has not its newspaper. It may readily be imagined that neither discipline nor unity of action can be established among so many combatants, and each one consequently fights under his own standard. All the political journals of the United States are, indeed, arrayed on the side of the administration or against it; but they attack and defend it in a thousand different ways. They cannot form those great currents of opinion which sweep away the strongest dikes. This division of the influence of the press produces other consequences scarcely less remarkable. The facility with which newspapers can be established produces a multitude of them; but as the competition prevents any considerable profit, persons of much capacity are rarely led to engage in these undertakings. Such is the number of the public prints that even if they were a source of wealth, writers of ability could not be found to direct them all. The journalists of the United States are generally in a very humble position, with a scanty education and a vulgar turn of mind.

. . .

It cannot be denied that the political effects of this extreme license of the press tend indirectly to the maintenance of public order. Individuals who already stand high in the esteem of their fellow citizens are afraid to write in the newspapers, and they are thus deprived of the most powerful instrument that they can use to excite the passions of the multitude to their own advantage.

. . .

But although the press is limited to these resources, its influence in America is immense. It causes political life to circulate through all the parts of that vast territory. Its eye is constantly open to detect the secret springs of political designs and to summon the leaders of all parties in turn to the bar of public opinion. It rallies the interests of the community round certain principles and draws up the creed of every party; for it affords a means of intercourse between those who hear and address each other without ever coming into immediate contact. When many organs of the press adopt the same line of conduct, their influence in the long run becomes irresistible, and public opinion, perpetually assailed from the same side, eventually yields to the attack. In the United States each separate journal exercises but little authority; but the power of the periodical press is second only to that of the people.

In the United States democracy perpetually brings new men to the conduct of public affairs, and the administration consequently seldom preserves consistency or order in its measures. But the general principles of the government are more stable and the chief opinions which regulate society are more durable there than in many other countries. When once the Americans have taken up an idea, whether it be well or ill founded, nothing is more difficult than to eradicate it from their minds. The same tenacity of opinion has been observed in England, where for the last century greater freedom of thought and more invincible prejudices have existed than in any other country of Europe. I attribute this to a cause that may at first sight appear to have an opposite tendency: namely, to the liberty of the press. The nations among whom this liberty exists cling to their opinions as much from pride as from conviction. They cherish them because they hold them to be just and because they chose them of their own free will; and they adhere to them, not only because they are true, but because they are their own.

. . .

Chapter XI

POLITICAL ASSOCIATIONS
IN THE UNITED STATES

In no country in the world has the principle of association
been more successfully used or applied to a greater multitude of objects than in America. Besides the permanent
associations which are established by law under the names
of townships, cities, and counties, a vast number of others
are formed and maintained by the agency of private
individuals.

The citizen of the United States is taught from infancy to
rely upon his own exertions in order to resist the evils and
the difficulties of life; he looks upon the social authority with
an eye of mistrust and anxiety, and he claims its assistance
only when he is unable to do without it. This habit may be
traced even in the schools, where the children in their games
are wont to submit to rules which they have themselves
established, and to punish misdemeanors which they have
themselves defined. The same spirit pervades every act of
social life. If a stoppage occurs in a thoroughfare and the
circulation of vehicles is hindered, the neighbors immediately form themselves into a deliberative body; and this
extemporaneous assembly gives rise to an executive power
which remedies the inconvenience before anybody has
thought of recurring to a pre-existing authority superior to
that of the persons immediately concerned. If some public
pleasure is concerned, an association is formed to give more
splendor and regularity to the entertainment. Societies are
formed to resist evils that are exclusively of a moral nature,

as to diminish the vice if intemperance. In the United States associations are established to promote the public safety, commerce, industry, morality, and religion. There is no end which the human will despairs of attaining through the combined power of individuals united into a society.

I shall have occasion hereafter to show the effects of association in civil life; I confine myself for the present to the political world. When once the right of association is recognized, the citizens may use it in different ways.

An association consists simply in the public assent which a number of individuals give to certain doctrines and in the engagement which they contract to promote in a certain manner the spread of those doctrines. The right of associating in this fashion almost merges with freedom of the press, but societies thus formed possess more authority than the press. When an opinion is represented by a society, it necessarily assumes a more exact and explicit form. It numbers its partisans and engages them in its cause; they, on the other hand, become acquainted with one another, and their zeal is increased by their number. An association unites into one channel the efforts of divergent minds and urges them vigorously towards the one end which it clearly points out.

The second degree in the exercise of the right of association is the power of meeting. When an association is allowed to establish centers of action at certain important points in the country, its activity is increased and its influence extended. Men have the opportunity of seeing one another; means of execution are combined; and opinions are maintained with a warmth and energy that written language can never attain.

Lastly, in the exercise of the right of political association there is a third degree: the partisans of an opinion may unite in electoral bodies and choose delegates to represent them in a central assembly. This is, properly speaking, the application of the representative system to a party.

. . .

The more I consider the independence of the press in its principal consequences, the more am I convinced that in the modern world it is the chief and, so to speak, the constitutive element of liberty. A nation that is determined to remain free is therefore right in demanding, at any price, the exercise of this independence. But the *unlimited* liberty of political association cannot be entirely assimilated to the liberty of the press. The one is at the same time less necessary and more dangerous than the other. A nation may confine it within certain limits without forfeiting any part of its self-directing power; and it may sometimes be obliged to do so in order to maintain its own authority.

. . .

It must be acknowledged that the unrestrained liberty of political association has not hitherto produced in the United States the fatal results that might perhaps be expected from it elsewhere. The right of association was imported from England, and it has always existed in America; the exercise of this privilege is now incorporated with the manners and customs of the people. At the present time the liberty of association has become a necessary guarantee against the tyranny of the majority. In the United States, as soon as a party has become dominant, all public authority passes into its hands; its private supporters occupy all the offices and have all the force of the administration at their disposal. As the most distinguished members of the opposite party cannot surmount the barrier that excludes them from power, they must establish themselves outside of it and oppose the whole moral authority of the minority to the physical power that domineers over it. Thus a dangerous expedient is used to obviate a still more formidable danger.

The omnipotence of the majority appears to me to be so full of peril to the American republics that the dangerous means used to bridle it seem to be more advantageous than prejudicial. And here I will express an opinion that may remind the reader of what I said when speaking of the freedom of townships. There are no countries in which associations are more needed to prevent the despotism of faction or the arbitrary power of a prince than those which are democratically constituted. In aristocratic nations the body of the nobles and the wealthy are in themselves natural associations which check the abuses of power. In countries where such associations do not exist, if private individuals cannot create an artificial and temporary substitute for them I can see no permanent protection against the most galling tyranny; and a great people may be oppressed with impunity by a small faction or by a single individual.

. . .

It cannot be denied that the unrestrained liberty of association for political purposes is the privilege which a people is longest in learning how to exercise. If it does not throw the nation into anarchy, it perpetually augments the chances of that calamity. On one point, however, this perilous liberty offers a security against dangers of another kind; in countries where associations are free, secret societies are unknown. In America there are factions, but no conspiracies.

The most natural privilege of man, next to the right of acting for himself, is that of combining his exertions with those of his fellow creatures and of acting in common with them. The right of association therefore appears to me almost as inalienable in its nature as the right of personal liberty. No legislator can attack it without impairing the foundations of society. Nevertheless, if the liberty of association is only a source of advantage and prosperity to some nations, it may be perverted or carried to excess by others, and from an element of life may be changed into a cause of destruction. A comparison of the different methods that associations pursue in those countries in which liberty is well understood and in those where liberty degenerates into license may be useful both to governments and to parties.

Most Europeans look upon association as a weapon which is to be hastily fashioned and immediately tried in the conflict. A society is formed for discussion, but the idea of impending action prevails in the minds of all those who constitute it. It is, in fact, an army; and the time given to speech serves to reckon up the strength and to animate the courage of the host, after which they march against the enemy. To the persons who compose it, resources which lie within the bounds of law may suggest themselves as means of success, but never as the only means.

Such, however, is not the manner in which the right of association is understood in the United States. In America the citizens who form the minority associate in order, first, to show their numerical strength and so to diminish the moral power of the majority; and, secondly, to stimulate competition and thus to discover those arguments that are most fitted to act upon the majority; for they always entertain hopes of drawing over the majority to their own side and then controlling the supreme power in its name. Political associations in the United States are therefore peaceable in their intentions and strictly legal in the means which they employ; and they assert with perfect truth that they aim at success only by lawful expedients.

. . .

Chapter XII

GOVERNMENT OF THE DEMOCRACY IN AMERICA

I am well aware of the difficulties that attend this part of my subject; but although every expression which I am about to use may clash, upon some points, with the feelings of the different parties which divide my country, I shall still speak my whole thought.

In Europe we are at a loss how to judge the true character and the permanent instincts of democracy, because in Europe two conflicting principles exist and we do not know what to attribute to the principles themselves and what to the passions that the contest produces. Such is not the case in America, however; there the people reign without impediment, and they have no perils to dread and no injuries to avenge. In America democracy is given up to its own propensities; its course is natural and its activity is unrestrained; there, consequently, its real character must be judged. And to no people can this inquiry be more vitally interesting than to the French nation, who are blindly driven onwards, by a daily and irresistible impulse, towards a state of things which may prove either despotic or republican, but which will assuredly be democratic.

I have already observed that universal suffrage has been adopted in all the states of the Union; it consequently exists in communities that occupy very different positions in the social scale. I have had opportunities of observing its effects in different localities and among races of men who are nearly strangers to each other in their language, their religion, and their modes of life; in Louisiana as well as in New England,

106

in Georgia as in Canada. I have remarked that universal suffrage is far from producing in America either all the good or all the evil consequences which may be expected from it in Europe, and that its effects generally differ very much from those which are attributed to it.

Many people in Europe are apt to believe without saying it, or to say without believing it, that one of the great advantages of universal suffrage is that it entrusts the direction of affairs to men who are worthy of the public confidence. They admit that the people are unable to govern of themselves, but they aver that the people always wish the welfare of the state and instinctively designate those who are animated by the same good will and who are the most fit to wield the supreme authority. I confess that the observations I made in America by no means coincide with these opinions. On my arrival in the United States I was surprised to find so much distinguished talent among the citizens and so little among the heads of the government. It is a constant fact that at the present day the ablest men in the United States are rarely placed at the head of affairs; and it must be acknowledged that such has been the result in proportion as democracy has exceeded all its former limits. The race of American statesmen has evidently dwindled most remarkably in the course of the last fifty years.

Several causes may be assigned for this phenomenon. It is impossible, after the most strenuous exertions, to raise the intelligence of the people above a certain level. Whatever may be the facilities of acquiring information, whatever may be the profusion of easy methods and cheap science, the human mind can never be instructed and developed without devoting considerable time to these objects.

The greater or lesser ease with which people can live without working is a sure index of intellectual progress. This boundary is more remote in some countries and more restricted in others, but it must exist somewhere as long as the people are forced to work in order to procure the means of subsistence; that is to say, as long as they continue to be the people. It is therefore quite as difficult to imagine a state in which all the citizens are very well informed as a state in which they are all wealthy; these two difficulties are correlative. I readily admit that the mass of the citizens sincerely wish to promote the welfare of the country; nay, more, I even grant that the lower classes mix fewer considerations of personal interest with their patriotism than the higher orders; but it is always more or less difficult for them to discern the best means of attaining the end which they sincerely desire. Long and patient observation and much acquired knowledge are requisite to form a just estimate of the character of a single individual. Men of the greatest genius often fail to do it, and can it be supposed that the common people will always succeed? The people have neither the time nor the means for an investigation of this kind. Their conclusions are hastily formed from a superficial inspection of the more prominent features of a question. Hence it often happens that mountebanks of all sorts are able to please the people, while their truest friends frequently fail to gain their confidence.

Moreover, democracy not only lacks that soundness of judgment which is necessary to select men really deserving of their confidence, but often have not the desire or the inclination to find them out. It cannot be denied that democratic institutions strongly tend to promote the feeling of envy in the human heart; not so much because they afford to everyone the means of rising to the same level with others as because those means perpetually disappoint the persons who employ them. Democratic institutions awaken and foster a passion for equality which they can never entirely satisfy. This complete equality eludes the grasp of the people at the very moment when they think they have grasped it, and "flies," as Pascal says, "with an eternal flight"; the people are excited in the pursuit of an advantage, which is more precious because it is not sufficiently remote to be unknown or sufficiently near to be enjoyed. The lower orders are agitated by the chance of success, they are irritated by its uncertainty; and they pass from the enthusiasm of pursuit to the exhaustion of ill success, and lastly to the acrimony of disappointment. Whatever transcends their own limitations appears to be an obstacle to their desires, and there is no superiority, however legitimate it may be, which is not irksome in their sight.

It has been supposed that the secret instinct which leads the lower orders to remove their superiors as much as possible from the direction of public affairs is peculiar to France. This is an error, however; the instinct to which I allude is not French, it is democratic; it may have been heightened by peculiar political circumstances, but it owes its origin to a higher cause.

In the United States the people do not hate the higher classes of society, but are not favorably inclined towards them and carefully exclude them from the exercise of authority. They do not fear distinguished talents, but are rarely fond of them. In general, everyone who rises without their aid seldom obtains their favor.

While the natural instincts of democracy induce the people to reject distinguished citizens as their rulers, an instinct not less strong induces able men to retire from the political arena, in which it is so difficult to retain their independence, or to advance without becoming servile.

. . .

I have already observed that the American statesmen of the present day are very inferior to those who stood at the head of affairs fifty years ago. This is as much a consequence of the circumstances as of the laws of the country. When America was struggling in the high cause of independence to throw off the yoke of another country, and when it was about to usher a new nation into the world, the spirits of its inhabitants were roused to the height which their great objects required. In this general excitement distinguished men were ready to anticipate the call of the community, and the people clung to them for support and placed them at their head. But such events are rare, and it is from the ordinary course of affairs that our judgment must be formed.

If passing occurrences sometimes check the passions of democracy, the intelligence and the morals of the community exercise an influence on them which is not less powerful and far more permanent. This is very perceptible in the United States.

In New England, where education and liberty are the daughters of morality and religion, where society has acquired age and stability enough to enable it to form principles and hold fixed habits, the common people are accustomed to respect intellectual and moral superiority and to submit to it without complaint, although they set at naught all those privileges which wealth and birth have introduced among mankind. In New England, consequently, the democracy makes a more judicious choice than it does elsewhere.

But as we descend towards the South, to those states in which the constitution of society is more recent and less strong, where instruction is less general and the principles of morality, religion, and liberty are less happily combined, we perceive that talents and virtues become more rare among those who are in authority.

Lastly, when we arrive at the new Southwestern states, in which the constitution of society dates but from yesterday and presents only an agglomeration of adventurers and speculators, we are amazed at the persons who are invested with public authority, and we are led to ask by what force, independent of legislation and of the men who direct it, the state can be protected and society be made to flourish.

There are certain laws of a democratic nature which contribute, nevertheless, to correct in some measure these dangerous tendencies of democracy. On entering the House of Representatives at Washington, one is struck by the vulgar demeanor of that great assembly. Often there is not a distinguished man in the whole number. Its members are almost all obscure individuals, whose names bring no associations to mind. They are mostly village lawyers, men in trade, or even persons belonging to the lower classes of society. In a country in which education is very general, it is said that the representatives of the people do not always know how to write correctly.

At a few yards' distance is the door of the Senate, which contains within a small space a large proportion of the celebrated men of America. Scarcely an individual is to be seen in it who has not had an active and illustrious career: the Senate is composed of eloquent advocates, distinguished generals, wise magistrates, and statesmen of note, whose arguments would do honor to the most remarkable parliamentary debates of Europe.

How comes this strange contrast, and why are the ablest citizens found in one assembly rather than in the other? Why is the former body remarkable for its vulgar elements, while the latter seems to enjoy a monopoly of intelligence and talent? Both of these assemblies emanate from the people; both are chosen by universal suffrage; and no voice has hitherto been heard to assert in America that the Senate is hostile to the interests of the people. From what cause, then, does so startling a difference arise? The only reason which appears to me adequately to account for it is that the House of Representatives is elected by the people directly, while the Senate is elected by elected bodies. The whole body of the citizens name the legislature of each state, and the Federal

Constitution converts these legislatures into so many electoral bodies, which return the members of the Senate. The Senators are elected by an indirect application of the popular vote; for the legislatures which appoint them are not aristocratic or privileged bodies, that elect in their own right, but they are chosen by the totality of the citizens; they are generally elected every year, and enough new members may be chosen every year to determine the senatorial appointments. But this transmission of the popular authority through an assembly of chosen men operates an important change in it by refining its discretion and improving its choice. Men who are chosen in this manner accurately represent the majority of the nation which governs them; but they represent only the elevated thoughts that are current in the community and the generous propensities that prompt its nobler actions rather than the petty passions that disturb or the vices that disgrace it.

The time must come when the American republics will be obliged more frequently to introduce the plan of election by an elected body into their system of representation or run the risk of perishing miserably among the shoals of democracy.

. . .

When elections recur only at long intervals, the state is exposed to violent agitation every time they take place. Parties then exert themselves to the utmost in order to gain a prize which is so rarely within their reach; and as the evil is almost irremediable for the candidates who fail, everything is to be feared from their disappointed ambition. If, on the other hand, the legal struggle is soon to be repeated, the defeated parties take patience.

When elections occur frequently, their recurrence keeps society in a feverish excitement and gives a continual instability to public affairs. Thus, on the one hand, the state is exposed to the perils of a revolution, on the other to perpetual mutability; the former system threatens the very existence of the government, the latter prevents any steady and consistent policy. The Americans have preferred the second of these evils to the first; but they were led to this conclusion by instinct more than by reason, for a taste for variety is one of the characteristic passions of democracy. Hence their legislation is strangely mutable.

. . .

Public officers in the United States are not separate from the mass of citizens; they have neither palaces nor guards nor ceremonial costumes. This simple exterior of persons in authority is connected not only with the peculiarities of the American character, but with the fundamental principles of society. In the estimation of the democracy a government is not a benefit, but a necessary evil. A certain degree of power must be granted to public officers, for they would be of no use without it. But the ostensible semblance of authority is by no means indispensable to the conduct of affairs, and it is needlessly offensive to the susceptibility of the public. The public officers themselves are well aware that the superiority over their fellow citizens which they derive from their authority they enjoy only on condition of putting themselves on a level with the whole community by their manners. A public officer in the Unites States is uniformly simple in his manners, accessible to all the world, attentive to all requests, and obliging in his replies. I was pleased by these characteristics of a democratic government; I admired the manly independence that respects the office more than the officer and thinks less of the emblems of authority than of the man who bears them.

In two kinds of government the magistrates exercise considerable arbitrary power: namely, under the absolute government of an individual, and under that of a democracy. This identical result proceeds from very similar causes.

In despotic states the fortune of no one is secure; public officers are not more safe than private persons. The sovereign, who has under his control the lives, the property, and sometimes the honor of the men whom he employs, thinks he has nothing to fear from them and allows them great latitude of action because he is convinced that they will not use it against him. In despotic states the sovereign is so much attached to his power that he dislikes the constraint even of his own regulations, and likes to see his agents acting irregularly and, as it were, by chance in order to be sure that their actions will never counteract his desires.

In democracies, as the majority has every year the right of taking away the power of the officers whom it had appointed, it has no reason to fear any abuse of their authority. As the people are always able to signify their will to those who conduct the government, they prefer leaving them to their own free action instead of prescribing an invariable rule of conduct, which would at once fetter their activity and the popular authority.

. . .

The authority which public men possess in America is so brief and they are so soon commingled with the ever changing population of the country that the acts of a community frequently leave fewer traces than events in a private family. The public administration is, so to speak, oral and traditional. But little is committed to writing, and that little is soon wafted away forever, like the leaves of the Sibyl, by the smallest breeze.

The only historical remains in the United States are the

newspapers; if a number be wanting, the chain of time is broken and the present is severed from the past. I am convinced that in fifty years it will be more difficult to collect authentic documents concerning the social condition of the Americans at the present day than it is to find remains of the administration of France during the Middle Ages; and if the United States were ever invaded by barbarians, it would be necessary to have recourse to the history of other nations in order to learn anything of the people who now inhabit them.

The instability of administration has penetrated into the habits of the people; it even appears to suit the general taste, and no one cares for what occurred before his time: no methodical system is pursued, no archives are formed, and no documents are brought together when it would be very easy to do so. Where they exist, little store is set upon them. I have among my papers several original public documents which were given to me in the public offices in answer to some of my inquiries. In America society seems to live from hand to mouth, like an army in the field. Nevertheless, the art of administration is undoubtedly a science, and no sciences can be improved if the discoveries and observations of successive generations are not connected together in the order in which they occur. One man in the short space of his life remarks a fact, another conceives an idea; the former invents a means of execution, the latter reduces a truth to a formula; and mankind gathers the fruits of individual experience on its way and gradually forms the sciences. But the persons who conduct the administration in America can seldom afford any instruction to one another; and when they assume the direction of society, they simply possess those attainments which are widely disseminated in the community, and no knowledge peculiar to themselves. Democracy, pushed to its furthest limits, is therefore prejudicial to the art of government; and for this reason it is better adapted to a people already versed in the conduct of administration than to a nation that is uninitiated in public affairs.

. . .

Before we can tell whether a democratic government is economical or not we must establish a standard of comparison. The question would be of easy solution if we were to draw a parallel between a democratic republic and an absolute monarchy. The public expenditure in the former would be found to be more considerable than in the latter; such is the case with all free states compared with those which are not so. It is certain that despotism ruins individuals by preventing them from producing wealth much more than by depriving them of what they have already produced; it dries up the source of riches, while it usually respects acquired property. Freedom, on the contrary, produces far more goods than it destroys; and the nations which are favored by free institutions invariably find that their resources increase even more rapidly than their taxes.

My present object is to compare free nations with one another and to point out the influence of democracy upon the finances of a state.

Communities as well as organic bodies are subject in their formation to certain fixed rules from which they cannot depart. They are composed of certain elements that are common to them at all times and under all circumstances. The people may always be mentally divided into three classes. The first of these classes consists of the wealthy; the second, of those who are in easy circumstances; and the third is composed of those who have little or no property and who subsist by the work that they perform for the two superior orders. The proportion of the individuals in these several divisions may vary according to the condition of society, but the divisions themselves can never be obliterated.

It is evident that each of these classes will exercise an

influence peculiar to its own instincts upon the administration of the finances of the state. If the first of the three exclusively possesses the leglislative power, it is probable that it will not be sparing of the public funds, because the taxes which are levied on a large fortune only diminish the sum of superfluities and are, in fact, but little felt. If the second class has the power of making the laws, it will certainly not be lavish of taxes, because nothing is so onerous as a large impost levied upon a small income. The government of the middle classes appears to me the most economical, I will not say the most enlightened, and certainly not the most generous, of free governments.

Let us now suppose that the legislative authority is vested in the lowest order: there are two striking reasons which show that the tendency of the expenditures will be to increase, not to diminish.

As the great majority of those who create the laws have no taxable property, all the money that is spent for the community appears to be spent to their advantage, at no cost of their own; and those who have some little property readily find means of so regulating the taxes that they weigh upon the wealthy and profit the poor, although the rich cannot take the same advantage when they are in possession of the government.

In countries in which the poor have the exclusive power of making the laws, no great economy of public expenditure ought to be expected; that expenditure will always be considerable, either because the taxes cannot weigh upon those who levy them, or because they are levied in such a manner as not to reach these poorer classes. In other words, the government of the democracy is the only one under which the power that votes the taxes escapes the payment of them.

In vain will it be objected that the true interest of the people is to spare the fortunes of the rich, since they must suffer in the long run from the general impoverishment which will ensue. Is it not the true interest of kings also, to render their subjects happy, and of nobles to admit recruits into their order on suitable grounds? If remote advantages had power to prevail over the passions and the exigencies of the moment, no such thing as a tyrannical sovereign or an exclusive aristocracy could ever exist.

Again, it may be objected that the poor never have the sole power of making the laws; but I reply that wherever universal suffrage has been established, the majority unquestionably exercises the legislative authority; and if it be proved that the poor always constitute the majority, may it not be added with perfect truth that in the countries in which they possess the elective franchise they possess the sole power of making the laws? It is certain that in all the nations of the world the greater number has always consisted of those persons who hold no property, or of those whose property is insufficient to exempt them from the necessity of working in order to procure a comfortable subsistence. Universal suffrage, therefore, in point of fact does invest the poor with the government of society.

The disastrous influence that popular authority may sometimes exercise upon the finances of a state was clearly seen in some of the democratic republics of antiquity, in which the public treasure was exhausted in order to relieve indigent citizens or to supply games and theatrical amusements for the populace. It is true that the representative system was then almost unknown, and that at the present time the influence of popular passions is less felt in the conduct of public affairs, but it may well be believed that in the end the delegate will conform to the principles of his constituents and favor their propensities as much as their interests.

The extravagance of democracy is less to be dreaded, however, in proportion as the people acquire a share of property, because, on the one hand, the contributions of the rich are then less needed, and, on the other, it is more difficult to impose taxes that will not reach the imposers. On this account universal suffrage would be less dangerous in France than in England, where nearly all the taxable property is vested in the hands of a few. America, where the great majority of the citizens possess some fortune, is in a still more favorable position than France.

There are further causes that may increase the amount of public expenditure in democratic countries. When an aristocracy governs, those who conduct the affairs of state are exempted, by their very station in society, from any want: content with their lot, power and renown are the only objects for which they strive; placed far above the obscure crowd, they do not always clearly perceive how the well-being of the mass of the people will redound to their own grandeur. They are not, indeed, callous to the sufferings of the poor; but they cannot feel those miseries as acutely as if they were themselves partakers of them. Provided that the people appear to submit to their lot, the rulers are satisfied and demand nothing further from the government. An aristocracy is more intent upon the means of maintaining than of improving its condition.

When, on the contrary, the people are invested with the supreme authority, they are perpetually seeking for something better, because they feel the hardship of their lot. The thirst for improvement extends to a thousand different ojects; it descends to the most trivial details, and especially to those changes which are accompanied with considerable expense, since the object is to improve the condition of the poor, who cannot pay for the improvement. Moreover, all democratic communities are agitated by an ill-defined excitement and a kind of feverish impatience that creates a multitude of innovations, almost all of which are expensive.

In monarchies and aristocracies those who are ambitious

flatter the natural taste which the rulers have for power and renown and thus often incite them to very costly undertakings. In democracies, where the rulers are poor and in want, they can be courted only by such means as will improve their well-being, and these improvements cannot take place without money. When a people begin to reflect on their situation, they discover a multitude of wants that they had not before been conscious of, and to satisfy these exigencies recourse must be had to the coffers of the state. Hence it happens that the public charges increase in proportion to the civilization of the country, and taxes are augmented as knowledge becomes more diffused.

The last cause which renders a democratic government dearer than any other is that a democracy does not always lessen its expenditures even when it wishes to do so, because it does not understand the art of being economical. As it frequently changes its purposes, and still more frequently its agents, its undertakings are often ill-conducted or left unfinished; in the former case the state spends sums out of all proportion to the end that it proposes to accomplish; in the latter the expense brings no return.

There is a powerful reason that usually induces democracies to economize upon the salaries of public officers. Those who fix the amount of the salaries, being very numerous, have but little chance of obtaining office so as to be in receipt of those salaries. In aristocratic countries, on the contrary, the individuals who appoint high salaries have almost always a vague hope of profiting by them. These appointments may be looked upon as a capital which they create for their own use, or at least as a resource for their children.

.   .   .

A distinction must be made when aristocracies and democracies accuse each other of facilitating corruption. In aristocratic governments, those who are placed at the head of affairs are rich men, who are desirous only of power. In democracies, statesmen are poor and have their fortunes to make. The consequence is that in aristocratic states the rulers are rarely accessible to corruption and have little craving for money, while the reverse is the case in democratic nations.

But in aristocracies, as those who wish to attain the head of affairs possess considerable wealth, and as the number of persons by whose assistance they may rise is comparatively small, the government is, if I may so speak, put up at auction. In democracies, on the contrary, those who are covetous of power are seldom wealthy, and the number of those who confer power is extremely great. Perhaps in democracies the number of men who might be bought is not smaller, but buyers are rarely to be found; and, besides, it would be necessary to buy so many persons at once that the attempt would be useless.

Many of the men who have governed France during the last forty years have been accused of making their fortunes at the expense of the state or its allies, a reproach which was rarely addressed to the public men of the old monarchy. But in France the practice of bribing electors is almost unknown, while it is notoriously and publicly carried on in England. In the United States I never heard anyone accused of spending his wealth in buying votes, but I have often heard the probity of public officers questioned; still more frequently have I heard their success attributed to low intrigues and immoral practices.

If, then, the men who conduct an aristocracy sometimes endeavor to corrupt the people, the heads of a democracy are themselves corrupt. In the former case the morality of the people is directly assailed; in the latter an indirect influence is exercised which is still more to be dreaded.

As the rulers of democratic nations are almost always

suspected of dishonorable conduct, they in some measure lend the authority of the government to the base practices of which they are accused. They thus afford dangerous examples, which discourage the struggles of virtuous independence and cloak with authority the secret designs of wickedness. If it be asserted that evil passions are found in all ranks of society, that they ascend the throne by hereditary right, and that we may find despicable characters at the head of aristocratic nations as well as in the bosom of a democracy, the plea has but little weight in my estimation. The corruption of men who have casually risen to power has a coarse and vulgar infection in it that renders it dangerous to the multitude. On the contrary, there is a kind of aristocratic refinement and an air of grandeur in the depravity of the great, which frequently prevent it from spreading abroad.

. . .

It is difficult to say what degree of effort a democratic government may be capable of making on the occurrence of a national crisis. No great democratic republic has hitherto existed in the world. To style the oligarchy which ruled over France in 1793 by that name would be an insult to the republican form of government. The United States affords the first example of the kind.

The American Union has now subsisted for half a century, and its existence has only once been attacked; namely, during the War of Independence. At the commencement of that long war, extraordinary efforts were made with enthusiasm for the service of the country. But as the contest was prolonged, private selfishness began to reappear. No money was brought into the public treasury; few recruits could be raised for the army; the people still wished to acquire independence, but would not employ the only means by which it could be obtained. "Tax laws," says

Hamilton, in *The Federalist* (No. 12), "have in vain been multipled; new methds to enforce the collection have in vain been tried; the public expectation has been uniformly disappointed; and the treasuries of the States have remained empty. The popular system of administration inherent in the nature of popular government, coinciding with the real scarcity of money incident to a languid and mutilated state of trade, has hitherto defeated every experiment for extensive collections, and has at length taught the different legislatures the folly of attempting them."

Since that period the United States has not had a single serious war to carry on. In order, therefore, to know what sacrifices democratic nations may impose upon themselves, we must wait until the American people are obliged to put half their entire income at the disposal of the government, as was done by the English; or to send forth a twentieth part of its population to the field of battle, as was done by France.

. . .

It is incontestable that, in times of danger, a free people display far more energy than any other. But I incline to believe that this is especially true of those free nations in which the aristocratic element preponderates. Democracy appears to me better adapted for the conduct of society in times of peace, or for a sudden effort of remarkable vigor, than for the prolonged endurance of the great storms that beset the political existence of nations. The reason is very evident; enthusiasm prompts men to expose themselves to dangers and privations; but without reflection they will not support them long. There is more calculation even in the impulses of bravery than is generally supposed; and although the first efforts are made by passion alone, perseverance is maintained only by a distinct view of what one is fighting for. A portion of what is dear to us is hazarded in order to save the remainder.

But it is this clear perception of the future, founded upon judgment and experience, that is frequently wanting in democracies. The people are more apt to feel than to reason; and if their present sufferings are great, it is to be feared that the still greater sufferings attendant upon defeat will be forgotten.

. . .

I am of opinion that a democratic government tends, in the long run, to increase the real strength of society; but it can never combine, upon a single point and at a given time, so much power as an aristocracy or an absolute monarchy. If a democratic country remained during a whole century subject to a republican government, it would probably at the end of that period be richer, more populous, and more prosperous than the neighboring despotic states. But during that century it would often have incurred the risk of being conquered by them.

The difficulty that a democracy finds in conquering the passions and subduing the desires of the moment with a view to the future is observable in the United States in the most trivial things. The people, surrounded by flatterers, find great difficulty in surmounting their inclinations; whenever they are required to undergo a privation or any inconvenience, even to attain an end sanctioned by their own rational conviction, they almost always refuse at first to comply. The deference of the Americans to the laws has been justly applauded; but it must be added that in America legislation is made by the people and for the people. Consequently, in the United States the law favors those classes that elsewhere are most interested in evading it. It may therefore be supposed that an offensive law of which the majority should not see the immediate utility would either not be enacted or not be obeyed.

In America there is no law against fraudulent bankruptcies, not because they are few, but because they are many. The dread of being prosecuted as a bankrupt is greater in the minds of the majority than the fear of being ruined by the bankruptcy of others; and a sort of guilty tolerance is extended by the public conscience to an offense which everyone condemns in his individual capacity. In the new states of the Southwest the citizens generally take justice into their own hands, and murders are of frequent occurrence. This arises from the rude manners and the ignorance of the inhabitants of those deserts, who do not perceive the utility of strengthening the law, and who prefer duels to prosecutions.

Someone observed to me one day in Philadelphia that almost all crimes in America are caused by the abuse of intoxicating liquors, which the lower classes can procure in great abundance because of their cheapness. "How comes it," said I, "that you do not put a duty upon brandy?" "Our legislators," rejoined my informant, "have frequently thought of this expedient; but the task is difficult: a revolt might be anticipated; and the members who should vote for such a law would be sure of losing their seats." "Whence I am to infer," replied I, "that drunkards are the majority in your country, and that temperance is unpopular."

When these things are pointed out to the American statesmen, they will answer: "Leave it to time, and experience of the evil will teach the people their true interests." This is frequently true: though a democracy is more liable to error than a monarch or a body of nobles, the chances of its regaining the right path when once it has acknowledged its mistake are greater also; because it is rarely embarrassed by interests that conflict with those of the majority and resist the authority of reason. But a democracy can obtain truth only as the result of experience; and many nations may perish while they are awaiting the consequences of their errors. The great privilege of the Americans does not consist in being more enlightened than other nations, but in being able to repair the faults they may commit.

. . .

We have seen that the Federal Constitution entrusts the permanent direction of the external interests of the nation to the President and the Senate, which tends in some degree to detach the general foreign policy of the Union from the direct control of the people. It cannot, therefore, be asserted with truth that the foreign affairs of the state are conducted by the democracy.

. . .

Foreign politics demand scarcely any of those qualities which are peculiar to a democracy; they require, on the contrary, the perfect use of almost all those in which it is deficient. Democracy is favorable to the increase of the internal resources of a state; it diffuses wealth and comfort, promotes public spirit, and fortifies the respect for law in all classes of society: all these are advantages which have only an indirect influence over the relations which one people bears to another. But a democracy can only with great difficulty regulate the details of an important undertaking, persevere in a fixed design, and work out its execution in spite of serious obstacles. It cannot combine its measures with secrecy or await their consequences with patience. These are qualities which more especially belong to an individual or an aristocracy; and they are precisely the qualities by which a nation, like an individual, attains a dominant position.

If, on the contrary, we observe the natural defects of aristocracy, we shall find that, comparatively speaking, they do not injure the direction of the external affairs of the state.

The capital fault of which aristocracies may be accused is that they work for themselves and not for the people. In foreign politics it is rare for the interest of the aristocracy to be distinct from that of the people.

The propensity that induces democracies to obey impulse rather than prudence, and to abandon a mature design for the gratification of a momentary passion, was clearly seen in America on the breaking out of the French Revolution. It was then as evident to the simplest capacity as it is at the present time that the interest of the Americans forbade them to take any part in the contest which was about to deluge Europe with blood, but which could not injure their own country. But the sympathies of the people declared themselves with so much violence in favor of France that nothing but the inflexible character of Washington and the immense popularity which he enjoyed could have prevented the Americans from declaring war against England. And even then the exertions which the austere reason of that great man made to repress the generous but imprudent passions of his fellow citizens nearly deprived him of the sole recompense which he ever claimed, that of his country's love. The majority reprobated his policy, but it was afterwards approved by the whole nation.

If the Constitution and the favor of the public had not entrusted the direction of the foreign affairs of the country to Washington, it is certain that the American nation would at that time have adopted the very measures which it now condemns.

Almost all the nations that have exercised a powerful influence upon the destinies of the world, by conceiving, following out, and executing vast designs, from the Romans to the English, have been governed by aristocratic institutions. Nor will this be a subject of wonder when we recollect that nothing in the world is so conservative in its views as an aristocracy. The mass of the people may be led astray by ignorance or passion; the mind of a king may be biased and made to vacillate in his designs, and, besides, a king is not immortal. But an aristocratic body is too numerous to be led astray by intrigue, and yet not numerous enough to yield readily to the intoxication of unreflecting passion. An aristocracy is a firm and enlightened body that never dies.

Chapter XIII

WHAT ARE THE REAL ADVANTAGES WHICH AMERICAN SOCIETY DERIVES FROM A DEMOCRATIC GOVERMENT

Before entering upon the present chapter I must remind the reader of what I have more than once observed in this book. The political Constitution of the United States appears to me to be one of the forms of government that a democracy may adopt; but I do not regard the American Constitution as the best, or as the only one, that a democratic people may establish. In showing the advantages which the Americans derive from the government of democracy, I am therefore very far from affirming, or believing, that similar advantages can be obtained only from the same laws.

The defects and weaknesses of a democratic government may readily be discovered; they can be proved by obvious facts, whereas their healthy influence becomes evident in ways which are not obvious and are, so to speak, hidden. A glance suffices to detect its faults, but its good qualities can be discerned only by long observation. The laws of the American democracy are frequently defective or incomplete; they sometimes attack vested rights, or sanction others which are dangerous to the community; and even if they were good, their frequency would still be a great evil. How comes it, then, that the American republics prosper and continue?

. . .

Democratic laws generally tend to promote the welfare of the greatest possible number; for they emanate from the majority of the citizens, who are subject to error, but who cannot have an interest opposed to their own advantage. The laws of an aristocracy tend, on the contrary, to concentrate wealth and power in the hands of the minority; because an aristocracy, by its very nature, constitutes a minority. It may therefore be asserted, as a general proposition, that the purpose of a democracy in its legislation is more useful to humanity than that of an aristocracy. This, however, is the sum total of its advantages.

Aristocracies are infinitely more expert in the science of legislation than democracies ever can be. They are possessed of a self-control that protects them from the errors of temporary excitement; and they form far-reaching designs, which they know how to mature till a favorable opportunity arrives. Aristocratic government proceeds with the dexterity of art; it understands how to make the collective force of all its laws converge at the same time to a given point. Such is not the case with democracies, whose laws are almost always ineffective or inopportune. The means of democracy are therefore more imperfect than those of aristocracy, and the measures that it unwittingly adopts are frequently opposed to its own cause; but the object it has in view is more useful.

Let us now imagine a community so organized by nature or by its constitution that it can support the transitory action of bad laws, and that it can await, without destruction, the general tendency of its legislation: we shall then conceive how a democratic government, notwithstanding its faults, may be best fitted to produce the prosperity of this community. This is precisely what has occurred in the United States; and I repeat what I have before remarked, that the great advantage of the Americans consists in their being able to commit faults which they may afterwards repair.

An analogous observation may be made respecting public officers. It is easy to perceive that American democracy frequently errs in the choice of the individuals to whom it entrusts the power of the administration; but it is more difficult to say why the state prospers under their rule. In the first place, it is to be remarked that if, in a democratic state, the governors have less honesty and less capacity than elsewhere, the governed are more enlightened and more attentive to their interests. As the people in democracies are more constantly vigilant in their affairs and more jealous of their rights, they prevent their representatives from abandoning that general line of conduct which their own interest prescribes. In the second place, it must be remembered that if the democratic magistrate is more apt to misuse his power, he possesses it for a shorter time. But there is yet another reason which is still more general and conclusive. It is no doubt of importance to the welfare of nations that they should be governed by men of talents and virtue; but it is perhaps still more important for them that the interests of those men should not differ from the interests of the community at large; for if such were the case, their virtues might become almost useless and their talents might be turned to a bad account. I have said that it is important that the interests of the persons in authority should not differ from or oppose the interests of the community at large; but I do not insist upon their having the same interests as the *whole* population, because I am not aware that such a state of things ever existed in any country.

No political form has hitherto been discovered that is equally favorable to the prosperity and the development of all the classes into which society is divided. These classes continue to form, as it were, so many distinct communities in the same nation; and experience has shown that it is no less dangerous to place the fate of these classes exclusively in the hands of any one of them than it is to make one people the arbiter of the destiny of another. When the rich alone govern, the interest of the poor is always endangered; and when the poor make the laws, that of the rich incurs very serious risks. The advantage of democracy does not consist, therefore, as has sometimes been asserted, in favoring the prosperity of all, but simply in contributing to the well-being of the greatest number.

The men who are entrusted with the direction of public affairs in the United States are frequently inferior, in both capacity and morality, to those whom an aristocracy would raise to power. But their interest is identified and mingled with that of the majority of their fellow citizens. They may frequently be faithless and frequently mistaken, but they will never systematically adopt a line of conduct hostile to the majority; and they cannot give a dangerous or exclusive tendency to the government.

The maladministration of a democratic magistrate, moreover, is an isolated fact, which has influence only during the short period for which he is elected. Corruption and incapacity do not act as common interests which may connect men permanently with one another. A corrupt or incapable magistrate will not combine his measures with another magistrate simply because the latter is as corrupt and incapable as himself; and these two men will never unite their endeavors to promote the corruption and inaptitude of their remote posterity. The ambition and the maneuvers of the one will serve, on the contrary, to unmask the other. The vices of a magistrate in democratic states are usually wholly personal.

But under aristocratic governments public men are swayed by the interest of their order, which, if it is sometimes confused with the interests of the majority, is very frequently distinct from them. This interest is the common and lasting bond that unites them; it induces them to coalesce and combine their efforts to attain an end which is not always the happiness of the greatest number; and it serves not only to connect the persons in authority with one another, but to unite them with a considerable portion of the community, since a numerous body of citizens belong to the aristocracy without being invested with official functions. The aristocratic magistrate is therefore constantly supported by a portion of the community as well as by the government of which he is a member.

The common purpose which in aristocracies connects the interest of the magistrates with that of a portion of their contemporaries identifies it also with that of future generations; they labor for the future as well as for the present. The aristocratic magistrate is urged at the same time towards the same point by the passions of the community, by his own, and, I may almost add, by those of his posterity. Is it, then, wonderful that he does not resist such repeated impulses? And, indeed, aristocracies are often carried away by their class spirit without being corrupted by it; and they unconsciously fashion society to their own ends and prepare it for their own descendants.

. . .

In the United States, where public officers have no class interests to promote, the general and constant influence of the government is beneficial, although the individuals who conduct it are frequently unskillful and sometimes contemptible. There is, indeed, a secret tendency in democratic institutions that makes the exertions of the citizens subservient to the prosperity of the community in spite of their vices and mistakes; while in aristocratic institutions there is a secret bias which, notwithstanding the talents and virtues of those who conduct the government, leads them to contribute to the evils that oppress their fellow creatures. In aristocratic governments public men may frequently do harm without intending it; and in democratic states they bring about good results of which they have never thought.

There is one sort of patriotic attachment which principally

arises from that instinctive, disinterested, and undefinable feeling which connects the affections of man with his birthplace. This natural fondness is united with a taste for ancient customs and a reverence for traditions of the past; those who cherish it love their country as they love the mansion of their fathers. They love the tranquillity that it affords them; they cling to the peaceful habits that they have contracted within its bosom; they are attached to the reminiscences that it awakens; and they are even pleased by living there in a state of obedience. This patriotism is sometimes stimulated by religious enthusiasm, and then it is capable of making prodigious efforts. It is in itself a kind of religion: it does not reason, but it acts from the impulse of faith and sentiment. In some nations the monarch is regarded as a personification of the country; and, the fervor of patriotism being converted into the fervor of loyalty, they take a sympathetic pride in his conquests, and glory in his power.

. . .

But, like all instinctive passions, this kind of patriotism incites great transient exertions, but no continuity of effort. It may save the state in critical circumstances, but often allows it to decline in times of peace. While the manners of a people are simple and its faith unshaken, while society is steadily based upon traditional institutions whose legitimacy has never been contested, this instinctive patriotism is wont to endure.

But there is another species of attachment to country which is more rational than the one I have been describing. It is perhaps less generous and less ardent, but it is more fruitful and more lasting: it springs from knowledge; it is nurtured by the laws; it grows by the exercise of civil rights; and, in the end, it is confounded with the personal interests of the citizen. A man comprehends the influence which the well-being of his country has upon his own; he is aware that the laws permit him to contribute to that prosperity, and he labors to promote it, first because it benefits him, and secondly because it is in part his own work.

But epochs sometimes occur in the life of a nation when the old customs of a people are changed, public morality is destroyed, religious belief shaken, and the spell of tradition broken, while the diffusion of knowledge is yet imperfect and the civil rights of the community are ill secured or confined within narrow limits. The country then assumes a dim and dubious shape in the eyes of the citizens; they no longer behold it in the soil which they inhabit, for that soil is to them an inanimate clod; nor in the usages of their forefathers, which they have learned to regard as a debasing yoke; nor in religion, for of that they doubt; nor in the laws, which do not originate in their own authority; nor in the legislator, whom they fear and despise. The country is lost to their senses; they can discover it neither under its own nor under borrowed features, and they retire into a narrow and unenlightened selfishness. They are emancipated from prejudice without having acknowledged the empire of reason; they have neither the instinctive patriotism of a monarchy nor the reflecting patriotism of a republic; but they have stopped between the two in the midst of confusion and distress.

In this predicament to retreat is impossible, for a people cannot recover the sentiments of their youth any more than a man can return to the innocent tastes of childhood; such things may be regretted, but they cannot be renewed. They must go forward and accelerate the union of private with public interests, since the period of disinterested patriotism is gone by forever.

I am certainly far from affirming that in order to obtain this result the exercise of political rights should be immediately granted to all men. But I maintain that the most powerful and perhaps the only means that we still possess of interesting men in the welfare of their country is to make them partakers in the government. At the present time civic zeal seems to me to be inseparable from the exercise of political rights; and I think that the number of citizens will be found to augment or decrease in Europe in proportion as those rights are extended.

How does it happen that in the United States, where the inhabitants have only recently immigrated to the land which they now occupy, and brought neither customs nor traditions with them there; where they met one another for the first time with no previous acquaintance; where, in short, the instinctive love of country can scarcely exist; how does it happen that everyone takes as zealous an interest in the affairs of his township, his county, and the whole state as if they were his own? It is because everyone, in his sphere, takes an active part in the government of society.

The lower orders in the United States understand the influence exercised by the general prosperity upon their own welfare; simple as this observation is, it is too rarely made by the people. Besides, they are accustomed to regard this prosperity as the fruit of their own exertions. The citizen looks upon the fortune of the public as his own, and he labors for the good of the state, not merely from a sense of pride or duty, but from what I venture to term cupidity.

It is unnecessary to study the institutions and the history of the Americans in order to know the truth of this remark, for their manners render it sufficiently evident. As the American participates in all that is done in his country, he thinks himself obliged to defend whatever may be censured in it; for it is not only his country that is then attacked, it is himself. The consequence is that his national pride resorts to a thousand artifices and descends to all the petty tricks of personal vanity.

Nothing is more embarrassing in the ordinary intercourse

of life than this irritable patriotism of the Americans. A stranger may be well inclined to praise many of the institutions of their country, but he begs permission to blame some things in it, a permission that is inexorably refused. America is therefore a free country in which, lest anybody should be hurt by your remarks, you are not allowed to speak freely of private individuals or of the state, of the citizens or of the authorities, of public or of private undertakings, or, in short, of anything at all except, perhaps, the climate and the soil; and even then Americans will be found ready to defend both as if they had co-operated in producing them.

In our times we must choose between the patriotism of all and the government of a few; for the social force and activity which the first confers are irreconcilable with the pledges of tranquillity which are given by the second.

. . .

The government of a democracy brings the notion of political rights to the level of the humblest citizens, just as the dissemination of wealth brings the notion of property within the reach of all men; to my mind, this is one of its greatest advantages. I do not say it is easy to teach men how to exercise political rights, but I maintain that, when it is possible, the effects which result from it are highly important; and I add that, if there ever was a time at which such an attempt ought to be made, that time is now. Do you not see that religious belief is shaken and the divine notion of right is declining, that morality is debased and the notion of moral right is therefore fading away? Argument is substituted for faith, and calculation for the impulses of sentiment. If, in the midst of this general disruption, you do not succeed in connecting the notion of right with that of private interest, which is the only immutable point in the human heart, what means will you have of governing the world except by fear? When I am told that the laws are weak and the people are turbulent, that passions are excited and the authority of virtue is paralyzed, and therefore no measures must be taken to increase the rights of the democracy, I reply that for these very reasons some measures of the kind ought to be taken; and I believe that governments are still more interested in taking them than society at large, for governments may perish, but society cannot die.

But I do not wish to exaggerate the example that America furnishes. There the people were invested with political rights at a time when they could not be abused, for the inhabitants were few in number and simple in their manners. As they have increased, the Americans have not augmented the power of the democracy; they have rather extended its domain.

. . .

It is not always feasible to consult the whole people, either directly or indirectly, in the formation of law; but it cannot be denied that, when this is possible, the authority of law is much augmented. This popular origin, which impairs the excellence and the wisdom of legislation, contributes much to increase its power. There is an amazing strength in the expression of the will of a whole people; and when it declares itself, even the imagination of those who would wish to contest it is overawed. The truth of this fact is well known by parties, and they consequently strive to make out a majority whenever they can. If they have not the greater number of voters on their side, they assert that the true majority abstained from voting; and if they are foiled even there, they have recourse to those persons who had no right to vote.

In the United States, except slaves, servants, and paupers supported by the townships, there is no class of persons who do not exercise the elective franchise and who do not indirectly contribute to make the laws. Those who wish to attack the laws must consequently either change the opinion of the nation or trample upon its decision.

A second reason, which is still more direct and weighty, may be adduced: in the United States everyone is personally interested in enforcing the obedience of the whole community to the law; for as the minority may shortly rally the majority to its principles, it is interested in professing that respect for the decrees of the legislator which it may soon have occasion to claim for its own. However irksome an enactment may be, the citizen of the United States complies with it, not only because it is the work of the majority, but because it is his own, and he regards it as a contract to which he is himself a party.

In the United States, then, that numerous and turbulent multitude does not exist who, regarding the law as their natural enemy, look upon it with fear and distrust. It is impossible, on the contrary, not to perceive that all classes display the utmost reliance upon the legislation of their country and are attached to it by a kind of parental affection.

I am wrong, however, in saying all classes; for as in America the European scale of authority is inverted, there the wealthy are placed in a position analogous to that of the poor in the Old World, and it is the opulent classes who frequently look upon law with suspicion. I have already observed that the advantage of democracy is not, as has been sometimes asserted, that it protects the interests of all, but simply that it protects those of the majority. In the United States, where the poor rule, the rich have always something to fear from the abuse of their power. This natural anxiety of the rich may produce a secret dissatisfaction; but society is not disturbed by it, for the same reason that withholds the confidence of the rich from the legislative authority makes them obey its mandates: their wealth, which prevents them from making the law, prevents them from withstanding it. Among civilized nations, only those who have nothing to lose ever revolt; and if the laws of a democracy are not always worthy of respect, they are always respected; for those who usually infringe the laws cannot fail to obey those which they have themselves made and by which they are benefited; while the citizens who might be interested in their infraction are induced, by their character and station, to submit to the decisions of the legislature, whatever they may be. Besides, the people in America obey the law, not only because it is their own work, but because it may be changed if it is harmful; a law is observed because, first, it is a self-imposed evil, and, secondly, it is an evil of transient duration.

On passing from a free country into one which is not free the traveler is struck by the change; in the former all is bustle and activity; in the latter everything seems calm and motionless. In the one, amelioration and progress are the topics of inquiry; in the other, it seems as if the community wished only to repose in the enjoyment of advantages already acquired. Nevertheless, the country which exerts itself so strenuously to become happy is generally more wealthy and prosperous than that which appears so contented with its lot; and when we compare them, we can scarcely conceive how so many new wants are daily felt in the former, while so few seems to exist in the latter.

If this remark is applicable to those free countries which have preserved monarchical forms and aristocratic institutions, it is still more so to democratic republics. In these states it is not a portion only of the people who endeavor to improve the state of society, but the whole community is engaged in the task; and it is not the exigencies and convenience of a single class for which provision is to be made, but the exigencies and convenience of all classes at once.

It is not impossible to conceive the suprising liberty that the Americans enjoy; some idea may likewise be formed of their extreme equality; but the political activity that pervades the United States must be seen in order to be understood. No sooner do you set foot upon American ground that you are stunned by a kind of tumult; a confused clamor is heard on every side, and a thousand simultaneous voices demand the satisfaction of their social wants. Everything is in motion around you; here the people of one quarter of a town are met to decide upon the building of a church; there the election of a representative is going on; a little farther, the delegates of a district are hastening to the town in order to consult upon some local improvements; in another place, the laborers in a village quit their plows to deliberate upon the project of a road or a public school. Meetings are called for the sole purpose of declaring their disapprobation of the conduct of the government; while in other assemblies citizens salute the authorities of the day as the fathers of their country. Societies are formed which regard drunkenness as the principal cause of the evils of the state, and solemnly bind themselves to give an example of temperance.

The great political agitation of American legislative bodies, which is the only one that attracts the attention of foreigners, is a mere episode, or a sort of continuation, of that universal movement which originates in the lowest classes of the people and extends successively to all the ranks of society. It is impossible to spend more effort in the pursuit of happiness.

It is difficult to say what place is taken up in the life of an inhabitant of the United States by his concern for politics. To take a hand in the regulation of society and to discuss it is his biggest concern and, so to speak, the only pleasure an American knows. This feeling pervades the most trifling habits of life; even the women frequently attend public meetings and listen to political harangues as a recreation from their household labors. Debating clubs are, to a certain extent, a substitute for theatrical entertainments: an American cannot converse, but he can discuss, and his talk falls into a dissertation. He speaks to you as if he was addressing a meeting; and if he should chance to become warm in the discussion, he will say "Gentlemen" to the person with whom he is conversing.

In some countries the inhabitants seem unwilling to avail themselves of the political privileges which the law gives them; it would seem that they set too high a value upon their time to spend it on the interests of the community; and they shut themselves up in a narrow selfishness, marked out by four sunk fences and a quickset hedge. But if an American were condemned to confine his activity to his own affairs, he would be robbed of one half of his existence; he would feel an immense void in the life which he is accustomed to lead, and his wretchedness would be unbearable. I am persuaded that if ever a despotism should be established in America, it will be more difficult to overcome the habits that freedom has formed than to conquer the love of freedom itself.

This ceaseless agitation which democratic government has introduced into the political world influences all social intercourse. I am not sure that, on the whole, this is not the greatest advantage of democracy; and I am less inclined to applaud it for what it does than for what it causes to be done.

It is incontestable that the people frequently conduct public business very badly; but it is impossible that the lower orders should take a part in public business without extending the circle of their ideas and quitting the ordinary routine of their thoughts. The humblest individual who co-operates in the government of society acquires a certain degree of self-respect; and as he possesses authority, he can command the services of minds more enlightened than his own. He is canvassed by a multitude of applicants, and in seeking to deceive him in a thousand ways, they really enlighten him. He takes a part in political undertakings which he did not originate, but which give him a taste for undertakings of the kind. New improvements are daily pointed out to him in the common property, and this gives him the desire of improving that property which is his own. He is perhaps neither happier nor better than those who came before him, but he is better informed and more active. I have no doubt that the democratic institutions of the United States, joined to the physical constitution of the country, are the cause (not the direct, as is so often asserted, but the indirect cause) of the prodigious commercial activity of the inhabitants. It is not created by the laws, but the people learn how to promote it by the experience derived from legislation.

When the opponents of democracy assert that a single man performs what he undertakes better than the government of all, it appears to me that they are right. The government of an individual, supposing an equality of knowledge on either side, is more consistent, more persevering, more uniform, and more accurate in details than that of a multitude, and it selects with more discrimination the men whom it employs. If any deny this, they have never seen a democratic government, or have judged upon partial evidence. It is true that, even when local circumstances and the dispositions of the people allow democratic institutions to exist, they do not display a regular and methodical system of government. Democratic liberty is far from accomplishing all its projects with the skill of an adroit despotism. It frequently abandons them before they have borne their fruits, or risks them when the consequences may be dangerous; but in the end it produces more than any absolute government; if it does fewer things well, it does a greater number of things. Under its sway the grandeur is not in what the public administration does, but in what is done without it or outside of it. Democracy does not give the people the most skillful government, but it produces what the ablest governments are frequently unable to create: namely, an all-pervading and restless activity, a superabundant force, and an energy which is inseparable from it and which may, however unfavorable circumstances may be, produce wonders. These are the true advantages of democracy

. . .

Chapter XIV

UNLIMITED POWER OF THE MAJORITY
IN THE UNITED STATES, AND
ITS CONSEQUENCES

The very essence of democratic government consists in the absolute sovereignty of the majority; for there is nothing in democratic states that is capable of resisting it. Most of the American constitutions have sought to increase this natural strength of the majority by artificial means.

Of all political institutions, the legislature is the one that is most easily swayed by the will of the majority. The Americans determined that the members of the legislature should be elected by the people *directly,* and for a *very brief term,* in order to subject them, not only to the general convictions, but even to the daily passions, of their constituents. The members of both houses are taken from the same classes in society and nominated in the same manner; so that the movements of the legislative bodies are almost as rapid, and quite as irresistible, as those of a single assembly. It is to a legislature thus constituted that almost all the authority of the government has been entrusted.

At the same time that the law increased the strength of those authorities which of themselves were strong, it enfeebled more and more those which were naturally weak. It deprived the representatives of the executive power of all stability and independence; and by subjecting them completely to the caprices of the legislature, it robbed them of the slender influence that the nature of a democratic government might have allowed them to exercise. In several states the judicial power was also submitted to the election of the majority; and in all of them its existence was made to depend on the pleasure of the legislative authority, since the representatives were empowered annually to regulate the stipend of the judges.

Custom has done even more than law. A proceeding is becoming more and more general in the United States which will, in the end, do away with the guarantees of representative government: it frequently happens that the voters, in electing a delegate, point out a certain line of conduct to him and impose upon him certain positive obligations that he is pledged to fulfill. With the exception of the tumult, this comes to the same thing as if the majority itself held its deliberations in the market-place.

Several particular circumstances combine to render the power of the majority in America not only preponderant, but irresistible. The moral authority of the majority is partly based upon the notion that there is more intelligence and wisdom in a number of men united than in a single individual, and that the number of the legislators is more important than their quality. The theory of equality is thus applied to the intellects of men; and human pride is thus assailed in its last retreat by a doctrine which the minority hesitate to admit, and to which they will but slowly assent. Like all other powers, and perhaps more than any other, the authority of the many rquires the sanction of time in order to appear legitimate. At first it enforces obedience by constraint; and its laws are not *respected* until they have been long maintained.

The right of governing society, which the majority supposes itself to derive from its superior intelligence, was introduced into the United States by the first settlers; and this idea, which of itself would be sufficient to create a free nation, has now been amalgamated with the customs of the people and the minor incidents of social life.

. . .

I have already spoken of the natural defects of democratic institutions; each one of them increases in the same ratio as the power of the majority. To begin with the most evident of them all, the mutability of the laws is an evil inherent in a democratic government, because it is natural to democracies to raise new men to power. But this evil is more or less perceptible in proportion to the authority and the means of action which the legislature possesses.

In America the authority exercised by the legislatures is supreme; nothing prevents them from accomplishing their wishes with celerity and with irresistible power, and they are supplied with new representatives every year. That is to say, the circumstances which contribute most powerfully to democratic instability, and which admit of the free application of caprice to the most important objects, are here in full operation. Hence America is, at the present day, the country beyond all others where laws last the shortest time. Almost all the American constitutions have been amended within thirty years; there is therefore not one American state which has not modified the principles of its legislation in that time. As for the laws themselves, a single glance at the archives of the different states of the Union suffices to convince one that in America the activity of the legislator never slackens. Not that the American democracy is naturally less stable than any other, but it is allowed to follow, in the formation of the laws, the natural instability of its desires.

The omnipotence of the majority and the rapid as well as absolute manner in which its decisions are executed in the United States not only render the law unstable, but exercise the same influence upon the execution of the law and the conduct of the administration. As the majority is the only power that it is important to court, all its projects are taken up with the greatest ardor; but no sooner is its attention distracted than all this ardor ceases; while in the free states of Europe, where the administration is at once independent and secure, the projects of the legislature continue to be executed even when its attention is directed to other objects.

In America certain improvements are prosecuted with much more zeal and activity than elsewhere; in Europe the same ends are promoted by much less social effort more continuously applied.

. . .

I hold it to be an impious and detestable maxim that, politically speaking, the people have a right to do anything; and yet I have asserted that all authority originates in the will of the majority. Am I, then, in contradiction with myself?

A general law, which bears the name of justice, has been made and sanctioned, not only by a majority of this or that people, but by a majority of mankind. The rights of every people are therefore confined within the limits of what is just. A nation may be considered as a jury which is empowered to represent society at large and to apply justice, which is its law. Ought such a jury, which represents society, to have more power than the society itself whose laws it executes?

When I refuse to obey an unjust law, I do not contest the right of the majority to command, but I simply appeal from the sovereignty of the people to the sovereignty of mankind. Some have not feared to assert that a people can never outstep the boundaries of justice and reason in those affairs which are peculiarly its own; and that consequently full power may be given to the majority by which it is represented. But this is the language of a slave.

A majority taken collectively is only an individual, whose opinions, and frequently whose interests, are opposed to those of another individual, who is styled a minority. If it be admitted that a man possessing absolute power may misuse that power by wronging his adversaries, why should not a majority be liable to the same reproach? Men do not change their characters by uniting with one another; nor does their patience in the presence of obstacles increase with their strength. For my own part, I cannot believe it; the power to do everything, which I should refuse to one of my equals, I will never grant to any number of them.

I do not think that, for the sake of preserving liberty, it is possible to combine several principles in the same government so as really to oppose them to one another. The form of government that is usually termed *mixed* has always appeared to me a mere chimera. Accurately speaking, there is no such thing as a *mixed government,* in the sense usually given to that word, because in all communities some one principle of action may be discovered which preponderates over the others. England in the last century, which has been especially cited as an example of this sort of government, was essentially an aristocratic state, although it comprised some great elements of democracy; for the laws and customs of the country were such that the aristocracy could not but preponderate in the long run and direct public affairs according to its own will. The error arose from seeing the interests of the nobles perpetually contending with those of the people, without considering the issue of the contest, which was really the important point. When a community actually has a mixed government—that is to say, when it is equally divided between adverse principles—it must either experience a revolution or fall into anarchy.

I am therefore of the opinion that social power superior to all others must always be placed somewhere; but I think that liberty is endangered when this power finds no obstacle which can retard its course and give it time to moderate its own vehemence.

Unlimited power is in itself a bad and dangerous thing. Human beings are not competent to exercise it with discretion. God alone can be omnipotent, because his wisdom and his justice are always equal to his power. There is no power on earth so worthy of honor in itself or clothed with rights so sacred that I would admit its uncontrolled and all-predominant authority. When I see that the right and the means of absolute command are conferred on any power whatever, be it called a people or a king, an aristocracy or a democracy, a monarchy or a republic, I say there is the germ of tyranny, and I seek to live elsewhere, under other laws.

In my opinion, the main evil of the present democratic institutions of the United States does not arise, as is often asserted in Europe, from their weakness, but from their irresistible strength. I am not so much alarmed at the excessive liberty which reigns in that country as at the inadequate securities which one finds there against tyranny.

When an individual or a party is wronged in the United States, to whom can he apply for redress? If to public opinion, public opinion constitutes the majority; if to the legislature, it represents the majority and implicitly obeys it; if to the executive power, it is appointed by the majority and serves as a passive tool in its hands. The public force consists of the majority under arms; the jury is the majority invested with the right of hearing judicial cases; and in certain states even the judges are elected by the majority. However iniquitous or absurd the measure of which you complain, you must submit to it as well as you can.

If, on the other hand, a legislative power could be so constituted as to represent the majority without necessarily being the slave of its passions, an executive so as to retain a proper share of authority, and a judiciary so as to remain independent of the other two powers, a government would be formed which would still be democratic while incurring scarcely any risk of tyranny.

I do not say that there is a frequent use of tyranny in America at the present day; but I maintain that there is no sure barrier against it, and that the causes which mitigate the government there are to be found in the circumstances and the manners of the country more than in its laws.

A distinction must be drawn between tyranny and arbitrary power. Tyranny may be exercised by means of the law itself, and in that case it is not arbitrary; arbitrary power may be exercised for the public good, in which case it is not tyrannical. Tyranny usually employs arbitrary means, but if necessary it can do without them.

In the United States the omnipotence of the majority, which is favorable to the legal despotism of the legislature, likewise favors the arbitrary authority of the magistrate. The majority has absolute power both to make the laws and to watch over their execution; and as it has equal authority over those who are in power and the community at large, it considers public officers as its passive agents and readily confides to them the task of carrying out its designs. The details of their office and the privileges that they are to enjoy are rarely defined beforehand. It treats them as a master does his servants, since they are always at work in his sight and he can direct or reprimand them at any instant.

In general, the American functionaries are far more independent within the sphere that is prescribed to them than the French civil officers. Sometimes, even, they are allowed by the popular authority to exceed those bounds; and as they are protected by the opinion and backed by the power of the majority, they dare do things that even a European, accustomed as he is to arbitrary power, is astonished at. By this means habits are formed in the heart of a free country which may some day prove fatal to its liberties.

It is in the examination of the exercise of thought in the United States that we clearly perceive how far the power of the majority surpasses all the powers with which we are acquainted in Europe. Thought is an invisible and subtle power that mocks all the efforts of tyranny. At the present time the most absolute monarchs in Europe cannot prevent certain opinions hostile to their authority from circulating in secret through their dominions and even in their courts. It is not so in America; as long as the majority is still undecided, discussion is carried on; but as soon as its decision is irrevocably pronounced, everyone is silent, and the friends as well as the opponents of the measure unite in assenting to its propriety. The reason for this is perfectly clear: no monarch is so absolute as to combine all the powers of society in his own hands and to conquer all opposition, as a majority is able to do, which has the right both of making and of executing the laws.

The authority of a king is physical and controls the actions of men without subduing their will. But the majority possesses a power that is physical and moral at the same time, which acts upon the will as much as upon the actions and represses not only all contest, but all controversy.

I know of no country in which there is so little independence of mind and real freedom of discussion as in America. In any constitutional state in Europe every sort of religious and political theory may be freely preached and disseminated; for there is no country in Europe so subdued by any single authority as not to protect the man who raises his voice in the cause of truth from the consequences of his hardihood. If he is unfortunate enough to live under an absolute government, the people are often on his side; if he inhabits a free country, he can, if necessary, find a shelter behind the throne. The aristocratic part of society supports him in some countries, and the democracy in others. But in a nation where democratic institutions exist, organized like those of the United States, there is but one authority, one element of strength and success, with nothing beyond it.

In America the majority raises formidable barriers around the liberty of opinion; within these barriers an author may write what he pleases, but woe to him if he goes beyond them. Not that he is in danger of an auto-da-fé, but he is exposed to continued obloquy and persecution. His political career is closed forever, since he has offended the only authority that is able to open it. Every sort of compensation, even that of celebrity, is refused to him. Before making public his opinions he thought he had sympathizers; now it seems to him that he has none any more since he has revealed himself to everyone; then those who blame him criticize loudly and those who think as he does keep quiet and move away without courage. He yields at length, overcome by the daily effort which he has to make, and subsides into silence, as if he felt remorse for having spoken the truth.

Fetters and headsmen were the coarse instruments that tyranny formerly employed; but the civilization of our age has perfect despotism itself, though it seemed to have nothing to learn. Monarchs had, so to speak, materialized oppression; the democratic republics of the present day have rendered it as entirely an affair of the mind as the will which it is intended to coerce. Under the absolute sway of one man the body was attacked in order to subdue the soul; but the soul escaped the blows which were directed against it and rose proudly superior. Such is not the course adopted by tyranny in democratic republics; there the body is left free, and the soul is enslaved. The master no longer says: "You are free to think differently from me and to retain your life, your property, and all that you possess; but you are henceforth a stranger among your people. You may retain your civil rights, but they will be useless to you, for you will never be chosen by your fellow citizens if you solicit their votes; and they will affect to scorn you if you ask for their esteem. You will remain among men, but you will be deprived of the rights of mankind. Your fellow creatures will shun you like an impure being; and even those who believe in your innocence will abandon you, lest they should be shunned in their turn. Go in peace! I have given you your life, but it is an existence worse than death."

Absolute monarchies had dishonored despotism; let us beware lest democratic republics should reinstate it and render it less odious and degrading in the eyes of the many by making it still more onerous to the few.

Works have been published in the proudest nations of the Old World expressly intended to censure the vices and the follies of the times: Labruyère inhabited the palace of Louis XIV when he composed his chapter upon the Great, and Molière criticized the courtiers in the plays that were acted before the court. But the ruling power in the United States is not to be made game of. The smallest reproach irritates its sensibility, and the slightest joke that has any foundation in truth renders it indignant; from the forms of its language up to the solid virtues of its character, everything must be made the subject of encomium. No writer, whatever be his eminence, can escape paying this tribute of adulation to his fellow citizens. The majority lives in the perpetual utterance of self-applause, and there are certain truths which the Americans can learn only from strangers or from experience.

If America has not as yet had any great writers, the reason is given in these facts; there can be no literary genius without freedom of opinion, and freedom of opinion does not exist in America. The Inquisition has never been able to prevent a vast number of anti-religious books from circulating in Spain. The empire of the majority succeeds much better in the United States, since it actually removes any wish to publish them. Unbelievers are to be met with in America, but there is no public organ of infidelity. Attempts have been made by some governments to protect morality by prohibiting licentious books. In the United States no one is punished for this sort of book, but no one is induced to write them; not because all the citizens are immaculate in conduct, but because the majority of the community is decent and orderly.

In this case the use of power is unquestionably good; and I am discussing the nature of the power itself. This irresistible authority is a constant fact, and its judicious exercise is only an accident.

The tendencies that I have just mentioned are as yet but slightly perceptible in political society, but they already exercise an unfavorable influence upon the national character of the Americans. I attribute the small number of distinguished men in political life to the ever increasing despotism of the majority in the United States.

When the American Revolution broke out, they arose in great numbers; for public opinion then served, not to tyrannize over, but to direct the exertions of individuals. Those celebrated men, sharing the agitation of mind common at that period, had a grandeur peculiar to themselves, which was reflected back upon the nation, but was by no means borrowed from it.

In absolute governments the great nobles who are nearest to the throne flatter the passions of the sovereign and voluntarily truckle to his caprices. But the mass of the nation does not degrade itself by servitude; it often submits from weakness, from habit, or from ignorance, and sometimes from loyalty. Some nations have been known to sacrifice their own desires to those of the sovereign with pleasure and pride, thus exhibiting a sort of independence of mind in the very act of submission. These nations are miserable, but they are not degraded. There is a great difference between doing what one does not approve, and feigning to approve what one does; the one is the weakness of a feeble person, the other befits the temper of a lackey.

In free countries, where everyone is more or less called upon to give his opinion on affairs of state, in democratic republics, where public life is incessantly mingled with domestic affairs, where the sovereign authority is accessible on every side, and where its attention can always be attracted by vociferation, more persons are to be met with who speculate upon its weaknesses and live upon ministering to its passions than in absolute monarchies. Not because men are naturally worse in these states than elsewhere, but the temptation is stronger and at the same time of easier access. The result is a more extensive debasement of character.

Democratic republics extend the practice of currying favor with the many and introduce it into all classes at once; this is the most serious reproach that can be addressed to them. This is especially true in democratic states organized like the American republics, where the power of the majority is so absolute and irresistible that one must give up one's rights as a citizen and almost abjure one's qualities as a man if one intends to stray from the track which it prescribes.

In that immense crowd which throngs the avenues to power in the United States, I found very few men who displayed that manly candor and masculine independence of opinion which frequently distinguished the Americans in former times, and which constitutes the leading feature in distinguished characters wherever they may be found. It seems at first sight as if all the minds of the Americans were formed upon one model, so accurately do they follow the same route. A stranger does, indeed, sometimes meet with Americans who dissent from the rigor of these formulas, with men who deplore the defects of the laws, the mutability and the ignorance of democracy, who even go so far as to observe the evil tendencies that impair the national character, and to point out such remedies as it might be possible to apply; but no one is there to hear them except yourself, and you, to whom these secret reflections are confided, are a stranger and a bird of passage. They are very ready to communicate truths which are useless to you, but they hold a different language in public.

If these lines are ever read in America, I am well assured of two things: in the first place, that all who peruse them will raise their voices to condemn me; and, in the second place, that many of them will acquit me at the bottom of their conscience.

. . .

Governments usually perish from impotence or from tyranny. In the former case, their power escapes from them; it is wrested from their grasp in the latter. Many observers who have witnessed the anarchy of democratic states have imagined that the government of those states was naturally weak and impotent. The truth is that when war is once begun between parties, the government loses its control over society. But I do not think that a democratic power is naturally without force or resources; say, rather, that it is almost always by the abuse of its force and the misemployment of its resources that it becomes a failure. Anarchy is almost always produced by its tyranny or its mistakes, but not by its want of strength.

It is important not to confuse stability with force, or the greatness of a thing with its duration. In democratic republics the power that directs society is not stable, for it often changes hands and assumes a new direction. But whichever way it turns, its force is almost irresistible. The governments of the American republics appear to me to be as much centralized as those of the absolute monarchies of Europe, and more energetic than they are. I do not, therefore, imagine that they will perish from weakness.

If ever the free institutions of America are destroyed, that event may be attributed to the omnipotence of the majority, which may at some future time urge the minorities to desperation and oblige them to have recourse to physical force. Anarchy will then be the result, but it will have been brought about by despotism.

Mr. Madison expresses the same opinion in *The Feder-*

alist, No. 51. "It is of great importance in a republic, not only to guard the society against the oppression of its rulers, but to guard one part of the society against the injustice of the other part. Justice is the end of government. It is the end of civil society. It ever has been, and ever will be, pursued until it be obtained, or until liberty be lost in the pursuit. In a society, under the forms of which the stronger faction can readily unite and oppress the weaker, anarchy may as truly be said to reign as in a state of nature, where the weaker individual is not secured against the violence of the stronger: and as, in the latter state, even the stronger individuals are prompted by the uncertainty of their condition to submit to a government which may protect the weak as well as themselves, so, in the former state, will the more powerful factions be gradually induced by a like motive to wish for a government which will protect all parties, the weaker as well as the more powerful. It can be little doubted, that, if the State of Rhode Island was separated from the Confederacy and left to itself, the insecurity of right under the popular form of government within such narrow limits would be displayed by such reiterated oppressions of the factious majorities, that some power altogether independent of the people would soon be called for by the voice of the very factions whose misrule had proved the necessity of it."

Jefferson also said: "The executive power in our government is not the only, perhaps not even the principle, object of my solicitude. The tyranny of the legislature is really the danger most to be feared, and will continue to be so for many years to come. The tyranny of the executive power will come in its turn, but at a more distant period."

I am glad to cite the opinion of Jefferson upon this subject rather than that of any other, because I consider him the most powerful advocate democracy has ever had.

Chapter XV

CAUSES WHICH MITIGATE THE TYRANNY OF THE MAJORITY IN THE UNITED STATES

I have already pointed out the distinction between a centralized government and a centralized administration. The former exists in America, but the latter is nearly unknown there. If the directing power of the American communities had both these instruments of government at its disposal and united the habit of executing its commands to the right of commanding; if, after having established the general principles of government, it descended to the details of their application; and if, having regulated the great interests of the country, it could descend to the circle of individual interests, freedom would soon be banished from the New World.

But in the United States the majority, which so frequently displays the tastes and the propensities of a despot, is still destitute of the most perfect instruments of tyranny.

In the American republics the central government has never as yet busied itself except with a small number of objects, sufficiently prominent to attract its attention. The secondary affairs of society have never been regulated by its authority; and nothing has hitherto betrayed its desire of even interfering in them. The majority has become more and more absolute, but has not increased the prerogatives of the central government; those great prerogatives have been confined to a certain sphere; and although the despotism of the majority may be galling upon one point, it cannot be said to extend to all. However the predominant party in the nation may be carried away by its passions, however ardent it may be in the pursuit of its projects, it cannot oblige all the citizens to comply with its desires in the same manner and at the same time throughout the country. When the central government which represents the majority has issued a decree, it must entrust the execution of its will to agents over whom it frequently has no control and whom it cannot perpetually direct. The townships, municipal bodies, and counties form so many concealed breakwaters, which check or part the tide of popular determination. If an oppressive law were passed, liberty would still be protected by the mode of executing that law; the majority cannot descend to the details and what may be called the puerilities of administrative tyranny. It does not even imagine that it can do so, for it has not a full consciousness of its authority. It knows only the extent of its natural powers, but is unacquainted with the art of increasing them.

This point deserves attention; for if a democratic republic, similar to that of the United States, were ever founded in a country where the power of one man had previously established a centralized administration and had sunk it deep into the habits and the laws of the people, I do not hesitate to assert that in such a republic a more insufferable despotism would prevail than in any of the absolute monarchies of Europe; or, indeed, than any that could be found on this side of Asia.

In visiting the Americans and studying their laws, we perceive that the authority they have entrusted to members of the legal profession, and the influence that these individuals exercise in the government, are the most powerful existing security against the excesses of democracy. This effect seems to me to result from a general cause, which it is useful to investigate, as it may be reproduced elsewhere.

Men who have made a special study of the laws derive from occupation certain habits of order, a taste for formalities, and a kind of instinctive regard for the regular connection of ideas, which naturally render them very hostile to the revolutionary spirit and the unreflecting passions of the multitude.

The special information that lawyers derive from their studies ensures them a separate rank in society, and they constitute a sort of privileged body in the scale of intellect. This notion of their superiority perpetually recurs to them in the practice of their profession: they are the masters of a science which is necessary, but which is not very generally known; they serve as arbiters between the citizens; and the habit of directing to their purpose the blind passions of parties in litigation inspires them with a certain contempt for the judgment of the multitude. Add to this that they naturally constitute a *body;* not by any previous understanding, or by an agreement that directs them to a common end; but the analogy of their studies and the uniformity of their methods connect their minds as a common interest might unite their endeavors.

Some of the tastes and the habits of the aristocracy may consequently be discovered in the characters of lawyers. They participate in the same instinctive love of order and formalities; and they entertain the same repugnance to the actions of the multitude, and the same secret contempt of the government of the people.

. . .

I do not, then, assert that *all* the members of the legal profession are at *all* times the friends of order and the opponents of innovation, but merely that most of them are usually so. In a community in which lawyers are allowed to occupy without opposition that high station which naturally belongs to them, their general spirit will be eminently conservative and anti-democratic. When an aristocracy excludes the leaders of that profession from its ranks, it excites enemies who are the more formidable as they are independent of the nobility by their labors and feel themselves to be their equals in intelligence though inferior in opulence and power. But whenever an aristocracy consents to impart some of its privileges to these same individuals, the two classes coalesce very readily and assume, as it were, family interests.

. . .

Lawyers are attached to public order beyond every other consideration, and the best security of public order is authority. It must not be forgotten, also, that if they prize freedom much, they generally value legality still more: they are less afraid of tyranny than of arbitrary power; and, provided the legislature undertakes of itself to deprive men of their independence, they are not dissatisfied.

I am therefore convinced that the prince who, in presence of an encroaching democracy, should endeavor to impair the judicial authority in his dominions, and to diminish the political influence of lawyers, would commit a great mistake: he would let slip the substance of authority to grasp the shadow. He would act more wisely in introducing lawyers into the government; and if he entrusted despotism to them under the form of violence, perhaps he would find it again in their hands under the external features of justice and law.

The government of democracy is favorable to the political power of lawyers; for when the wealthy, the noble, and the prince are excluded from the government, the lawyers take possession of it, in their own right, as it were, since they are the only men of information and sagacity, beyond the sphere of the people, who can be the object of the popular choice. If, then, they are led by their tastes towards the aristocracy and the prince, they are brought in contact with the people by their interests. They like the government of democracy without participating in its propensities and without imitating its weaknesses; whence they derive a twofold authority from it and over it. The people in democratic states do not mistrust the members of the legal profession, because it is known that they are interested to serve the popular cause; and the people listen to them without irritation, because they do not attribute to them any sinister designs. The lawyers do not, indeed, wish to overthrow the institutions of democracy, but they constantly endeavor to turn it away from its real direction by means that are foreign to its nature. Lawyers belong to the people by birth and interest, and to the aristocracy by habit and taste; they may be looked upon as the connecting link between the two great classes of society.

The profession of the law is the only aristocratic element that can be amalgamated without violence with the natural elements of democracy and be advantageously and permanently combined with them. I am not ignorant of the defects inherent in the character of this body of men; but without this admixture of lawyer-like sobriety with the democratic principle, I question whether democratic institutions could long be maintained; and I cannot believe that a republic could hope to exist at the present time if the influence of lawyers in public business did not increase in proportion to the power of the people.

. . .

In America there are no nobles or literary men, and the people are apt to mistrust the wealthy; lawyers consequently form the highest political class and the most cultivated portion of society. They have therefore nothing to gain by innovation, which adds a conservative interest to their natural taste for public order. If I were asked where I place the American aristocracy, I should reply without hesitation that it is not among the rich, who are united by no common tie, but that it occupies the judicial bench and the bar.

. . .

The influence of legal habits extends beyond the precise limits I have pointed out. Scarcely any political question arises in the United States that is not resolved, sooner or later, into a judicial question. Hence all parties are obliged to borrow, in their daily controversies, the ideas, and even the language, peculiar to judicial proceedings. As most public men are or have been legal practitioners, they introduce the customs and technicalities of their profession into the management of public affairs. The jury extends this habit to all classes. The language of the law thus becomes, in some measure, a vulgar tongue; the spirit of the law, which is produced in the schools and courts of justice, gradually penetrates beyond their walls into the bosom of society, where it descends to the lowest classes, so that at last the whole people contract the habits and the tastes of the judicial magistrate. The lawyers of the United States form a party which is but little feared and scarcely perceived, which has no badge peculiar to itself, which adapts itself with great flexibility to the exigencies of the time and accommodates itself without resistance to all the movements of the social body. But this party extends over the whole community and penetrates into all the classes which compose it; it acts upon the country imperceptibly, but finally fashions it to suit its own purposes.

Since my subject has led me to speak of the administration of justice in the United States, I will not pass over it without referring to the institution of the jury. Trial by jury may be considered in two separate points of view: as a judicial, and as a political institution. If it was my purpose to inquire how far trial by jury, especially in civil cases, ensures a good administration of justice, I admit that its utility might be contested. As the jury was first established when society was in its infancy and when courts of justice merely decided simple questions of fact, it is not an easy task to adapt it to the wants of a highly civilized community when the mutual relations of men are multiplied to a surprising extent and have assumed an enlightened and intellectual character.

My present purpose is to consider the jury as a political institution; any other course would divert me from my subject. Of trial by jury considered as a judicial institution I shall here say but little. When the English adopted trial by jury, they were a semi-barbarous people; they have since become one of the most enlightened nations of the earth, and their attachment to this institution seems to have increased with their increased cultivation. They have emigrated and colonized every part of the habitable globe; some have formed colonies, others independent states; the mother country has maintained its monarchical constitution; many of its offspring have founded powerful republics; but everywhere they have boasted of the privilege of trial by jury. They have established it, or hastened to re-establish it, in all their settlements. A judicial institution which thus obtains the suffrages of a great people for so long a series of ages, which is zealously reproduced at every stage of civilization, in all the climates of the earth, and under every form of human government, cannot be contrary to the spirit of justice.

But to leave this part of the subject. It would be a very narrow view to look upon the jury as a mere judicial institution; for however great its influence may be upon the decisions of the courts, it is still greater on the destinies of society at large. The jury is, above all, a political institution, and it must be regarded in this light in order to be duly appreciated.

By the jury I mean a certain number of citizens chosen by lot and invested with a temporary right of judging. Trial by jury, as applied to the repression of crime, appears to me an eminently republican element in the government, for the following reasons.

The institution of the jury may be aristocratic or democratic, according to the class from which the jurors are taken; but it always preserves its republican character, in that it places the real direction of society in the hands of the governed, or of a portion of the governed, and not in that of the government. Force is never more than a transient element of success, and after force comes the notion of right. A government able to reach its enemies only upon a field of battle would soon be destroyed. The true sanction of political laws is to be found in penal legislation; and if that sanction is wanting, the law will sooner or later lose its cogency. He who punishes the criminal is therefore the real master of society. Now, the institution of the jury raises the people itself, or at least a class of citizens, to the bench of judges. The institution of the jury consequently invests the people, or that class of citizens, with the direction of society.

In England the jury is selected from the aristocratic portion of the nation; the aristocracy makes the laws, applies the laws, and punishes infractions of the laws; everything is established upon a consistent footing, and England may with truth be said to constitute an aristocratic republic. In the United States the same system is applied to the whole people. Every American citizen is both an eligible and a legally qualified voter. The jury system as it is understood in America appears to me to be as direct and as extreme a consequence of the sovereignty of the people as universal suffrage. They are two instruments of equal power, which contribute to the supremacy of the majority. All the sovereigns who have chosen to govern by their own authority, and to direct society instead of obeying its directions, have destroyed or enfeebled the institution of the jury. The Tudor monarchs sent to prison jurors who refused to convict, and Napoleon caused them to be selected by his agents.

However clear most of these truths may seem to be, they do not command universal assent; and in France, at least, trial by jury is still but imperfectly understood. If the question arises as to the proper qualification of jurors, it is confined to a discussion of the intelligence and knowledge of the citizens who may be returned, as if the jury was merely a judicial institution. This appears to me the least important part of the subject. The jury is pre-eminently a political institution; it should be regarded as one form of the sovereignty of the people: when that sovereignty is repudiated, it must be rejected, or it must be adapted to the laws by which that sovereignty is established. The jury is that portion of the nation to which the execution of the laws is entrusted, as the legislature is that part of the nation which makes the laws; and in order that society may be governed in a fixed and uniform manner, the list of citizens qualified to serve on juries must increase and diminish with the list of electors. This I hold to be the point of view most worthy of the attention of the legislator; all that remains is merely accessory.

I am so entirely convinced that the jury is pre-eminently a political institution that I still consider it in this light when it is applied in civil causes. Laws are always unstable unless they are founded upon the customs of a nation: customs are the only durable and resisting power in a people. When the jury is reserved for criminal offenses, the people witness only its occasional action in particular cases; they become accustomed to do without it in the ordinary course of life, and it is considered as an instrument, but not as the only instrument, of obtaining justice.

When, on the contrary, the jury acts also on civil causes, its application is constantly visible; it affects all the interests of the community; everyone co-operates in its work: it thus penetrates into all the usages of life, it fashions the human mind to its peculiar forms, and is gradually associated with the idea of justice itself.

The institution of the jury, if confined to criminal causes, is always in danger; but when once it is introduced into civil proceedings, it defies the aggressions of time and man. If it had been as easy to remove the jury from the customs as from the laws of England, it would have perished under the Tudors; and the civil jury did in reality at that period save the liberties of England. In whatever manner the jury be applied, it cannot fail to exercise a powerful influence upon the national character; but this influence is prodigiously increased when it is introduced into civil causes. The jury, and more especially the civil jury, serves to communicate the spirit of the judges to the minds of all the citizens; and this spirit, with the habits which attend it, is the soundest preparation for free institutions. It imbues all classes with a respect for the thing judged and with the notion of right. If these two elements be removed, the love of independence becomes a mere destructive passion. It teaches men to practice equity; every man learns to judge his neighbor as he would himself be judged. And this is especially true of the jury in civil causes; for while the number of persons who have reason to apprehend a criminal prosecution is small, everyone is liable to have a lawsuit. The jury teaches every man not to recoil before the responsibility of his own actions and impresses him with that manly confidence without which no political virtue can exist. It invests each citizen with a kind of magistracy; it makes them all feel the duties which they are bound to discharge towards society and the part which they take in its government. By obliging men to turn their attention to other affairs than their own, it rubs off that private selfishness which is the rust of society.

The jury contributes powerfully to form the judgment and to increase the natural intelligence of a people; and this, in my opinion, is its greatest advantage. It may be regarded as a gratuitous public school, ever open, in which every juror learns his rights, enters into daily communication with the most learned and enlightened members of the upper classes, and becomes practically acquainted with the laws, which are brought within the reach of his capacity by the efforts of the bar, the advice of the judge, and even the passions of the parties. I think that the practical intelligence and political good sense of the Americans are mainly attributable to the long use that they have made of the jury in civil causes.

. . .

Chapter XVI

PRINCIPAL CAUSES WHICH TEND TO MAINTAIN THE DEMOCRATIC REPUBLIC IN THE UNITED STATES

A democratic republic exists in the United States; and the principal object of this book has been to explain the causes of its existence. Several of these causes have been involuntarily passed by, or only hinted at, as I was borne along by my subject. Others I have been unable to discuss at all; and those on which I have dwelt most are, as it were, buried in the details of this work.

I think, therefore, that before I proceed to speak of the future, I ought to collect within a small compass the reasons that explain the present. In this retrospective chapter I shall be brief, for I shall take care to remind the reader only very summarily of what he already knows and shall select only the most prominent of those facts that I have not yet pointed out.

All the causes which contribute to the maintenance of the democratic republic in the United States are reducible to three heads:

I. The peculiar and accidental situation in which Providence has placed the Americans.

II. The laws.

III. The manners and customs of the people.

A thousand circumstances independent of the will of man facilitate the maintenance of a democratic republic in the United States. Some of these are known, the others may easily be pointed out; but I shall confine myself to the principal ones.

The Americans have no neighbors and consequently they have no great wars, or financial crises, or inroads, or conquest, to dread; they require neither great taxes, nor large armies, nor great generals; and they have nothing to fear from a scourge which is more formidable to republics than all these evils combined: namely, military glory. It is impossible to deny the inconceivable influence that military glory exercises upon the spirit of a nation. General Jackson, whom the Americans have twice elected to be the head of their government, is a man of violent temper and very moderate talents; nothing in his whole career ever proved him qualified to govern a free people; and, indeed, the majority of the enlightened classes of the Union has always opposed him. But he was raised to the Presidency, and has been maintained there, solely by the recollection of a victory which he gained, twenty years ago, under the walls of New Orleans; a victory which was, however, a very ordinary achievement and which could only be remembered in a country where battles are rare. Now the people who are thus carried away by the illusions of glory are unquestionably the most cold and calculating, the most unmilitary, if I may so speak, and the most prosaic of all the nations of the earth.

America has no great capital city, whose direct or indirect influence is felt over the whole extent of the country; this I hold to be one of the first causes of the maintenance of republican institutions in the United States. In cities men cannot be prevented from concerting together and awakening a mutual excitement that prompts sudden and passionate resolutions. Cities may be looked upon as large assemblies, of which all the inhabitants are members; their populace exercise a prodigious influence upon the magistrates, and frequently execute their own wishes without the intervention of public officers.

To subject the provinces to the metropolis is therefore to place the destiny of the empire not only in the hands of a portion of the community, which is unjust, but in the hands of a populace carrying out its own impulses, which is very dangerous. The preponderance of capital cities is therefore a serious injury to the representative system; and it exposes modern republics to the same defect as the republics of antiquity, which all perished from not having known this system.

It would be easy for me to enumerate many secondary causes that have contributed to establish, and now concur to maintain, the democratic republic of the United States. But among these favorable circumstances I discern two principal ones, which I hasten to point out. I have already observed that the origin of the Americans, or what I have called their point of departure, may be looked upon as the first and most efficacious cause to which the present prosperity of the United States may be attributed. The Americans had the chances of birth in their favor; and their forefathers imported that equality of condition and of intellect into the country whence the democratic republic has very naturally taken its rise. Nor was this all; for besides this republican condition of society, the early settlers bequeathed to their descendants the customs, manners, and opinions that contribute most to the success of a republic. When I reflect upon the consequences of this primary fact, I think I see the destiny of America embodied in the first Puritan who landed on those shores, just as the whole human race was represented by the first man.

The chief circumstance which has favored the establishment and the maintenance of a democratic republic in the United States is the nature of the territory that the Americans inhabit. Their ancestors gave them the love of equality and of freedom; but God himself gave them the means of remaining equal and free, by placing them upon a boundless continent. General prosperity is favorable to the tability of all governments, but more particularly of a democratic one, which depends upon the will of the majority, and especially upon the will of that portion of the community which is most exposed to want. When the people rule, they must be rendered happy or they will overturn the state; and misery stimulates them to those excesses to which ambition rouses kings. The physical causes, independent of the laws, which promote general prosperity are more numerous in America than they ever have been in any other country in the world, at any other period of history. In the United States not only is legislation democratic, but Nature herself favors the cause of the people.

In what part of human history can be found anything similar to what is passing before our eyes in North America? The celebrated communities of antiquity were all founded in the midst of hostile nations, which they were obliged to subjugate before they could flourish in their place. Even the moderns have found, in some parts of South America, vast regions inhabited by a people of inferior civilization, who nevertheless had already occupied and cultivated the soil. To found their new states it was necessary to extirpate or subdue a numerous population, and they made civilization blush for its own success. But North America was inhabited only by wandering tribes, who had no thought of profiting by the natural riches of the soil; that vast country was still, properly speaking, an empty continent, a desert land awaiting its inhabitants.

. . .

That continent still presents, as it did in the primeval time, rivers that rise from never failing sources, green and moist solitudes, and limitless fields which the plowshare of the husbandman has never turned. In this state it is offered to man, not barbarous, ignorant, and isolated, as he was in the early ages, but already in possession of the most important secrets of nature, united to his fellow men, and instructed by the experience of fifty centuries. At this very time thirteen millions of civilized Europeans are peaceably spreading over those fertile plains, with whose resources and extent they are not yet themselves accurately acquainted. Three or four thousand soldiers drive before them the wandering races of the aborigines; these are followed by the pioneers, who pierce the woods, scare off the beasts of prey, explore the courses of the inland streams, and make ready the triumphal march of civilization across the desert.

Often, in the course of this work, I have alluded to the favorable influence of the material prosperity of America upon the institutions of that country. This reason had already been given by many others before me, and is the only one which, being palpable to the senses, as it were, is familiar to Europeans. I shall not, then, enlarge upon a subject so often handled and so well understood, beyond the addition of a few facts. An erroneous notion is generally entertained that the deserts of America are peopled by European emigrants who annually disembark upon the coasts of the New World, while the American population increase and multiply upon the soil which their forefathers tilled. The European settler usually arrives in the United States without friends and often without resources; in order to subsist, he is obliged to work for hire, and he rarely proceeds beyond that belt of industrious population which adjoins the ocean. The desert cannot be explored without capital or credit; and the body must be accustomed to the rigors of a new climate before it can be exposed in the midst of the forest. It is the Americans themselves who daily quit the spots which gave them birth, to acquire extensive domains in a remote region. Thus the European leaves his cottage for the transatlantic shores, and the American, who is born on that very coast, plunges in his turn into the wilds of central America. This double emigration is incessant; it begins in the middle of Europe, it crosses the Atlantic Ocean, and it advances over the solitudes of the New World. Millions of men are marching at once towards the same horizon; their language, their religion, their manners differ; their object is the same. Fortune has been promised to them somewhere in the West, and to the West they go to find it.

No event can be compared with this continuous removal of the human race, except perhaps those irruptions which caused the fall of the Roman Empire. Then, as well as now, crowds of men were impelled in the same direction, to meet and struggle on the same spot; but the designs of Providence were not the same. Then every new-comer brought with him destruction and death; now each one brings the elements of prosperity and life. The future still conceals from us the remote consequences of this migration of the Americans towards the West; but we can readily apprehend its immediate results. As a portion of the inhabitants annually leave the states in which they were born, the population of these states increases very slowly, although they have long been established. Thus in Connecticut, which yet contains only fifty-nine inhabitants to the square mile, the population has not been increased by more than one quarter in forty years, while that of England has been augmented by one third in the same period. The European emigrant always lands, therefore, in a country that is but half full, and where hands are in demand; he becomes a workman in easy circumstances, his son goes to seek his fortune in unpeopled regions and becomes a rich landowner. The former amasses the capital which the latter invests; and the stranger as well as the native is unacquainted with want.

The laws of the United States are extremely favorable to the division of property; but a cause more powerful than the laws prevents property from being divided to excess. This is very perceptible in the states which are at last beginning to be thickly peopled. Massachusetts is the most populous part of the Union, but it contains only eighty inhabitants to the square mile, which is much less than in France, where one hundred and sixty-two are reckoned to the same extent of country. But in Massachusetts estates are very rarely divided; the eldest son generally takes the land, and the others go to seek their fortune in the wilderness. The law has abolished the right of primogeniture, but circumstances have concurred to re-establish it under a form of which none can complain and by which no just rights are impaired.

A single fact will suffice to show the prodigious number of individuals who thus leave New England to settle in the wilds. We were assured in 1830 that thirty-six of the members of Congress were born in the little state of Connecticut. The population of Connecticut, which constitutes only one forty-third part of that of the United States, thus furnished one eighth of the whole body of representatives. The state of Connecticut of itself, however, sends only five delegates to Congress; and the thirty-one others sit for the new Western states. If these thirty-one individuals had remained in Connecticut, it is probable that, instead of becoming rich landowners, they would have remained humble laborers, that they would have lived in obscurity without being able to rise into public life, and that, far from becoming useful legislators, they might have been unruly citizens.

These reflections do not escape the observation of the Americans any more than of ourselves. "It cannot be doubted," says Chancellor Kent, in his *Treatise on American Law* (Vol. IV, p. 580), "that the division of landed estates must produce great evils, when it is carried to such excess as that each parcel of land is insufficient to support a family; but these disadvantages have never been felt in the United States, and many generations must elapse before they can be felt. The extent of our inhabited territory, the abundance of adjacent land, and the continual stream of emigration flowing from the shores of the Atlantic towards the interior of the country, suffice as yet, and will long suffice, to prevent the parcelling out of estates."

It would be difficult to describe the avidity with which the American rushes forward to secure this immense booty that fortune offers. In the pursuit he fearlessly braves the arrow of the Indian and the diseases of the forest; he is unimpressed by the silence of the woods; the approach of beasts of prey does not disturb him, for he is goaded onwards by a passion stronger than the love of life. Before him lies a boundless continent, and he urges onward as if time pressed and he was afraid of finding no room for his exertions. I have spoken of the emigration from the older states, but how shall I describe that which takes place from the more recent ones? Fifty years have scarcely elapsed since Ohio was founded; the greater part of its inhabitants were not born within its confines; its capital has been built only thirty years, and its territory is still covered by an immense extent of un-cultivated fields; yet already the population of Ohio is proceeding westward, and most of the settlers who descend to the fertile prairies of Illinois are citizens of Ohio. These men left their first country to improve their condition; they quit their second to ameliorate it still more; fortune awaits them everywhere, but not happiness. The desire of pros-perity has become an ardent and restless passion in their minds, which grows by what it feeds on. They early broke the ties that bound them to their natal earth, and they have contracted no fresh ones on their way. Emigration was at first necessary to them; and it soon becomes a sort of game of chance, which they pursue for the emotions it excites as much as for the gain it procures.

. . .

In Europe we are wont to look upon a restless disposition, an unbounded desire of riches, and an excessive love of independence as propensities very dangerous to society. Yet these are the very elements that ensure a long and peaceful future to the republics of America. Without these unquiet passions the population would collect in certain spots and would soon experience wants like those of the Old World, which it is difficult to satisfy; for such is the present good fortune of the New World that the vices of its inhabitants are scarcely less favorable to society than their virtues. These circumstances exercise a great influence on the estimation in which human actions are held in the two hemispheres. What we should call cupidity, the Americans frequently term a laudable industry; and they blame as faint-heartedness what we consider to be the virtue of moderate desires.

. . . .

At the present time America presents a field for human effort far more extensive than any sum of labor that can be applied to work it. In America too much knowledge cannot be diffused; for all knowledge, while it may serve him who possesses it, turns also to the advantage of those who are without it. New wants are not to be feared there, since they can be satisfied without difficulty; the growth of human passions need not be dreaded, since all passions may find an easy and a legitimate object; nor can men there be made too free, since they are scarcely ever tempted to misuse their liberties.

. . . .

The principal aim of this book has been to make known the laws of the United States; if this purpose has been accomplished, the reader is already enabled to judge for himself which are the laws that really tend to maintain the democratic republic, and which endanger its existence.

Three circumstances seem to me to contribute more than all others to the maintenance of the democratic republic in the United States.

The first is that federal form of government which the Americans have adopted, and which enables the Union to combine the power of a great republic with the security of a small one.

The second consists in those township institutions which limit the despotism of the majority and at the same time impart to the people a taste for freedom and the art of being free.

The third is to be found in the constitution of the judicial power. I have shown how the courts of justice serve to repress the excesses of democracy, and how they check and direct the impulses of the majority without stopping its activity.

I have previously remarked that the manners of the people may be considered as one of the great general causes to which the maintenance of a democratic republic in the United States is attributable. I here use the word *customs* with the meaning which the ancients attached to the word *mores;* for I apply it not only to manners properly so called—that is, to what might be termed *the habits of the heart*—but to the various notions and opinions current among men and to the mass of those ideas which constitute their character of mind. I comprise under this term, therefore, the whole moral and intellectual condition of a people. My intention is not to draw a picture of American customs, but simply to point out such features of them as are favorable to the maintenance of their political institutions.

By the side of every religion is to be found a political opinion, which is connected with it by affinity. If the human mind be left to follow its own bent, it will regulate the temporal and spiritual institutions of society in a uniform manner, and man will endeavor, if I may so speak, to *harmonize* earth with heaven.

The greatest part of British America was peopled by men who, after having shaken off the authority of the Pope, acknowledged no other religious supremacy: they brought with them into the New World a form of Christianity which I cannot better describe than by styling it a democratic and republican religion. This contributed powerfully to the establishment of a republic and a democracy in public affairs; and from the beginning, politics and religion contracted an alliance which has never been dissolved.

About fifty years ago Ireland began to pour a Catholic population into the United States; and on their part, the Catholics of America made proselytes, so that, at the present moment more than a million Christians professing the truths of the Church of Rome are to be found in the Union. These Catholics are faithful to the observances of their religion; they are fervent and zealous in the belief of their doctrines. Yet they constitute the most republican and the most democratic class in the United States. This fact may surprise the observer at first, but the causes of it may easily be discovered upon reflection.

I think that the Catholic religion has erroneously been regarded as the natural enemy of democracy. Among the various sects of Christians, Catholicism seems to me, on the contrary, to be one of the most favorable to equality of condition among men. In the Catholic Church the religious community is composed of only two elements: the priest and the people. The priest alone rises above the rank of his flock, and all below him are equal.

On doctrinal points the Catholic faith places all human capacities upon the same level; it subjects the wise and ignorant, the man of genius and the vulgar crowd, to the details of the same creed; it imposes the same observances upon the rich and the needy, it inflicts the same austerities upon the strong and the weak; it listens to no compromise with mortal man, but, reducing all the human race to the same standard, it confounds all the distinctions of society at the foot of the same altar, even as they are confounded in the sight of God. If Catholicism predisposes the faithful to obedience, it certainly does not prepare them for inequality; but the contrary may be said of Protestantism, which generally tends to make men independent more than to render them equal. Catholicism is like an absolute monarchy; if the sovereign be removed, all the other classes of society are more equal than in republics.

. . .

If, then, the Catholic citizens of the United States are not forcibly led by the nature of their tenets to adopt democratic and republican principles, at least they are not necessarily opposed to them; and their social position, as well as their limited number, obliges them to adopt these opinions. Most of the Catholics are poor, and they have no chance of taking a part in the government unless it is open to all the citizens. They constitute a minority, and all rights must be respected in order to ensure to them the free exercise of their own privileges. These two causes induce them, even unconsciously, to adopt political doctrines which they would perhaps support with less zeal if they were rich and preponderant.

The Catholic clergy of the United States have never attempted to oppose this political tendency; but they seek rather to justify it. The Catholic priests in America have divided the intellectual world into two parts: in the one they place the doctrines of revealed religion, which they assent to without discussion; in the other they leave those political truths which they believe the Deity has left open to free inquiry. Thus the Catholics of the United States are at the same time the most submissive believers and the most independent citizens.

It may be asserted, then, that in the United States no religious doctrine displays the slightest hostility to democratic and republican institutions. The clergy of all the different sects there hold the same language; their opinions are in agreement with the laws, and the human mind flows onwards, so to speak, in one undivided current.

.   .   .

I have just shown what the direct influence of religion upon politics is in the United States; but its indirect influence appears to me to be still more considerable, and it never instructs the Americans more fully in the art of being free than when it says nothing of freedom.

The sects that exist in the United States are innumerable. They all differ in respect to the worship which is due to the Creator; but they all agree in respect to the duties which are due from man to man. Each sect adores the Deity in its own peculiar manner, but all sects preach the same moral law in the name of God. If it be of the highest importance to man, as an individual, that his religion should be true, it is not so to society. Society has no future life to hope for or to fear; and provided the citizens profess a religion, the peculiar tenets of that religion are of little importance to its interests. Moreover, all the sects of the United States are comprised within the great unity of Christianity, and Christian morality is everywhere the same.

It may fairly be believed that a certain number of Americans pursue a peculiar form of worship from habit more than from conviction. In the United States the sovereign authority is religious, and consequently hypocrisy must be common; but there is no country in the world where the Christian religion retains a greater influence over the souls of men than in America; and there can be no greater proof of its utility and of its conformity to human nature than that its influence is powerfully felt over the most enlightened and free nation of the earth.

I have remarked that the American clergy in general, without even excepting those who do not admit religious liberty, are all in favor of civil freedom; but they do not support any particular political system. They keep aloof from parties and from public affairs. In the United States religion exercises but little influence upon the laws and upon the details of public opinion; but it directs the customs of the community, and, by regulating domestic life, it regulates the state.

I do not question that the great austerity of manners that is observable in the United States arises, in the first instance, from religious faith. Religion is often unable to restrain man from the numberless temptations which chance offers; nor can it check that passion for gain which everything contributes to arouse; but its influence over the mind of woman is supreme, and women are the protectors of morals. There is certainly no country in the world where the tie of marriage is more respected than in America or where conjugal happiness is more highly or worthily appreciated. In Europe almost all the disturbances of society arise from the irregularities of domestic life. To despise the natural bonds and legitimate pleasures of home is to contract a taste for excesses, a restlessness of heart, and fluctuating desires. Agitated by the tumultuous passions that frequently disturb his dwelling, the European is galled by the obedience which the legislative powers of the state exact. But when the American retires from the turmoil of public life to the bosom of his family, he finds in it the image of order and of peace. There his pleasures are simple and natural, his joys are innocent and calm; and as he finds that an orderly life is the surest path to happiness, he accustoms himself easily to moderate his opinions as well as his tastes. While the

European endeavors to forget his domestic troubles by agitating society, the American derives from his own home that love of order which he afterwards carries with him into public affairs.

. . .

The imagination of the Americans, even in its greatest flights, is circumspect and undecided; its impulses are checked and its works unfinished. These habits of restraint recur in political society and are singularly favorable both to the tranquillity of the people and to the durability of the institutions they have established. Nature and circumstances have made the inhabitants of the United States bold, as is sufficiently attested by the enterprising spirit with which they seek for fortune. If the mind of the Americans were free from all hindrances, they would shortly become the most daring innovators and the most persistent disputants in the world. But the revolutionists of America are obliged to profess an ostensible respect from Christian morality and equity, which does not permit them to violate wantonly the laws that oppose their designs; nor would they find it easy to surmount the scruples of their partisans even if they were able to get over their own. Hitherto no one in the United States has dared to advance the maxim that everything is permissible for the interests of society, an impious adage which seems to have been invented in an age of freedom to shelter all future tyrants. Thus, while the law permits the Americans to do what they please, religion prevents them from conceiving, and forbids them to commit, what is rash or unjust.

Religion in America takes no direct part in the government of society, but it must be regarded as the first of their political insitutions; for if it does not impart a taste for freedom, it facilitates the use of it. Indeed, it is in this same point of view that the inhabitants of the United States themselves look upon religious belief. I do not know whether all Americans have a sincere faith in their religion—for who can search the human heart?—but I am certain that they hold it to be indispensable to the maintenance of republican institutions. This opinion is not peculiar to a class of citizens or to a party, but it belongs to the whole nation and to every rank of society.

. . .

The philosophers of the eighteenth century explained in a very simple manner the gradual decay of religious faith. Religious zeal, said they, must necessarily fail the more generally liberty is established and knowledge diffused. Unfortunately, the facts by no means accord with their theory. There are certain populations in Europe whose unbelief is ony equaled by their ignorance and debasement; while in America, one of the freest and most enlightened nations in the world, the people fulfill with fervor all the outward duties of religion.

On my arrival in the United States the religious aspect of the country was the first thing that struck my attention; and the longer I stayed there, the more I perceived the great political consequences resulting from this new state of things. In France I had almost always seen the spirit of religion and the spirit of freedom marching in opposite directions. But in America I found they were intimately united and that they reigned in common over the same country. My desire to discover the causes of this phenomenon increased from day to day. In order to satisfy it I questioned the members of all the different sects; I sought especially the society of the clergy, who are the depositaries of the different creeds and are especially interested in their duration. As a member of the Roman Catholic Church, I was more particularly brought into contact with several of 'ts priests, with whom I became intimately acquainted. To each of these men I expressed my astonishment and explained my doubts. I found that they differed upon matters of detail alone, and that they all attributed the peaceful dominion of religion in their country mainly to the separation of church and state. I do not hesitate to affirm that during my stay in America I did not meet a single individual, of the clergy or the laity, who was not of the same opinion on this point.

This led me to examine more attentively than I had hitherto done the station which the American clergy occupy in political society. I learned with surprise that they filled no public appointments; I did not see one of them in the administration, and they are not even represented in the legislative assemblies. In several states the law excludes them from political life; public opinion excludes them in all. And when I came to inquire into the prevailing spirit of the clergy, I found that most of its members seemed to retire of their own accord from the exercise of power, and that they made it the pride of their profession to abstain from politics.

I heard them inveigh against ambition and deceit, under whatever political opinions these vices might chance to lurk; but I learned from their discourses that men are not guilty in the eye of God for any opinions concerning political government which they may profess with sincerity, any more than they are for their mistakes in building a house or in driving a furrow. I perceived that these ministers of the Gospel eschewed all parties, with the anxiety attendant upon personal interest. These facts convinced me that what I had been told was true; and it then became my object to investigate their causes and to inquire how it happened that the real authority of religion was increased by a state of things which diminished its apparent force. These causes did not long escape my researches.

As long as a religion rests only upon those sentiments which are the consolation of all affliction, it may attract the affections of all mankind. But if it be mixed up with the bitter passions of the world, it may be constrained to defend allies whom its interests, and not the principle of love, have given to it; or to repel as antagonists men who are still attached to it, however opposed they may be to the powers with which it is allied. The church cannot share the temporal power of the state without being the object of a portion of that animosity which the latter excites.

. . .

In proportion as a nation assumes a democratic condition of society and as communities display democratic propensities, it becomes more and more dangerous to connect religion with political institutions; for the time is coming when authority will be bandied from hand to hand, when political theories will succeed one another, and when men, laws, and constitutions will disappear or be modified from day to day, and this not for a season only, but unceasingly. Agitation and mutability are inherent in the nature of democratic republics, just as stagnation and sleepiness are the law of absolute monarchies.

If the Americans, who change the head of the government once in four years, who elect new legislators every two years, and renew the state officers every twelve months; if the Americans, who have given up the political world to the attempts of innovators, had not placed religion beyond their reach, where could it take firm hold in the ebb and flow of human opinions? Where would be that respect which belongs to it, amid the struggles of faction? And what would become of its immortality, in the midst of universal decay? The American clergy were the first to perceive this truth and to act in conformity with it. They saw that they must renounce their religious influence if they were to strive for political power, and they chose to give up the support of the state rather than to share its vicissitudes.

In America religion is perhaps less powerful than it has been at certain periods and among certain nations; but its influence is more lasting. It restricts itself to its own resources, but of these none can deprive it; its circle is limited, but it pervades it and holds it under undisputed control.

. . .

I have but little to add to what I have already said concerning the influence that the instruction and the habits of the Americans exercise upon the maintenance of their political institutions.

America has hitherto produced very few writers of distinction; it possesses no great historians and not a single eminent poet. The inhabitants of that country look upon literature properly so called with a kind of disapprobation; and there are towns of second-rate importance in Europe in which more literary works are annually published than in the twenty-four states of the Union put together. The spirit of the Americans is averse to general ideas; it does not seek theoretical discoveries. Neither politics nor manufactures direct them to such speculations; and although new laws are perpetually enacted in the United States, no great writers there have hitherto inquired into the general principles of legislation. The Americans have lawyers and commentators, but no jurists; and they furnish examples rather than lessons to the world. The same observation applies to the mechanical arts. In America the inventions of Europe are adopted with sagacity; they are perfected, and adapted with admirable skill to the wants of the country. Manufactures exist, but the science of manufacture is not cultivated; and they have good workmen, but very few inventors. Fulton was obliged to proffer his services to foreign nations for a long time before he was able to devote them to his own country.

The observer who is desirous of forming an opinion on the state of instruction among the Anglo-Americans must consider the same object from two different points of view. If he singles out only the learned, he will be astonished to find how few they are; but if he counts the ignorant, the American people will appear to be the most enlightened in the world. The whole population, as I observed in another place, is situated between these two extremes.

. . .

The Americans never use the word *peasant,* because they have no idea of the class which that term denotes; the ignorance of more remote ages, the simplicity of rural life, and the rusticity of the villager have not been preserved among them; and they are alike unacquainted with the virtues, the vices, the coarse habits, and the simple graces of an early stage of civilization. At the extreme borders of the confederate states, upon the confines of society and the wilderness, a population of bold adventurers have taken up their abode, who pierce the solitudes of the American woods and seek a country there in order to escape the poverty that awaited them in their native home. As soon as the pioneer reaches the place which is to serve him for a retreat, he fells a few trees and builds a log house. Nothing can offer a more miserable aspect than these isolated dwellings. The traveler who approaches one of them towards nightfall sees the flicker of the hearth flame through the chinks in the walls; and at night, if the wind rises, he hears the roof of boughs shake to and fro in the midst of the great forest trees. Who would not suppose that this poor hut is the asylum of rudeness and ignorance? Yet no sort of comparison can be drawn between the pioneer and the dwelling that shelters him. Everything about him is primitive and wild, but he is himself the result of the labor and experience of eighteen centuries. He wears the dress and speaks the language of cities; he is acquainted with the past, curious about the future, and ready for argument about the present; he is, in short, a highly civilized being, who consents for a time to inhabit the backwoods, and who penetrates into the wilds of the New World with the Bible, an axe, and some newspapers. It is difficult to imagine the incredible rapidity with which thought circulates in the midst of these deserts. I do not think that so much intellectual activity exists in the most enlightened and populous districts of France.

It cannot be doubted that in the United States the instruction of the people powerfully contributes to the support of the democratic republic; and such must always be the case, I believe, where the instruction which enlightens the understanding is not separated from the moral education which amends the heart. But I would not exaggerate this advantage, and I am still further from thinking, as so many people do think in Europe, that men can be instantaneously made citizens by teaching them to read and write. True information is mainly derived from experience; and if the Americans had not been gradually accustomed to govern themselves, their book-learning would not help them much at the present day.

I have lived much with the people in the United States, and I cannot express how much I admire their experience and their good sense. An American should never be led to speak of Europe, for he will then probably display much presumption and very foolish pride. He will take up with those crude and vague notions which are so useful to the ignorant all over the world. But if you question him respecting his own country, the cloud that dimmed his intelligence will immediately disperse; his language will become as clear and precise as his thoughts. He will inform you what his rights are and by what means he exercises them; he will be able to point out the customs which obtain in the political world. You will find that he is well acquainted with the rules of the administration, and that he is familiar with the mechanism of the laws. The citizen of the United States does not acquire his practical science and his positive notions from books; the instruction he has acquired may have prepared him for receiving those ideas, but it did not furnish them. The American learns to know the laws by participating in the act of legislation; and he takes a lesson in the forms of government from governing. The great work of society is ever going on before his eyes and, as it were, under his hands.

* * *

I have remarked that the maintenance of democratic institutions in the United States is attributable to the circumstances, the laws, and the customs of that country. Most Europeans are acquainted with only the first of these three causes, and they are apt to give it a preponderant importance that it does not really possess.

It is true that the Anglo-Americans settled in the New World in a state of social equality; the low-born and the noble were not to be found among them; and professional prejudices were always as unknown as the prejudices of birth. Thus, as the condition of society was democratic, the rule of democracy was established without difficulty. But this circumstance is not peculiar to the United States; almost all the American colonies were founded by men equal among themselves, or who became so by inhabiting them. In no one part of the New World have Europeans been able to create an aristocracy. Nevertheless, democratic institutions prosper nowhere but in the United States.

The American Union has no enemies to contend with; it stands in the wilds like an island in the ocean. But the

Spaniards of South America were no less isolated by nature; yet their position has not relieved them from the charge of standing armies. They make war upon one another when they have no foreign enemies to oppose; and the Anglo-American democracy is the only one that has hitherto been able to maintain itself in peace.

The territory of the Union presents a boundless field to human activity, and inexhaustible materials for labor. The passion for wealth takes the place of ambition, and the heat of faction is mitigated by a consciousness of prosperity. But in what portion of the globe shall we find more fertile plains, mightier rivers, or more unexplored and inexhaustible riches than in South America? Yet South America has been unable to maintain democratic institutions. If the welfare of nations depended on their being placed in a remote position, with an unbounded space of habitable territory before them, the Spaniards of South America would have no reason to complain of their fate. And although they might enjoy less prosperity than the inhabitants of the United States, their lot might still be such as to excite the envy of some nations in Europe. There are no nations upon the face of the earth, however, more miserable than those of South America.

Thus not only are physical causes inadequate to produce results analogous to those which occur in North America, but they cannot raise the population of South America above the level of European states, where they act in a contrary direction. Physical causes do not therefore affect the destiny of nations so much as has been supposed.

. . .

Other inhabitants of America have the same physical conditions of prosperity as the Anglo-Americans, but without their laws and their customs; and these people are miserable. The laws and customs of the Anglo-Americans are therefore that special and predominant cause of their greatness which is the object of my inquiry.

I am far from supposing that the American laws are preeminently good in themselves: I do not hold them to be applicable to all democratic nations; and several of them seem to me to be dangerous, even in the United States. But it cannot be denied that American legislation, taken as a whole, is extremely well adapted to the genius of the people and the nature of the country which it is intended to govern. American laws are therefore good, and to them must be attributed a large portion of the success that attends the government of democracy in America; but I do not believe them to be the principal cause of that success; and if they seem to me to have more influence than the nature of the country upon the social happiness of the Americans, there is still reason to believe that their effect is inferior to that produced by the customs of the people.

. . .

The customs of the Americans of the United States are, then, the peculiar cause which renders that people the only one of the American nations that is able to support a democratic government; and it is the influence of customs that produces the different degrees of order and prosperity which may be distinguished in the several Anglo-American democracies. Thus the effect which the geographical position of a country may have upon the duration of democratic institutions is exaggerated in Europe. Too much importance is attributed to legislation, too little to customs. These three great causes serve, no doubt, to regulate and direct American democracy; but if they were to be classed in their proper order, I should say that physical circumstances are less efficient than the laws, and the laws infinitely less so than the customs of the people. I am convinced that the most advantageous situation and the best possible laws cannot maintain a constitution in spite of the customs of a country; while the latter may turn to some advantage the most unfavorable positions and the worst laws. The importance of customs is a common truth to which study and experience incessantly direct our attention. It may be regarded as a central point in the range of observation, and the common termination of all my inquiries. So seriously do I insist upon this head that, if I have hitherto failed in making the reader feel the important influence of the practical experience, the habits, the opinions, in short, of the customs of the Americans upon the maintenance of their institutions, I have failed in the principal object of my work.

I have asserted that the success of democratic institutions in the United States is more attributable to the laws themselves and the customs of the people than to the nature of the country. But does it follow that the same causes would of themselves produce the same results if they were put in operation elsewhere; and if the country is no adequate substitute for laws and customs, can laws and manners in their turn take the place of a country? It will readily be understood that the elements of a reply to this question are wanting: other inhabitants are to be found in the New World besides the Anglo-Americans, and, as these are affected by the same physical circumstances as the latter, they may fairly be compared with them. But there are no nations out of America which have adopted the same laws and customs, though destitute of the physical advantages peculiar to the Anglo-Americans. No standard of comparison therefore exists, and we can only hazard an opinion.

It appears to me, in the first place, that a careful distinction must be made between the institutions of the United States and democratic institutions in general. When I reflect upon the state of Europe, its mighty nations, its populous cities, its formidable armies, and the complex nature of its politics, I cannot suppose that even the Anglo-

Americans, if they were transported to our hemisphere, with their ideas, their religion, and their customs, could exist without considerably altering their laws. But a democratic nation may be imagined organized differently from the American people. Is it, then, impossible to conceive a government really established upon the will of the majority, but in which the majority, repressing its natural instinct of equality, should consent, with a view to the order and the stability of the state, to invest a family or an individual with all the attributes of executive power? Might not a democratic society be imagined in which the forces of the nation would be more centralized than they are in the United States; where the people would exercise a less direct and less irresistible influence upon public affairs, and yet every citizen, invested with certain rights, would participate, within his sphere, in the conduct of the government? What I have seen among the Anglo-Americans induces me to believe that democratic institutions of this kind, prudently introduced into society so as gradually to mix with the habits and to be interfused with the opinions of the people, might exist in other countries besides America. If the laws of the United States were the only imaginable democratic laws or the most perfect which it is possible to conceive, I should admit that their success in America affords no proof of the success of democratic institutions in general in a country less favored by nature. But as the laws of America appear to me to be defective in several respects, and as I can readily imagine others, the peculiar advantages of that country do not prove to me that democratic institutions cannot succeed in a nation less favored by circumstances if ruled by better laws.

. . .

It may readily be discovered with what intention I undertook the foregoing inquiries. The question here discussed is interesting not only to the United States, but to the whole world; it concerns, not a nation only, but all mankind. If those nations whose social condition is democratic could remain free only while they inhabit uncultivated regions, we must despair of the future destiny of the human race; for democracy is rapidly acquiring a more extended sway, and the wilds are gradually peopled with men. If it were true that laws and customs are insufficient to maintain democratic institutions, what refuge would remain open to the nations, except the despotism of one man? I am aware that there are many worthy persons at the present time who are not alarmed at this alternative and who are so tired of liberty as to be glad of repose far from its storms. But these persons are ill acquainted with the haven towards which they are bound. Preoccupied by their remembrances, they judge of absolute power by what it has been and not by what it might become in our times.

If absolute power were re-established among the democratic nations of Europe, I am persuaded that it would assume a new form and appear under features unknown to our fathers. There was a time in Europe when the laws and the consent of the people had invested princes with almost unlimited authority, but they scarcely ever availed themselves of it. I do not speak of the prerogatives of the nobility, of the authority of high courts of justice, of corporations and their chartered rights, or of provincial privileges, which served to break the blows of sovereign authority and to keep up a spirit of resistance in the nation. Independently of these political institutions, which, however opposed they might be to personal liberty, served to keep alive the love of freedom in the mind and which may be esteemed useful in this respect, the manners and opinions of the nation confined the royal authority within barriers that were not less powerful because less conspicuous. Religion, the affections of the people, the benevolence of the prince, the sense of honor, family pride, provincial prejudices, custom, and public opinion limited the power of kings and restrained their authority within an invisible circle. The constitution of nations was despotic at that time, but their customs were free. Princes had the right, but they had neither the means nor the desire of doing whatever they pleased.

But what now remains of those barriers which formerly arrested tyranny? Since religion has lost its empire over the souls of men, the most prominent boundary that divided good from evil is overthown; everything seems doubtful and indeterminate in the moral world; kings and nations are guided by chance, and none can say where are the natural limits of despotism and the bounds of license. Long revolutions have forever destroyed the respect which surrounded the rulers of the state; and since they have been relieved from the burden of public esteem, princes may henceforward surrender themselves without fear to the intoxication of arbitrary power.

. . .

If men must really come to this point, that they are to be entirely emancipated or entirely enslaved, all their rights to be made equal or all to be taken away from them; if the rulers of society were compelled either gradually to raise the crowd to their own level or to allow all the citizens to fall below that of humanity, would not the doubts of many be resolved, the consciences of many be confirmed, and the community prepared to make great sacrifices with little difficulty? In that case the gradual growth of democratic manners and institutions should be regarded, not as the best, but as the only means of preserving freedom; and, without caring for the democratic form of government, it might be adopted as the most applicable, and the fairest remedy for the present ills of society.

It is difficult to make the people participate in the government, but it is still more difficult to supply them with experience and to inspire them with the feelings which they need in order to govern well. I grant that the wishes of the democracy are capricious, its instruments rude, its laws imperfect. But if it were true that soon no just medium would exist between the rule of democracy and the dominion of a single man, should we not rather incline towards the former than submit voluntarily to the latter? And if complete equality be our fate, is it not better to be leveled by free institutions than by a despot?

Those who, after having read this book, should imagine that my intention in writing it was to propose the laws and customs of the Anglo-Americans for the imitation of all democratic communities would make a great mistake; they must have paid more attention to the form than to the substance of my thought. My aim has been to show, by the example of America, that laws, and especially customs, may allow a democratic people to remain free. But I am very far from thinking that we ought to follow the example of the American democracy and copy the means that it has employed to attain this end; for I am well aware of the influence which the nature of a country and its political antecedents exercise upon its political constitution; and I should regard it as a great misfortune for mankind if liberty were to exist all over the world under the same features.

But I am of the opinion that if we do not succeed in gradually introducing democratic institutions into France, if we despair of imparting to all the citizens those ideas and sentiments which first prepare them for freedom and afterwards allow them to enjoy it, there will be no independence at all, either for the middle classes or for the nobility, for the poor or for the rich, but an equal tyranny over all; and I foresee that if the peaceable dominion of the majority is not founded among us in time, we shall sooner or later fall under the unlimited authority of a single man.

Chapter XVII

THE PRESENT AND PROBABLE FUTURE CONDITION OF THE THREE RACES THAT INHABIT THE TERRITORY OF THE UNITED STATES

The principal task that I had imposed upon myself is now performed: I have shown, as far as I was able, the laws and the customs of the American democracy. Here I might stop; but the reader would perhaps feel that I had not satisfied his expectations.

An absolute and immense democracy is not all that we find in America; the inhabitants of the New World may be considered from more than one point of view. In the course of this work my subject often led me to speak of the Indians and the Negroes, but I have never had time to stop in order to show what place these two races occupy in the midst of the democratic people whom I was engaged in describing. I have shown in what spirit and according to what laws the Anglo-American Union was formed; but I could give only a hurried and imperfect glance at the dangers which menace that confederation and could not furnish a detailed account of its chances of survival independently of its laws and manners. When speaking of the united republics, I hazarded no conjectures upon the permanence of republican forms in the New World; and when making frequent allusions to the commercial activity that reigns in the Union, I was unable to inquire into the future of the Americans as a commercial people.

These topics are collaterally connected with my subject

without forming a part of it; they are American without being democratic, and to portray democracy has been my principal aim. It was therefore necessary to postpone these questions, which I now take up as the proper termination of my work.

. . .

The territory now occupied or claimed by the American Union spreads from the shores of the Atlantic to those of the Pacific Ocean. On the east and west its limits are those of the continent itself. On the south it advances nearly to the tropics, and it extends upward to the icy regions of the north.

The human beings who are scattered over this space do not form, as in Europe, so many branches of the same stock. Three races, naturally distinct, and, I might almost say, hostile to each other, are discoverable among them at the first glance. Almost insurmountable barriers had been raised between them by education and law, as well as by their origin and outward characteristics; but fortune has brought them together on the same soil, where, although they are mixed, they do not amalgamate, and each race fulfills its destiny apart.

Among these widely differing families of men, the first that attracts attention, the superior in intelligence, in power, and in enjoyment, is the white, or European, the MAN pre-eminently so called; below him appear the Negro and the Indian. These two unhappy races have nothing in common, neither birth, nor features, nor language, nor habits. Their only resemblance lies in their misfortunes. Both of them occupy an equally inferior position in the country they inhabit; both suffer from tyranny; and if their wrongs are not the same, they originate from the same authors.

If we reason from what passes in the world, we should

almost say that the European is to the other races of mankind what man himself is to the lower animals: he makes them subservient to his use, and when he cannot subdue he destroys them. Oppression has, at one stroke, deprived the descendants of the Africans of almost all the privileges of humanity. The Negro of the United States has lost even the remembrance of this country; the language which his forefathers spoke is never heard around him; he abjured their religion and forgot their customs when he ceased to belong to Africa, without acquiring any claim to European privileges. But he remains half-way between the two communities, isolated between two races; sold by the one, repulsed by the other; finding not a spot in the universe to call by the name of country, except the faint image of a home which the shelter of his master's roof affords.

The Negro has no family: woman is merely the temporary companion of his pleasures, and his children are on an equality with himself from the moment of their birth. Am I to call it a proof of God's mercy, or a visitation of his wrath, that man, in certain states, appears to be insensible to his extreme wretchedness and almost obtains a depraved taste for the cause of his misfortunes? The Negro, plunged in this abyss of evils, scarcely feels his own calamitous situation. Violence made him a slave, and the habit of servitude gives him the thoughts and desires of a slave; he admires his tyrants more than he hates them, and finds his joy and his pride in the servile imitation of those who oppress him. His understanding is degraded to the level of his soul.

The Negro enters upon slavery as soon as he is born; nay, he may have been purchased in the womb, and have begun his slavery before he began his existence. Equally devoid of wants and of enjoyment, and useless to himself, he learns, with his first notions of existence, that he is the property of another, who has an interest in preserving his life, and that the care of it does not devolve upon himself; even the power of thought appears to him a useless gift of Providence, and he quietly enjoys all the privileges of his debasement.

If he becomes free, independence is often felt by him to be a heavier burden than slavery; for, having learned in the course of his life to submit to everything except reason, he is too unacquainted with her dictates to obey them. A thousand new desires beset him, and he has not the knowledge and energy necessary to resist them: these are masters which it is necessary to contend with, and he has learned only to submit and obey. In short, he is sunk to such a depth of wretchedness that while servitude brutalizes, liberty destroys him.

Oppression has been no less fatal to the Indian than to the Negro race, but its effects are different. Before the arrival of white men in the New World, the inhabitants of North America lived quietly in their woods, enduring the vicissitudes and practicing the virtues and vices common to savage nations. The Europeans, having dispersed the Indian tribes and driven them into the deserts, condemned them to a wandering life, full of inexpressible sufferings.

Savage nations are only controlled by opinion and custom. When the North American Indians had lost the sentiment of attachment to their country; when their families were dispersed, their traditions obscured, and the chain of their recollections broken; when all their habits were changed, and their wants increased beyond measure, European tyranny rendered them more disorderly and less civilized than they were before. The moral and physical condition of these tribes continually grew worse, and they became more barbarous as they became more wretched. Nevertheless, the Europeans have not been able to change the character of the Indians; and though they have had power to destroy, they have never been able to subdue and civilize them.

The lot of the Negro is placed on the extreme limit of servitude, while that of the Indian lies on the uttermost verge of liberty; and slavery does not produce more fatal effects upon the first than independence upon the second. The Negro has lost all property in his own person, and he cannot dispose of his existence without committing a sort of fraud. But the savage is his own master as soon as he is able to act; parental authority is scarcely known to him; he has never bent his will to that of any of his kind, nor learned the difference between voluntary obedience and a shameful subjection; and the very name of law is unknown to him. To be free, with him, signifies to escape from all the shackles of society. As he delights in this barbarous independence and would rather perish than sacrifice the least part of it, civilization has little hold over him.

The Negro makes a thousand fruitless efforts to insinuate himself among men who repulse him; he conforms to the tastes of his oppressors, adopts their opinions, and hopes by imitating them to form a part of their community. Having been told from infancy that his race is naturally inferior to that of the whites, he assents to the proposition and is ashamed of his own nature. In each of his features he discovers a trace of slavery, and if it were in his power, he would willingly rid himself of everything that makes him what he is.

The Indian, on the contrary, has his imagination inflated with the pretended nobility of his origin, and lives and dies in the midst of these dreams of pride. Far from desiring to conform his habits to ours, he loves his savage life as the distinguishing mark of his race and repels every advance to civilization, less, perhaps, from hatred of it than from a dread of resembling the Europeans. While he has nothing to oppose to our perfection in the arts but the resources of the wilderness, to our tactics nothing but undisciplined courage, while our well-digested plans are met only by the spontaneous instincts of savage life, who can wonder if he fails in this unequal contest?

The Negro, who earnestly desires to mingle his race with that of the European, cannot do so; while the Indian, who might succeed to a certain extent, disdains to make the attempt. The servility of the one dooms him to slavery, the pride of the other to death.

I remember that while I was traveling through the forests which still cover the state of Alabama, I arrived one day at the log house of a pioneer. I did not wish to penetrate into the dwelling of the American, but retired to rest myself for a while on the margin of a spring, which was not far off, in the woods. While I was in this place (which was in the neighborhood of the Creek territory), an Indian woman appeared, followed by a Negress, and holding by the hand a little white girl of five or six years, whom I took to be the daughter of the pioneer. A sort of barbarous luxury set off the costume of the Indian; rings of metal were hanging from her nostrils and ears, her hair, which was adorned with glass beads, fell loosely upon her shoulders; and I saw that she was not married, for she still wore that necklace of shells which the bride always deposits on the nuptial couch. The Negress was clad in squalid European garments. All three came and seated themselves upon the banks of the spring; and the young Indian, taking the child in her arms, lavished upon her such fond caresses as mothers give, while the Negress endeavored, by various little artifices, to attract the attention of the young Creole. The child displayed in her slightest gestures a consciousness of superiority that formed a strange contrast with her infantine weakness; as if she received the attentions of her companions with a sort of condescension. The Negress was seated on the ground before her mistress, watching her smallest desires and apparently divided between an almost maternal affection for the child and servile fear; while the savage, in the midst of her tenderness, displayed an air of freedom and pride which was almost ferocious. I had approached the group and was contemplating them in silence, but my curiosity was probably displeasing to the Indian woman, for she suddenly rose, pushed the child roughly from her, and, giving me an angry look, plunged into the thicket.

In the same place I had often chanced to see individuals together who belonged to the three races that people North America. I had perceived from many different traits the preponderance of the whites. But in the picture that I have just been describing there was something peculiarly touching; a bond of affection here united the oppressors with the oppressed, and the effort of Nature to bring them together rendered still more striking the immense distance placed between them by prejudice and the laws.

. . .

When the Indians were the sole inhabitants of the wilds whence they have since been expelled, their wants were few. Their arms were of their own manufacture, their only drink was the water of the brook, and their clothes consisted of the skins of animals, whose flesh furnished them with food.

The Europeans introduced among the savages of North America firearms, ardent spirits, and iron; they taught them to exchange for manufactured stuffs the rough garments that had previously satisfied their untutored simplicity. Having acquired new tastes, without the arts by which they could be gratified, the Indians were obliged to have recourse to the workmanship of the whites; but in return for their productions the savage had nothing to offer except the rich furs that still abounded in his woods. Hence the chase became necessary, not merely to provide for his subsistence, but to satisfy the frivolous desires of Europeans. He no longer hunted merely to obtain food, but to procure the only objects of barter which he could offer. While the wants of the natives were thus increasing, their resources continued to diminish.

From the moment when a European settlement is formed in the neighborhood of the territory occupied by the Indians, the beasts of chase take the alarm. Thousands of savages, wandering in the forests and destitute of any fixed dwelling, did not disturb them; but as soon as the continuous sounds of European labor are heard in their neighborhood, they begin to flee away and retire to the West, where their instinct teaches them that they will still find deserts of immeasurable extent. "The buffalo is constantly receding," say Messrs. Clarke and Cass in their *Report* of the year 1829; "a few years since they approached the base of the Alleghany; and a few years hence they may even be rare upon the immense plains which extend to the base of the Rocky Mountains." I have been assured that this effect of the approach of the whites is often felt at two hundred leagues' distance from their frontier. Their influence is thus exerted over tribes whose name is unknown to them, and who suffer the evils of usurpation long before they are acquainted with the authors of their distress.

Bold adventurers soon penetrate into the country the Indians have deserted, and when they have advanced about fifteen or twenty leagues from the extreme frontiers of the whites, they begin to build habitations for civilized beings in the midst of the wilderness. This is done without difficulty, as the territory of a hunting nation is ill defined; it is the common property of the tribe and belongs to no one in particular, so that individual interests are not concerned in protecting any part of it.

A few European families, occupying points very remote from one another, soon drive away the wild animals that remain between their places of abode. The Indians, who had previously lived in a sort of abundance, then find it difficult to subsist, and still more difficult to procure the articles of barter that they stand in need of. To drive away their game has the same effect as to render sterile the fields of our agriculturists; deprived of the means of subsistence, they are reduced, like famished wolves, to prowl through the forsaken woods in quest of prey. Their instinctive love of country attaches them to the soil that gave them birth, even after it has ceased to yield anything but misery and death. At length they are compelled to acquiesce and depart; they follow the traces of the elk, the buffalo, and the beaver and are guided by these wild animals in the choice of their future country. Properly speaking, therefore, it is not the Europeans who drive away the natives of America; it is famine, a happy distinction which had escaped the casuists of former times and for which we are indebted to modern discovery!

It is impossible to conceive the frightful sufferings that attend these forced migrations. They are undertaken by a people already exhausted and reduced; and the countries to which the new-comers betake themselves are inhabited by other tribes, which receive them with jealous hostility. Hunger is in the rear, war awaits them, and misery besets them on all sides. To escape from so many enemies, they separate, and each individual endeavors to procure secretly the means of supporting his existence by isolating himself, living in the immensity of the desert like an outcast in civilized society. The social tie, which distress had long since weakened, is then dissolved; they have no longer a country, and soon they will not be a people; their very families are obliterated; their common name is forgotten; their language perishes; and all traces of their origin disappear. Their nation has ceased to exist except in the recollection of the antiquaries of America and a few of the learned of Europe.

I should be sorry to have my reader suppose that I am coloring the picture too highly; I saw with my own eyes many of the miseries that I have just described, and was the witness of sufferings that I have not the power to portray.

At the end of the year 1831, while I was on the left bank of the Mississippi, at a place named by Europeans Memphis, there arrived a numerous band of Choctaws (or Chactas, as they are called by the French in Louisiana). These savages had left their country and were endeavoring to gain the right bank of the Mississippi, where they hoped to find an asylum that had been promised them by the American government. It was then the middle of winter, and the cold was unusually severe; the snow had frozen hard upon the ground, and the river was drifting huge masses of ice. The Indians had their families with them, and they brought in their train the wounded and the sick, with children newly born and old men upon the verge of death. They possessed neither tents nor wagons, but only their arms and some provisions. I saw them embark to pass the mighty river, and never will that solemn spectacle fade from my remembrance. No cry, no sob, was heard among the assembled crowd; all were silent. Their calamities were of ancient date, and they knew them to be irremediable. The Indians had all stepped into the bark that was to carry them across, but their dogs remained upon the bank. As soon as these animals perceived that their masters were finally leaving the shore, they set up a dismal howl and, plunging all together into the icy waters of the Mississippi, swam after the boat.

The expulsion of the Indians often takes place at the present day in a regular and, as it were, a legal manner. When the European population begins to approach the limit of the desert inhabited by a savage tribe, the government of the United States usually sends forward envoys who assemble the Indians in a large plain and, having first eaten and drunk with them, addressed them thus: "What have you to do in the land of your fathers? Before long, you must dig up their bones in order to live. In what respect is the country you inhabit better than another? Are there no woods, marshes, or prairies except where you dwell? And can you live nowhere but under your own sun? Beyond those mountains which you see at the horizon, beyond the lake which bounds your territory on the west, their lie vast countries where beasts of chase are yet found in great abundance; sell us your lands, then, and go to live happily in those solitudes." After holding this language, they spread before the eyes of the Indians firearms, woolen garments, kegs of brandy, glass necklaces, bracelets of tinsel, ear-rings, and looking-glasses. If, when they have beheld all these riches, they still hesitate, it is insinuated that they cannot refuse the required consent and that the government itself will not long have the power of protecting them in their rights. What are they to do? Half convinced and half compelled, they go to inhabit new deserts, where the importunate whites will not let them remain ten years in peace. In this manner do the Americans obtain, at a very low price, whole provinces, which the richest sovereigns of Europe could not purchase.

These are great evils; and it must be added that they appear to me to be irremediable. I believe that the Indian nations of North America are doomed to perish, and that whenever the Europeans shall be established on the shores of the Pacific Ocean, that race of men will have ceased to exist. The Indians had only the alternative of war or civilization; in other words, they must either destroy the Europeans or become their equals.

At the first settlement of the colonies they might have found it possible, by uniting their forces, to deliver themselves from the small bodies of strangers who landed on their continent. They several times attempted to do it, and were on the point of succeeding; but the disproportion of their resources at the present day, when compared with those of the whites, is too great to allow such an enterprise to be thought of. But from time to time among the Indians men of sagacity and energy foresee the final destiny that awaits the native population and exert themselves to unite all the tribes in common hostility to the Europeans; but their efforts are unavailing. The tribes which are in the neighborhood of the whites are too much weakened to offer an effectual resistance; while the others, giving way to that childish carelessness of the morrow which characterizes savage life, wait for the near approach of danger before they prepare to meet it; some are unable, others are unwilling, to act.

It is easy to foresee that the Indians will never civilize themselves, or that it will be too late when they may be inclined to make the experiment.

Civilization is the result of a long social process, which takes place in the same spot and is handed down from one generation to another, each one profiting by the experience of the last. Of all nations, those submit to civilization with the most difficulty who habitually live by the chase. Pastoral tribes, indeed, often change their place of abode; but they follow a regular order in their migrations and often return to their old stations, while the dwelling of the hunter varies with that of the animals he pursues.

Several attempts have been made to diffuse knowledge among the Indians, leaving unchecked their wandering propensities, by the Jesuits in Canada and by the Puritans in New England; but none of these endeavors have been crowned by any lasting success. Civilization began in the cabin, but soon retired to expire in the woods. The great error of these legislators for the Indians was their failure to understand that in order to succeed in civilizing a people it is first necessary to settle them permanently, which cannot be done without inducing them to cultivate the soil; the Indians ought in the first place to have been accustomed to agriculture. But not only are they destitute of this indispensable preliminary to civilization, they would even have great difficulty in acquiring it. Men who have once abandoned themselves to the restless and adventurous life of the hunter feel an insurmountable disgust for the constant and regular labor that tillage requires. We see this proved even in our own societies; but it is far more visible among races whose partiality for the chase is a part of their national character.

Independently of this general difficulty, there is another, which applies peculiarly to the Indians. They consider labor not merely as an evil, but as a disgrace; so that their pride contends against civilization as obstinately as their indolence.

There is no Indian so wretched as not to retain under his hut of bark a lofty idea of his personal worth; he considers the cares of industry as degrading occupations; he compares the plowman to the ox that traces the furrow; and in each of our handicrafts he can see only the labor of slaves. Not that he is devoid of admiration for the power and intellectual greatness of the whites; but although the result of our efforts surprises him, he despises the means by which we obtain it; and while he acknowledges our ascendancy, he still believes in his own superiority. War and hunting are the only pursuits that appear to him worthy of a man.

.   .   .

Several of the Southern tribes, considerably numerous, and among others the Cherokees and the Creeks, found themselves, as it were, surrounded by Europeans, who had landed on the shores of the Atlantic and, either descending the Ohio or proceeding up the Mississippi, arrived simultaneously upon their borders. These tribes had not been driven from place to place like their Northern brethren; but they had been gradually shut up within narrow limits, like game driven into an enclosure before the huntsmen plunge among them. The Indians, who were thus placed between civilization and death, found themselves obliged to live ignominiously by labor, like the whites. They took to agriculture and, without entirely forsaking their old habits or manners, sacrificed only as much as was necessary to their existence.

The Cherokees went further; they created a written language, established a permanent form of government, and, as everything proceeds rapidly in the New World, before all of them had clothes they set up a newspaper.

The development of European habits has been much accelerated among these Indians by the mixed race which has sprung up. Deriving intelligence from the father's side without entirely losing the savage customs of the mother, the half-blood forms the natural link between civilization and barbarism. Wherever this race has multiplied, the savage state has become modified and a great change has taken place in the manners of the people.

The success of the Cherokees proves that the Indians were capable of civilization, but it does not prove that they will succeed in it. This difficulty that the Indians find in submitting to civilization proceeds from a general cause, the influence of which it is almost impossible for them to escape. An attentive survey of history demonstrates that, in general, barbarous nations have raised themselves to civilization by degrees and by their own efforts. Whenever they derived knowledge from a foreign people, they stood towards them in the relation of conquerors, and not of a conquered nation. When the conquered nation is enlightened and the conquerors are half-savage, as in the invasion of the Roman Empire by the northern nations, or that of China by the Mongols, the power that victory bestows upon the barbarian is sufficient to keep up his importance among civilized men and permit him to rank as their equal until he becomes their rival. The one has might on his side, the other has intelligence; the former admires the knowledge and the arts of the conquered, the latter envies the power of the conquerors.

The barbarians at length admit civilized man into their palaces, and he in turn opens his schools to the barbarians. But when the side on which the physical force lies also possesses an intellectual superiority, the conquered party seldom becomes civilized; it retreats or is destroyed. It may therefore be said, in a general way, that savages go forth in arms to seek knowledge, but do not receive it when it comes to them.

If the Indian tribes that now inhabit the heart of the continent could summon up energy enough to attempt to civilize themselves, they might possibly succeed. Superior already to the barbarous nations that surround them, they would gradually gain strength and experience, and when the Europeans appear upon their borders, they would be in a state, if not to maintain their independence, at least to assert their right to the soil and to incorporate themselves with the conquerors. But it is the misfortune of Indians to be brought into contact with a civilized people, who are also (it must be owned) the most grasping nation on the globe, while they are still semi-barbarian; to find their masters in their instructors, and to receive knowledge and oppression at the same time. Living in the freedom of the woods, the North American Indian was destitute, but he had no feeling of inferiority towards anyone; as soon, however, as he desires to penetrate into the social scale of the whites, he can take only the lowest rank in society, for he enters ignorant and poor within the pale of science and wealth. After having led a life of agitation, beset with evils and dangers, but at the same time filled with proud emotions, he is obliged to submit to a wearisome, obscure, and degraded state. To gain by hard and ignoble labor the bread that nourishes him is in his eyes the only result of which civilization can boast; and even this he is not always sure to obtain.

When the Indians undertake to imitate their European neighbors, and to till the earth as they do, they are immediately exposed to a formidable competition. The white man is skilled in the craft of agriculture; the Indian is a rough beginner in an art with which he is unacquainted. The former reaps abundant crops without difficulty, the latter meets with a thousand obstacles in raising the fruits of the earth.

The European is placed among a population whose wants he knows and shares. The savage is isolated in the midst of a hostile people, with whose customs, language, and laws he is imperfectly acquainted, but without whose assistance he cannot live. He can procure only the materials of comfort by bartering his commodities for the goods of the European, for the assistance of his countrymen is wholly insufficient to supply his wants. Thus, when the Indian wishes to sell the produce of his labor, he cannot always find a purchaser, while the European readily obtains a market; the former can produce only at considerable cost what the latter sells at a low rate. Thus the Indian has no sooner escaped those evils to which barbarous nations are exposed than he is subjected to the still greater miseries of civilized communities; and he finds it scarcely less difficult to live in the midst of our abundance than in the depth of his own forest.

He has not yet lost the habits of his erratic life; the traditions of his fathers and his passion for the chase are still alive within him. The wild enjoyments that formerly animated him in the woods painfully excite his troubled imagination; the privations that he endured there appear less keen, his former perils less appalling. He contrasts the independence that he possessed among his equals with the servile position that he occupies in civilized society. On the other hand, the solitudes which were so long his free home are still at hand; a few hours' march will bring him back to them once more. The whites offer him a sum which seems to him considerable for the half-cleared ground whence he obtains sustenance with difficulty. This money of the

Europeans may possibly enable him to live a happy and tranquil life far away from them; and he quits the plow, resumes his native arms, and returns to the wilderness forever. The condition of the Creeks and Cherokees, to which I have already alluded, sufficiently corroborates the truth of this sad picture.

The Indians, in the little which they have done, have unquestionably displayed as much natural genius as the peoples of Europe in their greatest undertakings; but nations as well as men require time to learn, whatever may be their intelligence and their zeal. While the savages were endeavoring to civilize themselves, the Europeans continued to surround them on every side and to confine them within narrower limits; the two races gradually met, and they are now in immediate contact with each other. The Indian is already superior to his barbarous parent, but he is still far below his white neighbor. With their resources and acquired knowledge, the Europeans soon appropriated to themselves most of the advantages that the natives might have derived from the possession of the soil: they have settled among them, have purchased land at a low rate, or have occupied it by force, and the Indians have been ruined by a competition which they had not the means of sustaining. They were isolated in their own country, and their race constituted only a little colony of troublesome strangers in the midst of a numerous and dominant people.

Washington said in one of his messages to Congress: "We are more enlightened and more powerful than the Indian nations; we are therefore bound in honor to treat them with kindness, and even with generosity." But this virtuous and high-minded policy has not been followed. The rapacity of the settlers is usually backed by the tyranny of the government. Although the Cherokees and the Creeks are established upon territory which they inhabited before the arrival of the Europeans, and although the Americans have frequently treated with them as with foreign nations, the surrounding states have not been willing to acknowledge them as an independent people and have undertaken to subject these children of the woods to Anglo-American magistrates, laws, and customs. Destitution had driven these unfortunate Indians to civilization, and oppression now drives them back to barbarism: many of them abandon the soil which they had begun to clear and return to the habits of savage life.

If we consider the tyrannical measures that have been adopted by the legislatures of the Southern states, the conduct of their governors, and the decrees of their courts of justice, we shall be convinced that the entire expulsion of the Indians is the final result to which all the efforts of their policy are directed. The Americans of that part of the Union look with jealousy upon the lands which the natives still possess; they are aware that these tribes have not yet lost the traditions of savage life, and before civilization has permanently fixed them to the soil it is intended to force them to depart by reducing them to despair. The Creeks and Cherokees, oppressed by the several states, have appealed to the central government, which is by no means insensible to their misfortunes and is sincerely desirous of saving the remnant of the natives and of maintaining them in the free possession of that territory which the Union has guaranteed to them. But when it seeks to carry out this plan, the several states set up a tremendous resistance, and so it makes up its mind not to take the easier way, and to let a few savage tribes perish, since they are already half-decimated, in order not to endanger the safety of the American Union.

But the Federal government, which is not able to protect the Indians, would fain mitigate the hardships of their lot; and with this intention it has undertaken to transport them into remote regions at the public cost.

Between the 33rd and 37th degrees of north latitude lies a

vast tract of country that has taken the name of Arkansas, from the principal river that waters it. It is bounded on one side by the confines of Mexico, on the other by the Mississippi. Numberless streams cross it in every direction; the climate is mild and the soil productive, and it is inhabited only by a few wandering hordes of savages. The government of the Union wishes to transport the broken remnants of the indigenous population of the South to the portion of this country that is nearest to Mexico and at a great distance from the American settlements.

We were assured, towards the end of the year 1831, that 10,000 Indians had already gone to the shores of the Arkansas, and fresh detachments were constantly following them. But Congress has been unable to create a unanimous determination in those whom it is disposed to protect. Some, indeed, joyfully consent to quit the seat of oppression; but the most enlightened members of the community refuse to abandon their recent dwellings and their growing crops; they are of opinion that the work of civilization, once interrupted, will never be resumed; they fear that those domestic habits which have been so recently contracted may be irrevocably lost in the midst of a country that is still barbarous and where nothing is prepared for the subsistence of an agricultural people; they know that their entrance into those wilds will be opposed by hostile hordes, and that they have lost the energy of barbarians without having yet acquired the resources of civilization to resist their attacks. Moreover, the Indians readily discover that the settlement which is proposed to them is merely temporary. Who can assure them that they will at length be allowed to dwell in peace in their new retreat? The United States pledges itself to maintain them there, but the territory which they now occupy was formerly secured to them by the most solemn oaths. The American government does not indeed now rob them of their lands, but it allows perpetual encroachments on them. In a few years the same white population that now flocks around them will doubtless track them anew to the solitudes of the Arkansas; they will then be exposed to the same evils, without the same remedies; and as the limits of the earth will at last fail them, their only refuge is the grave.

The Union treats the Indians with less cupidity and violence than the several states, but the two governments are alike deficient in good faith. The states extend what they call the benefits of their laws to the Indians, believing that the tribes will recede rather than submit to them; and the central government, which promises a permanent refuge to these unhappy beings in the West, is well aware of its inability to secure it to them. Thus the tyranny of the states obliges the savages to retire; the Union, by its promises and resources, facilitates their retreat; and these measures tend to precisely the same end.

"By the will of our Father in heaven, the Governor of the whole world," said the Cherokees in their petition to Congress, "the red man of America has become small, and the white man great and renowned. When the ancestors of the people of these United States first came to the shores of America, they found the red man strong: though he was ignorant and savage, yet he received them kindly and gave them dry land to rest their weary feet. They met in peace and shook hands in token of friendship. Whatever the white man wanted and asked of the Indian, the latter willingly gave. At that time the Indian was the lord, and the white man the suppliant. But now the scene has changed. The strength of the red man has become weakness. As his neighbors increased in numbers, his power became less and less; and now, of the many and powerful tribes who once covered these United States, only a few are to be seen—a few whom a sweeping pestilence has left. The Northern tribes, who were once so numerous and powerful, are now nearly extinct.

Thus it has happened to the red man in America. Shall we, who are remnants, share the same fate?

"The land on which we stand we have received as an inheritance from our fathers, who possessed it from time immemorial, as a gift from our common Father in heaven. They bequeathed it to us as their children, and we have sacredly kept it, as containing the remains of our beloved men. This right of inheritance we have never ceded nor ever forfeited. Permit us to ask what better right can the people have to a country than the right of inheritance and immemorial peaceable possession? We know it is said of late by the state of Georgia and by the Executive of the United States that we have forfeited this right; but we think this is said gratuitously. At what time have we made the forfeit? What great crime have we committed whereby we must forever be divested of our country and rights? Was it when we were hostile to the United States and took part with the King of Great Britain during the struggle for independence? If so, why was not this forfeiture declared in the first treaty of peace between the United States and our beloved men? Why was not such an article as the following inserted in the treaty: 'The United States give peace to the Cherokees, but, for the part they took in the late war, declare them to be but tenants at will, to be removed when the convenience of the states within those chartered limits they live shall require it'? That was the proper time to assume such a possession. But it was not thought of; nor would our forefathers have agreed to any treaty whose tendency was to deprive them of their rights and their country."

Such is the language of the Indians; what they say is true; what they foresee seems inevitable. From whichever side we consider the destinies of the aborigines of North America, their calamities appear irremediable: if they continue barbarous, they are forced to retire; if they attempt to civilize themselves, the contact of a more civilized community subjects them to oppression and destitution. They perish if they continue to wander from waste to waste, and if they attempt to settle they still must perish. The assistance of Europeans is necessary to instruct them, but the approach of Europeans corrupts and repels them into savage life. They refuse to change their habits as long as their solitudes are their own, and it is too late to change them when at last they are forced to submit.

The Spaniards pursued the Indians with bloodhounds, like wild beasts; they sacked the New World like a city taken by storm, with no discernment or compassion; but destruction must cease at last and frenzy has a limit: the remnant of the Indian population which had escaped the massacre mixed with its conquerors and adopted in the end their religion and their manners. The conduct of the Americans of the United States towards the aborigines is characterized, on the other hand, by a singular attachment to the formalities of law. Provided that the Indians retain their barbarous condition, the Americans take no part in their affairs; they treat them as independent nations and do not possess themselves of their hunting-grounds without a treaty of purchase; and if an Indian nation happens to be so encroached upon as to be unable to subsist upon their territory, they kindly take them by the hand and transport them to a grave far from the land of their fathers.

The Spaniards were unable to exterminate the Indian race by those unparalleled atrocities which brand them with indelible shame, nor did they succeed even in wholly depriving it of its rights; but the Americans of the United States have accomplished this twofold purpose with singular felicity, tranquilly, legally, philanthropically, without shedding blood, and without violating a single great principle of morality in the eyes of the world. It is impossible to destroy men with more respect for the laws of humanity.

The Indians will perish in the same isolated condition in which they have lived, but the destiny of the Negroes is in some measure interwoven with that of the Europeans. These two races are fastened to each other without intermingling; and they are alike unable to separate entirely or to combine. The most formidable of all the ills that threaten the future of the Union arises from the presence of a black population upon its territory; and in contemplating the cause of the present embarrassments, or the future dangers of the United States, the observer is invariably led to this as a primary fact.

Generally speaking, men must make great and unceasing efforts before permanent evils are created; but there is one calamity which penetrated furtively into the world, and which was at first scarcely distinguishable amid the ordinary abuses of power: it originated with an individual whose name history has not preserved; it was wafted like some accursed germ upon a portion of the soil; but it afterwards nurtured itself, grew without effort, and spread naturally with the society to which it belonged. This calamity is slavery. Christianity suppressed slavery, but the Christians of the sixteenth century re-established it, as an exception, indeed, to their social system, and restricted to one of the races of mankind; but the wound thus inflicted upon humanity, though less extensive, was far more difficult to cure.

It is important to make an accurate distinction between slavery itself and its consequences. The immediate evils produced by slavery were very nearly the same in antiquity as they are among the moderns, but the consequences of these evils were different. The slave among the ancients belonged to the same race as his master, and was often the superior of the two in education and intelligence. Freedom was the only distinction between them; and when freedom was conferred, they were easily confounded together. The ancients, then, had a very simple means of ridding them-

selves of slavery and its consequences: that of enfranchise-
ment; and they succeeded as soon as they adopted this
measure generally. Not but that in ancient states the vestiges
of servitude subsisted for some time after servitude itself was
abolished. There is a natural prejudice that prompts men to
despise whoever has been their inferior long after he has
become their equal; and the real inequality that is produced
by fortune or by law is always succeeded by an imaginary
inequality that is implanted in the manners of the people.
But among the ancients this secondary consequence of
slavery had a natural limit; for the freedman bore so entire a
resemblance to those born free that it soon became impossible to distinguish him from them.

The greatest difficulty in antiquity was that of altering the
law; among the moderns it is that of altering the customs,
and as far as we are concerned, the real obstacles begin
where those of the ancients left off. This arises from the
circumstance that among the moderns the abstract and
transient fact of slavery is fatally united with the physical
and permanent fact of color. The tradition of slavery
dishonors the race, and the peculiarity of the race perpetuates the tradition of slavery. No African has ever
voluntarily emigrated to the shores of the New World,
whence it follows that all the blacks who are now found
there are either slaves or freedmen. Thus the Negro transmits the eternal mark of his ignominy to all his descendants;
and although the law may abolish slavery, God alone can
obliterate the traces of its existence.

The modern slave differs from his master not only in his
condition but in his origin. You may set the Negro free, but
you cannot make him otherwise than an alien to the
European. Nor is this all; we scarcely acknowledge the
common features of humanity in this stranger whom slavery
has brought among us. His physiognomy is to our eyes

hideous, his understanding weak, his tastes low; and we are almost inclined to look upon him as a being intermediate between man and the brutes. The moderns, then, after they have abolished slavery, have three prejudices to contend against, which are less easy to attack and far less easy to conquer than the mere fact of servitude: the prejudice of the master, the prejudice of the race, and the prejudice of color.

It is difficult for us, who have had the good fortune to be born among men like ourselves by nature and our equals by law, to conceive the irreconcilable differences that separate the Negro from the European in America. But we may derive some faint notion of them from analogy. France was formerly a country in which numerous inequalities existed that had been created by law. Nothing can be more fictitious than a purely legal inferiority, nothing more contrary to the instinct of mankind than these permanent divisions established between beings evidently similar. Yet these divisions existed for ages; they still exist in many places; and everywhere they have left imaginary vestiges, which time alone can efface. If it be so difficult to root out an inequality that originates solely in the law, how are those distinctions to be destroyed which seem to be based upon the immutable laws of Nature herself? When I remember the extreme difficulty with which aristocratic bodies, of whatever nature they may be, are commingled with the mass of the people, and the exceeding care which they take to preserve for ages the ideal boundaries of their caste inviolate, I despair of seeing an aristocracy disappear which is founded upon visible and indelible signs. Those who hope that the Europeans will ever be amalgamated with the Negroes appear to me to delude themselves. I am not led to any such conclusion by my reason or by the evidence of facts. Hitherto wherever the whites have been the most powerful, they have held the blacks in degradation or in slavery;

wherever the Negroes have been strongest, they have destroyed the whites: this has been the only balance that has ever taken place between the two races.

I see that in a certain portion of the territory of the United States at the present day the legal barrier which separated the two races is falling away, but not that which exists in the manners of the country; slavery recedes, but the prejudice to which it has given birth is immovable. Whoever has inhabited the United States must have perceived that in those parts of the Union in which the Negroes are no longer slaves they have in no wise drawn nearer to the whites. On the contrary, the prejudice of race appears to be stronger in the states that have abolished slavery than in those where it still exists; and nowhere is it so intolerant as in those states where servitude has never been known.

It is true that in the North of the Union marriages may be legally contracted between Negroes and whites; but public opinion would stigmatize as infamous a man who should connect himself with a Negress, and it would be difficult to cite a single instance of such a union. The electoral franchise has been conferred upon the Negroes in almost all the states in which slavery has been abolished, but if they come forward to vote, their lives are in danger. If oppressed, they may bring an action at law, but they will find none but whites among their judges; and although they may legally serve as jurors, prejudice repels them from that office. The same schools do not receive the children of the black and of the European. In the theaters gold cannot procure a seat for the servile race beside their former masters; in the hospitals they lie apart; and although they are allowed to invoke the same God as the whites, it must be at a different altar and in their own churches, with their own clergy. The gates of heaven are not closed against them, but their inferiority is continued to the very confines of the other world. When the Negro dies, his bones are cast aside, and the distinction of condition prevails even in the equality of death. Thus the Negro is free, but he can share neither the rights, nor the pleasures, nor the labor, nor the afflictions, nor the tomb of him whose equal he has been declared to be; and he cannot meet him upon fair terms in life or in death.

In the South, where slavery still exists, the Negroes are less carefully kept apart; they sometimes share the labors and the recreations of the whites; the whites consent to intermix with them to a certain extent, and although legislation treats them more harshly, the habits of the people are more tolerant and compassionate. In the South the master is not afraid to raise his slave to his own standing, because he knows that he can in a moment reduce him to the dust at pleasure. In the North the white no longer distinctly perceives the barrier that separates him from the degraded race, and he shuns the Negro with the more pertinacity since he fears lest they should some day be confounded together.

Among the Americans of the South, Nature sometimes reasserts her rights and restores a transient equality between the blacks and the whites; but in the North pride restrains the most imperious of human passions. The American of the Northern states would perhaps allow the Negress to share his licentious pleasures if the laws of his country did not declare that she may aspire to be the legitimate partner of his bed, but he recoils with horror from her who might become his wife.

Thus it is in the United States that the prejudice which repels the Negroes seems to increase in proportion as they are emancipated, and inequality is sanctioned by the manners while it is effaced from the laws of the country. But if the relative position of the two races that inhabit the United States is such as I have described, why have the Americans abolished slavery in the North of the Union, why do they maintain it in the South, and why do they aggravate its hardships? The answer is easily given. It is not for the good of the Negroes, but for that of the whites, that measures are taken to abolish slavery in the United States.

. . .

A century had scarcely elapsed since the foundation of the colonies when the attention of the planters was struck by the extraordinary fact that the provinces which were comparatively destitute of slaves increased in population, in wealth, and in prosperity more rapidly than those which contained many of them.

. . .

This truth was most satisfactorily demonstrated when civilization reached the banks of the Ohio. The stream that the Indians had distinguished by the name of Ohio, or the Beautiful River, waters one of the most magnificent valleys which have ever been made the abode of man. Undulating lands extend upon both shores of the Ohio, whose soil affords inexhaustible treasures to the laborer; on either bank the air is equally wholesome and the climate mild; and each of them forms the extreme frontier of a vast state: that which follows the numerous windings of the Ohio upon the left is called Kentucky; that upon the right bears the name of the river. These two states differ only in a single respect: Kentucky has admitted slavery, but the state of Ohio has prohibited the existence of slaves within its borders. Thus the traveler who floats down the current of the Ohio to the spot where that river falls into the Mississippi may be said to sail between liberty and servitude; and a transient inspection of surrounding objects will convince him which of the two is more favorable to humanity.

Upon the left bank of the stream the population is sparse; from time to time one descries a troop of slaves loitering in the half-desert fields; the primeval forest reappears at every turn; society seems to be asleep, man to be idle, and nature alone offers a scene of activity and life.

From the right bank, on the contrary, a confused hum is heard, which proclaims afar the presence of industry; the fields are covered with abundant harvests; the elegance of the dwellings announces the taste and activity of the laborers; and man appears to be in the enjoyment of that wealth and contentment which is the reward of labor.

The state of Kentucky was founded in 1775, the state of Ohio only twelve years later; but twelve years are more in America than half a century in Europe; and at the present day the population of Ohio exceeds that of Kentucky by two hundred and fifty thousand souls. These different effects of slavery and freedom may readily be understood; and they suffice to explain many of the differences which we notice between the civilization of antiquity and that of our own time.

Upon the left bank of the Ohio labor is confounded with the idea of slavery, while upon the right bank it is identified with that of prosperity and improvement; on the one side it is degraded, on the other it is honored. On the former territory no white laborers can be found, for they would be afraid of assimilating themselves to the Negroes; all the work is done by slaves; on the latter no one is idle, for the white population extend their activity and intelligence to every kind of employment. Thus the men whose task it is to cultivate the rich soil of Kentucky are ignorant and apathetic, while those who are active and enlightened either do nothing or pass over into Ohio, where they may work without shame.

It is true that in Kentucky the planters are not obliged to pay the slaves whom they employ, but they derive small profits from their labor, while the wages paid to free workmen would be returned with interest in the value of their services. The free workman is paid, but he does his work quicker than the slave; and rapidity of execution is one of the great elements of economy. The white sells his services, but they are purchased only when they may be useful; the black can claim no remuneration for his toil, but the expense of his maintenance is perpetual; he must be supported in his old age as well as in manhood, in his profitless infancy as well as in the productive years of youth, in sickness as well as in health. Payment must equally be made in order to obtain the services of either class of men: the free workman receives his wages in money; the slave in education, in food, in care, and in clothing. The money which a master spends in the maintenance of his slaves goes gradually and in detail, so that it is scarcely perceived; the salary of the free workman is paid in a round sum and appears to enrich only him who receives it; but in the end the slave has cost more than the free servant, and his labor is less productive.

The influence of slavery extends still further: it affects the character of the master and imparts a peculiar tendency to his ideas and tastes. Upon both banks of the Ohio the character of the inhabitants is enterprising and energetic, but this vigor is very differently exercised in the two states. The white inhabitant of Ohio, obliged to subsist by his own exertions, regards temporal prosperity as the chief aim of his existence; and as the country which he occupies presents inexhaustible resources to his industry, and ever varying lures to his activity, his acquisitive ardor surpasses the ordinary limits of human cupidity: he is tormented by the desire of wealth, and he boldly enters upon every path that fortune opens to him; he becomes a sailor, a pioneer, an artisan, or a cultivator with the same indifference, and supports with equal constancy the fatigues and the dangers incidental to these various professions; the resources of his intelligence are astonishing, and his avidity in the pursuit of gain amounts to a species of heroism.

But the Kentuckian scorns not only labor but all the undertakings that labor promotes; as he lives in an idle independence, his tastes are those of an idle man; money has lost a portion of its value in his eyes; he covets wealth much less than pleasure and excitement; and the energy which his neighbor devotes to gain turns with him to a passionate love of field sports and military exercises; he delights in violent bodily exertion, he is familiar with the use of arms, and is accustomed from a very early age to expose his life in single combat. Thus slavery prevents the whites not only from becoming opulent, but even from desiring to become so.

As the same causes have been continually producing opposite effects for the last two centuries in the British colonies of North America, they have at last established a striking difference between the commercial capacity of the inhabitants of the South and those of the North. At the present day it is only the Northern states that are in possession of shipping, manufactures, railroads, and canals. This difference is perceptible not only in comparing the North with the South, but in comparing the several Southern states. Almost all those who carry on commercial operations or endeavor to turn slave labor to account in the most southern districts of the Union have emigrated from the North. The natives of the Northern states are constantly spreading over that portion of the American territory where they have less to fear from competition; they discover resources there which escaped the notice of the inhabitants; and as they comply with a system which they do not approve, they succeed in turning it to better advantage than those who first founded and who still maintain it.

Were I inclined to continue this parallel, I could easily prove that almost all the differences which may be noticed between the characters of the Americans in the Southern and in the Northern states have originated in slavery; but this would divert me from my subject, and my present intention is not to point out all the consequences of servitude, but those effects which it has produced upon the material prosperity of the countries that have admitted it.

The influence of slavery upon the production of wealth must have been very imperfectly known in antiquity, as slavery then obtained throughout the civilized world, and the nations that were unacquainted with it were barbarians. And, indeed, Christianity abolished slavery only by advocating the claims of the slave; at the present time it may be attacked in the name of the master, and upon this point interest is reconciled with morality.

As these truths became apparent in the United States, slavery receded before the progress of experience. Servitude had begun in the South and had thence spread towards the North, but it now retires again. Freedom, which started from the North, now descends uninterruptedly towards the South. Among the great states, Pennsylvania now constitutes the extreme limit of slavery to the North; but even within those limits the slave system is shaken: Maryland, which is immediately below Pennsylvania, is preparing for its abolition; and Virginia, which comes next to Maryland, is already discussing its utility and its dangers.

No great change takes place in human institutions without involving among its causes the law of inheritance. When the law of primogeniture obtained in the South, each family was represented by a wealthy individual, who was neither compelled nor induced to labor; and he was surrounded, as by parasitic plants, by the other members of his family, who were then excluded by law from sharing the common inheritance, and who led the same kind of life as himself. The same thing then occurred in all the families of the South which still happens in the noble families of some countries in Europe: namely, that the younger sons remain in the same state of idleness as their elder brother, without being as rich as he is. This identical result seems to be produced in Europe and in America by wholly analogous causes. In the South of the United States the whole race of whites formed an aristocratic body, headed by a certain number of privileged individuals, whose wealth was permanent and whose leisure was hereditary. These leaders of the American nobility kept alive the traditional prejudices of the white race, in the body of which they were the representatives, and maintained idleness in honor. This aristocracy contained many who were poor, but none who would work; its members preferred want to labor; consequently Negro laborers and slaves met with no competition; and, whatever opinion might be entertained as to the utility of their industry, it was necessary to employ them, since there was no one else to work.

No sooner was the law of primogeniture abolished than fortunes began to diminish and all the families of the country were simultaneously reduced to a state in which labor became necessary to existence; several of them have since entirely disappeared, and all of them learned to look forward to the time when it would be necessary for everyone to provide for his own wants. Wealthy individuals are still to be met with, but they no longer constitute a compact and hereditary body, nor have they been able to adopt a line of conduct in which they could persevere and which they could infuse into all ranks of society. The prejudice that stigmatized labor was, in the first place, abandoned by common consent, the number of needy men was increased, and the needy were allowed to gain a subsistence by labor without blushing for their toil. Thus one of the most immediate consequences of the equal division of estates has been to create a class of free laborers. As soon as competition began between the free laborer and the slave, the inferiority of the latter became manifest and slavery was attacked in its fundamental principle, which is the interest of the master.

As slavery recedes, the black population follows its retrograde course and returns with it towards those tropical regions whence it originally came. However singular this fact may at first appear to be, it may readily be explained. Although the Americans abolish the principle of slavery, they do not set their slaves free. To illustrate this remark, I will quote the example of the state of New York. In 1788 this state prohibited the sale of slaves within its limits, which was an indirect method of prohibiting the importation of them. Thenceforward the number of Negroes could only increase according to the ratio of the natural increase of population. But eight years later, a more decisive measure was taken, and it was enacted that all children born of slave parents after the 4th of July 1799 should be free. No increase could then take place, and although slaves still existed, slavery might be said to be abolished.

As soon as a Northern state thus prohibited the importation, no slaves were brought from the South to be sold in its markets. On the other hand, as the sale of slaves was forbidden in that state, an owner could no longer get rid of his slave (who thus became a burdensome possession) otherwise than by transporting him to the South. But when a Northern state declared that the son of the slave should be born free, the slave lost a large portion of his market value, since his posterity was no longer included in the bargain, and the owner had then a strong interest in transporting him to the South. Thus the same law prevents the slaves of the South from coming North and drives those of the North to the South.

But there is another cause more powerful than any that I have described. The want of free hands is felt in a state in proportion as the number of slaves decreases. But in proportion as labor is performed by free hands, slave labor becomes less productive; and the slave is then a useless or onerous possession, whom it is important to export to the South, where the same competition is not to be feared. Thus the abolition of slavery does not set the slave free, but merely transfers him to another master, and from the North to the South.

The emancipated Negroes and those born after the abolition of slavery do not, indeed, migrate from the North to the South; but their situation with regard to the Europeans is not unlike that of the Indians; they remain half civilized and deprived of their rights in the midst of a population that is far superior to them in wealth and knowledge, where they are exposed to the tyranny of the laws and the intolerance of the people. On some accounts they are still more to be pitied than the Indians, since they are haunted by the reminiscence of slavery, and they cannot claim possession of any part of the soil. Many of them perish miserably, and the rest congregate in the great towns, where they perform the meanest offices and lead a wretched and precarious existence.

If, moreover, the number of Negroes were to continue to grow in the same proportion during the period when they did not have their liberty, yet, with the number of the whites increasing at a double rate after the abolition of slavery, the Negroes would soon be swallowed up in the midst of an alien population.

A district which is cultivated by slaves is in general less populous than a district cultivated by free labor; moreover, America is still a new country, and a state is therefore not half peopled when it abolishes slavery. No sooner is an end put to slavery than the want of free labor is felt, and a crowd of enterprising adventurers immediately arrives from all parts of the country, who hasten to profit by the fresh resources which are then opened to industry. The soil is soon divided among them, and a family of white settlers takes possession of each portion. Besides, European immigration is exclusively directed to the free states; for what would a poor immigrant do who crosses the Atlantic in search of ease and happiness if he were to land in a country where labor is stigmatized as degrading?

Thus the white population grows by its natural increase, and at the same time by the immense influx of immigrants; while the black population receives no immigrants and is upon its decline. The proportion that existed between the two races is soon inverted. The Negroes constitute a scanty remnant, a poor tribe of vagrants, lost in the midst of an immense people who own the land; and the presence of the blacks is only marked by the injustice and the hardships of which they are the victims.

In several of the Western states the Negro race never made its appearance, and in all the Northern states it is rapidly declining. Thus the great question of its future condition is confined within a narrow circle, where it becomes less formidable, though not more easy of solution. The more we descend towards the South, the more difficult it becomes to abolish slavery with advantage; and this arises from several physical causes which it is important to point out.

The first of these causes is the climate: it is well known that, in proportion as Europeans approach the tropics, labor becomes more difficult to them. Many of the Americans even assert that within a certain latitude it is fatal to them, while the Negroes can work there without danger; but I do not think that this opinion, which is so favorable to the indolence of the inhabitants of the South, is confirmed by experience. The southern parts of the Union are not hotter than the south of Italy and of Spain; and it may be asked why the European cannot work as well there as in the latter two countries. If slavery has been abolished in Italy and in Spain without causing the destruction of the masters, why should not the same thing take place in the Union? I cannot believe that nature has prohibited the Europeans in Georgia and the Floridas, under pain of death, from raising the means of subsistence from the soil; but their labor would unquestionably be more irksome and less productive to them than to the inhabitants of New England. As the free workman thus loses a portion of his superiority over the slave in the Southern states, there are fewer inducements to abolish slavery.

All the plants of Europe grow in the northern parts of the Union; the South has special products of its own. It has been observed that slave labor is a very expensive method of cultivating cereal grain. The farmer of grainland in a country where slavery is unknown habitually retains only a small number of laborers in his service, and at seed-time and harvest he hires additional hands, who live at his cost for only a short period. But the agriculturist in a slave state is obliged to keep a large number of slaves the whole year round in order to sow his fields and to gather in his crops, although their services are required only for a few weeks; for slaves are unable to wait till they are hired and to subsist by their own labor in the meantime, like free laborers; in order to have their services, they must be bought. Slavery, independently of its general disadvantages, is therefore still more inapplicable to countries in which grain is cultivated than to those which produce crops of a different kind. The cultivation of tobacco, of cotton, and especially of sugar-cane demands, on the other hand, unremitting attention; and women and children are employed in it, whose services are of little use in the cultivation of wheat. Thus slavery is naturally more fitted to the countries from which these productions are derived.

Tobacco, cotton, and sugar-cane are exclusively grown in the South, and they form the principle sources of the wealth of those states. If slavery were abolished, the inhabitants of the South would be driven to this alternative: they must either change their system of cultivation, and then they would come into competition with the more active and more experienced inhabitants of the North; or, if they continued to cultivate the same produce without slave labor, they would have to support the competition of the other states of the South, which might still retain their slaves. Thus peculiar reasons for maintaining slavery exist in the South which do not operate in the North.

But there is yet another motive, which is more cogent than all the others: the South might, indeed, rigorously speaking, abolish slavery; but how should it rid its territory of the black population? Slaves and slavery are driven from the North by the same law; but this twofold result cannot be hoped for in the South.

In proving that slavery is more natural and more advantageous in the South than in the North, I have shown that the number of slaves must be far greater in the former. It was to the Southern settlements that the first Africans were brought, and it is there that the greatest number of them have always been imported. As we advance towards the South, the prejudice that sanctions idleness increases in power. In the states nearest to the tropics there is not a single white laborer; the Negroes are consequently much more numerous in the South than in the North. And, as I have already observed, this disproportion increases daily, since the Negroes are transferred to one part of the Union as soon as slavery is abolished in the other. Thus the black population augments in the South, not only by its natural fecundity, but by the compulsory emigration of the Negroes from the North; and the African race has causes of increase in the South very analogous to those which accelerate the growth of the European race in the North.

In the state of Maine there is one Negro in three hundred inhabitants; in Massachusetts, one in one hundred; in New

York, two in one hundred; in Pennsylvania, three in the same number; in Maryland, thirty four; in Virginia, forty-two; and lastly, in South Carolina, fifty-five per cent of the inhabitants are black. Such was the proportion of the black population to the whites in the year 1830. But this proportion is perpetually changing, as it constantly decreases in the North and augments in the South.

It is evident that the most southern states of the Union cannot abolish slavery without incurring great dangers, which the North had no reason to apprehend when it emancipated its black population. I have already shown how the Northern states made the transition from slavery to freedom, by keeping the present generation in chains and setting their descendants free; by this means the Negroes are only gradually introduced into society; and while the men who might abuse their freedom are kept in servitude, those who are emancipated may learn the art of being free before they become their own masters. But it would be difficult to apply this method in the South. To declare that all the Negroes born after a certain period shall be free is to introduce the principle and the notion of liberty into the heart of slavery; the blacks whom the law thus maintains in a state of slavery from which their children are delivered are astonished at so unequal a fate, and their astonishment is only the prelude to their impatience and irritation. Thenceforward slavery loses, in their eyes, that kind of moral power which it derived from time and habit; it is reduced to a mere palpable abuse of force. The Northern states had nothing to fear from the contrast, because in them the blacks were few in number, and the white population was very considerable. But if this faint dawn of freedom were to show two millions of men their true position, the oppressors would have reason to tremble. After having enfranchised the children of their slaves, the Europeans of the Southern states would very shortly be obliged to extend the same benefit to the whole black population.

. . .

Thus the inhabitants of the South, while abolishing slavery, would not be able, like their Northern countrymen, to initiate the slaves gradually into a state of freedom; they have no means of perceptibly diminishing the black population, and they would remain unsupported to repress its excesses. Thus in the course of a few years a great people of free Negroes would exist in the heart of a white nation of equal size.

The same abuses of power that now maintain slavery would then become the source of the most alarming perils to the white population of the South. At the present time the descendants of the Europeans are the sole owners of the land and the absolute masters of all labor; they alone possess wealth, knowledge, and arms. The black is destitute of all these advantages, but can subsist without them because he is a slave. If he were free, and obliged to provide for his own subsistence, would it be possible for him to remain without these things and to support life? Or would not the very instruments of the present superiority of the white while slavery exists expose him to a thousand dangers if it were abolished?

As long as the Negro remains a slave, he may be kept in a condition not far removed from that of the brutes; but with his liberty he cannot but acquire a degree of instruction that will enable him to appreciate his misfortunes and to discern a remedy for them. Moreover, there exists a singular principle of relative justice which is firmly implanted in the human heart. Men are much more forcibly struck by those inequalities which exist within the same class than by those which may be noted between different classes. One can understand slavery, but how allow several millions of citizens to exist under a load of eternal infamy and hereditary wretchedness? In the North the population of freed Negroes feels these hardships and indignities, but its numbers and its powers are small, while in the South it would be numerous and strong.

As soon as it is admitted that the whites and the emancipated blacks are placed upon the same territory in the situation of two foreign communities, it will readily be understood that there are but two chances for the future: the Negroes and the whites must either wholly part or wholly mingle. I have already expressed my conviction as to the latter event. I do not believe that the white and black races will ever live in any country upon an equal footing. But I believe the difficulty to be still greater in the United States than elsewhere. An isolated individual may surmount the prejudices of religion, of his country, or of his race; and if this individual is a king, he may effect surprising changes in society; but a whole people cannot rise, as it were, above itself. A despot who should subject the Americans and their former slaves to the same yoke might perhaps succeed in commingling their races; but as long as the American democracy remains at the head of affairs, no one will undertake so difficult a task; and it may be foreseen that the freer the white population of the United States becomes, the more isolated will it remain.

I have previously observed that the mixed race is the true bond of union between the Europeans and the Indians; just so, the mulattoes are the true means of transition between the white and the Negro; so that wherever mulattoes abound, the intermixture of the two races is not impossible. In some parts of America the European and the Negro races are so crossed with one another that it is rare to meet with a man who is entirely black or entirely white; when they have arrived at this point, the two races may really be said to be combined, or, rather, to have been absorbed in a third race, which is connected with both without being identical with either.

Of all Europeans, the English are those who have mixed least with the Negroes. More mulattoes are to be seen in the South of the Union than in the North, but infinitely fewer than in any other European colony. Mulattoes are by no means numerous in the United States; they have no force peculiar to themselves, and when quarrels originating in differences of color take place, they generally side with the whites, just as the lackeys of the great in Europe assume the contemptuous airs of nobility towards the lower orders.

The pride of origin, which is natural to the English, is singularly augmented by the personal pride that democratic liberty fosters among the Americans: the white citizen of the United States is proud of his race and proud of himself. But if the whites and the Negroes do not intermingle in the North of the Union, how should they mix in the South? Can it be supposed for an instant that an American of the Southern states, placed, as he must forever be, between the white man, with all his physical and moral superiority, and the Negro, will ever think of being confounded with the latter? The Americans of the Southern states have two powerful passions which will always keep them aloof: the first is the fear of being assimilated to the Negroes, their former slaves; and the second, the dread of sinking below the whites, their neighbors.

If I were called upon to predict the future, I should say that the abolition of slavery in the South will, in the common course of things, increase the repugnance of the white population for the blacks. I base this opinion upon the analogous observation I have already made in the North. I have remarked that the white inhabitants of the North avoid the Negroes with increasing care in proportion as the legal barriers of separation are removed by the legislature; and why should not the same result take place in the South? In the North the whites are deterred from intermingling with the blacks by an imaginary danger; in the South, where the danger would be real, I cannot believe that the fear would be less.

If, on the other hand, it be admitted (and the fact is unquestionable) that the colored population perpetually accumulate in the extreme South and increase more rapidly than the whites; and if, on the other hand, it be allowed that it is impossible to foresee a time at which the whites and the blacks will be so intermingled as to derive the same benefits from society, must it not be inferred that the blacks and the whites will, sooner or later, come to open strife in the Southern states? But if it be asked what the issue of the struggle is likely to be, it will readily be understood that we are here left to vague conjectures. The human mind may succeed in tracing a wide circle, as it were, which includes the future; but within that circle chance rules, and eludes all our foresight. In every picture of the future there is a dim spot which the eye of the understanding cannot penetrate. It appears, however, extremely probable that in the West Indies islands the white race is destined to be subdued, and upon the continent the blacks.

In the West Indies the white planters are isolated amid an immense black population; on the continent the blacks are placed between the ocean and an innumerable people, who already extend above them, in a compact mass, from the icy confines of Canada to the frontiers of Virginia, and from the banks of the Missouri to the shores of the Atlantic. If the white citizens of North America remain united, it is difficult to believe that the Negroes will escape the destruction which menaces them; they must be subdued by want or by the sword. But the black population accumulated along the coast of the Gulf of Mexico have a chance of success if the American Union should be dissolved when the struggle between the two races begins. The Federal tie once broken, the people of the South could not rely upon any lasting succor from their Northern countrymen. The latter are well aware that the danger can never reach them; and unless they are constrained to march to the assistance of the South by a positive obligation, it may be foreseen that the sympathy of race will be powerless.

Yet, at whatever period the strife may break out, the whites of the South, even if they are abandoned to their own resources, will enter the lists with an immense superiority of knowledge and the means of warfare; but the blacks will have numerical strength and the energy of despair upon their side, and these are powerful resources to men who have taken up arms. The fate of the white population of the Southern states will perhaps be similar to that of the Moors in Spain. After having occupied the land for centuries, it will perhaps retire by degrees to the country whence its ancestors came and abandon to the Negroes the possession of a territory which Providence seems to have destined for them, since they can subsist and labor in it more easily than the whites.

The danger of a conflict between the white and the black inhabitants of the Southern states of the Union (a danger which, however remote it may be, is inevitable) perpetually haunts the imagination of the Americans, like a painful dream. The inhabitants of the North make it a common topic of conversation, although directly they have nothing to fear from it; but they vainly endeavor to devise some means of obviating the misfortunes which they foresee. In the Southern states the subject is not discussed: the planter does not allude to the future in conversing with strangers; he does not communicate his apprehensions to his friends; he seeks to conceal them from himself. But there is something more alarming in the tacit forebodings of the South than in the clamorous fears of the North.

This all-pervading disquietude has given birth to an

undertaking as yet but little known, which, however, may change the fate of a portion of the human race. From apprehension of the dangers that I have just described, some American citizens have formed a society for the purpose of exporting to the coast of Guinea, at their own expense, such free Negroes as may be willing to escape from the oppression to which they are subject.

In 1820 the society to which I allude formed a settlement in Africa, on the seventh degree of north latitude, which bears the name of Liberia. The most recent intelligence informs us that two thousand five hundred Negroes are collected there. They have introduced the democratic institutions of America into the country of their forefathers. Liberia has a representative system of government, Negro jurymen, Negro magistrates, and Negro priests; churches have been built, newspapers established, and, by a singular turn in the vicissitudes of the world, white men are prohibited from establishing themselves within the settlement.

This is indeed a strange caprice of fortune. Two hundred years have now elapsed since the inhabitants of Europe undertook to tear the Negro from his family and his home in order to transport him to the shores of North America. Now the European settlers are engaged in sending back the descendants of those very Negroes to the continent whence they were originally taken: the barbarous Africans have learned civilization in the midst of bondage and have become acquainted with free political institutions in slavery. Up to the present time Africa has been closed against the arts and sciences of the whites, but the inventions of Europe will perhaps penetrate into those regions now that they are introduced by Africans themselves. The settlement of Liberia is founded upon a lofty and fruitful idea; but, whatever may be its results with regard to Africa, it can afford no remedy to the New World.

In twelve years the Colonization Society has transported two thousand five hundred Negroes to Africa; in the same space of time about seven hundred thousand blacks were born in the United States. If the colony of Liberia were able to receive thousands of new inhabitants every year, and if the Negroes were in a state to be sent thither with advantage; if the Union were to supply the society with annual subsidies, and to transport the Negroes to Africa in government vessels, it would still be unable to counterpoise the natural increase of population among the blacks; and as it could not remove as many men in a year as are born upon its territory within that time, it could not prevent the growth of the evil which is daily increasing in the states. The Negro race will never leave those shores of the American continent to which it was brought by the passions and the vices of Europeans; and it will not disappear from the New World as long as it continues to exist. The inhabitants of the United States may retard the calamities which they apprehend, but they cannot now destroy their efficient cause.

I am obliged to confess that I do not regard the abolition of slavery as a means of warding off the struggle of the two races in the Southern states. The Negroes may long remain slaves without complaining; but if they are once raised to the level of freemen, they will soon revolt at being deprived of almost all their civil rights; and as they cannot become the equals of the whites, they will speedily show themselves as enemies. In the North everything facilitated the emancipation of the slaves, and slavery was abolished without rendering the free Negroes formidable, since their number was too small for them ever to claim their rights. But such is not the case in the South. The question of slavery was a commercial and manufacturing question for the slave-owners in the North; for those of the South it is a question of life and death. God forbid that I should seek to justify the principle of Negro slavery, as has been done by some

American writers! I say only that all the countries which formerly adopted that execrable principle are not equally able to abandon it at the present time.

When I contemplate the condition of the South, I can discover only two modes of action for the white inhabitants of those States: namely, either to emancipate the Negroes and to intermingle with them, or, remaining isolated from them, to keep them in slavery as long as possible. All intermediate measures seem to me likely to terminate, and that shortly, in the most horrible of civil wars and perhaps in the extirpation of one or the other of the two races. Such is the view that the Americans of the South take of the question, and they act consistently with it. As they are determined not to mingle with the Negroes, they refuse to emancipate them.

Not that the inhabitants of the South regard slavery as necessary to the wealth of the planter; on this point many of them agree with their Northern countrymen, in freely admitting that slavery is prejudicial to their interests; but they are convinced that the removal of this evil would imperil their own existence. The instruction which is now diffused in the South has convinced the inhabitants that slavery is injurious to the slave-owner, but it has also shown them, more clearly than before, that it is almost an impossibility to get rid of it. Hence arises a singular contrast: the more the utility of slavery is contested, the more firmly is it established in the laws; and while its principle is gradually abolished in the North, that selfsame principle gives rise to more and more rigorous consequences in the South.

The legislation of the Southern states with regard to slaves presents at the present day such unparalleled atrocities as suffice to show that the laws of humanity have been totally perverted, and to betray the desperate position of the community in which that legislation has been promulgated. The Americans of this portion of the Union have not, indeed, augmented the hardships of slavery; on the contrary, they have bettered the physical condition of the slaves. The only means by which the ancients maintained slavery were fetters and death; the Americans of the South of the Union have discovered more intellectual securities for the duration of their power. They have employed their despotism and their violence against the human mind. In antiquity precautions were taken to prevent the slave from breaking his chains; at the present day measures are adopted to deprive him even of the desire for freedom. The ancients kept the bodies of their slaves in bondage, but placed no restraint upon the mind and no check upon education; and they acted consistently with their established principle, since a natural termination of slavery then existed, and one day or other the slave might be set free and become the equal of his master. But the Americans of the South, who do not admit that the Negroes can ever be commingled with themselves, have forbidden them, under severe penalties, to be taught to read or write; and as they will not raise them to their own level, they sink them as nearly as possible to that of the brutes.

The hope of liberty had always been allowed to the slave, to cheer the hardships of his condition. But the Americans of the South are well aware that emancipation cannot but be dangerous when the freed man can never be assimilated to his former master. To give a man his freedom and to leave him in wretchedness and ignominy is nothing less than to prepare a future chief for a revolt of the slaves. Moreover, it has long been remarked that the presence of a free Negro vaguely agitates the minds of his less fortunate brethren, and conveys to them a dim notion of their rights. The Americans of the South have consequently taken away from slave-owners the right of emancipating their slaves in most cases.

I happened to meet an old man, in the South of the Union, who had lived in illicit intercourse with one of his Negresses and had had several children by her, who were born the slaves of their father. He had, indeed, frequently thought of bequeathing to them at least their liberty; but years had elapsed before he could surmount the legal obstacles to their emancipation, and meanwhile his old age had come and he was about to die. He pictured to himself his sons dragged from market to market and passing from the authority of a parent to the rod of the stranger, until these horrid anticipations worked his expiring imagination into frenzy. When I saw him, he was a prey to all the anguish of despair; and I then understood how awful is the retribution of Nature upon those who have broken her laws.

These evils are unquestionably great, but they are the necessary and foreseen consequences of the very principle of modern slavery. When the Europeans chose their slaves from a race differing from their own, which many of them considered as inferior to the other races of mankind, and any notion of intimate union with which they all repelled with horror, they must have believed that slavery would last forever, since there is no intermediate state that can be durable between the excessive inequality produced by servitude and the complete equality that originates in independence. The Europeans did imperfectly feel this truth, but without acknowledging it even to themselves. Whenever they have had to do with Negroes, their conduct has been dictated either by their interest and their pride or by their compassion. They first violated every right of humanity by their treatment of the Negro, and they afterwards informed him that those rights were precious and inviolable. They opened their ranks to their slaves, and when the latter tried to come in, they drove them forth in scorn. Desiring slavery, they have allowed themselves unconsciously to be swayed in spite of themselves towards liberty, without having the courage to be either completely iniquitous or completely just.

If it is impossible to anticipate a period at which the

Americans of the South will mingle their blood with that of the Negroes, can they allow their slaves to become free without compromising their own security? And if they are obliged to keep that race in bondage in order to save their own families, may they not be excused for availing themselves of the means best adapted to that end? The events that are taking place in the Southern states appear to me to be at once the most horrible and the most natural results of slavery. When I see the order of nature overthrown, and when I hear the cry of humanity in its vain struggle against the laws, my indignation does not light upon the men of our own time who are the instruments of these outrages; but I reserve my execration for those who, after a thousand years of freedom, brought back slavery into the world once more.

Whatever may be the efforts of the Americans of the South to maintain slavery, they will not always succeed. Slavery, now confined to a single tract of the civilized earth, attacked by Christianity as unjust and by political economy as prejudicial, and now contrasted with democratic liberty and the intelligence of our age, cannot survive. By the act of the master, or by the will of the slave, it will cease; and in either case great calamities may be expected to ensue. If liberty be refused to the Negroes of the South, they will in the end forcibly seize it for themselves; if it be given, they will before long abuse it.

Chapter XVIII

THE CHANCES OF DURATION OF THE AMERICAN UNION

The maintenance of the existing institutions of the several states depends in part upon the maintenance of the Union itself. We must therefore first inquire into the probable fate of the Union. One point may be assumed at once: if the present confederation were dissolved, it appears to me to be incontestable that the states of which it is now composed would not return to their original isolated condition, but that several unions would then be formed in the place of one. It is not my intention to inquire into the principles upon which these new unions would probably be established, but merely to show what the causes are which may effect the dismemberment of the existing confederation.

. . .

When the national government, independently of the prerogatives inherent in its nature, is invested with the right of regulating the mixed objects of sovereignty, it possesses a preponderant influence. Not only are its own rights extensive, but all the rights which it does not possess exist by its sufferance; and it is to be feared that the provincial governments may be deprived by it of their natural and necessary prerogatives.

When, on the other hand, the provincial governments are invested with the power of regulating those same affairs of mixed interest, an opposite tendency prevails in society. The preponderant force resides in the province, not in the nation; and it may be apprehended that the national government may, in the end, be stripped of the privileges that are necessary to its existence.

Single nations have therefore a natural tendency to centralization, and confederations to dismemberment.

It now remains to apply these general principles to the American Union. The several states necessarily retained the right of regulating all purely local affairs. Moreover, these same states kept the rights of determining the civil and political competency of the citizens, of regulating the reciprocal relations of the members of the community, and of dispensing justice—rights which are general in their nature, but do not necessarily appertain to the national government. We have seen that the government of the Union is invested with the power of acting in the name of the whole nation in those cases in which the nation has to appear as a single and undivided power; as, for instance, in foreign relations, and in offering a common resistance to a common enemy; in short, in conducting those affairs which I have styled exclusively national.

In this division of the rights of sovereignty the share of the Union seems at first sight more considerable than that of the states, but a more attentive investigation shows it to be less so. The undertakings of the government of the Union are more vast, but it has less frequent occasion to act at all. Those of the state governments are comparatively small, but they are incessant and they keep alive the authority which they represent. The government of the Union watches over the general interests of the country; but the general interests of a people have but a questionable influence upon individual happiness, while state interests produce an immediate effect upon the welfare of the inhabitants. The Union secures the independence and the greatness of the nation, which do not immediately affect private citizens; but the several states maintain the liberty, regulate the rights, protect the fortune, and secure the life and the whole future prosperity of every citizen.

. . .

The Americans have, therefore, much more to hope and to fear from the states than from the Union; and, according to the natural tendency of the human mind, they are more likely to attach themselves strongly to the former than to the latter. In this respect their habits and feelings harmonize with their interests.

. . .

The Union is a vast body, which presents no definite object to patriotic feeling. The forms and limits of the state are distinct and circumscribed, since it represents a certain number of objects that are familiar to the citizens and dear to them all. It is identified with the soil; with the right of property and the domestic affections; with the recollections of the past, the labors of the present, and the hopes of the future. Patriotism, then, which is frequently a mere extension of individual selfishness, is still directed to the state and has not passed over to the Union. Thus the tendency of the interests, the habits, and the feelings of the people is to center political activity in the states in preference to the Union.

It is easy to estimate the different strength of the two governments by noting the manner in which they exercise their respective powers. Whenever the government of a state addresses an individual or an assembly of individuals, its language is clear and imperative, and such is also the tone of the Federal government when it speaks to individuals; but no sooner has it anything to do with a state than it begins to parley, to explain its motives and justify its conduct, to argue, to advise, and, in short, anything but to command. If doubts are raised as to limits of the constitutional powers of either government, the state government prefers its claim with boldness and takes prompt and energetic steps to support it. Meanwhile the government of the Union reasons; it appeals to the interests, the good sense, the glory of the nation; it temporizes, it negotiates, and does not consent to act until it is reduced to the last extremity. At first sight it might readily be imagined that it is the state government which is armed with the authority of the nation and that Congress represents a single state.

The Federal government is, therefore, notwithstanding the precautions of those who founded it, naturally so weak that, more than any other, it requires the free consent of the governed to enable it to exist. It is easy to perceive that its object is to enable the states to realize with facility their determination of remaining united; and as long as this preliminary condition exists, it is wise, strong, and active. The Constitution fits the government to control individuals and easily to surmount such obstacles as they may be inclined to offer, but it was by no means established with a view to the possible voluntary separation of one or more of the states from the Union.

If the sovereignty of the Union were to engage in a struggle with that of the states at the present day, its defeat may be confidently predicted; and it is not probable that such a struggle would be seriously undertaken. As often as a steady resistance is offered to the Federal government, it will be found to yield. Experience has hitherto shown that whenever a state has demanded anything with perseverance and resolution, it has invariably succeeded; and that if it has distinctly refused to act, it was left to do as it thought fit.

. . .

However strong a government may be, it cannot easily escape from the consequences of a principle which it has once admitted as the foundation of its constitution. The Union was formed by the voluntary agreement of the states; and these, in uniting together, have not forfeited their sovereignty, nor have they been reduced to the condition of one and the same people. If one of the states chose to withdraw its name from the contract, it would be difficult to disprove its right of doing so, and the Federal government would have no means of maintaining its claims directly, either by force or by right. In order to enable the Federal government easily to conquer the resistance that may be offered to it by any of its subjects, it would be necessary that one or more of them should be specially interested in the existence of the Union, as has frequently been the case in the history of confederations.

. . .

In America the existing Union is advantageous to all the states, but it is not indispensable to any one of them. Several of them might break the Federal tie without compromising the welfare of the others, although the sum of their joint prosperity would be less. As the existence and the happiness of none of the states are wholly dependent on the present Constitution, none of them would be disposed to make great personal sacrifices to maintain it. On the other hand, there is no state which seems hitherto to have been by its ambition much interested in the maintenance of the existing Union. They certainly do not all exercise the same influence in the Federal councils; but no one can hope to domineer over the rest or to treat them as its inferiors or as its subjects.

It appears to me unquestionable that if any portion of the Union seriously desired to separate itself from the other states, they would not be able, nor indeed would they attempt, to prevent it; and that the present Union will last only as long as the states which compose it choose to continue members of the confederation. If this point be admitted, the question becomes less difficult; and our object is, not to inquire whether the states of the existing Union are capable of separating, but whether they will choose to remain united.

Among the various reasons that tend to render the existing Union useful to the Americans, two principal ones are especially evident to the observer. Although the Americans are, as it were, alone upon their continent, commerce gives them for neighbors all the nations with which they trade. Notwithstanding their apparent isolation, then, the Americans need to be strong, and they can be strong only by remaining united. If the states were to split, not only would they diminish the strength that they now have against foreigners, but they would soon create foreign powers upon their own territory. A system of inland custom-houses would then be established; the valleys would be divided by imaginary boundary lines; the courses of the rivers would be impeded, and a multitude of hindrances would prevent the Americans from using that vast continent which Providence has given them for a dominion. At present they have no invasion to fear, and consequently no standing armies to maintain, no taxes to levy. If the Union were dissolved, all these burdensome things would before long be required. The Americans are, then, most deeply interested in the maintenance of their Union. On the other hand, it is almost impossible to discover any private interest that might now tempt a portion of the Union to separate from the other states.

.   .   .

It is indeed easy to discover different interests in the different parts of the Union, but I am unacquainted with any that are hostile to one another. The Southern states are almost exclusively agricultural. The Northern states are more peculiarly commercial and manufacturing. The states of the West are at the same time agricultural and manufacturing. In the South the crops consist of tobacco, rice, cotton, and sugar; in the North and the West, of wheat and corn. These are different sources of wealth, but union is the means by which these sources are opened and rendered equally advantageous to all.

The North, which ships the produce of the Anglo-Americans to all parts of the world and brings back the produce of the globe to the Union, is evidently interested in maintaining the confederation in its present condition, in order that the number of American producers and consumers may remain as large as possible. The North is the most natural agent of communication between the South and the West of the Union on the one hand, and the rest of the world on the other; the North is therefore interested in the union and prosperity of the South and the West, in order that they may continue to furnish raw materials for its manufactures, and cargoes for its shipping.

The South and the West, on their side, are still more directly interested in the preservation of the Union and the prosperity of the North. The produce of the South is, for the most part, exported beyond seas; the South and the West consequently stand in need of the commercial resources of the North. They are likewise interested in the maintenance of a powerful fleet by the Union, to protect them efficaciously. The South and the West have no vessels, but willingly contribute to the expense of a navy, for if the fleets of Europe were to blockade the ports of the South and the delta of the Mississippi, what would become of the rice of the Carolinas, the tobacco of Virginia, and the sugar and cotton that grow in the valley of the Mississippi? Every portion of the Federal budget does, therefore, contribute to the maintenance of material interests that are common to all the federated states.

Independently of this commercial utility, the South and

the West derive great political advantages from their union with each other and with the North. The South contains an enormous slave population, a population which is already alarming and still more formidable for the future. The states of the West occupy a single valley; the rivers that intersect their territory rise in the Rocky Mountains or in the Alleghenies, and fall into the Mississippi, which bears them onwards to the Gulf of Mexico. The Western states are consequently entirely cut off, by their position, from the traditions of Europe and the civilization of the Old World. The inhabitants of the South, then, are induced to support the Union in order to avail themselves of its protection against the blacks; and the inhabitants of the West, in order not to be excluded from a free communication with the rest of the globe and shut up in the wilds of central America. The North cannot but desire the maintenance of the Union in order to remain, as it now is, the connecting link between that vast body and the other parts of the world.

The material interests of all the parts of the Union are, then, intimately connected; and the same assertion holds true respecting those opinions and sentiments that may be termed the immaterial interests of men.

. . .

The observer who examines what is passing in the United States upon this principle will readily discover that their inhabitants, though divided into twenty-four distinct sovereignties, still constitute a single people; and he may perhaps be led to think that the Anglo-American Union is more truly a united society than some nations of Europe which live under the same legislation and the same prince.

Although the Anglo-Americans have several religious sects, they all regard religion in the same manner. They are not always agreed upon the measures that are most conducive to good government, and they vary upon some of the forms of government which it is expedient to adopt; but they are unanimous upon the general principles that ought to rule human society. From Maine to the Floridas, and from the Missouri to the Atlantic Ocean, the people are held to be the source of all legitimate power. The same notions are entertained respecting liberty and equality, the liberty of the press, the right of association, the jury, and the responsibility of the agents of government.

If we turn from their political and religious opinions to the moral and philosophical principles that regulate the daily actions of life and govern their conduct, we still find the same uniformity. The Anglo-Americans acknowledge the moral authority of the reason of the community as they acknowledge the political authority of the mass of citizens; and they hold that public opinion is the surest arbiter of what is lawful or forbidden, true or false. The majority of them believe that a man by following his own interest, rightly understood, will be led to do what is just and good. They hold that every man is born in possession of the right of self-government, and that no one has the right of constraining his fellow creatures to be happy. They have all a lively faith in the perfectibility of man, they judge that the diffusion of knowledge must necessarily be advantageous, and the consequences of ignorance fatal; they all consider society as a body in a state of improvement, humanity as a changing scene, in which nothing is, or ought to be, permanent; and they admit that what appears to them today to be good, may be superseded by something better tomorrow. I do not give all these opinions as true, but as American opinions.

Not only are the Anglo-Americans united by these common opinions, but they are separated from all other nations by a feeling of pride. For the last fifty years no pains have been spared to convince the inhabitants of the United States that they are the only religious, enlightened, and free people. They perceive that, for the present, their own democratic institutions prosper, while those of other countries fail; hence they conceive a high opinion of their superiority and are not very remote from believing themselves to be a distinct species of mankind.

Thus the dangers that threaten the American Union do not originate in diversity of interests or of opinions, but in the various characters and passions of the Americans. The men who inhabit the vast territory of the United States are almost all the issue of a common stock; but climate, and more especially slavery, have gradually introduced marked differences between the British settler of the Southern states and the British settler of the North. In Europe it is generally believed that slavery has rendered the interests of one part of the Union contrary to those of the other, but I have not found this to be the case. Slavery has not created interests in the South contrary to those of the North, but it has modifed the character and changed the habits of the natives of the South.

. . .

In the Southern states the more pressing wants of life are always supplied; the inhabitants, therefore, are not occupied with the material cares of life, from which they are relieved by others; and their imagination is diverted to more captivating and less definite objects. The American of the South is fond of grandeur, luxury, and renown, of gayety, pleasure, and, above all, of idleness; nothing obliges him to exert himself in order to subsist; and as he has no necessary occupations, he gives way to indolence and does not even attempt what would be useful.

But the equality of fortunes and the absence of slavery in the North plunge the inhabitants in those material cares which are disdained by the white population of the South. They are taught from infancy to combat want and to place wealth above all the pleasures of the intellect or the heart. The imagination is extinguished by the trivial details of life, and the ideas become less numerous and less general, but far more practical, clearer, and more precise. As prosperity is the sole aim of exertion, it is excellently well attained; nature and men are turned to the best pecuniary advantage; and society is dexterously made to contribute to the welfare of each of its members, while individual selfishness is the source of general happiness.

The American of the North has not only experience but knowledge; yet he values science not as an enjoyment, but as a means, and is only anxious to seize its useful applications. The American of the South is more given to act upon impulse; he is more clever, more frank, more generous, more intellectual, and more brilliant. The former, with a greater degree of activity, common sense, information, and general aptitude, has the characteristic good and evil qualities of the middle classes. The latter has the tastes, the prejudices, the weaknesses, and the magnanimity of all aristocracies.

If two men are united in society who have the same interests, and, to a certain extent, the same opinions, but different characters, different acquirements, and a different style of civilization, it is most probable that these men will not agree. The same remark is applicable to a society of nations.

Slavery, then, does not attack the American Union directly in its interests, but indirectly in its manners.

.

All the states of the Union are carried forward at the same time towards prosperity, but all cannot grow and prosper at the same rate. In the North of the Union the detached branches of the Allegheny chain, extending as far as the Atlantic Ocean, form spacious roads and ports, constantly accessible to the largest vessels. But from the Potomac, following the shore, to the mouth of the Mississippi, the coast is sandy and flat. In this part of the Union the mouths of almost all the rivers are obstructed; and the few harbors that exist among these inlets do not offer the same depth to vessels and present, for commerce, facilities less extensive than those of the North.

The first and natural cause of inferiority is united to another cause proceeding from the laws. We have seen that slavery, which is abolished in the North, still exists in the South; and I have pointed out its fatal consequences upon the prosperity of the planter himself.

. . .

It is difficult to imagine a durable union of a nation that is rich and strong with one that is poor and weak, even if it were proved that the strength and wealth of the one are not the causes of the weakness and poverty of the other. But union is still more difficult to maintain at a time when one partly is losing strength and the other is gaining it. This rapid and disproportionate increase of certain states threatens the independence of the others. New York might perhaps succeed, with its two million inhabitants and its forty representatives, in dictating to the other states in Congress. But even if the more powerful states make no attempt to oppress the smaller ones, the danger still exists; for there is amost as much in the possibility of the act as in the act itself. The weak generally mistrust the justice and the reason of the strong. The states that increase less rapidly than the others look upon those that are more favored by fortune with envy and suspicion. Hence arise the deep-seated uneasiness and ill-defined agitation which are observable in the South and which form so striking a contrast to the confidence and prosperity which are common to other parts of the Union. I am inclined to think that the hostile attitude taken by the South recently is attributable to no other cause. The inhabitants of the Southern states are, of all the Americans, those who are most interested in the maintenance of the Union; they would assuredly suffer most from being left to themselves; and yet they are the only ones who threaten to break the tie of confederation. It is easy to perceive that the South, which has given four Presidents to the Union, which perceives that it is losing its federal influence and that the number of its representatives in Congress is diminishing from year to year, while those of the Northern and Western states are increasing, the South, which is peopled with ardent and irascible men, is becoming more and more irritated and alarmed. Its inhabitants reflect upon their present position and remember their past influence, with the melancholy uneasiness of men who suspect oppression. If they discover a law of the Union that is not unequivocally favorable to their interests, they protest against it as an abuse of force; and if their ardent remonstrances are not listened to, they threaten to quit an association that loads them with burdens while it deprives them of the profits. "The Tariff," said the inhabitants of Carolina in 1832, "enriches the North and ruins the South; for, if this were not the case, to what can we attribute the continually increasing power and wealth of the North, with its inclement skies and arid soil; while the South, which may be styled the garden of America, is rapidly declining."

If the changes which I have described were gradual, so that each generation at least might have time to disappear with the order of things under which it had lived, the danger would be less; but the progress of society in America is precipitate and almost revolutionary. The same citizen may have lived to see his state take the lead in the Union and afterwards become powerless in the Federal assemblies; and an Anglo-American republic has been known to grow as rapidly as a man, passing from birth and infancy to maturity in the course of thirty years. It must not be imagined, however, that the states that lose their preponderance also lose their population or their riches; no stop is put to their prosperity, and they even go on to increase more rapidly than any kingdom in Europe. But they believe themselves to be impoverished because their wealth does not augment as rapidly as that of their neighbors; and they think that their power is lost because they suddenly come in contact with a power greater than their own. Thus they are more hurt in their feelings and their passions than in their interests. But this is amply sufficient to endanger the maintenance of the Union. If kings and peoples had only had their true interests in view ever since the beginning of the world, war would scarcely be known among mankind.

Thus the prosperity of the United States is the source of their most serious dangers, since it tends to create in some of the federal states that intoxication which accompanies a rapid increase of fortune, and to awaken in others those feelings of envy, mistrust, and regret which usually attend the loss of it. The Americans contemplate this extraordinary progress with exultation; but they would be wiser to consider it with sorrow and alarm. The Americans of the United States must inevitably become one of the greatest nations in the world; their offspring will cover almost the whole of North America; the continent that they inhabit is their dominion, and it cannot escape them. What urges them to take possession of it so soon? Riches, power, and renown cannot fail to be theirs at some future time, but they rush upon this immense fortune as if but a moment remained for them to make it their own.

I think that I have demonstrated that the existence of the present confederation depends entirely on the continued assent of all the confederates; and starting from this principle, I have inquired into the causes that may induce some of the states to separate from the others. The Union may, however, perish in two different ways: one of the federated states may choose to retire from the compact, and so forcibly to sever the Federal tie; and it is to this supposition that most of the remarks that I have made apply; or the authority of the Federal government may be gradually lost by the simultaneous tendency of the united republics to resume their independence. The central power, successively stripped of all its prerogatives and reduced to impotence by tacit consent, would become incompetent to fulfill its purpose, and the second union would perish, like the first, by a sort of senile imbecility. The gradual weakening of the Federal tie, which may finally lead to the dissolution of the Union, is a distinct circumstance that may produce a variety of minor consequences before it operates so violent a change. The confederation might still exist although its government were reduced to such a degree of inanition as to paralyze the nation, to cause internal anarchy, and to check the general prosperity of the country.

After having investigated the causes that may induce the Anglo-Americans to disunite, it is important to inquire whether, if the Union continues to survive, their government will extend or contract its sphere of action, and whether it will become more energetic or more weak.

The Americans are evidently disposed to look upon their condition with alarm. They perceive that in most of the nations of the world the exercise of the rights of sovereignty tends to fall into a few hands, and they are dismayed by the idea that it may be so in their own country. Even the statesmen feel, or affect to feel, these fears; for in America centralization is by no means popular, and there is no surer means of courting the majority than by inveighing against the encroachments of the central power. The Americans do not perceive that the countries in which this alarming tendency to centralization exists are inhabited by a single people, while the Union is composed of different communities, a fact that is sufficient to baffle all the inferences which might be drawn from analogy. I confess that I am inclined to consider these fears of a great number of Americans as purely imaginary. Far from participating in their dread of the consolidation of power in the hands of the Union, I think that the Federal government is visibly losing strength. To prove this assertion, I shall not have recourse to any remote occurrences, but to circumstances which I have myself witnessed and which belong to our own time.

An attentive examination of what is going on in the United States will easily convince us that two opposite tendencies exist there, like two currents flowing in contrary directions in the same channel. The Union has now existed for forty-five years, and time has done away with many provincial prejudices which were at first hostile to its power. The patriotic feeling that attached each of the Americans to his own state has become less exclusive, and the different parts of the Union have become more amicable as they have become better acquainted with each other. The post, that great instrument of intercourse, now reaches into the backwoods; and steamboats have established daily means of communication between the different points of the coast. An inland navigation of unexampled rapidity conveys commodities up and down the rivers of the country. And to these facilities of nature and art may be added those restless cravings, that busy-mindedness and love of pelf, which are constantly urging the American into active life and bringing him into contact with his fellow citizens. He crosses the country in every direction; he visits all the various populations of the land. There is not a province in France in which the natives are so well known to one another as the thirteen millions of men who cover the territory of the United States.

While the Americans intermingle, they assimilate; the differences resulting from their climate, their origin, and their institutions diminish; and they all draw nearer and nearer to the common type. Every year thousands of men leave the North to settle in different parts of the Union; they bring with them their faith, their opinions, and their manners, and as they are more enlightened than the men among whom they are about to dwell, they soon rise to the head of affairs and adapt society to their own advantage. This continual emigration of the North to the South is peculiarly favorable to the fusion of all the different provincial characters into one national character. The civilization of the North appears to be the common standard, to which the whole nation will one day be assimilated.

. . .

And yet a careful examination of the history of the United States for the last forty-five years will readily convince us that the Federal power is declining; nor is it difficult to explain the causes of this phenomenon. When the Constitution of 1789 was promulgated, the nation was a prey to anarchy; the Union which succeeded this confusion excited much dread and hatred, but it was warmly supported because it satisfied an imperious want. Although it was then more attacked than it is now, the Federal power soon reached the maximum of its authority, as is usually the case with a government that triumphs after having braced its strength by the struggle. At that time the interpretation of the Constitution seemed to extend rather than to repress the Federal sovereignty; and the Union offered, in several respects, the appearance of a single and undivided people, directed in its foreign and internal policy by a single government. But to attain this point the people had risen, to some extent, above itself.

The Constitution had not destroyed the individuality of the states, and all communities, of whatever nature they may be, are impelled by a secret instinct towards independence. This propensity is still more decided in a country like

America, in which every village forms a sort of republic, accustomed to govern itself. It therefore cost the states an effort to submit to the Federal supremacy; and all efforts, however successful, necessarily subside with the causes in which they originated.

As the Federal government consolidated its authority, America resumed its rank among the nations, peace returned to its frontiers, and public credit was restored; confusion was succeeded by a fixed state of things, which permitted the full and free exercise of industrious enterprise. It was this very prosperity that made the Americans forget the cause which had produced it; and when once the danger was passed, the energy and the patriotism that had enabled them to brave it disappeared from among them. Delivered from the cares that oppressed them, they easily returned to their ordinary habits and gave themselves up without resistance to their natural inclinations. When a powerful government no longer appeared to be necessary, they once more began to think it irksome. Everything prospered under the Union, and the states were not inclined to abandon the Union; but they desired to render the action of the power which represented it as light as possible. The general principle of union was adopted, but in every minor detail there was a tendency to independence. The principle of confederation was every day more easily admitted and more rarely applied, so that the Federal government, by creating order and peace, brought about its own decline.

. .

The Constitution gave to the Federal government the right of providing for the national interests; and it had been held that no other authority was so fit to superintend the internal improvements that affected the prosperity of the whole Union, such, for instance, as the cutting of canals. But the states were alarmed at a power that could thus dispose of a portion of their territory; they were afraid that the central government would by this means acquire a formidable patronage within their own limits, and exercise influence which they wished to reserve exclusively to their own agents. The Democratic Party, which has constantly opposed the increase of the Federal authority, accused Congress of usurpation, and the chief magistrate of ambition. The central government was intimidated by these clamors, and it finally acknowledged its error, promising to confine its influence for the future within the circle that was prescribed to it.

The Constitution confers upon the Union the right of treating with foreign nations. The Indian tribes which border upon the frontiers of the United States had usually been regarded in this light. As long as these savages consented to retire before the civilized settlers, the Federal right was not contested; but as soon as an Indian tribe attempted to fix its residence upon a given spot, the adjacent states claimed possession of the lands and a right of sovereignty over the natives. The central government soon recognized both these claims; and after it had concluded treaties with the Indians as independent nations, it gave them up as subjects to the legislative tyranny of the states.

. . . .

The slightest observation in the United States enables one to appreciate the advantages that the country derives from the Bank of the United States. These advantages are of several kinds, but one of them is peculiarly striking to the stranger. The notes of the bank are taken upon the borders of the wilderness for the same value as at Philadelphia, where the bank conducts its operations.

But the Bank of the United States is the object of great animosity. Its directors proclaimed their hostility to the President, and they were accused, not without probability, of having abused their influence to thwart his election. The President therefore attacked the establishment with all the warmth of personal enmity; and he was encouraged in the pursuit of his revenge by the conviction that he was supported by the secret inclinations of the majority. The bank may be regarded as the great monetary tie of the Union, just as Congress is the great legislative tie; and the same passions that tend to render the states independent of the central power contributed to the overthrow of the bank.

The Bank of the United States always held a great number of the notes issued by the state banks, which it can at any time oblige them to convert into cash. It has itself nothing to fear from a similar demand, as the extent of its resources enables it to meet all claims. But the existence of the provincial banks is thus threatened and their operations are restricted, since they are able to issue only a quantity of notes duly proportioned to their capital. They submitted with impatience to this salutary control. The newspapers that they bought over, and the President, whose interest rendered him their instrument, attacked the bank with the greatest vehemence. They roused the local passions and the blind democratic instinct of the country to aid their cause; and they asserted that the bank directors formed a permanent aristocratic body, whose influence would ultimately be felt in the government and affect those principles of equality upon which society rests in America.

The contest between the bank and its opponents was only an incident in the great struggle which is going on in America between the states and the central power, between the spirit of democratic independence and that of a proper distribution and subordination of power. I do not mean that the enemies of the bank were identically the same individuals who on other points attacked the Federal government, but I assert that the attacks directed against the Bank of the United States originated in the same propensities that militate against the Federal government, and that the very numerous opponents of the former afford a deplorable symptom of the decreasing strength of the latter.

But the Union has never shown so much weakness as on the celebrated question of the tariff. The wars of the French Revolution and of 1812 had created manufacturing establishments in the North of the Union, by cutting off free communication between America and Europe. When peace was concluded and the channel of intercourse reopened by which the produce of Europe was transmitted to the New World, the Americans thought fit to establish a system of import duties for the twofold purpose of protecting their incipient manufactures and of paying off the amount of the debt contracted during the war. The Southern states, which have no manufactures to encourage and which are exclusively agricultural, soon complained of this measure. I do not pretend to examine here whether their complaints were well or ill founded, but only to recite the facts.

As early as 1820 South Carolina declared in a petition to Congress that the tariff was "unconstitutional, oppressive, and unjust." And the states of Georgia, Virginia, North Carolina, Alabama, and Mississippi subsequently remonstrated against it with more or less vigor. But Congress, far from lending an ear to these complaints, raised the scale of tariff duties in the years 1824 and 1828 and recognized anew the principle on which it was founded. A doctrine was then proclaimed, or rather revived, in the South, which took the name of Nullification.

I have shown in the proper place that the object of the Federal Constitution was not to form a league, but to create a national government. The Americans of the United States form one and the same people, in all the cases which are specified by that Constitution; and upon these points the will of the nation is expressed, as it is in all constitutional nations, by the voice of the majority. When the majority has once spoken, it is the duty of the minority to submit. Such is the sound legal doctrine, and the only one that agrees with the text of the Constitution and the known intention of those who framed it.

The partisans of Nullification in the South maintain, on the contrary, that the intention of the Americans in uniting was not to combine themselves into one and the same people, but that they meant only to form a league of independent states; and that each state, consequently, retains its entire sovereignty, if not *de facto,* at least *de jure,* and has the right of putting its own construction upon the laws of Congress and of suspending their execution within the limits of its own territory if they seem unconstitutional and unjust.

The entire doctrine of Nullification is comprised in a sentence uttered by Vice President Calhoun, the head of that party in the South, before the Senate of the United States, in 1833: "The Constitution is a compact to which the States were parties in their sovereign capacity: now, whenever a compact is entered into by parties which acknowledge no common arbiter to decide in the last resort, each of them has a right to judge for itself in relation to the nature, extent, and obligations of the instrument." It is evident that such a doctrine destroys the very basis of the Federal Constitution and brings back the anarchy from which the Americans were delivered by the act of 1789.

When South Carolina perceived that Congress turned a deaf ear to its remonstrances, it threatened to apply the doctrine of Nullification to the Federal tariff law. Congress persisted in its system, and at length the storm broke out. In the course of 1832 the people of South Carolina named a national convention to consult upon the extraordinary measures that remained to be taken; and on the 24th of November of the same year this convention promulgated a law, under the form of a decree, which annulled the Federal tariff law, forbade the levy of the duties which that law commands, and refused to recognize the appeal that might be made to the Federal courts of law. This decree was only to be put in execution in the ensuing month of February; and it was intimated that if Congress modified the tariff before that period, South Carolina might be induced to proceed no further with her menaces; and a vague desire was afterwards expressed of submitting the question to an extraordinary assembly of all the federated states. In the meantime South Carolina armed her militia and prepared for war.

But Congress, which had slighted its suppliant subjects, listened to their complaints as soon as they appeared with arms in their hands. A law was passed by which the tariff duties were to be gradually reduced for ten years, until they were brought so low as not to exceed the supplies necessary to the government. Thus Congress completely abandoned the principle of the tariff and substituted a mere fiscal impost for a system of protective duties. The government of the Union, to conceal its defeat, had recourse to an expedient that is much in vogue with feeble governments. It yielded the point *de facto,* but remained inflexible upon the principles; and while it was altering the tariff law, it passed another bill by which the President was invested with extraordinary powers enabling him to overcome by force a resistance which was then no longer to be feared.

But South Carolina did not consent to leave the Union in the enjoyment of these scanty appearances of success: the same national convention that had annulled the tariff bill met again and accepted the proffered concession; but at the same time it declared its unabated perseverance in the doctrine of Nullification; and to prove what it said, it annulled the law investing the President with extraordinary powers, although it was very certain that the law would never be carried into effect.

Almost all the controversies of which I have been

speaking have taken place under the Presidency of General Jackson; and it cannot be denied that in the question of the tariff he has supported the rights of the Union with energy and skill. I think, however, that the conduct of this President of the Federal government may be reckoned as one of the dangers that threaten its continuance.

Some persons in Europe have formed an opinion of the influence of General Jackson upon the affairs of his country which appears highly extravagant to those who have seen the subject nearer at hand. We have been told that General Jackson has won battles; that he is an energetic man, prone by nature and habit to the use of force, covetous of power, and a despot by inclination. All this may be true; but the inferences which have been drawn from these truths are very erroneous. It has been imagined that General Jackson is bent on establishing a dictatorship in America, introducing a military spirit, and giving a degree of influence to the central authority that cannot but be dangerous to provincial liberties. But in America the time for similar undertakings, and the age for men of this kind, has not yet come; if General Jackson had thought of exercising his authority in this manner, he would infallibly have forfeited his political station and compromised his life; he has not been so imprudent as to attempt anything of the kind.

Far from wishing to extend the Federal power, the President belongs to the party which is desirous of limiting that power to the clear and precise letter of the Constitution, and which never puts a construction upon that act favorable to the government of the Union; far from standing forth as the champion of centralization, General Jackson is the agent of the state jealousies; and he was placed in his lofty station by the passions that are most opposed to the central government. It is by perpetually flattering these passions that he maintains his station and his popularity. General Jackson is the slave of the majority: he yields to its wishes, its propensities, and its demands—say, rather, anticipates and forestalls them.

Whenever the governments of the states come into collision with that of the Union, the President is generally the first to question his own rights; he almost always outstrips the legislature; and when the extent of the Federal power is controverted, he takes part, as it were, against himself; he conceals his official interests, and labors to diminish his own dignity. Not, indeed, that he is naturally weak or hostile to the Union; for when the majority decided against the claims of Nullification, he put himself at their head, asserted distinctly and energetically the doctrines which the nation held, and was the first to recommend force; but General Jackson appears to me, if I may use the American expression, to be a Federalist by taste and a Republican by calculation.

General Jackson stoops to gain the favor of the majority; but when he feels that his popularity is secure, he overthrows all obstacles in the pursuit of the objects which the community approves or of those which it does not regard with jealousy. Supported by a power that his predecessors never had, he tramples on his personal enemies, whenever they cross his path, with a facility without example; he takes upon himself the responsibility of measures that no one before him would have ventured to attempt. He even treats the national representatives with a disdain approaching to insult; he puts his veto on the laws of Congress and frequently neglects even to reply to that powerful body. He is a favorite who sometimes treats his master roughly. The power of General Jackson perpetually increases, but that of the President declines; in his hands the Federal government is strong, but it will pass enfeebled into the hands of his successor.

I am strangely mistaken if the Federal government of the United States is not constantly losing strength, retiring gradually from public affairs, and narrowing its circle of action. It is naturally feeble, but it now abandons even the appearance of strength. On the other hand, I thought that I noticed a more lively sense of independence and a more decided attachment to their separate governments in the states. The Union is desired, but only as a shadow; they wish it to be strong in certain cases and weak in all others; in time of warfare it is to be able to concentrate all the forces of the nation and all the resources of the country in its hands, and in time of peace its existence is to be scarcely perceptible, as if this alternate debility and vigor were natural or possible.

I do not see anything for the present that can check this general tendency of opinion; the causes in which it originated do not cease to operate in the same direction. The change will therefore go on, and it may be predicted that unless some extraordinary event occurs, the government of the Union will grow weaker and weaker every day.

I think, however, that the period is still remote at which the Federal power will be entirely extinguished by its inability to protect itself and to maintain peace in the country. The Union is sanctioned by the manners and desires of the people; its results are palpable, its benefits visible. When it is perceived that the weakness of the Federal government compromises the existence of the Union, I do not doubt that a reaction will take place with a view to increase its strength.

The government of the United States is, of all the federal governments which have hitherto been established, the one that is most naturally destined to act. As long as it is only indirectly assailed by the interpretation of its laws and as long as its substance is not seriously impaired, a change of opinion, an internal crisis, or a war may restore all the vigor that it requires. What I have been most anxious to establish is simply this: Many people in France imagine that a change of opinion is going on in the United States which is favorable to a centralization of power in the hands of the President and the Congress. I hold that a contrary tendency may distinctly be observed. So far is the Federal government, as it grows old, from acquiring strength and from threatening the sovereignty of the states that I maintain it to be growing weaker and the sovereignty of the Union alone to be in danger. Such are the facts that the present time discloses. The future conceals the final result of this tendency and the events which may check, retard, or accelerate the changes I have described; I do not pretend to be able to remove the veil that hides them.

Chapter XIX

OF THE REPUBLICAN INSTITUTIONS OF THE UNITED STATES, AND THEIR CHANCES OF DURATION

The dismemberment of the Union, by introducing war into the heart of those states which are now federated, with standing armies, a dictatorship, and heavy taxation, might eventually compromise the fate of republican institutions. But we ought not to confound the future prospects of the republic with those of the Union. The Union is an accident, which will last only as long as circumstances favor it; but a republican form of government seems to me the natural state of the Americans, which nothing but the continued action of hostile causes, always acting in the same direction, could change into a monarchy. The Union exists principally in the law which formed it; one revolution, one change in public opinion, might destroy it forever; but the republic has a deeper foundation to rest upon.

What is understood by a republican government in the United States is the slow and quiet action of society upon itself. It is a regular state of things really founded upon the enlightened will of the people. It is a conciliatory government, under which resolutions are allowed time to ripen, and in which they are deliberately discussed, and are executed only when mature. The republicans in the United States set a high value upon morality, respect religious belief, and acknowledge the existence of rights. They profess to think that a people ought to be moral, religious, and temperate in proportion as it is free. What is called the

276

republic in the United States is the tranquil rule of the majority, which, after having had time to examine itself and to give proof of its existence, is the common source of all the powers of the state. But the power of the majority itself is not unlimited. Above it in the moral world are humanity, justice, and reason; and in the political world, vested rights.

.

The ideas that the Americans have adopted respecting the republic render it easy for them to live under it and ensure its duration. With them, if the republic is often bad practically, at least it is good theoretically; and in the end the people always act in conformity to it.

It was impossible at the foundation of the states, and it would still be difficult, to establish a central administration in America. The inhabitants are dispersed over too great a space and separated by too many natural obstacles for one man to undertake to direct the details of their existence. America is therefore pre-eminently the country of state and municipal government.

.

In the United States, therefore, the mass of the institutions of the country is essentially republican; and in order permanently to destroy the laws which form the basis of the republic, it would be necessary to abolish all the laws at once.

In the United States the sovereignty of the people is not an isolated doctrine, bearing no relation to the prevailing habits and ideas of the people; it may, on the contrary, be regarded as the last link of a chain of opinions which binds the whole Anglo-American world. That Providence has given to every human being the degree of reason necessary to direct himself in the affairs that interest him exclusively is the grand maxim upon which civil and political society rests in the United States.

. . .

Thus in the United States the fundamental principle of the republic is the same which governs the greater part of human actions; republican notions insinuate themselves into all the ideas, opinions, and habits of the Americans and are formally recognized by the laws; and before the laws could be altered, the whole community must be revolutionized. In the United States even the religion of most of the citizens is republican, since it submits the truths of the other world to private judgment, as in politics the care of their temporal interests is abandoned to the good sense of the people. Thus every man is allowed freely to take that road which he thinks will lead him to heaven, just as the law permits every citizen to have the right of choosing his own government.

. . .

If republican principles are to perish in America, they can yield only after a laborious social process, often interrupted and as often resumed; they will have many apparent revivals and will not become totally extinct until an entirely new people have succeeded to those who now exist. There is no symptom or presage of the approach of such a revolution. There is nothing more striking to a person newly arrived in the United States than the kind of tumultuous agitation in which he finds political society. The laws are incessantly changing, and at first sight it seems impossible that a people so fickle in its desires should avoid adopting, within a short space of time, a completely new form of government. But such apprehensions are premature; the instability that affects political institutions is of two kinds, which ought not to be confounded. The first, which modifies secondary laws, is not incompatible with a very settled state of society. The other shakes the very foundations of the constitution and attacks the fundamental principles of legislation; this species of instability is always followed by troubles and revolutions, and the nation that suffers under it is in a violent and transitory state.

Experience shows that these two kinds of legislative instability have no necessary connection, for they have been found united or separate, according to times and circumstances. The first is common in the United States, but not the second: the Americans often change their laws, but the foundations of the Constitution are respected.

. . .

The inhabitants of the United States constitute a great civilized people, which fortune has placed in the midst of an uncultivated country, at a distance of three thousand miles from the central point of civilization. America consequently stands in daily need of Europe. The Americans will no doubt ultimately succeed in producing or manufacturing at home most of the articles that they require; but the two continents can never be independent of each other, so numerous are the natural ties between their wants, their ideas, their habits, and their manners.

The Union has peculiar commodities which have now become necessary to us, as they cannot be cultivated or can be raised only at an enormous expense upon the soil of Europe. The Americans consume only a small portion of this produce, and they are willing to sell us the rest. Europe is therefore the market of America, as America is the market of Europe.

. . .

The inhabitants of the United States experience all the wants and all the desires that result from an advanced civilization; and as they are not surrounded, as in Europe, by a community skillfully organized to satisfy them, they are often obliged to procure for themselves the various articles that education and habit have rendered necessaries. In America it sometimes happens that the same person tills his field, builds his dwelling, fashions his tools, makes his shoes, and weaves the coarse stuff of which his clothes are composed. This is prejudicial to the excellence of the work, but it powerfully contributes to awaken the intelligence of the workman. Nothing tends to materialize man and to deprive his work of the faintest trace of mind more than the extreme division of labor. In a country like America, where men devoted to special occupations are rare, a long apprenticeship cannot be required from anyone who embraces a profession. The Americans therefore change their means of gaining a livelihood very readily, and they suit their occupations to the exigencies of the moment. Men are to be met with who have successively been lawyers, farmers, merchants, ministers of the Gospel, and physicians. If the American is less perfect in each craft than the European, at least there is scarcely any trade with which he is utterly unacquainted. His capacity is more general, and the circle of his intelligence is greater.

The inhabitants of the United States are never fettered by the axioms of their profession; they escape from all the prejudices of their present station; they are not more attached to one line of operation than to another; they are not more prone to employ an old method than a new one; they have no rooted habits, and they easily shake off the influence that the habits of other nations might exercise upon them, from a conviction that their country is unlike any other and that its situation is without a precedent in the world. America is a land of wonders, in which everything is in constant motion and every change seems an improvement. The idea of novelty is there indissolubly connected with the idea of amelioration. No natural boundary seems to be set to the efforts of man; and in his eyes what is not yet done is only what he has not yet attempted to do.

This perpetual change which goes on in the United States, these frequent vicissitudes of fortune, these unforeseen fluctuations in private and public wealth, serve to keep the minds of the people in a perpetual feverish agitation, which admirably invigorates their exertions and keeps them, so to speak, above the ordinary level of humanity. The whole life of an American is passed like a game of chance, a revolutionary crisis, or a battle. As the same causes are continually in operation throughout the country, they ultimately impart an irresistible impulse to the national character. The American, taken as a chance specimen of his countrymen, must then be a man of singular warmth in his desires, enterprising, fond of adventure and, above all, of novelty. The same bent is manifest in all that he does: he introduces it into his political laws, his religious doctrines, his theories of social economy, and his domestic occupations; he bears it with him in the depth of the backwoods as well as in the business of the city. It is this same passion, applied to maritime commerce, that makes him the cheapest and the quickest trader in the world.

. . .

CONCLUSION

I am approaching the close of my inquiry; hitherto, in speaking of the future destiny of the United States, I have endeavored to divide my subject into distinct portions in order to study each of them with more attention. My present object is to embrace the whole from one point of view; the remarks I shall make will be less detailed, but they will be more sure. I shall perceive each object less distinctly, but I shall descry the principal facts with more certainty. A traveler who has just left a vast city climbs the neighboring hill; as he goes farther off, he loses sight of the men whom he has just quitted; their dwellings are confused in a dense mass; he can no longer distinguish the public squares and can scarcely trace out the great thoroughfares; but his eye has less difficulty in following the boundaries of the city, and for the first time he sees the shape of the whole. Such is the future destiny of the British race in North America to my eye; the details of the immense picture are lost in the shade, but I conceive a clear idea of the entire subject.

The territory now occupied or possessed by the United States of America forms about one twentieth of the habitable earth. But extensive as these bounds are, it must not be supposed that the Anglo-American race will always remain within them; indeed, it has already gone far beyond them.

There was a time when we also might have created a great French nation in the American wilds, to counterbalance the influence of the English on the destinies of the New World. France formerly possessed a territory in North America scarcely less extensive than the whole of Europe. The three greatest rivers of that continent then flowed within her dominions. The Indian tribes that dwelt between the mouth of the St. Lawrence and the delta of the Mississippi were unaccustomed to any other tongue than ours; and all the European settlements scattered over that immense region recalled the traditions of our country. Louisburg, Montmorency, Duquesne, St. Louis, Vincennes, New Orleans (for such were the names they bore) are words dear to France and familiar to our ears.

But a course of circumstances which it would be tedious to enumerate has deprived us of this magnificent inheritance. Wherever the French settlers were numerically weak and partially established, they have disappeared; those who remain are collected on a small extent of country and are now subject to other laws. The 400,000 French inhabitants of Lower Canada constitute at the present time the remnant of an old nation lost in the midst of a new people. A foreign population is increasing around them unceasingly and on all sides, who already penetrate among the former masters of the country, predominate in their cities, and corrupt their language. This population is identical with that of the United States; it is therefore with truth that I asserted that the British race is not confined within the frontiers of the Union, since it already extends to the northeast.

To the northwest nothing is to be met with but a few insignificant Russian settlements; but to the southwest Mexico presents a barrier to the Anglo-Americans. Thus the Spaniards and the Anglo-Americans are, properly speaking, the two races that divide the possession of the New World. The limits of separation between them have been settled by treaty; but although the conditions of that treaty are favorable to the Anglo-Americans, I do not doubt that they will shortly infringe it. Vast provinces extending beyond the frontiers of the Union towards Mexico are still destitute of inhabitants. The natives of the United States will people these solitary regions before their rightful occupants. They will take possession of the soil and establish social institutions, so that when the legal owner at length arrives, he will find the wilderness under cultivation, and strangers quietly settled in the midst of his inheritance.

The lands of the New World belong to the first occupant; they are the natural reward of the swiftest pioneer. Even the countries that are already peopled will have some difficulty in securing themselves from this invasion. I have already alluded to what is taking place in the province of Texas. The inhabitants of the United States are perpetually migrating to Texas, where they purchase land; and although they conform to the laws of the country, they are gradually founding the empire of their own language and their own manners. The province of Texas is still part of the Mexican dominions, but it will soon contain no Mexicans; the same thing has occurred wherever the Anglo-Americans have come in contact with a people of a different origin.

It cannot be denied that the British race has acquired an amazing preponderance over all other European races in the New World; and it is very superior to them in civilization, industry, and power. As long as it is surrounded only by wilderness or thinly peopled countries, as long as it encounters on its route no dense population through which it cannot work its way, it will assuredly continue to spread. The lines marked out by treaties will not stop it, but it will everywhere overleap these imaginary barriers.

The geographical position of the British race in the New World is peculiarly favorable to its rapid increase. Above its northern frontiers the icy regions of the Pole extend; and a few degrees below its southern confines lies the burning climate of the Equator. The Anglo-Americans are therefore placed in the most temperate and habitable zone of the continent.

It is generally supposed that the prodigious increase of population in the United States is posterior to their Declaration of Independence, but this is an error. The population increased as rapidly under the colonial system as at the present day; that is to say, it doubled in about twenty-two years. But this proportion, which is now applied to millions of inhabitants, was then applied to thousands; and the same fact which was scarcely noticeable a century ago is now evident to every observer.

The English in Canada, who are dependent on a king, augment and spread almost as rapidly as the British settlers of the United States, who live under a republican government. During the War of Independence, which lasted eight years, the population continued to increase without intermission in the same ratio. Although powerful Indian nations allied with the English existed at that time on the western frontiers, the emigration westward was never checked. While the enemy laid waste the shores of the Atlantic, Kentucky, the western parts of Pennsylvania, and the states of Vermont and of Maine were filling with inhabitants. Nor did the unsettled state of things which succeeded the war prevent the increase of the population or stop its progress across the wilds. Thus the difference of laws, the various conditions of peace and war, of order or anarchy, have exercised no perceptible influence upon the continued development of the Anglo-Americans. This may be readily understood, for no causes are sufficiently general to exercise a simultaneous influence over the whole of so extensive a territory. One portion of the country always offers a sure retreat from the calamities that afflict another part; and however great may be the evil, the remedy that is at hand is greater still.

It must not, then, be imagined that the impulse of the British race in the New World can be arrested. The dismemberment of the Union and the hostilities that might ensue, the abolition of republican institutions and the tyrannical government that might succeed, may retard this impulse, but they cannot prevent the people from ultimately fulfilling their destinies. No power on earth can shut out the immigrants from that fertile wilderness which offers resources to all industry and a refuge from all want. Future events, whatever they may be, will not deprive the Americans of their climate or their inland seas, their great rivers or their exuberant soil. Nor will bad laws, revolutions, and anarchy be able to obliterate that love of prosperity and spirit of enterprise which seem to be the distinctive characteristics of their race or extinguish altogether the knowledge that guides them on their way.

Thus in the midst of the uncertain future one event at least is sure. At a period that may be said to be near, for we are speaking of the life of a nation, the Anglo-Americans alone will cover the immense space contained between the polar regions and the tropics, extending from the coasts of the Atlantic to those of the Pacific Ocean. The territory that will probably be occupied by the Anglo-Americans may perhaps equal three quarters of Europe in extent. The climate of the Union is, on the whole, preferable to that of Europe, and its natural advantages are as great; it is therefore evident that its population will at some future time be proportionate to our own.

. .

The time will therefore come when one hundred and fifty million men will be living in North America, equal in condition, all belonging to one family, owing their origin to the same cause, and preserving the same civilization, the same language, the same religion, the same habits, the same manners, and imbued with the same opinions, propagated under the same forms. The rest is uncertain, but this is certain; and it is a fact new to the world, a fact that the imagination strives in vain to grasp.

There are at the present time two great nations in the world, which started from different points, but seem to tend towards the same end. I allude to the Russians and the Americans. Both of them have grown up unnoticed; and while the attention of mankind was directed elsewhere, they have suddenly placed themselves in the front rank among the nations, and the world learned their existence and their greatness at almost the same time.

All other nations seem to have nearly reached their natural limits, and they have only to maintain their power; but these are still in the act of growth. All the others have stopped, or continue to advance with extreme difficulty; these alone are proceeding with ease and celerity along a path to which no limit can be perceived. The American struggles against the obstacles that nature opposes to him; the adversaries of the Russian are men. The former combats the wilderness and savage life; the latter, civilization with all its arms. The conquests of the American are therefore gained by the plowshare; those of the Russian by the sword. The Anglo-American relies upon personal interest to accomplish his ends and gives free scope to the unguided strength and common sense of the people; the Russian centers all the authority of society in a single arm. The principal instrument of the former is freedom; of the latter, servitude. Their starting-point is different and their courses are not the same; yet each of them seems marked out by the will of Heaven to sway the destinies of half the globe.

Democracy in America

SECOND PART

Author's Preface

TO THE SECOND PART

The Americans have a democratic state of society, which has naturally suggested to them certain laws and certain political manners. It has also created in their minds many feelings and opinions which were unknown in the old aristocratic societies of Europe. It has destroyed or modified the old relations of men to one another and has established new ones. The aspect of civil society has been as much altered as the face of the political world.

I have treated of the former subject in the work which I published, five years ago, on American Democracy; the latter is the object of the present book. These two Parts complete each other and form but a single work.

But I must warn the reader immediately against an error that would be very prejudicial to me. Because I attribute so many different effects to the principle of equality, it might be inferred that I consider this principle as the only cause of everything that takes place in our day. This would be attributing to me a very narrow view of things.

A multitude of the opinions, sentiments, and instincts that belong to our times owe their origin to circumstances that have nothing to do with the principle of equality or are even hostile to it. Thus, taking the United States for example, I could easily prove that the nature of the country, the origin of its inhabitants, the religion of the early settlers, their acquired knowledge, their previous habits, have exercised, and still do exercise, independently of democracy, an immense influence upon their modes of thought and feeling. Other causes, equally independent of the principle of equality, would be found in Europe and would explain much of what is passing there.

I recognize the existence and the efficiency of all these various causes; but my subject does not lead me to speak of them. I have not undertaken to point out the origin and nature of all our inclinations and all our ideas; I have only endeavored to show how far both of them are affected by the equality of men's conditions.

As I am firmly convinced that the democratic revolution which we are now beholding is an irresistible fact, against which it would be neither desirable nor prudent to contend, some persons perhaps may be surprised that, in the course of this book, I have often applied language of strong censure to the democratic communities which this revolution has created. The simple reason is, that precisely because I was not an opponent of democracy I wished to speak of it with all sincerity. Men will not receive the truth from their enemies, and it is very seldom offered to them by their friends; on this very account I have frankly uttered it. I believed that many persons would take it upon themselves to inform men of the benefits which they might hope to receive from the establishment of equality, while very few would venture to point out from afar the dangers with which it would be attended. It is principally towards these dangers, therefore, that I directed my gaze; and, believing that I had clearly discerned what they are, it would have been cowardice to say nothing about them.

I hope the same impartiality will be found in this second work which people seemed to observe in its predecessor. Placed between the conflicting opinions that divide my countrymen, I have endeavored for the time to stifle in my own bosom the sympathy or the aversion that I felt for either. If the readers of my book find in it a single phrase intended to flatter either of the great parties that have agitated our country, or any one of the petty factions that in our day harass and weaken it, let them raise their voices and accuse me.

The subject that I wished to cover by my investigations is immense, for it includes most of the feelings and opinions produced by the new condition of the world's affairs. Such a subject certainly exceeds my strength, and in the treatment of it I have not been able to satisfy myself. But even if I could not attain the goal towards which I strove, my readers will at least do me this justice, that I conceived and pursued my enterprise in a spirit which could make me worthy of succeeding.

FIRST BOOK

INFLUENCE OF DEMOCRACY ON THE ACTION OF INTELLECT IN THE UNITED STATES

Chapter I

PHILOSOPHICAL METHOD OF THE AMERICANS

I think that in no country in the civilized world is less attention paid to philosophy than in the United States. The Americans have no philosophical school of their own, and they care but little for all the schools into which Europe is divided, the very names of which are scarcely known to them.

Yet it is easy to perceive that almost all the inhabitants of the United States use their minds in the same manner, and direct them according to the same rules; that is to say, without ever having taken the trouble to define the rules, they have a philosophical method common to the whole people.

To evade the bondage of system and habit, of family maxims, class opinions, and, in some degree, of national prejudices; to accept tradition only as a means of information, and existing facts only as a lesson to be used in doing otherwise and doing better; to seek the reason of things for oneself, and in oneself alone; to tend to results without being bound to means, and to strike through the form to the substance—such are the principal characteristics of what I shall call the philosophical method of the Americans.

But if I go further and seek among these characteristics the principal one, which includes almost all the rest, I discover that in most of the operations of the mind each American appeals only to the individual effort of his own understanding.

. . .

In the midst of the continual movement that agitates a democratic community, the tie that unites one generation to another is relaxed or broken; every man there readily loses all trace of the ideas of his forefathers or takes no care about them.

Men living in this state of society cannot derive their belief from the opinions of the class to which they belong; for, so to speak, there are no longer any classes, or those which still exist are composed of such mobile elements that the body can never exercise any real control over its members.

As to the influence which the intellect of one man may have on that of another, it must necessarily be very limited in a country where the citizens, placed on an equal footing, are all closely seen by one another; and where, as no signs of incontestable greatness or superiority are perceived in any one of them, they are constantly brought back to their own reason as the most obvious and proximate source of truth. It is not only confidence in this or that man which is destroyed, but the disposition to trust the authority of any man whatsoever. Everyone shuts himself up tightly within himself and insists upon judging the world from there.

The practice of Americans leads their minds to other habits, to fixing the standard of their judgment in themselves alone. As they perceive that they succeed in resolving without assistance all the little difficulties which their practical life presents, they readily conclude that everything in the world may be explained, and that nothing in it transcends the limits of the understanding. Thus they fall to denying what they cannot comprehend; which leaves them but little faith for whatever is extraordinary and an almost insurmountable distaste for whatever is supernatural. As it is on their own testimony that they are accustomed to rely, they like to discern the object which engages their attention with extreme clearness; they therefore strip off as much as possible all that covers it; they rid themselves of whatever separates them from it, they remove whatever conceals it from sight, in order to view it more closely and in the broad light of day. This disposition of mind soon leads them to condemn forms, which they regard as useless and inconvenient veils placed between them and the truth.

. . .

There are no revolutions that do not shake existing belief, enervate authority, and throw doubts over commonly received ideas. Every revolution has more or less the effect of releasing men to their own conduct and of opening before the mind of each one of them an almost limitless perspective. When equality of conditions succeeds a protracted conflict between the different classes of which the elder society was composed, envy, hatred, and uncharitableness, pride and exaggerated self-confidence seize upon the human heart, and plant their sway in it for a time. This, independently of equality itself, tends powerfully to divide men, to lead them to mistrust the judgment of one other, and to seek the light of truth nowhere but in themselves. Everyone then attempts to be his own sufficient guide and makes it his boast to form his own opinions on all subjects. Men are no longer bound together by ideas, but by interests; and it would seem as if human opinions were reduced to a sort of intellectual dust, scattered on every side, unable to collect, unable to cohere.

Thus that independence of mind which equality supposes to exist is never so great, never appears so excessive, as at the time when equality is beginning to establish itself and in the course of that painful labor by which it is established. That sort of intellectual freedom which equality may give ought, therefore, to be very carefully distinguished from the anarchy which revolution brings. Each of these two things must be separately considered in order not to conceive exaggerated hopes or fears of the future.

I believe that the men who will live under the new forms of society will make frequent use of their private judgment, but I am far from thinking that they will often abuse it. This is attributable to a cause which is more generally applicable to democratic countries, and which, in the long run, must restrain, within fixed and sometimes narrow limits, individual freedom of thought.

I shall proceed to point out this cause in the next chapter.

Chapter II

OF THE PRINCIPAL SOURCE OF BELIEF
AMONG DEMOCRATIC NATIONS

At different periods dogmatic belief is more or less common. It arises in different ways, and it may change its object and its form; but under no circumstances will dogmatic belief cease to exist, or, in other words, men will never cease to entertain some opinions on trust and without discussion. If everyone undertook to form all his own opinions and to seek for truth by isolated paths struck out by himself alone, it would follow that no considerable number of men would ever unite in any common belief.

But obviously without such common belief no society can prosper; say, rather, no society can exist; for without ideas held in common there is no common action, and without common action there may still be men, but there is no social body. In order that society should exist and, *a fortiori,* that a society should prosper, it is necessary that the minds of all the citizens should be rallied and held together by certain predominant ideas; and this cannot be the case unless each of them sometimes draws his opinions from the common source and consents to accept certain matters of belief already formed.

If I now consider man in his isolated capacity, I find that dogmatic belief is not less indispensable to him in order to live alone than it is to enable him to co-operate with his fellows. If man were forced to demonstrate for himself all the truths of which he makes daily use, his task would never end. He would exhaust his strength in preparatory demonstrations without ever advancing beyond them. As, from the shortness of his life, he has not the time, nor, from the limits of his intelligence, the capacity, to act in this way, he is reduced to take on trust a host of facts and opinions which he has not had either the time or the power to verify for himself, but which men of greater ability have found out, or which the crowd adopts. On this groundwork he raises for himself the structure of his own thoughts; he is not led to proceed in this manner by choice, but is constrained by the inflexible law of his condition. There is no philosopher in the world so great but that he believes a million things on the faith of other people and accepts a great many more truths than he demonstrates.

This is not only necessary but desirable. A man who should undertake to inquire into everything for himself could devote to each thing but little time and attention. His task would keep his mind in perpetual unrest, which would prevent him from penetrating to the depth of any truth or of making his mind adhere firmly to any conviction. His intellect would be at once independent and powerless. He must therefore make his choice from among the various objects of human belief and adopt many opinions without discussion in order to search the better into that smaller number which he sets apart for investigation. It is true that whoever receives an opinion on the word of another does so far enslave his mind, but it is a salutary servitude, which allows him to make a good use of freedom.

A principle of authority must then always occur, under all circumstances, in some part or other of the moral and intellectual world. Its place is variable, but a place it necessarily has. The independence of individual minds may be greater or it may be less; it cannot be unbounded. Thus the question is, not to know whether any intellectual authority exists in an age of democracy, but simply where it resides and by what standard it is to be measured.

I have shown in the preceding chapter how equality of

conditions leads men to entertain a sort of instinctive incredulity of the supernatural and a very lofty and often exaggerated opinion of human understanding. The men who live at a period of social equality are not therefore easily led to place that intellectual authority to which they bow either beyond or above humanity. They commonly seek for the sources of truth in themselves or in those who are like themselves. This would be enough to prove that at such periods no new religion could be established, and that all schemes for such a purpose would be not only impious, but absurd and irrational. It may be foreseen that a democratic people will not easily give credence to divine missions; that they will laugh at modern prophets; and that they will seek to discover the chief arbiter of their belief within, and not beyond, the limits of their kind.

When the ranks of society are unequal, and men unlike one another in condition, there are some individuals wielding the power of superior intelligence, learning, and enlightenment, while the multitude are sunk in ignorance and prejudice. Men living at these aristocratic periods are therefore naturally induced to shape their opinions by the standard of a superior person, or a superior class of persons, while they are averse to recognizing the infallibility of the mass of the people.

The contrary takes place in ages of equality. The nearer the people are drawn to the common level of an equal and similar condition, the less prone does each man become to place implicit faith in a certain man or a certain class of men. But his readiness to believe the multitude increases, and opinion is more than ever mistress of the world. Not only is common opinion the only guide which private judgment retains among a democratic people, but among such a people it possesses a power infinitely beyond what it has elsewhere. At periods of equality men have no faith in one another, by reason of their common resemblance; but this very resemblance gives them almost unbounded confidence in the judgment of the public; for it would seem probable that, as they are all endowed with equal means of judging, the greater truth should go with the greater number.

When the inhabitant of a democratic country compares himself individually with all those about him, he feels with pride that he is the equal of any one of them; but when he comes to survey the totality of his fellows and to place himself in contrast with so huge a body, he is instantly overwhelmed by the sense of his own insignificance and weakness. The same equality that renders him independent of each of his fellow citizens, taken severally, exposes him alone and unprotected to the influence of the greater number. The public, therefore, among a democratic people, has a singular power, which aristocratic nations cannot conceive; for it does not persuade others to its beliefs, but it imposes them and makes them permeate the thinking of everyone by a sort of enormous pressure of the mind of all upon the individual intelligence.

In the United States the majority undertakes to supply a multitude of ready-made opinions for the use of individuals, who are thus relieved from the necessity of forming opinions of their own. Everybody there adopts great numbers of theories, on philosophy, morals, and politics, without inquiry, upon public trust; and if we examine it very closely, it will be perceived that religion itself holds sway there much less as a doctrine of revelation than as a commonly received opinion.

. . .

Thus intellectual authority will be different, but it will not be diminished; and far from thinking that it will disappear, I augur that it may readily acquire too much preponderance and confine the action of private judgment within narrower limits than are suited to either the greatness or the happiness of the human race. In the principle of equality I very clearly discern two tendencies; one leading the mind of every man to untried thoughts, the other prohibiting him from thinking at all. And I perceive how, under the dominion of certain laws, democracy would extinguish that liberty of the mind to which a democratic social condition is favorable; so that, after having broken all the bondage once imposed on it by ranks or by men, the human mind would be closely fettered to the general will of the greatest number.

If the absolute power of a majority were to be substituted by democratic nations for all the different powers that checked or retarded overmuch the energy of individual minds, the evil would only have changed character. Men would not have found the means of independent life; they would simply have discovered (no easy task) a new physiognomy of servitude. There is, and I cannot repeat it too often, there is here matter for profound reflection to those who look on freedom of thought as a holy thing and who hate not only the despot, but despotism. For myself, when I feel the hand of power lie heavy on my brow, I care but little to know who oppresses me; and I am not the more disposed to pass beneath the yoke because it is held out to me by the arms of a million men.

Chapter III

WHY THE AMERICANS SHOW MORE APTITUDE AND TASTE FOR GENERAL IDEAS THAN THEIR FOREFATHERS, THE ENGLISH

The Deity does not regard the human race collectively. He surveys at one glance and severally all the beings of whom mankind is composed; and He discerns in each man the resemblances that assimilate him to all his fellows, and the differences that distinguish him from them. God, therefore, stands in no need of general ideas; that is to say, He never feels the necessity of collecting a considerable number of analogous objects under the same form for greater convenience in thinking.

Such, however, is not the case with man. If the human mind were to attempt to examine and pass a judgment on all the individual cases before it, the immensity of detail would soon lead it astray and it would no longer see anything. In this strait, man has recourse to an imperfect but necessary expedient, which at the same time assists and demonstrates his weakness.

Having superficially considered a certain number of objects and noticed their resemblance, he assigns to them a common name, sets them apart, and proceeds onwards.

General ideas are no proof of the strength, but rather of the insufficiency of the human intellect; for there are in nature no beings exactly alike, no things precisely identical, no rules indiscriminately and alike applicable to several objects at once. The chief merit of general ideas is that they

304 DEMOCRACY IN AMERICA

enable the human mind to pass a rapid judgment on a great many objects at once; but, on the other hand, the notions they convey are never other than incomplete, and they always cause the mind to lose as much in accuracy as it gains in comprehensiveness.

As social bodies advance in civilization, they acquire the knowledge of new facts and they daily lay hold almost unconsciously of some particular truths. The more truths of this kind a man apprehends, the more general ideas he is naturally led to conceive. A multitude of particular facts cannot be seen separately without at last discovering the common tie that connects them. Several individuals lead to the notion of the species, several species to that of the genus. Hence the habit and the taste for general ideas will always be greatest among a people of ancient culture and extensive knowledge.

But there are other reasons which impel men to generalize their ideas or which restrain them from doing so.

The Americans are much more addicted to the use of general ideas than the English and entertain a much greater relish for them. This appears very singular at first, when it is remembered that the two nations have the same origin, that they lived for centuries under the same laws, and that they still incessantly interchange their opinions and their manners. This contrast becomes much more striking still if we fix our eyes on our own part of the world and compare together the two most enlightened nations that inhabit it. It would seem as if the mind of the English could tear itself only reluctantly and painfully away from the observation of particular facts, to rise from them to their causes, and that it only generalizes in spite of itself. Among the French, on the contrary, the taste for general ideas would seem to have grown to so ardent a passion that it must be satisfied on every occasion. I am informed every morning when I wake that some general and eternal law has just been discovered which I never heard mentioned before. There is not a mediocre scribbler who does not try his hand at discovering truths applicable to a great kingdom and who is not very ill pleased with himself if he does not succeed in compressing the human race into the compass of an article.

So great a dissimilarity between two very enlightened nations surprises me. If I again turn my attention to England and observe the events which have occurred there in the last half-century, I think I may affirm that a taste for general ideas increases in that country in proportion as its ancient constitution is weakened.

The state of civilization is therefore insufficient by itself to explain what suggests to the human mind the love of general ideas or diverts it from them.

When the conditions of men are very unequal and the inequalities are permanent, individual men gradually become so dissimilar that each class assumes the aspect of a distinct race. Only one of these classes is ever in view at the same instant; and, losing sight of that general tie which binds them all within the vast bosom of mankind, the observation invariably rests, not on man, but on certain men. Those who live in this aristocratic state of society never, therefore, conceive very general ideas respecting themselves; and that is enough to imbue them with a habitual distrust of such ideas and an instinctive aversion for them.

He, on the contrary, who inhabits a democratic country sees around him on every hand men differing but little from one another; he cannot turn his mind to any one portion of mankind without expanding and dilating his thought till it embraces the whole. All the truths that are applicable to himself appear to him equally and similarly applicable to each of his fellow citizens and fellow men. Having contracted the habit of generalizing his ideas in the study which engages him most and interests him most, he transfers the same habit to all his pursuits; and thus it is that the craving to discover general laws in everything, to include a great number of objects under the same formula, and to explain a mass of facts by a single cause becomes an ardent and sometimes an undiscerning passion in the human mind.

. . .

In the ages of equality all men are independent of each other, isolated, and weak. The movements of the multitude are not permanently guided by the will of any individuals; at such times humanity seems always to advance of itself. In order, therefore, to explain what is passing in the world, man is driven to seek for some great causes, which, acting in the same manner on an our fellow creatures, thus induce them all voluntarily to pursue the same track. This again naturally leads the human mind to conceive general ideas and superinduces a taste for them.

I have already shown in what way the equality of conditions leads every man to investigate truth for himself. It may readily be perceived that a method of this kind must insensibly beget a tendency to general ideas in the human mind. When I repudiate the traditions of rank, professions, and birth, when I escape from the authority of example to seek out, by the single effort of my reason, the path to be followed, I am inclined to derive the motives of my opinions from human nature itself, and this leads me necessarily, and almost unconsciously, to adopt a great number of very general notions.

All that I have here said explains why the English display much less aptitude and taste for the generalization of ideas than their American progeny, and still less again than their neighbors the French; and likewise why the English of the present day display more than their forefathers did.

The English have long been a very enlightened and a very aristocratic nation; their enlightened condition urged them constantly to generalize, and their aristocratic habits confined them to the particular. Hence arose that philosophy, at once bold and timid, broad and narrow, which has hitherto prevailed in England and which still obstructs and stagnates so many minds in that country.

Independently of the causes I have pointed out in what goes before, others may be discerned less apparent, but no less efficacious, which produce among almost every democratic people a taste, and frequently a passion, for general ideas. A distinction must be made between ideas of this kind. Some of them are the result of slow, minute, and conscientious labor of the mind, and these extend the sphere of human knowledge; others spring up at once from the first rapid exercise of the wits and beget none but very superficial and uncertain notions.

Men who live in ages of equality have a great deal of curiosity and little leisure; their life is so practical, so confused, so excited, so active, that but little time remains to them for thought. Such men are prone to general ideas because they are thereby spared the trouble of studying particulars; they contain, if I may so speak, a great deal in a little compass, and give, in a little time, a great return. If, then, on a brief and inattentive investigation, they think they discern a common relation between certain objects, inquiry is not pushed any further; and without examining in detail how far these several objects agree or differ, they are hastily arranged under one formula, in order to pass another subject.

One of the distinguishing characteristics of a democratic period is the taste that all men have for easy success and present enjoyment. This occurs in the pursuits of the intellect as well as in all others. Most of those who live in a time of equality are full of an ambition equally alert and indolent: they want to obtain great success immediately, but they would prefer to avoid great effort. These conflicting tendencies lead straight to the search for general ideas, by the aid of which they flatter themselves that they can delineate vast objects with little pains and draw the attention of the public without much trouble.

And I do not know that they are wrong in thinking so. For their readers are as much averse to investigating anything to the bottom as they are; and what is generally sought in the productions of mind is easy pleasure and information without labor.

If aristocratic nations do not make sufficient use of general ideas, and frequently treat them with inconsiderate disdain, it is true, on the other hand, that a democratic people is always ready to carry ideas of this kind to excess and to espouse them with injudicious warmth.

Chapter IV

WHY THE AMERICANS HAVE NEVER BEEN SO EAGER AS THE FRENCH FOR GENERAL IDEAS IN POLITICAL AFFAIRS

I have observed that the Americans show a less decided taste for general ideas than the French. This is especially true in politics.

Although the Americans infuse into their legislation far more general ideas than the English, and although they strive more than the latter to adjust the practice of affairs to theory, no political bodies in the United States have ever shown so much love for general ideas as the Constituent Assembly and the Convention in France. At no time has the American people laid hold on ideas of this kind with the passionate energy of the French people in the eighteenth century, or displayed the same blind confidence in the value and absolute truth of any theory.

This difference between the Americans and the French originates in several causes, but principally in the following one. The Americans are a democratic people who have always directed public affairs themselves. The French are a democratic people who for a long time could only speculate on the best manner of conducting them. The social condition of the French led them to conceive very general ideas on the subject of government, while their political constitution prevented them from correcting those ideas by experiment and from gradually detecting their insufficiency; whereas in America the two things constantly balance and correct each other.

It may seem at first sight that this is very much opposed to what I have said before, that democratic nations derive their love of theory from the very excitement of their active life. A more attentive examination will show that there is nothing contradictory in the proposition.

Men living in democratic countries eagerly lay hold of general ideas because they have but little leisure and because these ideas spare them the trouble of studying particulars. This is true, but it is only to be understood of those matters which are not the necessary and habitual subjects of their thoughts. Mercantile men will take up very eagerly, and without any close scrutiny, all the general ideas on philosophy, politics, science, or the arts which may be presented to them; but for such as relate to commerce, they will not receive them without inquiry or adopt them without reserve. The same thing applies to statesmen with regard to general ideas in politics.

If, then, there is a subject upon which a democratic people is peculiarly liable to abandon itself, blindly and extravagantly, to general ideas, the best corrective that can be used will be to make that subject a part of their daily practical occupation. They will then be compelled to enter into details, and the details will teach them the weak points of the theory. This remedy may frequently be a painful one, but its effect is certain.

Thus it happens that the democratic institutions which compel every citizen to take a practical part in the government moderate that excessive taste for general theories in politics which the principle of equality suggests.

Chapter V

HOW RELIGION IN THE UNITED STATES AVAILS ITSELF OF DEMOCRATIC TENDENCIES

I have shown in a preceding chapter that men cannot do without dogmatic belief, and even that it is much to be desired that such belief should exist among them. I now add that, of all the kinds of dogmatic belief, the most desirable appears to me to be dogmatic belief in matters of religion; and this is a clear inference, even from no higher consideration than the interests of this world.

There is hardly any human action, however particular it may be, that does not originate in some very general idea men have conceived of the Deity, of his relation to mankind, of the nature of their own souls, and of their duties to their fellow creatures. Nor can anything prevent these ideas from being the common spring from which all the rest emanates.

Men are therefore immeasurably interested in acquiring fixed ideas of God, of the soul, and of their general duties to their Creator and their fellow men; for doubt on these first principles would abandon all their actions to chance and would condemn them in some way to disorder and impotence.

This, then, is the subject on which it is most important for each of us to have fixed ideas; and unhappily it is also the subject on which it is most difficult for each of us, left to himself, to settle his opinions by the sole force of his reason. None but minds singularly free from the ordinary cares of life, minds at once penetrating, subtle, and trained by thinking, can, even with much time and care, sound the depths of these truths that are so necessary. And, indeed, we see that philosophers are themselves almost always surrounded with uncertainties; that at every step the natural light which illuminates their path grows dimmer and less secure; and that, in spite of all their efforts, they have discovered as yet only a few conflicting notions, on which the mind of man has been tossed about for thousands of years without ever firmly grasping the truth or finding novelty even in its errors. Studies of this nature are far above the average capacity of men; and, even if the majority of mankind were capable of such pursuits, it is evident that leisure to cultivate them would still be wanting.

Fixed ideas about God and human nature are indispensable to the daily practice of men's lives; but the practice of their lives prevents them from acquiring such ideas.

. . .

General ideas respecting God and human nature are therefore the ideas above all others which it is most suitable to withdraw from the habitual action of private judgment and in which there is most to gain and least to lose by recognizing a principle of authority.

The first object and one of the principal advantages of religion is to furnish to each of these fundamental questions a solution that is at once clear, precise, intelligible, and lasting, to the mass of mankind. There are religions that are false and very absurd, but it may be affirmed that any religion which remains within the circle I have just traced, without pretending to go beyond it (as many religions have attempted to do, for the purpose of restraining on every side the free movement of the human mind), imposes a salutary restraint on the intellect; and it must be admitted that, if it does not save men in another world, it is at least very conducive to their happiness and their greatness in this.

This is especially true of men living in free countries.

When the religion of a people is destroyed, doubt gets hold of the higher powers of the intellect and half paralyzes all the others. Every man accustoms himself to having only confused and changing notions on the subjects most interesting to his fellow creatures and himself. His opinions are ill-defended and easily abandoned; and, in despair of ever solving by himself the hard problems respecting the destiny of man, he ignobly submits to think no more about them.

Such a condition cannot but enervate the soul, relax the springs of the will, and prepare a people for servitude. Not only does it happen in such a case that they allow their freedom to be taken from them; they frequently surrender it themselves. When there is no longer any principle of authority in religion any more than in politics, men are speedily frightened at the aspect of this unbounded independence. The constant agitation of all surrounding things alarms and exhausts them. As everything is at sea in the sphere of the mind, they determine at least that the mechanism of society shall be firm and fixed; and as they cannot resume their ancient belief, they assume a master.

For my own part, I doubt whether man can ever support at the same time complete religious independence and entire political freedom. And I am inclined to think that if faith be wanting in him he must be subject; and if he be free, he must believe.

Perhaps, however, this great utility of religions is still more obvious among nations where equality of conditions prevails than among others. It must be acknowledged that equality, which brings great benefits into the world, nevertheless suggests to men (as will be shown hereafter) some very dangerous propensities. It tends to isolate them from one another, to concentrate every man's attention upon himself; and it lays open the soul to an inordinate love of material gratification.

The greatest advantage of religion is to inspire diametrically contrary principles. There is no religion that does not place the object of man's desires above and beyond the treasures of earth and that does not naturally raise his soul to regions far above those of the senses. Nor is there any which does not impose on man some duties towards his kind and thus draw him at times from the contemplation of himself. This is found in the most false and dangerous religions.

Religious nations are therefore naturally strong on the very point on which democratic nations are weak; this shows of what importance it is for men to preserve their religion as their conditions become more equal.

I have neither the right nor the intention of examining the supernatural means that God employs to infuse religious belief into the heart of man. I am at this moment considering religions in a purely human point of view; my object is to inquire by what means they may most easily retain their sway in the democratic ages upon which we are entering.

. . .

I find that for religions to maintain their authority, humanly speaking, in democratic ages, not only must they confine themselves strictly within the circle of spiritual matters, but their power also will depend very much on the nature of the belief they inculcate, on the external forms they assume, and on the obligations they impose.

The preceding observation, that equality leads men to very general and very vast ideas, is principally to be understood in respect to religion. Men who are similar and equal in the world readily conceive the idea of the one God, governing every man by the same laws and granting to every man future happiness on the same conditions. The idea of the unity of mankind constantly leads them back to the idea of the unity of the Creator; while on the contrary in a state of society where men are broken up into very unequal ranks, they are apt to devise as many deities as there are nations, castes, classes, or families, and to trace a thousand private roads to heaven.

. . .

It seems evident that the more the barriers are removed which separate one nation from another and one citizen from another, the stronger is the bent of the human mind, as if by its own impulse, towards the idea of a single and all-powerful Being, dispensing equal laws in the same manner to every man. In democratic ages, then, it is particularly important not to allow the homage paid to secondary agents to be confused with the worship due to the Creator alone.

Another truth is no less clear, that religions ought to have fewer external observances in democratic periods than at any others.

In speaking of philosophical method among the Americans I have shown that nothing is more repugnant to the human mind in an age of equality than the idea of subjection to forms. Men living at such times are impatient of figures; to their eyes, symbols appear to be puerile artifices used to conceal or to set off truths that should more naturally be bared to the light of day; they are unmoved by ceremonial observances and are disposed to attach only a secondary importance to the details of public worship.

Those who have to regulate the external forms of religion in a democratic age should pay close attention to these natural propensities of the human mind in order not to run counter to them unnecessarily.

I firmly believe in the necessity of forms, which fix the human mind in the contemplation of abstract truths and aid it in embracing them warmly and holding them with firmness. Nor do I suppose that it is possible to maintain a religion without external observances; but, on the other hand, I am persuaded that in the ages upon which we are entering it would be peculiarly dangerous to multiply them beyond measure, and that they ought rather to be limited to as much as is absolutely necessary to perpetuate the doctrine itself, which is the substance of religion, of which the ritual is only the form. A religion which became more insistent in details, more inflexible, and more burdened with small observances during the time that men became more equal would soon find itself limited to a band of fanatic zealots in the midst of a skeptical multitude.

I anticipate the objection that, as all religions have general and eternal truths for their object, they cannot thus shape themselves to the shifting inclinations of every age without forfeiting their claim to certainty in the eyes of mankind. To this I reply again that the principal opinions which constitute a creed, and which theologians call articles of faith, must be very carefully distinguished from the accessories connected with them. Religions are obliged to hold fast to the former, whatever be the peculiar spirit of the age; but they should take good care not to bind themselves in the same manner to the latter at a time when everything is in transition and when the mind, accustomed to the moving pageant of human affairs, reluctantly allows itself to be fixed on any point. The permanence of external and secondary things seems to me to have a chance of enduring only when civil society is itself static; under any other circumstances I am inclined to regard it as dangerous.

We shall see that of all the passions which originate in or are fostered by equality, there is one which it renders peculiarly intense, and which it also infuses into the heart of every man; I mean the love of well-being. The taste for well-being is the prominent and indelible feature of democratic times.

It may be believed that a religion which should undertake to destroy so deep-seated a passion would in the end be destroyed by it; and if it attempted to wean men entirely from the contemplation of the good things of this world in order to devote their faculties exclusively to the thought of another, it may be foreseen that the minds of men would at length escape its grasp, to plunge into the exclusive enjoyment of present and material pleasures.

The chief concern of religion is to purify, to regulate, and to restrain the excessive and exclusive taste for well-being that men feel in periods of equality; but it would be an error to attempt to overcome it completely or to eradicate it. Men cannot be cured of the love of riches, but they may be persuaded to enrich themselves by none but honest means.

This brings me to a final consideration, which comprises, as it were, all the others. The more the conditions of men are equalized and assimilated to each other, the more important is it for religion, while it carefully abstains from the daily turmoil of secular affairs, not needlessly to run counter to the ideas that generally prevail or to the permanent interests that exist in the mass of the people. For as public opinion grows to be more and more the first and most irresistible of existing powers, the religious principle has no external support strong enough to enable it long to resist its attacks. This is not less true of a democratic people ruled by a despot than of a republic. In ages of equality kings may often command obedience, but the majority always commands belief; to the majority, therefore, deference is to be paid in whatever is not contrary to the faith.

I showed in the first Part of this work how the American clergy stand aloof from secular affairs. This is the most obvious but not the only example of their self-restraint. In America religion is a distinct sphere, in which the priest is sovereign, but out of which he takes care never to go. Within its limits he is master of the mind; beyond them he leaves men to themselves and surrenders them to the independence and instability that belong to their nature and their age. I have seen no country in which Christianity is clothed with fewer forms, figures, and observances than in the United States, or where it presents more distinct, simple, and general notions to the mind. Although the Christians of America are divided into a multitude of sects, they all look upon their religion in the same light. This applies to Roman Catholicism as well as to the other forms of belief. There are no Roman Catholic priests who show less taste for the minute individual observances, for extraordinary or peculiar means of salvation, or who cling more to the spirit and less to the letter of the law than the Roman Catholic priests of the United States. Nowhere is that doctrine of the church which prohibits the worship reserved to God alone from being offered to the saints more clearly inculcated or more generally followed. Yet the Roman Catholics of America are very submissive and very sincere.

Another remark is applicable to the clergy of every communion. The American ministers of the Gospel do not attempt to draw or to fix all the thoughts of man upon the life to come; they are willing to surrender a portion of his heart to the cares of the present, seeming to consider the goods of this world as important, though secondary, objects. If they take no part themselves in productive labor, they are at least interested in its progress and they applaud its results; and while they never cease to point to the other world as the great object of the hopes and fears of the believer, they do not forbid him honestly to court prosperity in this. Far from attempting to show that these things are distinct and contrary to one another, they study rather to find out on what point they are most nearly and closely connected.

All the American clergy know and respect the intellectual supremacy exercised by the majority; they never sustain any but necessary conflicts with it. They take no share in the altercations of parties, but they readily adopt the general opinions of their country and their age, and they allow themselves to be borne away without opposition in the current of feeling and opinion by which everything around them is carried along. They endeavor to amend their contemporaries, but they do not quit fellowship with them. Public opinion is therefore never hostile to them; it rather supports and protects them, and their belief owes its authority at the same time to the strength which is its own and to that which it borrows from the opinions of the majority.

Thus it is that by respecting all democratic tendencies not absolutely contrary to herself and by making use of several of them for her own purposes, religion sustains a successful struggle with that spirit of individual independence which is her most dangerous opponent.

Chapter VI

THE PROGRESS OF ROMAN CATHOLICISM IN THE UNITED STATES

America is the most democratic country in the world, and it is at the same time (according to reports worthy of belief) the country in which the Roman Catholic religion makes most progress. At first sight this is surprising.

Two things must here be accurately distinguished: quality makes men want to form their own opinions; but, on the other hand, it imbues them with the taste and the idea of unity, simplicity, and impartiality in the power that governs society. Men living in democratic times are therefore very prone to shake off all religious authority; but if they consent to subject themselves to any authority of this kind, they choose at least that it should be single and uniform. Religious powers not radiating from a common center are naturally repugnant to their minds; and they almost as readily conceive that there should be no religion as that there should be several.

At the present time, more than in any preceding age, Roman Catholics are seen to lapse into infidelity, and Protestants to be converted to Roman Catholicism. If you consider Catholicism within its own organization, it seems to be losing; if you consider it from outside, it seems to be gaining. Nor is this difficult to explain. The men of our days are naturally little disposed to believe; but as soon as they have any religion, they immediately find in themselves a latent instinct that urges them unconsciously towards Catholicism. Many of the doctrines and practices of the Roman Catholic Church astonish them, but they feel a secret admiration for its discipline, and its great unity attracts them. If Catholicism could at length withdraw itself from the political animosities to which it has given rise, I have hardly any doubt but that the same spirit of the age which appears to be so opposed to it would become so favorable as to admit of its great and sudden advancement.

One of the most ordinary weaknesses of the human intellect is to seek to reconcile contrary principles and to purchase peace at the expense of logic. Thus there have ever been and will ever be men who, after having submitted some portion of their religious belief to the principle of authority, will seek to exempt several other parts of their faith from it and to keep their minds floating at random between liberty and obedience. But I am inclined to believe that the number of these thinkers will be less in democratic than in other ages, and that our posterity will tend more and more to a division into only two parts, some relinquishing Christianity entirely and others returning to the Church of Rome.

Chapter VII

WHAT CAUSES DEMOCRATIC NATIONS TO INCLINE TOWARDS PANTHEISM

I shall show hereafter how the preponderant taste of a democratic people for very general ideas manifests itself in politics, but I wish to point out at present its principal effect on philosophy.

It cannot be denied that pantheism has made great progress in our age. The writings of a part of Europe bear visible marks of it: the Germans introduce it into philosophy, and the French into literature. Most of the works of imagination published in France contain some opinions or some tinge caught from pantheistic doctrines or they disclose some tendency to such doctrines in their authors. This appears to me not to proceed only from an accidental, but from a permanent cause.

When the conditions of society are becoming more equal and each individual man becomes more like all the rest, more weak and insignificant, a habit grows up of ceasing to notice the citizens and considering only the people, of overlooking individuals to think only of their kind. At such times the human mind seeks to embrace a multitude of different objects at once, and it constantly strives to connect a variety of consequences with a single cause. The idea of unity so possesses man and is sought by him so generally that if he thinks he has found it, he readily yields himself to repose in that belief. Not content with the discovery that there is nothing in the world but a creation and a Creator, he is still embarrassed by this primary division of things and seeks to expand and simplify his conception by including God and the universe in one great whole.

If there is a philosophical system which teaches that all things material and immaterial, visible and invisible, which the world contains are to be considered only as the several parts of an immense Being, who alone remains eternal amidst the continual change and ceaseless transformation of all that constitutes him, we may readily infer that such a system, although it destroy the individuality of man, or rather because it destroys that individuality, will have secret charms for men living in democracies. All their habits of thought prepare them to conceive it and predispose them to adopt it. It naturally attracts and fixes their imagination; it fosters the pride while it soothes the indolence of their minds.

Among the different systems by whose aid philosophy endeavors to explain the universe I believe pantheism to be one of those most fitted to seduce the human mind in democratic times. Against it all who abide in their attachment to the true greatness of man should combine and struggle.

Chapter VIII

HOW EQUALITY SUGGESTS TO THE AMERICANS THE IDEA OF THE INDEFINITE PERFECTIBILITY OF MAN

Equality suggests to the human mind several ideas that would not have originated from any other source, and it modifies almost all those previously entertained. I take as an example the idea of human perfectibility, because it is one of the principal notions that the intellect can conceive and because it constitutes of itself a great philosophical theory, which is everywhere to be traced by its consequences in the conduct of human affairs.

Although man has many points of resemblance with the brutes, one trait is peculiar to himself: he improves; they are incapable of improvement. Mankind could not fail to discover this difference from the beginning. The idea of perfectibility is therefore as old as the world; equality did not give birth to it, but has imparted to it a new character.

When the citizens of a community are classed according to rank, profession, or birth and when all men are forced to follow the career which chance has opened before them, everyone thinks that the utmost limits of human power are to be discerned in proximity to himself, and no one seeks any longer to resist the inevitable law of his destiny. Not, indeed, that an aristocratic people absolutely deny man's faculty of self-improvement, but they do not hold it to be indefinite; they can conceive amelioration, but not change: they imagine that the future condition of society may be better, but not essentially different; and, while they admit that humanity has made progress and may still have some to make, they assign to it beforehand certain impassable limits.

. . .

In proportion as castes disappear and the classes of society draw together, as manners, customs, and laws vary, because of the tumultuous intercourse of men, as new facts arise, as new truths are brought to light, as ancient opinions are dissipated and others take their place, the image of an ideal but always fugitive perfection presents itself to the human mind. Continual changes are then every instant occurring under the observation of every man; the position of some is rendered worse, and he learns but too well that no people and no individual, however enlightened they may be, can lay claim to infallibility; the condition of others is improved, whence he infers that man is endowed with an indefinite faculty for improvement. His reverses teach him that none have discovered absolute good; his success stimulates him to the never ending pursuit of it. Thus, forever seeking, forever falling to rise again, often disappointed, but not discouraged, he tends unceasingly towards that unmeasured greatness so indistinctly visible at the end of the long track which humanity has yet to tread.

It can hardly be believed how many facts naturally flow from the philosophical theory of the indefinite perfectibility of man or how strong an influence it exercises even on those who, living entirely for the purposes of action and not of thought, seem to conform their actions to it without knowing anything about it.

I accost an American sailor and inquire why the ships of his country are built so as to last for only a short time; he answers without hesitation that the art of navigation is every day making such rapid progress that the finest vessel would become almost useless if it lasted beyond a few years. In these words, which fell accidentally, and on a particular subject, from an uninstructed man, I recognize the general and systematic idea upon which a great people direct all their concerns.

Aristocratic nations are naturally too liable to narrow the scope of human perfectibility; democratic nations, to expand it beyond reason.

Chapter IX

THE EXAMPLE OF THE AMERICANS DOES NOT PROVE THAT A DEMOCRATIC PEOPLE CAN HAVE NO APTITUDE AND NO TASTE FOR SCIENCE, LITERATURE, OR ART

It must be acknowledged that in few of the civilized nations of our time have the higher sciences made less progress than in the United States; and in few have great artists, distinguished poets, or celebrated writers been more rare. Many Europeans, struck by this fact, have looked upon it as a natural and inevitable result of equality; and they have thought that if a democratic state of society and democratic institutions were ever to prevail over the whole earth, the human mind would gradually find its beacon lights grow dim, and men would relapse into a period of darkness.

To reason thus is, I think, to confound several ideas that it is important to divide and examine separately; it is to mingle, unintentionally, what is democratic with what is only American.

The religion professed by the first immigrants and bequeathed by them to their descendants, simple in its forms, austere and almost harsh in its principles, and hostile to external symbols and to ceremonial pomp, is naturally unfavorable to the fine arts and yields only reluctantly to the pleasures of literature. The Americans are a very old and a very enlightened people, who have fallen upon a new and unbounded country, where they may extend themselves at pleasure and which they may fertilize without difficulty.

This state of things is without a parallel in the history of the world. In America everyone finds facilities unknown elsewhere for making or increasing his fortune. The spirit of gain is always eager, and the human mind, constantly diverted from the pleasures of imagination and the labors of the intellect, is there swayed by no impulse but the pursuit of wealth. Not only are manufacturing and commercial classes to be found in the United States, as they are in all other countries, but, what never occurred elsewhere, the whole community is simultaneously engaged in productive industry and commerce.

I am convinced, however, that if the Americans had been alone in the world, with the freedom and the knowledge acquired by their forefathers and the passions which are their own, they would not have been slow to discover that progress cannot long be made in the application of the sciences without cultivating the theory of them; that all the arts are perfected by one another: and, however absorbed they might have been by the pursuit of the principal object of their desires, they would speedily have admitted that it is necessary to turn aside from it occasionally in order the better to attain it in the end.

The taste for the pleasures of mind, moreover, is so natural to the heart of civilized man that among the highly civilized nations, which are least disposed to give themselves up to these pursuits, a certain number of persons is always to be found who take part in them. This intellectual craving, once felt, would very soon have been satisfied.

But at the very time when the Americans were naturally inclined to require nothing of science but its special applications to the useful arts and the means of rendering life comfortable, learned and literary Europe was engaged in exploring the common sources of truth and in improving at the same time all that can minister to the pleasures or satisfy the wants of man.

At the head of the enlightened nations of the Old World the inhabitants of the United States more particularly identified one to which they were closely united by a common origin and by kindred habits. Among this people they found distinguished men of science, able artists, writers of eminence; and they were enabled to enjoy the treasures of the intellect without laboring to amass them. In spite of the ocean that intervenes, I cannot consent to separate America from Europe. I consider the people of the United States as that portion of the English people who are commissioned to explore the forests of the New World, while the rest of the nation, enjoying more leisure and less harassed by the drudgery of life, may devote their energies to thought and enlarge in all directions the empire of mind.

The position of the Americans is therefore quite exceptional, and it may be believed that no democratic people will ever be placed in a similar one. Their strictly Puritanical origin, their exclusively commercial habits, even the country they inhabit, which seems to divert their minds from the pursuit of science, literature, and the arts, the proximity of Europe, which allows them to neglect these pursuits without relapsing into barbarism, a thousand special causes, of which I have only been able to point out the most important, have singularly concurred to fix the mind of the American upon purely practical objects. His passions, his wants, his education, and everything about him seem to unite in drawing the native of the United States earthward; his religion alone bids him turn, from time to time, a transient and distracted glance to heaven. Let us cease, then, to view all democratic nations under the example of the American people, and attempt to survey them at length with their own features.

It is possible to conceive a people not subdivided into any castes or scale of ranks, among whom the law, recognizing no privileges, should divide inherited property into equal shares, but which at the same time should be without knowledge and without freedom. Nor is this an empty hypothesis: a despot may find that it is his interest to render his subjects equal and to leave them ignorant, in order more easily to keep them slaves. Not only would a democratic people of this kind show neither aptitude nor taste for science, literature, or art, but it would probably never arrive at the possession of them. The law of descent would of itself provide for the destruction of large fortunes at each succeeding generation, and no new fortunes would be acquired. The poor man, without either knowledge or freedom, would not so much as conceive the idea of raising himself to wealth; and the rich man would allow himself to be degraded to poverty, without a notion of self-defense. Between these two members of the community complete and invincible equality would soon be established. No one would then have time or taste to devote himself to the pursuits or pleasures of the intellect, but all men would remain paralyzed in a state of common ignorance and equal servitude.

When I conceive a democratic society of this kind, I fancy myself in one of those low, close, and gloomy abodes where the light which breaks in from without soon faints and fades away. A sudden heaviness overpowers me, and I grope through the surrounding darkness to find an opening that will restore me to the air and the light of day. But all this is not applicable to men already enlightened who retain their freedom after having abolished those peculiar and hereditary rights which perpetuated the tenure of property in the hands of certain individuals or certain classes.

When men living in a democratic state of society are enlightened, they readily discover that they are not confined and fixed by any limits which force them to accept their present fortune. They all, therefore, conceive the idea of increasing it. If they are free, they all attempt it, but all do not succeed in the same manner. The legislature, it is true, no longer grants privileges, but nature grants them. As natural inequality is very great, fortunes become unequal as soon as every man exerts all his faculties to get rich.

The law of descent prevents the establishment of wealthy families, but it does not prevent the existence of wealthy individuals. It constantly brings back the members of the community to a common level, from which they as constantly escape; and the inequality of fortunes augments in proportion as their knowledge is diffused and their liberty increased.

.   .   .

Free and democratic communities, then, will always contain a multitude of people enjoying opulence or a competency. The wealthy will not be so closely linked to one another as the members of the former aristocratic class of society; their inclinations will be different, and they will scarcely ever enjoy leisure as secure or complete; but they will be far more numerous than those who belonged to that class of society could ever be. These persons will not be strictly confined to the cares of practical life, and they will still be able, though in different degrees, to indulge in the pursuits and pleasures of the intellect. In those pleasures they will indulge, for if it is true that the human mind leans on one side to the limited, the material, and the useful, it naturally rises on the other to the infinite, the spiritual, and the beautiful. Physical wants confine it to the earth, but as soon as the tie is loosened, it will rise of itself.

Not only will the number of those who can take an interest in the productions of mind be greater, but the taste for intellectual enjoyment will descend step by step even to those who in aristocratic societies seem to have neither time nor ability to indulge in them.

.   .   .

As soon as the multitude begins to take an interest in the labors of the mind, it finds out that to excel in some of them is a powerful means of acquiring fame, power, or wealth. The restless ambition that equality begets instantly takes this direction, as it does all others. The number of those who cultivate science, letters, and the arts, becomes immense. The intellectual world starts into prodigious activity; everyone endeavors to open for himself a path there and to draw the eyes of the public after him. Something analogous occurs to what happens in society in the United States politically considered. What is done is often imperfect, but the attempts are innumerable; and although the results of individual effort are commonly very small, the total amount is always very large.

It is therefore not true to assert that men living in democratic times are naturally indifferent to science, literature and the arts; only it must be acknowledged that they cultivate them after their own fashion and bring to the task their own peculiar qualifications and deficiencies.

Chapter X

WHY THE AMERICANS ARE MORE ADDICTED TO PRACTICAL THAN TO THEORETICAL SCIENCE

If a democratic state of society and democratic institutions do not retard the onward course of the human mind, they incontestably guide it in one direction in preference to another. Their efforts, thus circumscribed, are still exceedingly great, and I may be pardoned if I pause for a moment to contemplate them.

I had occasion, in speaking of the philosophical method of the American people, to make several remarks that it is necessary to make use of here.

Equality begets in man the desire of judging of everything for himself; it gives him in all things a taste for the tangible and the real, a contempt for tradition and for forms. These general tendencies are principally discernible in the peculiar subject of this chapter.

Those who cultivate the sciences among a democratic people are always afraid of losing their way in visionary speculation. They mistrust systems; they adhere closely to facts and study facts with their own senses. As they do not easily defer to the mere name of any fellow man, they are never inclined to rest upon any man's authority; but, on the contrary, they are unremitting in their efforts to find out the weaker points of their neighbor's doctrine. Scientific precedents have little weight with them; they are never long detained by the subtlety of the schools nor ready to accept big words for sterling coin; they penetrate, as far as they can, into the principal parts of the subject that occupies them, and they like to expound them in the popular language. Scientific pursuits then follow a freer and safer course, but a less lofty one.

The mind, it appears to me, may divide science into three parts.

The first comprises the most theoretical principles and those more abstract notions whose application is either unknown or very remote.

The second is composed of those general truths that still belong to pure theory, but lead nevertheless by a straight and short road to practical results.

Methods of application and means of execution make up the third.

Each of these different portions of science may be separately cultivated, although reason and experience prove that no one of them can prosper long if it is absolutely cut off from the two others.

In America the purely practical part of science is admirably understood, and careful attention is paid to the theoretical portion which is immediately requisite to application. On this head the Americans always display a clear, free, original, and inventive power of mind. But hardly anyone in the United States devotes himself to the essentially theoretical and abstract portion of human knowledge. In this respect the Americans carry to excess a tendency that is, I think, discernible, though in a less degree, among all democratic nations.

Nothing is more necessary to the culture of the higher sciences or of the more elevated departments of science than meditation; and nothing is less suited to meditation than the structure of democratic society. We do not find there, as among an aristocratic people, one class that keeps quiet because it is well off; and another that does not venture to stir because it despairs of improving its condition. Everyone is in motion, some in quest of power, others of gain. In the midst of this universal tumult, this incessant conflict of jarring interests, this continual striving of men after fortune, where is that calm to be found which is necessary for the deeper combinations of the intellect? How can the mind dwell upon any single point when everything whirls around it, and man himself is swept and beaten onwards by the heady current that rolls all things in its course?

You must make the distinction between the sort of permanent agitation that is characteristic of a peaceful democracy and the tumultuous and revolutionary movements that almost always attend the birth and growth of democratic society. When a violent revolution occurs among a highly civilized people, it cannot fail to give a sudden impulse to their feelings and ideas. This is more paticularly true of democratic revolutions, which stir up at once all the classes of which a people is composed and beget at the same time inordinate ambition in the breast of every member of the community. The French made surprising advances in the exact sciences at the very time at which they were finishing the destruction of the remains of their former feudal society; yet this sudden fecundity is not to be attributed to democracy, but to the unexampled revolution that attended its growth. What happened at that period was a special incident, and it would be unwise to regard it as the test of a general principle.

Great revolutions are not more common among democratic than among other nations; I am even inclined to believe that they are less so. But there prevails among those populations a small, distressing motion, a sort of incessant jostling of men, which annoys and disturbs the mind without exciting or elevating it.

Men who live in democratic communities not only seldom indulge in meditation, but they naturally entertain very little esteem for it. A democratic state of society and democratic institutions keep the greater part of men in constant activity; and the habits of mind that are suited to an active life are not always suited to a contemplative one. The man of action is frequently obliged to content himself with the best he can get because he would never accomplish his purpose if he chose to carry every detail to perfection. He has occasion perpetually to rely on ideas that he has not had leisure to search to the bottom; for he is much more frequently aided by the seasonableness of an idea than by its strict accuracy; and in the long run he risks less in making use of some false principles than in spending his time in establishing all his principles on the basis of truth. The world is not led by long or learned demonstrations; a rapid glance at particular incidents, the daily study of the fleeting passions of the multitude, the accidents of the moment, and the art of turning them to account decide all its affairs.

In the ages in which active life is the condition of almost everyone, men are generally led to attach an excessive value to the rapid bursts and superficial conceptions of the intellect, and on the other hand to undervalue unduly its slower and deeper labors. This opinion of the public influences the judgment of the men who cultivate the sciences; they are persuaded that they may succeed in those pursuits without meditation, or are deterred from such pursuits as demand it.

There are several methods of studying the sciences. Among a multitude of men you will find a selfish, mercantile, and trading taste for the discoveries of the mind, which must not be confounded with that disinterested passion which is kindled in the heart of a few. A desire to utilize knowledge is one thing; the pure desire to know is another. I do not doubt that in a few minds and at long intervals an ardent, inexhaustible love of truth springs up, self-supported and living in ceaseless fruition, without ever attaining full satisfaction. It is this ardent love, this proud, disinterested love of what is true, that raises men to the abstract sources of truth, to draw their mother knowledge thence

The future will prove whether these passions, at once so rare and so productive, come into being and into growth as easily in the midst of democratic as in aristocratic communities. For myself, I confess that I am slow to believe it.

In aristocratic societies the class that gives the tone to opinion and has the guidance of affairs, being permanently and hereditarily placed above the multitude, naturally conceives a lofty idea of itself and of man. It loves to invent for him noble pleasures, to carve out splendid objects for his ambition. Aristocracies often commit very tyrannical and inhuman actions, but they rarely entertain groveling thoughts; and they show a kind of haughty contempt of little pleasures, even while they indulge in them. The effect is to raise greatly the general pitch of society. In aristocratic ages vast ideas are commonly entertained of the dignity, the power, and the greatness of man. These opinions exert their influence on those who cultivate the sciences as well as on the rest of the community. They facilitate the natural impulse of the mind to the highest regions of thought, and they naturally prepare it to conceive a sublime, almost a divine love of truth.

Men of science at such periods are consequently carried away towards theory; and it even happens that they frequently conceive an inconsiderate contempt for practice. "Archimedes," says Plutarch, "was of so lofty a spirit that he never condescended to write any treatise on the manner of constructing all these engines of war. And as he held this science of inventing and putting together engines, and all arts generally speaking which tended to any useful end in practice, to be vile, low, and mercenary, he spent his talents and his studious hours in writing only of those things whose beauty and subtlety had in them no admixture of necessity." Such is the aristocratic aim of science; it cannot be the same in democratic nations.

The greater part of the men who constitute these nations

are extremely eager in the pursuit of actual and physical gratification. As they are always dissatisfied with the position that they occupy and are always free to leave it, they think of nothing but the means of changing their fortune or increasing it. To minds thus predisposed, every new method that leads by a shorter road to wealth, every machine that spares labor, every instrument that diminishes the cost of production, every discovery that facilitates pleasures or augments them, seems to be the grandest effort of the human intellect. It is chiefly from these motives that a democratic people addicts itself to scientific pursuits, that it understands and respects them. In aristocratic ages science is more particularly called upon to furnish gratification to the mind; in democracies, to the body.

You may be sure that the more democratic, enlightened, and free a nation is, the greater will be the number of these interested promoters of scientific genius and the more will discoveries immediately applicable to productive industry confer on their authors gain, fame, and even power. For in democracies the working class take a part in public affairs; and public honors as well as pecuniary remuneration may be awarded to those who deserve them.

In a community thus organized, it may easily be conceived that the human mind may be led insensibly to the neglect of theory; and that it is urged, on the contrary, with unparalleled energy, to the applications of science, or at least to that portion of theoretical science which is necessary to those who make such applications. In vain will some instinctive inclination raise the mind towards the loftier spheres of the intellect; interest draws it down to the middle zone. There it may develop all its energy and restless activity and bring forth wonders. These very Americans who have not discovered one of the general laws of mechanics have introduced into navigation an instrument that changes the aspect of the world.

Assuredly I do not contend that the democratic nations of our time are destined to witness the extinction of the great luminaries of man's intelligence, or even that they will never bring new lights into existence. At the age at which the world has now arrived, and among so many cultivated nations perpetually excited by the fever of productive industry, the bonds that connect the different parts of science cannot fail to strike the observer; and the taste for practical science itself, if it is enlightened, ought to lead men not to neglect theory. In the midst of so many attempted applications of so many experiments repeated every day, it is almost impossible that general laws should not frequently be brought to light; so that great discoveries would be frequent, though great inventors may be few.

I believe, moreover, in high scientific vocations. If the democratic principle does not, on the one hand, induce men to cultivate science for its own sake, on the other it enormously increases the number of those who do cultivate it. Nor is it credible that among so great a multitude a speculative genius should not from time to time arise inflamed by the love of truth alone. Such a one, we may be sure, would dive into the deepest mysteries of nature, whatever the spirit of his country and his age. He requires no assistance in his course; it is enough that he is not checked in it. All that I mean to say is this: permanent inequality of conditions leads men to confine themselves to the arrogant and sterile research for abstract truths, while the social condition and the institutions of democracy prepare them to seek the immediate and useful practical results of the sciences. This tendency is natural and inevitable; it is curious to be acquainted with it, and it may be necessary to point it out.

Chapter XI

IN WHAT SPIRIT THE AMERICANS CULTIVATE THE ARTS

It would be to waste the time of my readers and my own if I strove to demonstrate how the general mediocrity of fortunes, the absence of superfluous wealth, the universal desire for comfort, and the constant efforts by which everyone attempts to procure it make the taste for the useful predominate over the love of the beautiful in the heart of man. Democratic nations, among whom all these things exist, will therefore cultivate the arts that serve to render life easy in preference to those whose object is to adorn it. They will habitually prefer the useful to the beautiful, and they will require that the beautiful should be useful.

But I propose to go further, and, after having pointed out this first feature, to sketch several others.

It commonly happens that in the ages of privilege the practice of almost all the arts becomes a privilege, and that every profession is a separate sphere of action, into which it is not allowable for everyone to enter. Even when productive industry is free, the fixed character that belongs to aristocratic nations gradually segregates all the persons who practice the same art till they form a distinct class, always composed of the same families, whose members are all known to each other and among whom a public opinion of their own and a species of corporate pride soon spring up. In a class or guild of this kind each artisan has not only his fortune to make, but his reputation to preserve. He is not exclusively swayed by his own interest or even by that of his customer, but by that of the body to which he belongs; and the interest of that body is that each artisan should produce the best possible workmanship. In aristocratic ages the object of the arts is therefore to manufacture as well as possible, not with the greatest speed or at the lowest cost.

When, on the contrary, every profession is open to all, when a multitude of persons are constantly embracing and abandoning it, and when its several members are strangers, indifferent to and because of their numbers hardly seen by each other, the social tie is destroyed, and each workman, standing alone, endeavors simply to gain the most money at the least cost. The will of the customer is then his only limit. But at the same time a corresponding change takes place in the customer also. In countries in which riches as well as power are concentrated and retained in the hands of a few, the use of the greater part of this world's goods belongs to a small number of individuals, who are always the same. Necessity, public opinion, or moderate desires exclude all others from the enjoyment of them. As this aristocratic class remains fixed at the pinnacle of greatness on which it stands, without diminution or increase, it is always acted upon by the same wants and affected by them in the same manner. The men of whom it is composed naturally derive from their superior and hereditary position a taste for what is extremely well made and lasting. This affects the general way of thinking of the nation in relation to the arts. It often occurs among such a people that even the peasant will rather go without the objects he covets than procure them in a state of imperfection. In aristocracies, then, the handicraftsmen work for only a limited number of fastidious customers; the profit they hope to make depends principally on the perfection of their workmanship.

Such is no longer the case when, all privileges being abolished, ranks are intermingled and men are forever rising or sinking in the social scale. Among a democratic people a number of citizens always exists whose patrimony is divided and decreasing. They have contracted, under more prosperous circumstances, certain wants, which remain after the means of satisfying such wants are gone; and they are anxiously looking out for some surreptitious method of providing for them. On the other hand, there is always in democracies a large number of men whose fortune is on the increase, but whose desires grow much faster than their fortunes, and who gloat upon the gifts of wealth in anticipation, long before they have means to obtain them. Such men are eager to find some short cut to these gratifications, already almost within their reach. From the combination of these two causes the result is that in democracies there is always a multitude of persons whose wants are above their means and who are very willing to take up with imperfect satisfaction rather than abandon the object of their desires altogether.

The artisan readily understands these passions, for he himself partakes in them. In an aristocracy he would seek to sell his workmanship at a high price to the few; he now conceives that the more expeditious way of getting rich is to sell them at a low price to all. But there are only two ways of lowering the price of commodities. The first is to discover some better, shorter, and more ingenious method of producing them; the second is to manufacture a larger quantity of goods, nearly similar, but of less value. Among a democratic population all the intellectual faculties of the workman are directed to these two objects: he strives to invent methods that may enable him not only to work better, but more quickly and more cheaply; or if he cannot succeed in that, to diminish the intrinsic quality of the thing he makes, without rendering it wholly unfit for the use for which it is intended. When none but the wealthy had watches, they were almost all very good ones; few are now made that are worth much, but everybody has one in his pocket. Thus the democratic principle not only tends to direct the human mind to the useful arts, but it induces the artisan to produce with great rapidity many imperfect commodities, and the consumer to content himself with these commodities.

Not that in democracies the arts are incapable, in case of need, of producing wonders. This may occasionally be so if customers appear who are ready to pay for time and trouble. In this rivalry of every kind of industry, in the midst of this immense competition and these countless experiments, some excellent workmen are formed who reach the utmost limits of their craft. But they rarely have an opportunity of showing what they can do; they are scrupulously sparing of their powers; they remain in a state of accomplished mediocrity, which judges itself, and, though well able to shoot beyond the mark before it, aims only at what it hits. In aristocracies, on the contrary, workmen always do all they can; and when they stop, it is because they have reached the limit of their art.

. . .

This leads me to speak of those arts which are called, by way of distinction, the fine arts. I do not believe that it is a necessary effect of a democratic social condition and of democratic institutions to diminish the number of those who cultivate the fine arts, but these causes exert a powerful influence on the manner in which these arts are cultivated. Many of those who had already contracted a taste for the fine arts are impoverished; on the other hand, many of those who are not yet rich begin to conceive that taste, at least by imitation; the number of consumers increases, but opulent and fastidious consumers become more scarce. Something analogous to what I have already pointed out in the useful arts then takes place in the fine arts; the productions of artists are more numerous, but the merit of each production is diminished. No longer able to soar to what is great, they cultivate what is pretty and elegant, and appearance is more attended to than reality.

In aristocracies a few great pictures are produced; in democratic countries a vast number of insignificant ones. In the former statues are raised of bronze; in the latter, they are modeled in plaster.

When I arrived for the first time at New York, by that part of the Atlantic Ocean which is called the East River, I was surprised to perceive along the shore, at some distance from the city, a number of little palaces of white marble, several of which were of classic architecture. When I went the next day to inspect more closely one which had particularly attracted my notice, I found that its walls were of whitewashed brick, and its columns of painted wood. All the edifices that I had admired the night before were of the same kind.

The social condition and the institutions of democracy impart, moreover, certain peculiar tendencies to all the imitative arts, which it is easy to point out. They frequently withdraw them from the delineation of the soul to fix them exclusively on that of the body, and they substitute the representation of motion and sensation for that of sentiment and thought; in a word, they put the real in the place of the ideal.

. . .

This remark as to the manner of treating a subject is no less applicable to its choice. The painters of the Renaissance generally sought far above themselves, and away from their own time, for mighty subjects which left to their imagination an unbounded range. Our painters often employ their talents in the exact imitation of the details of private life, which they have always before their eyes; and they are forever copying trivial objects, the originals of which are only too abundant in nature.

Chapter XII

WHY THE AMERICANS RAISE SOME INSIGNIFICANT MONUMENTS AND OTHERS THAT ARE VERY GRAND

I have just observed that in democratic ages monuments of the arts tend to become more numerous and less important. I now hasten to point out the exception to this rule.

In a democratic community individuals are very weak, but the state, which represents them all and contains them all in its grasp, is very powerful. Nowhere do citizens appear so insignificant as in a democratic nation; nowhere does the nation itself appear greater or does the mind more easily take in a wide survey of it. In democratic communities the imagination is compressed when men consider themselves; it expands indefinitely when they think of the state. Hence it is that the same men who live on a small scale in cramped dwellings frequently aspire to gigantic splendor in the erection of their public monuments.

The Americans have traced out the circuit of an immense city on the site which they intend to make their capital, but which up to the present time is hardly more densely peopled than Pontoise, though, according to them, it will one day contain a million inhabitants. They have already rooted up trees for ten miles around lest they should interfere with the future citizens of this imaginary metropolis. They have erected a magnificent palace for Congress in the center of the city and have given it the pompous name of the Capitol.

The several states of the Union are every day planning and erecting for themselves prodigious undertakings which would astonish the engineers of the great European nations.

Thus democracy not only leads men to a vast number of inconsiderable productions; it also leads them to raise some monuments on the largest scale; but between these two extremes there is a blank. A few scattered specimens of enormous buildings can therefore teach us nothing of the social condition and the institutions of the people by whom they were raised. I may add, though the remark is outside my subject, that they do not make us better acquainted with its greatness, its civilization, and its real prosperity. Whenever a power of any kind is able to make a whole people co-operate in a single undertaking, that power, with a little knowledge and a great deal of time, will succeed in obtaining something enormous from efforts so multiplied. But this does not lead to the conclusion that the people are very happy, very enlightened, or even very strong.

Chapter XIII

LITERARY CHARACTERISTICS
OF DEMOCRATIC TIMES

When a traveler goes into a bookseller's shop in the United States and examines the American books on the shelves, the number of works appears very great, while that of known authors seems, on the contrary, extremely small. He will first find a multitude of elementary treatises, destined to teach the rudiments of human knowledge. Most of these books were written in Europe; the Americans reprint them, adapting them to their own use. Next comes an enormous quantity of religious works, Bibles, sermons, edifying anecdotes, controversial divinity, and reports of charitable societies; lastly appears the long catalogue of political pamphlets. In America parties do not write books to combat each other's opinions, but pamphlets, which are circulated for a day with incredible rapidity and then expire.

In the midst of all these obscure productions of the human brain appear the more remarkable works of a small number of authors whose names are, or ought to be, known to Europeans.

Although America is perhaps in our days the civilized country in which literature is least attended to, still a large number of persons there take an interest in the productions of the mind and make them, if not the study of their lives, at least the charm of their leisure hours. But England supplies these readers with most of the books that they require. Almost all important English books are republished in the United States. The literary genius of Great Britain still darts its rays into the recesses of the forests of the New World.

There is hardly a pioneer's hut that does not contain a few odd volumes of Shakespeare. I remember that I read the feudal drama of *Henry V* for the first time in a log cabin.

Not only do the Americans constantly draw upon the treasures of English literature, but it may be said with truth that they find the literature of England growing on their own soil. The larger part of that small number of men in the United States who are engaged in the composition of literary works are English in substance and still more so in form. Thus they transport into the midst of democracy the ideas and literary fashions that are current among the aristocratic nation they have taken for their model. They paint with colors borrowed from foreign manners; and as they hardly ever represent the country they were born in as it really is, they are seldom popular there.

The citizens of the United States are themselves so convinced that it is not for them that books are published, that before they can make up their minds upon the merit of one of their authors, they generally wait till his fame has been ratified in England; just as in pictures the author of an original is held entitled to judge of the merit of a copy.

The inhabitants of the United States have, then, at present, properly speaking, no literature. The only authors whom I acknowledge as American are the journalists. They indeed are not great writers, but they speak the language of their country and make themselves heard. Other authors are aliens; they are to the Americans what the imitators of the Greeks and Romans were to us at the revival of learning, an object of curiosity, not of general sympathy. They amuse the mind, but they do not act upon the manners of the people.

I have already said that this state of things is far from originating in democracy alone, and that the causes of it must be sought for in several peculiar circumstances independent of the democratic principle. If the Americans, retaining the same laws and social condition, had had a different origin and had been transported into another country, I do not question that they would have had a literature. Even as they are, I am convinced that they will ultimately have one; but its character will be different from that which marks the American literary productions of our time, and that character will be peculiarly its own. Nor is it impossible to trace this character beforehand.

In an aristocratic people, among whom letters are cultivated, I suppose that intellectual occupations, as well as the affairs of government, are concentrated in a ruling class. The literary as well as the political career is almost entirely confined to this class, or to those nearest to it in rank. These premises suffice for a key to all the rest.

When a small number of the same men are engaged at the same time upon the same objects, they easily concert with one another and agree upon certain leading rules that are to govern them each and all. If the object that attracts the attention of these men is literature, the productions of the mind will soon be subjected by them to precise canons, from which it will no longer be allowable to depart. If these men occupy a hereditary position in the country, they will be naturally inclined, not only to adopt a certain number of fixed rules for themselves, but to follow those which their forefathers laid down for their own guidance; their code will be at once strict and traditional. As they are not necessarily engrossed by the cares of daily life, as they have never been so, any more than their fathers were before them, they have learned to take an interest, for several generations back, in the labors of mind. They have learned to understand literature as an art, to love it in the end for its own sake, and to feel a scholar-like satisfaction in seeing men conform to its rules. Nor is this all: the men of whom I speak began and will end their lives in easy or affluent circumstances; hence they have naturally conceived a taste for carefully chosen gratifications and a love of refined and delicate pleasures.

Moreover, a kind of softness of mind and heart, which they frequently contract in the midst of this long and peaceful enjoyment of so much welfare, leads them to put aside, even from their pleasures, whatever might be too startling or too acute. They had rather be amused than intensely excited; they wish to be interested, but not to be carried away.

Now let us fancy a great number of literary performances executed by the men, or for the men, whom I have just described, and we shall readily conceive a style of literature in which everything will be regular and prearranged. The slightest work will be carefully wrought in its least details; art and labor will be conspicuous in everything; each kind of writing will have rules of its own, from which it will not be allowed to swerve and which distinguish it from all others. Style will be thought of almost as important as thought, and the form will be no less considered than the matter; the diction will be polished, measured and uniform. The tone of the mind will be always dignified, seldom very animated, and writers will care more to perfect what they produce than to multiply their productions. It will sometimes happen that the members of the literary class, always living among themselves and writing for themselves alone, will entirely lose sight of the rest of the world, which will infect them with a false and labored style; they will lay down minute literary rules for their exclusive use, which will insensibly lead them to deviate from common sense and finally to transgress the bounds of nature. By dint of striving after a mode of parlance different from the popular, they will arrive at a sort of aristocratic jargon which is hardly less remote from pure language than is the coarse dialect of the people. Such are the natural perils of literature among aristocracies. Every aristocracy that keeps itself entirely aloof from the people becomes impotent, a fact which is as true in literature as it is in politics.

Let us now turn the picture and consider the other side of

it: let us transport ourselves into the midst of a democracy not unprepared by ancient traditions and present culture to partake in the pleasures of mind. Ranks are there intermingled and identified; knowledge and power are both infinitely subdivided and, if I may use the expression, scattered on every side. Here, then, is a motley multitude whose intellectual wants are to be supplied. These new votaries of the pleasures of mind have not all received the same education; they do not resemble their fathers; nay, they perpetually differ from themselves, for they live in a state of incessant change of place, feelings, and fortunes. The mind of each is therefore unattached to that of his fellows by tradition or common habits; and they have never had the power, the inclination, or the time to act together. It is from the bosom of this heterogeneous and agitated mass, however, that authors spring; and from the same source their profits and their fame are distributed.

I can without difficulty understand that under these circumstances I must expect to meet in the literature of such a people with but few of those strict conventional rules which are admitted by readers and writers in aristocratic times. If it should happen that the men of some one period were agreed upon any such rules, that would prove nothing for the following period; for among democratic nations each new generation is a new people. Among such nations, then, literature will not easily be subjected to strict rules, and it is impossible that any such rules should ever be permanent.

In democracies it is by no means the case that all who cultivate literature have received a literary education; and most of those who have some tinge of belles-lettres are engaged either in politics or in a profession that only allows them to taste occasionally and by stealth the pleasures of mind. These pleasures, therefore, do not constitute the principal charm of their lives, but they are considered as a transient and necessary recreation amid the serious labors of life. Such men can never acquire a sufficiently intimate knowledge of the art of literature to appreciate its more delicate beauties; and the minor shades of expression must escape them. As the time they can devote to letters is very short, they seek to make the best use of the whole of it. They prefer books which may be easily procured, quickly read, and which require no learned researches to be understood. They ask for beauties self-profferred and easily enjoyed; above all, they must have what is unexpected and new. Accustomed to the struggle, the crosses, and the monotony of practical life, they require strong and rapid emotions, startling passages, truths or errors brilliant enough to rouse them up and to plunge them at once, as if by violence, into the midst of the subject.

Why should I say more, or who does not understand what is about to follow before I have expressed it? Taken as a whole, literature in democratic ages can never present, as it does in the periods of aristocracy, an aspect of order, regularity, science, and art; its form, on the contrary, will ordinarily be slighted, sometimes despised. Style will frequently be fantastic, incorrect, overburdened, and loose, almost always vehement and bold. Authors will aim at rapidity of execution more than at perfection of detail. Small productions will be more common than bulky books; there will be more wit than erudition, more imagination than profundity; and literary performances will bear marks of an untutored and rude vigor of thought, frequently of great variety and singular fecundity. The object of authors will be to astonish rather than to please, and to stir the passions more than to charm the taste.

Here and there, indeed, writers will doubtless occur who will choose a different track and who, if they are gifted with superior abilities, will succeed in finding readers in spite of their defects or their better qualities; but these exceptions will be rare, and even the authors who so depart from the received practice in the main subject of their works will always relapse into it in some lesser details.

I have just depicted two extreme conditions, but nations never leap from the first to the second; they reach it only by stages and through infinite gradation. In the progress that an educated people makes from the one to the other, there is almost always a moment when the literary genius of democratic nations coinciding with that of aristocratic nations, both seek to establish their sway jointly over the human mind. Such epochs are transient, but very brilliant; they are fertile without exuberance, and animated without confusion. The French literature of the eighteenth century may serve as an example.

I should say more than I mean if I were to assert that the literature of a nation is always subordinate to its social state and its political constitution. I am aware that, independently of these causes, there are several others which confer certain characteristics on literary productions; but these appear to me to be the chief. The relations that exist between the social and political condition of a people and the genius of its authors are always numerous; whoever knows the one is never completely ignorant of the other.

Chapter XIV

THE TRADE OF LITERATURE

Democracy not only infuses a taste for letters among the trading classes, but introduces a trading spirit into literature.

In aristocracies readers are fastidious and few in number; in democracies they are far more numerous and far less difficult to please. The consequence is that among aristocratic nations no one can hope to succeed without great exertion, and this exertion may earn great fame, but can never procure much money; while among democratic nations a writer may flatter himself that he will obtain at a cheap rate a moderate reputation and a large fortune. For this purpose he need not be admired; it is enough that he is liked.

The ever increasing crowd of readers and their continual craving for something new ensure the sale of books that nobody much esteems.

In democratic times the public frequently treat authors as kings do their courtiers; they enrich and despise them. What more is needed by the venal souls who are born in courts or are worthy to live there?

Democratic literature is always infested with a tribe of writers who look upon letters as a mere trade; and for some few great authors who adorn it, you may reckon thousands of idea-mongers.

Chapter XV

THE STUDY OF GREEK AND LATIN LITERATURE IS PECULIARLY USEFUL IN DEMOCRATIC COMMUNITIES

What was called the People in the most democratic republics of antiquity was very unlike what we designate by that term. In Athens all the citizens took part in public affairs; but there were only twenty thousand citizens to more than three hundred and fifty thousand inhabitants. All the rest were slaves, and discharged the greater part of those duties which belong at the present day to the lower or even to the middle classes. Athens, then, with her universal suffrage, was, after all, merely an aristocratic republic, in which all the nobles had an equal right to the government.

The struggle between the patricians and plebeians of Rome must be considered in the same light: it was simply an internal feud between the elder and younger branches of the same family. All belonged to the aristocracy and all had the aristocratic spirit.

It is to be remarked, moreover, that, among the ancients books were always scarce and dear, and that very great difficulties impeded their publication and circulation. These circumstances concentrated literary tastes and habits among a small number of men, who formed a small literary aristocracy out of the choicer spirits of the great political aristocracy. Accordingly, nothing goes to prove that literature was ever treated as a trade among the Greeks and Romans.

These communities, which were not only aristocracies, but very polished and free nations, of course imparted to their literary productions the special defects and merits that characterize the literature of aristocratic times. And indeed a very superficial survey of the works of ancient authors will suffice to convince us that if those writers were sometimes deficient in variety and fertility in their subjects, or in boldness, vivacity, and power of generalization in their thoughts, they always displayed exquisite care and skill in their details. Nothing in their works seems to be done hastily or at random; every line is written for the eye of the connoisseur and is shaped after some conception of ideal beauty. No literature places those fine qualities in which the writers of democracies are naturally deficient in bolder relief than that of the ancients; no literature, therefore, ought to be more studied in democratic times. This study is better suited than any other to combat the literary defects inherent in those times; as for their natural literary qualities, these will spring up of their own accord without its being necessary to learn to acquire them.

It is important that this point should be clearly understood. A particular study may be useful to the literature of a people without being appropriate to its social and political wants. If men were to persist in teaching nothing but the literature of the dead languages in a community where everyone is habitually led to make vehement exertions to augment or to maintain his fortune, the result would be a very polished, but a very dangerous set of citizens. For as their social and political condition would give them every day a sense of wants, which their education would never teach them to supply, they would perturb the state, in the name of the Greeks and Romans, instead of enriching it by their productive industry.

It is evident that in democratic communities the interest of individuals as well as the security of the commonwealth demands that the education of the greater number should be scientific, commercial, and industrial rather than literary.

Greek and Latin should not be taught in all the schools; but it is important that those who, by their natural disposition or their fortune, are destined to cultivate letters or prepared to relish them should find schools where a complete knowledge of ancient literature may be acquired and where the true scholar may be formed. A few excellent universities would do more towards the attainment of this object than a multitude of bad grammar-schools, where superfluous matters, badly learned, stand in the way of sound instruction in necessary studies.

All who aspire to literary excellence in democratic nations ought frequently to refresh themselves at the springs of ancient literature; there is no more wholesome medicine for the mind. Not that I hold the literary productions of the ancients to be irreproachable, but I think that they have some special merits, admirably calculated to counterbalance our peculiar defects. They are a prop on the side on which we are in most danger of falling.

Chapter XVI

HOW AMERICAN DEMOCRACY HAS MODIFIED THE ENGLISH LANGUAGE

If the reader has rightly understood what I have already said on the subject of literature in general, he will have no difficulty in understanding that species of influence which a democratic social condition and democratic institutions may exercise over language itself, which is the chief instrument of thought.

American authors may truly be said to live rather in England than in their own country, since they constantly study the English writers and take them every day for their models. But it is not so with the bulk of the population, which is more immediately subjected to the peculiar causes acting upon the United States. It is not, then, to the written, but to the spoken language that attention must be paid if we would detect the changes which the idiom of an aristocratic people may undergo when it becomes the language of a democracy.

Englishmen of education, and more competent judges than I can be of the nicer shades of expression, have frequently assured me that the language of the educated classes in the United States is notably different from that of the educated classes in Great Britain. They complain, not only that the Americans have brought into use a number of new words (the difference and the distance between the two countries might suffice to explain that much), but that these new words are more especially taken from the jargon of parties, the mechanical arts, or the language of trade. In addition to this, they assert that old English words are often used by the Americans in new acceptations; and lastly, that the inhabitants of the United States frequently intermingle phraseology in the strangest manner, and sometimes place words together which are always kept apart in the language of the mother country. These remarks, which were made to me at various times by persons who appeared to be worthy of credit, led me to reflect upon the subject; and my reflections brought me, by theoretical reasoning, to the same point at which my informants had arrived by practical observation.

In aristocracies language must naturally partake of that state of repose in which everything remains. Few new words are coined because few new things are made; and even if new things were made, they would be designated by known words, whose meaning had been determined by tradition.

. . .

The constant agitation that prevails in a democratic community tends unceasingly, on the contrary, to change the character of the language, as it does the aspect of affairs. In the midst of this general stir and competition of minds, many new ideas are formed, old ideas are lost, or reappear, or are subdivided into an infinite variety of minor shades. The consequence is that many words must fall into desuetude, and others must be brought into use.

Besides, democratic nations love change for its own sake, and this is seen in their language as much as in their politics. Even when they have no need to change words, they sometimes have the desire.

The genius of a democratic people is not only shown by the great number of words they bring into use, but also by the nature of the ideas these new words represent. Among such a people the majority lays down the law in language as well as in everything else; its prevailing spirit is as manifest in this as in other respects. But the majority is more engaged in business than in study, in political and commercial interests than in philosophical speculation or literary pursuits. Most of the words coined or adopted for its use will bear the mark of these habits; they will mainly serve to express the wants of business, the passions of party, or the details of the public administration. In these departments the language will constantly grow, while it will gradually lose ground in metaphysics and theology.

. . .

The most common expedient employed by democratic nations to make an innovation in language consists in giving an unwonted meaning to an expression already in use. This method is very simple, prompt, and convenient; no learning is required to use it correctly and ignorance itself rather facilitates the practice; but that practice is most dangerous to the language. When a democratic people double the meaning of a word in this way, they sometimes render the meaning which it retains as ambiguous as that which it acquires. An author begins by a slight deflection of a known expression from its primitive meaning, and he adapts it, thus modified, as well as he can to his subject. A second writer twists the sense of the expression in another way; a third takes possession of it for another purpose; and as there is no common appeal to the sentence of a permanent tribunal that may definitively settle the meaning of the word, it remains in an unsettled condition. The consequence is that writers hardly ever appear to dwell upon a single thought, but they always seem to aim at a group of ideas, leaving the reader to judge which of them has been hit.

This is a deplorable consequence of democracy. I had rather that the language should be made hideous with words imported from the Chinese, the Tatars, or the Hurons than that the meaning of a word in our own language should become indeterminate. Harmony and uniformity are only secondary beauties in composition: many of these things are conventional, and, strictly speaking, it is possible to do without them; but without clear phraseology there is no good language.

The principle of equality necessarily introduces several other changes into language.

In aristocratic ages, when each nation tends to stand aloof from all others and likes to have a physiognomy of its own, it often happens that several communities which have a common origin become nevertheless strangers to each other; so that, without ceasing to understand the same language, they no longer all speak it in the same manner. In these ages each nation is divided into a certain number of classes, which see but little of each other and do not intermingle. Each of these classes contracts and invariably retains habits of mind peculiar to itself and adopts by choice certain terms which afterwards pass from generation to generation, like their estates. The same idiom then comprises a language of the poor and a language of the rich, a language of the commoner and a language of the nobility, a learned language and a colloquial one. The deeper the divisions and the more impassable the barriers of society become, the more must this be the case. I would lay a wager that among the castes of India there are amazing variations of language, and that there is almost as much difference between the language of a pariah and that of a Brahmin as there is in their dress.

When, on the contrary, men, being no longer restrained by ranks, meet on terms of constant intercourse, when castes are destroyed and the classes of society are recruited from and intermixed with each other, all the words of a language are mingled. Those which are unsuitable to the greater number perish; the remainder form a common store, whence everyone chooses pretty nearly at random. Almost all the different dialects that divided the idioms of European nations are manifestly declining; there is no patois in the New World, and it is disappearing every day from the old countries.

The influence of this revolution in social condition is as much felt in style as it is in language. Not only does everyone use the same words, but a habit springs up of using them without discrimination. The rules which style had set up are almost abolished: the line ceases to be drawn between the expressions which seem by their very nature vulgar and others which appear to be refined. Persons springing from different ranks of society carry with them the terms and expressions they are accustomed to use into whatever circumstances they may enter; thus the origin of words is lost like the origin of individuals, and there is as much confusion in language as there is in society.

I am aware that in the classification of words there are rules which do not belong to one form of society any more than to another, but which are derived from the nature of things. Some expressions and phrases are vulgar because the ideas they are meant to express are low in themselves; others are of a higher character because the objects they are intended to designate are naturally lofty. No intermixture of ranks will ever efface these differences. But the principle of equality cannot fail to root out whatever is merely conventional and arbitrary in the forms of thought. Perhaps the necessary classification that I have just pointed out will always be less respected by a democratic people than by any other, because among such a people there are no men who are permanently disposed, by education, culture, and leisure, to study the natural laws of language and who cause those laws to be respected by their own observance of them.

I shall not leave this topic without touching on a feature of democratic languages that is, perhaps, more characteristic of them than any other. It has already been shown that democratic nations have a taste and sometimes a passion for general ideas, and that this arises from their peculiar merits and defects. This liking for general ideas is displayed in democratic languages by the continual use of generic terms or abstract expressions and by the manner in which they are employed. This is the great merit and the great imperfection of these languages.

Democratic nations are passionately addicted to generic terms and abstract expressions because these modes of speech enlarge thought and assist the operations of the mind by enabling it to include many objects in a small compass. A democratic writer will be apt to speak of *capacities* in the abstract for men of capacity and without specifying the objects to which their capacity is applied; he will talk about *actualities* to designate in one word the things passing before his eyes at the moment; and, in French, he will comprehend under the term *éventualités* whatever may happen in the universe, dating from the moment at which he speaks. Democratic writers are perpetually coining abstract words of this kind, in which they sublimate into further abstraction the abstract terms of the language. Moreover, to render their mode of speech more succinct, they personify the object of these abstract terms and make it act like a real person. Thus they would say in French: *La force des choses veut que les capacités gouvernent*.

I cannot better illustrate what I mean than by my own example. I have frequently used the word *equality* in an absolute sense; nay, I have personified equality in several places; thus I have said that equality does such and such things or refrains from doing others. It may be affirmed that the writers of the age of Louis XIV would not have spoken in this manner; they would never have thought of using the word *equality* without applying it to some particular thing; and they would rather have renounced the term altogether than have consented to make it a living personage.

These abstract terms which abound in democratic languages, and which are used on every occasion without attaching them to any particular fact, enlarge and obscure the thoughts they are intended to convey; they render the mode of speech more succinct and the idea contained in it less clear. But with regard to language, democratic nations prefer obscurity to labor.

Chapter XVII

OF SOME SOURCES OF POETRY
AMONG DEMOCRATIC NATIONS

Many different meanings have been given to the word *poetry*. It would weary my readers if I were to discuss which of these definitions ought to be selected; I prefer telling them at once that which I have chosen. In my opinion, Poetry is the search after, and the delineation of, the Ideal.

The Poet is he who, by suppressing a part of what exists, by adding some imaginary touches to the picture, and by combining certain real circumstances that do not in fact happen together, completes and extends the work of nature. Thus the object of poetry is not to represent what is true, but to adorn it and to present to the mind some loftier image. Verse, regarded as the ideal beauty of language, may be eminently poetical; but verse does not of itself constitute poetry.

I now proceed to inquire whether among the actions, the sentiments, and the opinions of democratic nations there are any which lead to a conception of the ideal, and which may for this reason be considered as natural sources of poetry.

It must, in the first place, be acknowledged that the taste for ideal beauty, and the pleasure derived from the expression of it, are never so intense or so diffused among a democratic as among an aristocratic people. In aristocratic nations it sometimes happens that the body acts as it were spontaneously, while the higher faculties are bound and burdened by repose. Among these nations the people will often display poetic tastes, and their fancy sometimes ranges beyond and above what surrounds them.

But in democracies the love of physical gratification, the notion of bettering one's condition, the excitement of competition, the charm of anticipated success, are so many spurs to urge men onward in the active professions they have embraced, without allowing them to deviate for an instant from the track. The main stress of the faculties is to this point. The imagination is not extinct, but its chief function is to devise what may be useful and to represent what is real. The principle of equality not only diverts men from the description of ideal beauty; it also diminishes the number of objects to be described.

Aristocracy, by maintaining society in a fixed position, is favorable to the solidity and duration of positive religions as well as to the stability of political institutions. Not only does it keep the human mind within a certain sphere of belief, but it predisposes the mind to adopt one faith rather than another. An aristocratic people will always be prone to place intermediate powers between God and man. In this respect it may be said that the aristocratic element is favorable to poetry. When the universe is peopled with supernatural beings, not palpable to sense, but discovered by the mind, the imagination ranges freely; and poets, finding a thousand subjects to delineate, also find a countless audience to take an interest in their productions.

In democratic ages it sometimes happens, on the contrary, that men are as much afloat in matters of faith as they are in their laws. Skepticism then draws the imagination of poets back to earth and confines them to the real and visible world. Even when the principle of equality does not disturb religious conviction, it tends to simplify it and to divert attention from secondary agents, to fix it principally on the Supreme Power.

Aristocracy naturally leads the human mind to the contemplation of the past and fixes it there. Democracy, on the contrary, gives men a sort of instinctive distaste for what is ancient. In this respect aristocracy is far more favorable to poetry; for things commonly grow larger and more obscure as they are more remote, and for this twofold reason they are better suited to the delineation of the ideal.

After having deprived poetry of the past, the principle of equality robs it in part of the present. Among aristocratic nations there is a certain number of privileged personages whose situation is, as it were, without and above the condition of man; to these, power, wealth, fame, wit, refinement, and distinction in all things appear peculiarly to belong. The crowd never sees them very closely or does not watch them in minute details, and little is needed to make the description of such men poetical. On the other hand, among the same people you will meet with classes so ignorant, low, and enslaved that they are no less fit objects for poetry, from the excess of their rudeness and wretchedness, than the former are from their greatness and refinement. Besides, as the different classes of which an aristocratic community is composed are widely separated and imperfectly acquainted with each other, the imagination may always present them with some addition to, or some subtraction from, what they really are.

In democratic communities, where men are all insignificant and very much alike, each man instantly sees all his fellows when he surveys himself. The poets of democratic ages, therefore, can never take any man in particular as the subject of a piece; for an object of slender importance, which is distinctly seen on all sides, will never lend itself to an ideal conception.

Thus the principle of equality, in proportion as it has established itself in the world, has dried up most of the old springs of poetry. Let us now attempt to see what new ones it may disclose.

I am persuaded that in the end democracy diverts the imagination from all that is external to man and fixes it on man alone. Democratic nations may amuse themselves for a while with considering the productions of nature, but they are excited in reality only by a survey of themselves. Here, and here alone, the true sources of poetry among such nations are to be found; and it may be believed that the poets who neglect to draw their inspirations hence will lose all sway over the minds which they would enchant, and will be left in the end with none but unimpassioned spectators of their transports.

I have shown how the ideas of progress and of the indefinite perfectibility of the human race belong to democratic ages. Democratic nations care but little for what has been, but they are haunted by visions of what will be; in this direction their unbounded imagination grows and dilates beyond all measure. Here, then, is the widest range open to the genius of poets, which allows them to remove their performances to a sufficient distance from the eye. Democracy, which shuts the past against the poet, opens the future before him.

As all the citizens who compose a democratic community are nearly equal and alike, the poet cannot dwell upon any one of them; but the nation itself invites the exercise of his powers. The general similitude of individuals, which renders any one of them taken separately an improper subject of poetry, allows poets to include them all in the same imagery and to take a general survey of the people itself. Democratic nations have a clearer perception than any others of their own aspect; and an aspect so imposing is admirably fitted to the delineation of the ideal.

I readily admit that the Americans have no poets; I cannot allow that they have no poetic ideas. In Europe people talk a great deal of the wilds of America, but the Americans themselves never think about them; they are insensible to the wonders of inanimate nature and they may be said not to perceive the mighty forests that surround them till they fall beneath the hatchet. Their eyes are fixed upon another sight: the American people views its own march across these wilds, draining swamps, turning the course of rivers, peopling solitudes, and subduing nature. This magnificent image of themselves does not meet the gaze of the Americans at intervals only; it may be said to haunt every one of them in his least as well as in his most important actions and to be always flitting before his mind.

Nothing conceivable is so petty, so insipid, so crowded with paltry interests—in one word, so anti-poetic—as the life of a man in the United States. But among the thoughts which it suggests, there is always one that is full of poetry, and this is the hidden nerve which gives vigor to the whole frame.

In aristocratic ages each people as well as each individual is prone to stand separate and aloof from all others. In democratic ages the extreme fluctuations of men and the impatience of their desires keep them perpetually on the move, so that the inhabitants of different countries intermingle, see, listen to, and borrow from each other. It is not only the members of the same community, then, who grow more alike, communities themselves are assimilated to one another, and the whole assemblage presents to the eye of the spectator one vast democracy, each citizen of which is a nation. This displays the aspect of mankind for the first time in the broadest light. All that belongs to the existence of the human race taken as a whole, to its vicissitudes and its future, becomes an abundant mine of poetry.

The poets who lived in aristocratic ages have been eminently successful in their delineations of certain incidents in the life of a people or a man; but none of them ever ventured to include within his performances the destinies of mankind, a task which poets writing in democratic ages may attempt.

At that same time at which every man, raising his eyes above his country, begins at length to discern mankind at large, the Deity is more and more manifest to the human mind in full and entire majesty. If in democratic ages faith in positive religion be often shaken and the belief in intermediate agents, by whatever name they are called, be overcast, on the other hand men are disposed to conceive a far broader idea of Providence itself, and its interference in human affairs assumes a new and more imposing appearance to their eyes. Looking at the human race as one great whole, they easily conceive that its destinies are regulated by the same design; and in the actions of every individual they are led to acknowledge a trace of that universal and eternal plan by which God rules our race. This consideration may be taken as another prolific source of poetry which is opened in democratic times.

Democratic poets will always appear trivial and frigid if they seek to invest gods, demons, or angels with corporeal forms and if they attempt to draw them down from heaven to dispute the supremacy of earth. But if they strive to connect the great events they commemorate with the general providential designs that govern the universe and, without showing the finger of the Supreme Governor, reveal the thoughts of the Supreme Mind, their works will be admired and understood, for the imagination of their contemporaries takes this direction of its own accord.

It may be foreseen in like manner that poets living in democratic times will prefer the delineation of passions and ideas to that of persons and achievements. The language, the dress, and the daily actions of men in democracies are repugnant to conceptions of the ideal. These things are not poetical in themselves; and if it were otherwise, they would cease to be so, because they are too familiar to all those to whom the poet would speak of them. This forces the poet constantly to search below the external surface which is palpable to the senses, in order to read the inner soul; and nothing lends itself more to the delineation of the ideal than the scrutiny of the hidden depths in the immaterial nature of man. I need not traverse earth and sky to discover a wondrous object woven of contrasts, of infinite greatness and littleness, of intense gloom and amazing brightness, capable at once of exciting pity, admiration, terror, contempt. I have only to look at myself. Man springs out oɪ nothing, crosses time, and disappears forever in the bosom of God; he is seen but for a moment, wandering on the verge of the two abysses, and there he is lost.

If man were wholly ignorant of himself, he would have no poetry in him; for it is impossible to describe what the mind does not conceive. If man clearly discerned his own nature, his imagination would remain idle and would have nothing to add to the picture. But the nature of man is sufficiently disclosed for him to know something of himself, and sufficiently obscure for all the rest to be plunged in thick darkness, in which he gropes forever, and forever in vain, to lay hold on some completer notion of his being.

Among a democratic people poetry will not be fed with legends or the memorials of old traditions. The poet will not attempt to people the universe with supernatural beings, in whom his readers and his own fancy have ceased to believe; nor will he coldly personify virtues and vices, which are better received under their own features. All these resources fail him; but Man remains, and the poet needs no more. The destinies of mankind, man himself taken aloof from his country and his age and standing in the presence of Nature and of God, with his passions, his doubts, his rare prosperities and inconceivable wretchedness, will become the chief, if not the sole, theme of poetry among these nations.

Experience may confirm this assertion if we consider the productions of the greatest poets who have appeared since the world has been turned to democracy. The authors of our age who have so admirably delineated the features of Faust, Childe Harold, René, and Jocelyn did not seek to record the actions of an individual, but to enlarge and to throw light on some of the obscurer recesses of the human heart.

Such are the poems of democracy. The principle of equality does not, then, destroy all the subjects of poetry: it renders them less numerous, but more vast.

Chapter XVIII

WHY AMERICAN WRITERS AND ORATORS OFTEN USE AN INFLATED STYLE

I have frequently noticed that the Americans, who generally treat of business in clear, plain language, devoid of all ornament and so extremely simple as to be often coarse, are apt to become inflated as soon as they attempt a more poetical diction. They then vent their pomposity from one end of a harangue to the other; and to hear them lavish imagery on every occasion, one might fancy that they never spoke of anything with simplicity.

The English less frequently commit a similar fault. The cause of this may be pointed out without much difficulty. In democratic communities, each citizen is habitually engaged in the contemplation of a very puny object: namely, himself. If he ever raises his looks higher, he perceives only the immense form of society at large or the still more imposing aspect of mankind. His ideas are all either extremely minute and clear or extremely general and vague; what lies between is a void. When he has been drawn out of his own sphere, therefore, he always expects that some amazing object will be offered to his attention; and it is on these terms alone that he consents to tear himself for a moment from the petty, complicated cares that form the charm and the excitement of his life.

This appears to me sufficiently to explain why men in democracies, whose concerns are in general so paltry, call upon their poets for conceptions so vast and descriptions so unlimited.

The authors, on their part, do not fail to obey a propensity of which they themselves partake; they perpetually inflate their imaginations, and, expanding them beyond all bounds, they not infrequently abandon the great in order to reach the gigantic. By these means they hope to attract the observation of the multitude and to fix it easily upon themselves; nor are their hopes disappointed, for as the multitude seeks for nothing in poetry but objects of vast dimensions, it has neither the time to measure with accuracy the proportions of all the objects set before it nor a taste sufficiently correct to perceive at once in what respect they are out of proportion. The author and the public at once vitiate one another.

We have also seen that among democratic nations the sources of poetry are grand, but not abundant. They are soon exhausted; and poets, not finding the elements of the ideal in what is real and true, abandon them entirely and create monsters. I do not fear that the poetry of democratic nations will prove insipid or that it will fly too near the ground; I rather apprehend that it will be forever losing itself in the clouds and that it will range at last to purely imaginary regions. I fear that the productions of democratic poets may often be surcharged with immense and incoherent imagery, with exaggerated descriptions and strange creations; and that the fantastic beings of their brain may sometimes make us regret the world of reality.

Chapter XIX

SOME OBSERVATIONS ON THE DRAMA AMONG DEMOCRATIC NATIONS

When the revolution that has changed the social and political state of an aristocratic people begins to penetrate into literature, it generally first manifests itself in the drama, and it always remains conspicuous there.

The spectator of a dramatic piece is, to a certain extent, taken by surprise by the impression it conveys. He has no time to refer to his memory or to consult those more able to judge than himself. It does not occur to him to resist the new literary tendencies that begin to be felt by him; he yields to them before he knows what they are.

Authors are very prompt in discovering which way the taste of the public is thus secretly inclined. They shape their productions accordingly; and the literature of the stage, after having served to indicate the approaching literary revolution, speedily completes it altogether. If you would judge beforehand of the literature of a people that is lapsing into democracy, study its dramatic productions.

The literature of the stage, moreover, even among aristocratic nations, constitutes the most democratic part of their literature. No kind of literary gratification is so much within the reach of the multitude as that which is derived from theatrical representations. Neither preparation nor study is required to enjoy them; they lay hold on you in the midst of your prejudices and your ignorance. When the yet untutored love of the pleasures of mind begins to affect a class of the community, it immediately draws them to the stage. The theaters of aristocratic nations have always been filled with spectators not belonging to the aristocracy. At the theater alone, the higher ranks mix with the middle and the lower classes; there alone do the former consent to listen to the opinion of the latter, or at least to allow them to give an opinion at all. At the theater men of cultivation and of literary attainments have always had more difficulty than elsewhere in making their taste prevail over that of the people and in preventing themselves from being carried away by the latter. The pit has frequently made laws for the boxes.

If it be difficult for an aristocracy to prevent the people from getting the upper hand in the theater, it will readily be understood that the people will be surpreme there when democratic principles have crept into the laws and customs, when ranks are intermixed, when minds as well as fortunes are brought more nearly together, and when the upper class has lost, with its hereditary wealth, its power, its traditions, and its leisure. The tastes and propensities natural to democratic nations in respect to literature will therefore first be discernible in the drama, and it may be foreseen that they will break out there with vehemence. In written productions the literary canons of aristocracy will be gently, gradually, and, so to speak, legally modified; at the theater they will be riotously overthrown.

The drama brings out most of the good qualities and almost all the defects inherent in democratic literature. Democratic communities hold erudition very cheap and care but little for what occurred at Rome and Athens; they want to hear something that concerns themselves, and the delineation of the present age is what they demand.

.   .   .

The refined tastes and the arrogant bearing of an aristocracy, when it manages the stage, will rarely fail to lead it to make a kind of selection in human nature. Some of the conditions of society claim its chief interest, and the scenes that delineate their manners are preferred upon the stage. Certain virtues, and even certain vices, are thought more particularly to deserve to figure there; and they are applauded while all others are excluded. On the stage, as well as elsewhere, an aristocratic audience wishes to meet only persons of quality and to be moved only by the misfortunes of kings. The same remark applies to style: an aristocracy is apt to impose upon dramatic authors certain modes of expression that give the key in which everything is to be delivered. By these means the stage frequently comes to delineate only one side of man, or sometimes even to represent what is not to be met with in human nature at all, to rise above nature and to go beyond it.

In democratic communities the spectators have no such preferences, and they rarely display any such antipathies: they like to see on the stage the medley of conditions, feelings, and opinions that occurs before their eyes. The drama becomes more striking, more vulgar, and more true. Sometimes, however, those who write for the stage in democracies also transgress the bounds of human nature; but it is on a different side from their predecessors. By seeking to represent in minute detail the little singularities of the present moment and the peculiar characteristics of certain personages, they forget to portray the general features of the race.

When the democratic classes rule the stage, they introduce as much license in the manner of treating subjects as in the choice of them. As the love of the drama is, of all literary tastes, that which is most natural to democratic nations, the number of authors and of spectators, as well as of theatrical representations, is constantly increasing among these communities. Such a multitude, composed of elements so different and scattered in so many different places, cannot acknowledge the same rules or submit to the same laws. No agreement is possible among judges so numerous, who do not know when they may meet again, and therefore each pronounces his own separate opinion on the piece. If the effect of democracy is generally to question the authority of all literary rules and conventions, on the stage it abolishes them altogether and puts in their place nothing but the caprice of each author and each public.

. . .

The Americans, when they go to the theater, very broadly display all the different propensities that I have here described; but it must be acknowledged that as yet very few of them go to the theater at all. Although playgoers and plays have prodigiously increased in the United States in the last forty years, the population indulge in this kind of amusement only with the greatest reserve. This is attributable to peculiar causes, which the reader is already acquainted with and of which a few words will suffice to remind him.

The Puritans who founded the American republics not only were enemies to amusements, but they professed an especial abhorrence for the stage. They considered it as an abominable pastime; and as long as their principles prevailed with undivided sway, scenic performances were wholly unknown among them. These opinions of the first fathers of the colonies have left very deep traces on the minds of their descendants.

The extreme regularity of habits and the great strictness of morals that are observable in the United States have as yet little favored the growth of dramatic art. There are no dramatic subjects in a country which has witnessed no great political catastrophes and in which love invariably leads by a straight and easy road to matrimony. People who spend every day in the week in making money, and Sunday in

THE DRAMA AMONG DEMOCRACIES

going to church, have nothing to invite the Muse of Comedy.

A single fact suffices to show that the stage is not very popular in the United States. The Americans, whose laws allow of the utmost freedom, and even license of language in all other respects, have nevertheless subjected their dramatic authors to a sort of censorship. Theatrical performances can take place only by permission of the municipal authorities. This may serve to show how much communities are like individuals; they surrender themselves unscrupulously to their ruling passions and afterwards take the greatest care not to yield too much to the vehemence of tastes that they do not possess.

No portion of literature is connected by closer or more numerous ties with the present condition of society than the drama. The drama of one period can never be suited to the following age if in the interval an important revolution has affected the manners and laws of the nation.

The great authors of a preceding age may be read, but pieces written for a different public will not attract an audience. The dramatic authors of the past live only in books. The traditional taste of certain individuals, vanity, fashion, or the genius of an actor may sustain or resuscitate for a time the aristocratic drama among a democracy; but it will speedily fall away of itself, not overthrown, but abandoned.

Chapter XX

SOME CHARACTERISTICS OF HISTORIANS IN DEMOCRATIC TIMES

Historians who write in aristocratic ages are inclined to refer all occurrences to the particular will and character of certain individuals; and they are apt to attribute the most important revolutions in slight accidents. They trace out the smallest causes with sagacity, and frequently leave the greatest unperceived.

Historians who live in democratic ages exhibit precisely opposite characteristics. Most of them attribute hardly any influence to the individual over the destiny of the race, or to citizens over the fate of a people; but, on the other hand, they assign great general causes to all petty incidents. These contrary tendencies explain each other.

When the historian of aristocratic ages surveys the theater of the world, he at once perceives a very small number of prominent actors who manage the whole piece. These great personages, who occupy the front of the stage, arrest attention and fix it on themselves; and while the historian is bent on penetrating the secret motives which make these persons speak and act, the others escape his memory. The importance of the things that some men are seen to do gives him an exaggerated estimate of the influence that one man may possess, and naturally leads him to think that in order to explain the impulses of the multitude, it is necessary to refer them to the particular influence of some one individual.

When, on the contrary, all the citizens are independent of one another, and each of them is individually weak, no one is seen to exert a great or still less a lasting power over the community. At first sight individuals appear to be absolutely devoid of any influence over it, and society would seem to advance alone by the free and voluntary action of all the men who compose it. This naturally prompts the mind to search for that general reason which operates upon so many men's faculties at once and turns them simultaneously in the same direction.

I am very well convinced that even among democratic nations the genius, the vices, or the virtues of certain individuals retard or accelerate the natural current of a people's history; but causes of this secondary and fortuitous nature are infinitely more various, more concealed, more complex, less powerful, and consequently less easy to trace, in periods of equality than in ages of aristocracy, when the task of the historian is simply to detach from the mass of general events the particular influence of one man or of a few men. In the former case the historian is soon wearied by the toil, his mind loses itself in this labyrinth, and, in his inability clearly to discern or conspicuously to point out the influence of individuals, he denies that they have any. He prefers talking about the characteristics of race, the physical conformation of the country, or the genius of civilization, and thus abridges his own labors and satisfies his reader better at less cost.

M. de Lafayette says somewhere in his *Memoirs* that the exaggerated system of general causes affords surprising consolations to second-rate statesmen. I will add that its effects are not less consolatory to second-rate historians; it can always furnish a few mighty reasons to extricate them from the most difficult part of their work, and it indulges the indolence or incapacity of their minds while it confers upon them the honors of deep thinking.

For myself, I am of the opinion that, at all times, one great portion of the events of this world are attributable to very general facts and another to special influences. These two kinds of cause are always in operation; only their proportion varies. General facts serve to explain more things in democratic than in aristocratic ages, and fewer things are then assignable to individual influences. During periods of aristocracy the reverse takes place: special influences are stronger, general causes weaker; unless, indeed, we consider as a general cause the fact itself of the inequality of condition, which allows some individuals to baffle the natural tendencies of all the rest.

The historians who seek to describe what occurs in democratic societies are right, therefore, in assigning much to general causes and in devoting their chief attention to discover them; but they are wrong in wholly denying the special influence of individuals because they cannot easily trace or follow it.

The historians who live in democratic ages not only are prone to assign a great cause to every incident, but are also given to connect incidents together so as to deduce a system from them. In aristocratic ages, as the attention of historians is constantly drawn to individuals, the connection of events escapes them; or rather they do not believe in any such connection. To them, the thread of history seems constantly to be broken by the course of one man's life. In democratic ages, on the contrary, as the historian sees much more of actions than of actors, he may easily establish some kind of sequence and methodical order among the former.

Ancient literature, which is so rich in fine historical compositions, does not contain a single great historical system, while the poorest of modern literatures abound with them. It would appear that the ancient historians did not make sufficient use of those general theories which our historical writers are ever ready to carry to excess.

Those who write in democratic ages have another more dangerous tendency. When the traces of individual action upon nations are lost, it often happens that you see the world move without the impelling force being evident. As it becomes extremely difficult to discern and analyze the reasons that, acting separately on the will of each member of the community, concur in the end to produce movement in the whole mass, men are led to believe that this movement is involuntary and that societies unconsciously obey some superior force ruling over them. But even when the general fact that governs the private volition of all individuals is supposed to be discovered upon the earth, the principle of human free-will is not made certain. A cause sufficiently extensive to affect millions of men at once and sufficiently strong to bend them all together in the same direction may well seem irresistible, having seen that mankind do yield to it, the mind is close upon the inference that mankind cannot resist it.

Historians who live in democratic ages, then, not only deny that the few have any power of acting upon the destiny of a people, but deprive the people themselves of the power of modifying their own condition, and they subject them either to an inflexible Providence or to some blind necessity. According to them, each nation is indissolubly bound by its position, its origin, its antecedents, and its character to a certain lot that no efforts can ever change. They involve generation in generation, and thus, going back from age to age, and from necessity to necessity, up to the origin of the world, they forge a close and enormous chain, which girds and binds the human race. To their minds it is not enough to show what events have occurred: they wish to show that events could not have occurred otherwise. They take a nation arrived at a certain stage of its history and affirm that it could not but follow the track that brought it thither. It is easier to make such an assertion than to show how the nation might have adopted a better course.

In reading the historians of aristocratic ages, and especially those of antiquity, it would seem that, to be master of his lot and to govern his fellow creatures, man requires only to be master of himself. In perusing the historical volumes which our age has produced, it would seem that man is utterly powerless over himself and over all around him. The historians of antiquity taught how to command; those of our time teach only how to obey; in their writings the author often appears great, but humanity is always diminutive.

If this doctrine of necessity, which is so attractive to those who write history in democratic ages, passes from authors to their readers till it infects the whole mass of the community and gets possession of the public mind, it will soon paralyze the activity of modern society and reduce Christians to the level of the Turks.

Moreover, I would observe that such doctrines are peculiarly dangerous at the period at which we have arrived. Our contemporaries are only too prone to doubt of human free-will, because each of them feels himself confined on every side by his own weakness; but they are still willing to acknowledge the strength and independence of men united in society. Do not let this principle be lost sight of, for the great object in our time is to raise the faculties of men, not to complete their prostration.

Chapter XXI

OF PARLIAMENTARY ELOQUENCE
IN THE UNITED STATES

Among aristocratic nations all the members of the community are connected with and dependent upon each other; the graduated scale of different ranks acts as a tie which keeps everyone in his proper place and the whole body in subordination. Something of the same kind always occurs in the political assemblies of these nations. Parties naturally range themselves under certain leaders, whom they obey by a sort of instinct, which is only the result of habits contracted elsewhere. They carry the manners of general society into the lesser assemblage.

In democratic countries it often happens that a great number of citizens are tending to the same point; but each one moves thither, or at least flatters himself that he moves only of his own accord. Accustomed to regulate his doings by personal impulse alone, he does not willingly submit to dictation from without. This taste and habit of independence accompany him into the councils of the nation. If he consents to connect himself with other men in the prosecution of the same purpose, at least he chooses to remain free to contribute to the common success after his own fashion. Hence it is that in democratic countries parties are so impatient of control and are never manageable except in moments of great public danger. Even then the authority of leaders, which under such circumstances may be able to make men act or speak, hardly ever reaches the extent of making them keep silence.

Among aristocratic nations the members of political

assemblies are at the same time members of the aristocracy. Each of them enjoys high established rank in his own right; and the position that he occupies in the assembly is often less important in his eyes than that which he fills in the country. This consoles him for playing no part in the discussion of public affairs and restrains him from too eagerly attempting to play an insignificant one.

In America it generally happens that a representative becomes somebody only from his position in the assembly. He is therefore perpetually haunted by a craving to acquire importance there, and he feels a petulant desire to be constantly obtruding his opinions upon his fellow members. His own vanity is not the only stimulant which urges him on in this course, but also that of his constituents and the continual necessity of propitiating them. Among aristocratic nations a member of the legislature is rarely in strict dependence upon his constituents: he is frequently to them a sort of unavoidable representative; sometimes they are themselves strictly dependent upon him, and if, at length, they reject him, he may easily get elected elsewhere or, retiring from public life, he may still enjoy the pleasures of splendid idleness. In a democratic country, like the United States, a representative has hardly ever a lasting hold on the minds of his constituents. However small an electoral body may be, the fluctuations of democracy are constantly changing its aspect; it must therefore be courted unceasingly. A representative is never sure of his supporters, and, if they forsake him, he is left without a resource; for his natural position is not sufficiently elevated for him to be easily known to those not close to him; and, with the complete state of independence prevailing among the people, he cannot hope that his friends or the government will send him down to be returned by an electoral body unacquainted with him. The seeds of his fortune, therefore, are sown in his own neighborhood; from that nook of earth he must start, to raise himself to command the people and to influence the destinies of the world. Thus it is natural that in democratic countries the members of political assemblies should think more of their constituents than of their party, while in aristocracies they think more of their party than of their constituents.

But what ought to be said to gratify constituents is not always what ought to be said in order to serve the party to which representatives profess to belong. The general interest of a party frequently demands that members belonging to it should not speak on great questions which they understand imperfectly; that they should speak but little on those minor questions, which impede the great ones; lastly, and for the most part, that they should not speak at all. To keep silence is the most useful service that an indifferent spokesman can render to the commonwealth.

Constituents, however, do not think so. The population of a district send a representative to take a part in the government of a country because they entertain a very high notion of his merits. As men appear greater in proportion to the littleness of the objects by which they are surrounded, it may be assumed that the opinion entertained of the delegate will be so much the higher as talents are more rare among his constituents. It will therefore frequently happen that the less constituents ought to expect from their representative, the more they anticipate from him; and however incompetent he may be, they will not fail to call upon him for signal exertions, corresponding to the rank they have conferred upon him.

Independently of his position as a legislator of the state, electors also regard their representative as the natural patron of the constituency in the legislature; they almost consider him as the proxy of each of his supporters, and they flatter themselves that he will not be less zealous in defense of their private interests than of those of the country. Thus

electors are well assured beforehand that the representative
of their choice will be an orator, that he will speak often if he
can, and that, in case he is forced to refrain, he will strive at
any rate to compress into his less frequent orations an
inquiry into all the great questions of state, combined with a
statement of all the petty grievances they have themselves to
complain of; so that, even though he is not able to come
forward frequently, he should on each occasion prove what
he is capable of doing; and that, instead of perpetually
lavishing his powers, he should occasionally condense them
in a small compass, so as to furnish a sort of complete and
brilliant epitome of his constituents and of himself. On these
terms they will vote for him at the next election.

These conditions drive worthy men of humble abilities to
despair; who, knowing their own powers, would never
voluntarily have come forward. But thus urged on, the
representative begins to speak, to the great alarm of his
friends; and rushing imprudently into the midst of the most
celebrated orators, he perplexes the debate and wearies the
House.

All laws that tend to make the representative more
dependent on the elector affect not only the conduct of the
legislators, as I have remarked elsewhere, but also their
language. They exercise a simultaneous influence on affairs
themselves and on the manner in which affairs are discussed.

There is hardly a member of Congress who can make up
his mind to go home without having dispatched at least one
speech to his constituents, or who will endure any inter-
ruption until he has introduced into his harangue whatever
useful suggestions may be made touching the four-and-
twenty states of which the Union is composed, and especially the district that he represents. He therefore presents to
the mind of his auditors a succession of great general truths
(which he himself comprehends and expresses only con-
fusedly) and of petty minutiæ, which he is but too able to

discover and to point out. The consequence is that the debates of that great assembly are frequently vague and perplexed and that they seem to drag their slow length along rather than to advance towards a distinct object. Some such state of things will, I believe, always arise in the public assemblies of democracies.

SECOND BOOK

INFLUENCE OF DEMOCRACY ON THE FEELINGS OF THE AMERICANS

Chapter I

WHY DEMOCRATIC NATIONS SHOW A MORE ARDENT AND ENDURING LOVE OF EQUALITY THAN OF LIBERTY

The first and most intense passion that is produced by equality of condition is, I need hardly say, the love of that equality. My readers will therefore not be surprised that I speak of this feeling before all others.

Everybody has remarked that in our time, and especially in France, this passion for equality is every day gaining ground in the human heart. It has been said a hundred times that our contemporaries are far more ardently and tenaciously attached to equality than to freedom; but as I do not find that the causes of the fact have been sufficiently analyzed, I shall endeavor to point them out.

It is possible to imagine an extreme point at which freedom and equality would meet and blend. Let us suppose that all the people take a part in the government, and that each of them has an equal right to take part in it. As no one is different from his fellows, none can exercise a tyrannical power; men will be perfectly free because they are all entirely equal; and they will all be perfectly equal because they are entirely free. To this ideal state democratic nations tend. This is the only complete form that equality can assume upon earth; but there are a thousand others which, without being equally perfect, are not less cherished by those nations.

The principle of equality may be established in civil society without prevailing in the political world. There may be equal rights of indulging in the same pleasures, of entering the same professions, of frequenting the same places; in a word, of living in the same manner and seeking wealth by the same means, although all men do not take an equal share in the government. A kind of equality may even be established in the political world though there should be no political freedom there. A man may be the equal of all his countrymen save one, who is the master of all without distinction and who selects equally from among them all the agents of his power. Several other combinations might be easily imagined by which very great equality would be united to institutions more or less free or even to institutions wholly without freedom.

Although men cannot become absolutely equal unless they are entirely free, and consequently equality, pushed to its furthest extent, may be confounded with freedom, yet there is good reason for distinguishing the one from the other. The taste which men have for liberty and that which they feel for equality are, in fact, two different things; and I am not afraid to add that among democratic nations they are two unequal things.

Upon close inspection it will be seen that there is in every age some peculiar and preponderant fact with which all others are connected; this fact almost always gives birth to some pregnant idea or some ruling passion, which attracts to itself and bears away in its course all the feelings and opinions of the time; it is like a great stream towards which each of the neighboring rivulets seems to flow.

Freedom has appeared in the world at different times and under various forms; it has not been exclusively bound to any social condition, and it is not confined to democracies. Freedom cannot, therefore, form the distinguishing characteristic of democratic ages. The peculiar and preponderant fact that marks those ages as its own is the equality of condition; the ruling passion of men in those periods is the love of this equality. Do not ask what singular charm the men of democratic ages find in being equal, or what special reasons they may have for clinging so tenaciously to equality rather than to the other advantages that society holds out to them: equality is the distinguishing characteristic of the age they live in; that of itself is enough to explain that they prefer it to all the rest.

But independently of this reason there are several others which will at all times habitually lead men to prefer equality to freedom.

If a people could ever succeed in destroying, or even in diminishing the equality that prevails in its own body, they could do so only by long and laborious efforts. Their social condition must be modified, their laws abolished, their opinions superseded, their habits changed, their manners corrupted. But political liberty is more easily lost; to neglect to hold it fast is to allow it to escape. Therefore not only do men cling to equality because it is dear to them; they also adhere to it because they think it will last forever.

That political freedom in its excesses may compromise the tranquillity, the property, the lives of individuals is obvious even to narrow and unthinking minds. On the contrary, none but attentive and clear-sighted men perceive the perils with which equality threatens us, and they commonly avoid pointing them out. They know that the calamities they apprehend are remote and flatter themselves that they will only fall upon future generations, for which the present generation takes but little thought. The evils that freedom sometimes brings with it are immediate; they are apparent to all, and all are more or less affected by them. The evils that extreme equality may produce are slowly disclosed; they creep gradually into the social frame; they are seen only at intervals; and at the moment at which they become most violent, habit already causes them to be no longer felt.

The advantages that freedom brings are shown only by the lapse of time, and it is always easy to mistake the cause in which they originate. The advantages of equality are immediate, and they may always be traced from their source.

Political liberty bestows exalted pleasures from time to time upon a certain number of citizens. Equality every day confers a number of small enjoyments on every man. The charms of equality are every instant felt and are within the reach of all; the noblest hearts are not insensible to them, and the most vulgar souls exult in them. The passion that equality creates must therefore be at once strong and general. Men cannot enjoy political liberty unpurchased by some sacrifices, and they never obtain it without great exertions. But the pleasures of equality are self-proffered; each of the petty incidents of life seems to occasion them, and in order to taste them, nothing is required but to live.

Democratic nations are at all times fond of equality, but there are certain epochs at which the passion they entertain for it swells to the height of fury. This occurs at the moment when the old social system, long menaced, is overthrown after a severe internal struggle, and the barriers of rank are at length thrown down. At such times men pounce upon equality as their booty, and they cling to it as to some precious treasure which they fear to lose. The passion for equality penetrates on every side into men's hearts, expands there, and fills them entirely. Tell them not that by this blind surrender of themselves to an exclusive passion they risk their dearest interests; they are deaf. Show them not freedom escaping from their grasp while they are looking another way; they are blind, or rather they can discern but one object to be desired in the universe.

What I have said is applicable to all democratic nations; what I am about to say concerns the French alone. Among most modern nations, and especially among all those of the continent of Europe, the taste and the idea of freedom began to exist and to be developed only at the time when social conditions were tending to equality and as a consequence of that very equality. Absolute kings were the most efficient levelers of ranks among their subjects. Among these nations equality preceded freedom; equality was therefore a fact of some standing when freedom was still a novelty; the one had already created customs, opinions, and laws belonging to it when the other, alone and for the first time, came into actual existence. Thus the latter was still only an affair of opinion and of taste while the former had already crept into the habits of the people, possessed itself of their manners, and given a particular turn to the smallest actions in their lives. Can it be wondered at that the men of our own time prefer the one to the other?

I think that democratic communities have a natural taste for freedom; left to themselves, they will seek it, cherish it, and view any privation of it with regret. But for equality their passion is ardent, insatiable, incessant, invincible; they call for equality in freedom; and if they cannot obtain that, they still call for equality in slavery. They will endure poverty, servitude, barbarism, but they will not endure aristocracy.

This is true at all times, and especially in our own day. All men and all powers seeking to cope with this irresistible passion will be overthrown and destroyed by it. In our age freedom cannot be established without it, and despotism itself cannot reign without its support.

Chapter II

OF INDIVIDUALISM IN DEMOCRATIC COUNTRIES

I have shown how it is that in ages of equality every man seeks for his opinions within himself; I am now to show how it is that in the same ages all his feelings are turned towards himself alone. *Individualism* is a novel expression, to which a novel idea has given birth. Our fathers were only acquainted with *egoïsme* (selfishness). Selfishness is a passionate and exaggerated love of self, which leads a man to connect everything with himself and to prefer himself to everything in the world. Individualism is a mature and calm feeling, which disposes each member of the community to sever himself from the mass of his fellows and to draw apart with his family and his friends, so that after he has thus formed a little circle of his own, he willingly leaves society at large to itself. Selfishness originates in blind instinct; individualism proceeds from erroneous judgment more than from depraved feelings; it originates as much in deficiencies of mind as in perversity of heart.

Selfishness blights the germ of all virtue; individualism, at first, only saps the virtues of public life; but in the long run it attacks and destroys all others and is at length absorbed in downright selfishness. Selfishness is a vice as old as the world, which does not belong to one form of society more than to another; individualism is of democratic origin, and it threatens to spread in the same ratio as the equality of condition.

Among aristocratic nations, as families remain for centuries in the same condition, often on the same spot, all generations become, as it were, contemporaneous. A man almost always knows his forefathers and respects them; he thinks he already sees his remote descendants and he loves them. He willingly imposes duties on himself towards the former and the latter, and he will frequently sacrifice his personal gratifications to those who went before and to those who will come after him. Aristocratic institutions, moreover, have the effect of closely binding every man to several of his fellow citizens. As the classes of an aristocratic people are strongly marked and permanent, each of them is regarded by its own members as a sort of lesser country, more tangible and more cherished than the country at large. As in aristocratic communities all the citizens occupy fixed positions, one above another, the result is that each of them always sees a man above himself whose patronage is necessary to him, and below himself another man whose co-operation he may claim. Men living in aristocratic ages are therefore almost always closely attached to something placed out of their own sphere, and they are often disposed to forget themselves. It is true that in these ages the notion of human fellowship is faint and that men seldom think of sacrificing themselves for mankind; but they often sacrifice themselves for other men. In democratic times, on the contrary, when the duties of each individual to the race are much more clear, devoted service to any one man becomes more rare; the bond of human affection is extended, but it is relaxed.

Among democratic nations new families are constantly springing up, others are constantly falling away, and all that remain change their condition; the woof of time is every instant broken and the track of generations effaced. Those who went before are soon forgotten; of those who will come after, no one has any idea: the interest of man is confined to those in close propinquity to himself. As each class gradually approaches others and mingles with them, its members become undifferentiated and lose their class identity for each other. Aristocracy had made a chain of all the members of the community, from the peasant to the king; democracy breaks that chain and severs every link of it.

As social conditions become more equal, the number of persons increases who, although they are neither rich nor powerful enough to exercise any great influence over their fellows, have nevertheless acquired or retained sufficient education and fortune to satisfy their own wants. They owe nothing to any man, they expect nothing from any man; they acquire the habit of always considering themselves as standing alone, and they are apt to imagine that their whole destiny is in their own hands.

Thus not only does democracy make every man forget his ancestors, but it hides his descendants and separates his contemporaries from him; it throws him back forever upon himself alone and threatens in the end to confine him entirely within the solitude of his own heart.

Chapter III

INDIVIDUALISM STRONGER AT THE CLOSE OF A DEMOCRATIC REVOLUTION THAN AT OTHER PERIODS

The period when the construction of democratic society upon the ruins of an aristocracy has just been completed is especially that at which this isolation of men from one another and the selfishness resulting from it most forcibly strike the observer. Democratic communities not only contain a large number of independent citizens, but are constantly filled with men who, having entered but yesterday upon their independent condition, are intoxicated with their new power.

. . .

It is, then, commonly at the outset of democratic society that citizens are most disposed to live apart. Democracy leads men not to draw near to their fellow creatures; but democratic revolutions lead them to shun each other and perpetuate in a state of equality the animosities that the state of inequality created.

The great advantage of the Americans is that they have arrived at a state of democracy without having to endure a democratic revolution, and that they are born equal instead of becoming so.

Chapter IV

THAT THE AMERICANS COMBAT THE EFFECTS OF INDIVIDUALISM BY FREE INSTITUTIONS

Despotism, which by its nature is suspicious, sees in the separation among men the surest guarantee of its continuance, and it usually makes every effort to keep them separate. No vice of the human heart is so acceptable to it as selfishness: a despot easily forgives his subjects for not loving him, provided they do not love one another. He does not ask them to assist him in governing the state; it is enough that they do not aspire to govern it themselves. He stigmatizes as turbulent and unruly spirits those who would combine their exertions to promote the prosperity of the community; and, perverting the natural meaning of words, he applauds as good citizens those who have no sympathy for any but themselves.

Thus the vices which despotism produces are precisely those which equality fosters. These two things perniciously complete and assist each other. Equality places men side by side, unconnected by any common tie; despotism raises barriers to keep them asunder; the former predisposes them not to consider their fellow creatures, the latter makes general indifference a sort of public virtue.

Despotism, then, which is at all times dangerous, is more particularly to be feared in democratic ages. It is easy to see that in those same ages men stand most in need of freedom. When the members of a community are forced to attend to public affairs, they are necessarily drawn from the circle of their own interests and snatched at times from self-observation. As soon as a man begins to treat of public affairs in public, he begins to perceive that he is not so independent of his fellow men as he had at first imagined, and that in order to obtain their support he must often lend them his co-operation.

When the public govern, there is no man who does not feel the value of public goodwill, or who does not endeavor to court it by drawing to himself the esteem and affection of those among whom he is to live. Many of the passions which congeal and keep asunder human hearts are then obliged to retire and hide below the surface. Pride must be dissembled; disdain dares not break out; selfishness fears its own self. Under a free government, as most public offices are elective, the men whose elevated minds or aspiring hopes are too closely circumscribed in private life constantly feel that they cannot do without the people who surround them. Men learn at such times to think of their fellow men from ambitious motives; and they frequently find it, in a manner, their interest to forget themselves.

. . .

The Americans have combated by free institutions the tendency of equality to keep men asunder, and they have subdued it. The legislators of America did not suppose that a general representation of the whole nation would suffice to ward off a disorder at once so natural to the frame of democratic society and so fatal; they also thought that it would be well to infuse political life into each portion of the territory in order to multiply to an infinite extent opportunities of acting in concert for all the members of the community and to make them constantly feel their mutual dependence. The plan was a wise one. The general affairs of a country engage the attention only of leading politicians, who assemble from time to time in the same places; and as they often lose sight of each other afterwards, no lasting ties are established between them. But if the object be to have the local affairs of a district conducted by the men who reside there, the same persons are always in contact, and they are, in a manner, forced to be acquainted and to adapt themselves to one another.

It is difficult to draw a man out of his own circle to interest him in the destiny of the state, because he does not clearly understand what influence the destiny of the state can have upon his own lot. But if it is proposed to make a road cross the end of his estate, he will see at a glance that there is a connection between this small public affair and his greatest private affairs; and he will discover, without its being shown to him, the close tie that unites private to general interest. Thus far more may be done by entrusting to the citizens the administration of minor affairs than by surrendering to them in the control of important ones, towards interesting them in the public welfare and convincing them that they constantly stand in need of one another in order to provide for it. A brilliant achievement may win for you the favor of a people at one stroke; but to earn the love and respect of the population that surrounds you, a long succession of little services rendered and of obscure good deeds, a constant habit of kindness, and an established reputation for disinterestedness will be required. Local freedom, then, which leads a great number of citizens to value the affection of their neighbors and of their kindred, perpetually brings men together and forces them to help one another in spite of the propensities that sever them.

. . .

It would be unjust to suppose that the patriotism and the zeal that every American displays for the welfare of his fellow citizens are wholly insincere. Although private interest directs the greater part of human actions in the United States as well as elsewhere, it does not regulate them all. I must say that I have often seen Americans make great and real sacrifices to the public welfare; and I have noticed a hundred instances in which they hardly ever failed to lend faithful support to one another. The free institutions which the inhabitants of the United States possess, and the political rights of which they make so much use, remind every citizen, and in a thousand ways, that he lives in society. They every instant impress upon his mind the notion that it is the duty as well as the interest of men to make themselves useful to their fellow creatures; and as he sees no particular ground of animosity to them, since he is never either their master or their slave, his heart readily leans to the side of kindness. Men attend to the interests of the public, first by necessity, afterwards by choice; what was intentional becomes an instinct, and by dint of working for the good of one's fellow citizens, the habit and the taste for serving them are at length acquired.

Many people in France consider equality of condition as one evil and political freedom as a second. When they are obliged to yield to the former, they strive at least to escape from the latter. But I contend that in order to combat the evils which equality may produce, there is only one effectual remedy: namely, political freedom.

Chapter V

OF THE USE WHICH THE AMERICANS
MAKE OF PUBLIC ASSOCIATIONS
IN CIVIL LIFE

I do not propose to speak of those political associations by the aid of which men endeavor to defend themselves against the despotic action of a majority or against the aggressions of regal power. That subject I have already treated. If each citizen did not learn, in proportion as he individually becomes more feeble and consequently more incapable of preserving his freedom single-handed, to combine with his fellow citizens for the purpose of defending it, it is clear that tyranny would unavoidably increase together with equality.

Only those associations that are formed in civil life without reference to political objects are here referred to. The political associations that exist in the United States are only a single feature in the midst of the immense assemblage of associations in that country. Americans of all ages, all conditions, and all dispositions constantly form associations. They have not only commercial and manufacturing companies, in which all take part, but associations of a thousand other kinds, religious, moral, serious, futile, general or restricted, enormous or diminutive. The Americans make associations to give entertainments, to found seminaries, to build inns, to construct churches, to diffuse books, to send missionaries to the antipodes; in this manner they found hospitals, prisons, and schools. If it is proposed to inculcate some truth or to foster some feeling by the encouragement of a great example, they form a society. Wherever at the head of some new undertaking you see the

403

government in France, or a man of rank in England, in the United States you will be sure to find an association.

I met with several kinds of associations in America of which I confess I had no previous notion; and I have often admired the extreme skill with which the inhabitants of the United States succeed in proposing a common object for the exertions of a great many men and inducing them voluntarily to pursue it.

I have since traveled over England, from which the Americans have taken some of their laws and many of their customs; and it seemed to me that the principle of association was by no means so constantly or adroitly used in that country. The English often perform great things singly, whereas the Americans form associations for the smallest undertakings. It is evident that the former people consider association as a powerful means of action, but the latter seem to regard it as the only means they have of acting.

Thus the most democratic country on the face of the earth is that in which men have, in our time, carried to the highest perfection the art of pursuing in common the object of their common desires and have applied this new science to the greatest number of purposes. Is this the result of accident, or is there in reality any necessary connection between the principle of association and that of equality?

Aristocratic communities always contain, among a multitude of persons who by themselves are powerless, a small number of powerful and wealthy citizens, each of whom can achieve great undertakings single-handed. In aristocratic societies men do not need to combine in order to act, because they are strongly held together. Every wealthy and powerful citizen constitutes the head of a permanent and compulsory association, composed of all those who are dependent upon him or whom he makes subservient to the execution of his designs.

Among democratic nations, on the contrary, all the

citizens are independent and feeble; they can do hardly anything by themselves, and none of them can oblige his fellow men to lend him their assistance. They all, therefore, become powerless if they do not learn voluntarily to help one another. If men living in democratic countries had no right and no inclination to associate for political purposes, their independence would be in great jeopardy, but they might long preserve their wealth and their cultivation: whereas if they never acquired the habit of forming associations in ordinary life, civilization itself would be endangered. A people among whom individuals lost the power of achieving great things single-handed, without acquiring the means of producing them by united exertions, would soon relapse into barbarism.

Unhappily, the same social condition that renders associations so necessary to democratic nations renders their formation more difficult among those nations than among all others. When several members of an aristocracy agree to combine, they easily succeed in doing so; as each of them brings great strength to the partnership, the number of its members may be very limited; and when the members of an association are limited in number, they may easily become mutually acquainted, understand each other, and establish fixed regulations. The same opportunities do not occur among democratic nations, where the associated members must always be very numerous for their association to have any power.

I am aware that many of my countrymen are not in the least embarrassed by this difficulty. They contend that the more enfeebled and incompetent the citizens become, the more able and active the government ought to be rendered in order that society at large may execute what individuals can no longer accomplish. They believe this answers the whole difficulty, but I think they are mistaken.

A government might perform the part of some of the

largest American companies, and several states, members of the Union, have already attempted it; but what political power could ever carry on the vast multitude of lesser undertakings which the American citizens perform every day, with the assistance of the principle of association? It is easy to foresee that the time is drawing near when man will be less and less able to produce, by himself alone, the commonest necessaries of life. The task of the governing power will therefore perpetually increase, and its very efforts will extend it every day. The more it stands in the place of associations, the more will individuals, losing the notion of combining together, require its assistance: these are causes and effects that unceasingly create each other. Will the administration of the country ultimately assume the management of all the manufactures which no single citizen is able to carry on? And if a time at length arrives when, in consequence of the extreme subdivision of landed property, the soil is split into an infinite number of parcels, so that it can be cultivated only by companies of tillers, will it be necessary that the head of the government should leave the helm of state to follow the plow? The morals and the intelligence of a democratic people would be as much endangered as its business and manufactures if the government ever wholly usurped the place of private companies.

Feelings and opinions are recruited, the heart is enlarged, and the human mind is developed only by the reciprocal influence of men upon one another. I have shown that these influences are almost null in democratic countries; they must therefore be artificially created, and this can only be accomplished by associations.

When the members of an aristocratic community adopt a new opinion or conceive a new sentiment, they give it a station, as it were, beside themselves, upon the lofty platform where they stand; and opinions or sentiments so conspicuous to the eyes of the multitude are easily introduced into the minds or hearts of all around. In democratic countries the governing power alone is naturally in a condition to act in this manner, but it is easy to see that its action is always inadequate, and often dangerous. A government can no more be competent to keep alive and to renew the circulation of opinions and feelings among a great people than to manage all the speculations of productive industry. No sooner does a government attempt to go beyond its political sphere and to enter upon this new track than it exercises, even unintentionally, an insupportable tyranny; for a government can only dictate strict rules, the opinions which it favors are rigidly enforced, and it is never easy to discriminate between its advice and its commands. Worse still will be the case if the government really believes itself interested in preventing all circulation of ideas; it will then stand motionless and oppressed by the heaviness of voluntary torpor. Governments, therefore, should not be the only active powers; associations ought, in democratic nations, to stand in lieu of those powerful private individuals whom the equality of conditions has swept away.

As soon as several of the inhabitants of the United States have taken up an opinion or a feeling which they wish to promote in the world, they look out for mutual assistance; and as soon as they have found one another out, they combine. From that moment they are no longer isolated men, but a power seen from afar, whose actions serve for an example and whose language is listened to. The first time I heard in the United States that a hundred thousand men had bound themselves publicly to abstain from spirituous liquors, it appeared to me more like a joke than a serious engagement, and I did not at once perceive why these temperate citizens could not content themselves with drinking water by their own firesides. I at last understood that these hundred thousand Americans, alarmed by the progress of drunkenness around them, had made up their minds to patronize temperance. They acted in just the same way as a man of high rank who should dress very plainly in order to inspire the humbler orders with a contempt of luxury. It is probable that if these hundred thousand men had lived in France, each of them would singly have memorialized the government to watch the public houses all over the kingdom.

Nothing, in my opinion, is more deserving of our attention than the intellectual and moral associations of America. The political and industrial associations of that country strike us forcibly; but the others elude our observation, or if we discover them, we understand them imperfectly because we have hardly ever seen anything of the kind. It must be acknowledged, however, that they are as necessary to the American people as the former, and perhaps more so. In democratic countries the science of association is the mother of science; the progress of all the rest depends upon the progress it has made.

Among the laws that rule human societies there is one which seems to be more precise and clear than all others. If men are to remain civilized or to become so, the art of associating together must grow and improve in the same ratio in which the equality of conditions is increased.

Chapter VI

OF THE RELATION BETWEEN PUBLIC ASSOCIATIONS AND THE NEWSPAPERS

When men are no longer united among themselves by firm and lasting ties, it is impossible to obtain the co-operation of any great number of them unless you can persuade every man whose help you require that his private interest obliges him voluntarily to unite his exertions to the exertions of all the others. This can be habitually and conveniently effected only by means of a newspaper; nothing but a newspaper can drop the same thought into a thousand minds at the same moment. A newspaper is an adviser that does not require to be sought, but that comes of its own accord and talks to you briefly every day of the common weal, without distracting you from your private affairs.

Newspapers therefore become more necessary in proportion as men become more equal and individualism more to be feared. To suppose that they only serve to protect freedom would be to diminish their importance: they maintain civilization. I shall not deny that in democratic countries newspapers frequently lead the citizens to launch together into very ill-digested schemes; but if there were no newspapers there would be no common activity. The evil which they produce is therefore much less than that which they cure.

The effect of a newspaper is not only to suggest the same purpose to a great number of persons, but to furnish means for executing in common the designs which they may have singly conceived. The principal citizens who inhabit an aristocratic country discern each other from afar; and if they wish to unite their forces, they move towards each other, drawing a multitude of men after them. In democratic countries, on the contrary, it frequently happens that a great number of men who wish or who want to combine cannot accomplish it because they are very insignificant and lost amid the crowd, they cannot see and do not know where to find one another. A newspaper then takes up the notion or the feeling that had occurred simultaneously, but singly, to each of them. All are then immediately guided towards this beacon; and these wandering minds, which had long sought each other in darkness, at length meet and unite. The newspaper brought them together, and the newspaper is still necessary to keep them united.

. . .

Consequently, there is a necessary connection between public associations and newspapers: newspapers make associations, and associations make newspapers; and if it has been correctly advanced that associations will increase in number as the conditions of men become more equal, it is not less certain that the number of newspapers increases in proportion to that of associations. Thus it is in America that we find at the same time the greatest number of associations and of newspapers.

This connection between the number of newspapers and that of associations leads us to the discovery of a further connection between the state of the periodical press and the form of the administration in a country, and shows that the number of newspapers must diminish or increase among a democratic people in proportion as its administration is more or less centralized. For among democratic nations the exercise of local powers cannot be entrusted to the principal members of the community as in aristocracies. Those powers must be either abolished or placed in the hands of very large numbers of men, who then in fact constitute an association permanently established by law for the purpose of administering the affairs of a certain extent of territory; and they require a journal to bring to them every day, in the midst of their own minor concerns, some intelligence of the state of their public weal. The more numerous local powers are, the greater is the number of men in whom they are vested by law; and as this want is hourly felt, the more profusely do newspapers abound.

The extraordinary subdivision of administrative power has much more to do with the enormous number of American newspapers than the great political freedom of the country and the absolute liberty of the press. If all the inhabitants of the Union had the suffrage, but a suffrage which should extend only to the choice of their legislators in Congress, they would require but few newspapers, because they would have to act together only on very important, but very rare, occasions. But within the great national association lesser associations have been established by law in every county, every city, and indeed in every village, for the purposes of local administration. The laws of the country thus compel every American to co-operate every day of his life with some of his fellow citizens for a common purpose, and each one of them requires a newspaper to inform him what all the others are doing.

. . .

Chapter VII

RELATION OF CIVIL TO POLITICAL ASSOCIATIONS

There is only one country on the face of the earth where the citizens enjoy unlimited freedom of association for political purposes. This same country is the only one in the world where the continual exercise of the right of association has been introduced into civil life and where all the advantages which civilization can confer are procured by means of it.

In all the countries where political associations are prohibited, civil associations are rare. It is hardly probable that this is the result of accident, but the inference should rather be that there is a natural and perhaps a necessary connection between these two kinds of associations.

Certain men happen to have a common interest in some concern; either a commercial undertaking is to be managed, or some speculation in manufactures to be tried: they meet, they combine, and thus, by degrees, they become familiar with the principle of association. The greater the multiplicity of small affairs, the more do men, even without knowing it, acquire facility in prosecuting great undertakings in common.

Civil associations, therefore, facilitate political association; but, on the other hand, political association singularly strengthens and improves associations for civil purposes. In civil life every man may, strictly speaking, fancy that he can provide for his own wants; in politics he can fancy no such thing. When a people, then, have any knowledge of public life, the notion of associations and the wish to coalesce present themselves every day to the minds of the whole community; whatever natural repugnance may restrain men from acting in concert, they will always be ready to combine for the sake of a party. Thus political life makes the love and practice of association more general; it imparts a desire of union and teaches the means of combination to numbers of men who otherwise would have always lived apart.

. . .

Chapter VIII

HOW THE AMERICANS COMBAT INDIVIDUALISM BY THE PRINCIPLE OF SELF-INTEREST RIGHTLY UNDERSTOOD

When the world was managed by a few rich and powerful individuals, these persons loved to entertain a lofty idea of the duties of man. They were fond of professing that it is praiseworthy to forget oneself and that good should be done without hope of reward, as it is by the Deity himself. Such were the standard opinions of that time in morals.

I doubt whether men were more virtuous in aristocratic ages than in others, but they were incessantly talking of the beauties of virtue, and its utility was only studied in secret. But since the imagination takes less lofty flights, and every man's thoughts are centered in himself, moralists are alarmed by this idea of self-sacrifice and they no longer venture to present it to the human mind. They therefore content themselves with inquiring whether the personal advantage of each member of the community does not consist in working for the good of all; and when they have hit upon some point on which private interest and public interest meet and amalgamate, they are eager to bring it into notice. Observations of this kind are gradually multiplied; what was only a single remark becomes a general principle, and it is held as a truth that man serves himself in serving his fellow creatures and that his private interest is to do good.

I have already shown, in several parts of this work, by what means the inhabitants of the United States almost always manage to combine their own advantage with that of their fellow citizens; my present purpose is to point out the general rule that enables them to do so. In the United States hardly anybody talks of the beauty of virtue, but they maintain that virtue is useful and prove it every day. The American moralists do not profess that men ought to sacrifice themselves for their fellow creatures *because* it is noble to make such sacrifices, but they boldly aver that such sacrifices are as necessary to him who imposes them upon himself as to him for whose sake they are made.

They have found out that, in their country and their age, man is brought home to himself by an irresistible force; and, losing all hope of stopping that force, they turn all their thoughts to the direction of it. They therefore do not deny that every man may follow his own interest, but they endeavor to prove that it is the interest of every man to be virtuous. I shall not here enter into the reasons they allege, which would divert me from my subject; suffice it to say that they have convinced their fellow countrymen.

Montaigne said long ago: "Were I not to follow the straight road for its straightness, I should follow it for having found by experience that in the end it is commonly the happiest and most useful track." The doctrine of interest rightly understood is not then new, but among the Americans of our time it finds universal acceptance; it has become popular there; you may trace it at the bottom of all their actions, you will remark it in all they say. It is as often asserted by the poor man as by the rich. In Europe the principle of interest is much grosser than it is in America, but it is also less common and especially it is less avowed; among us, men still constantly feign great abnegations which they no longer feel.

The Americans, on the other hand, are fond of explaining almost all the actions of their lives by the principle of self-interest rightly understood; they show with complacency how an enlightened regard for themselves constantly prompts them to assist one another and inclines them willingly to sacrifice a portion of their time and property to the welfare of the state. In this respect I think they frequently fail to do themselves justice; for in the United States as well as elsewhere people are sometimes seen to give way to those disinterested and spontaneous impulses that are natural to man; but the Americans seldom admit that they yield to emotions of this kind; they are more anxious to do honor to their philosophy than to themselves.

I might here pause without attempting to pass a judgment on what I have described. The extreme difficulty of the subject would be my excuse, but I shall not avail myself of it; and I had rather that my readers, clearly perceiving my object, would refuse to follow me than that I should leave them in suspense.

The principle of self-interest rightly understood is not a lofty one, but it is clear and sure. It does not aim at mighty objects, but attains without exertion all those at which it aims. As it lies within the reach of all capacities, everyone can without difficulty learn and retain it. By its admirable conformity to human weaknesses it easily obtains great dominion; nor is that dominion precarious, since the principle checks one personal interest by another, and uses, to direct the passions, the very same instrument that excites them.

The principle of self-interest rightly understood produces no great acts of self-sacrifice, but it suggests daily small acts of self-denial. By itself it cannot suffice to make a man virtuous; but it disciplines a number of persons in habits of regularity, temperance, moderation, foresight, self-command; and if it does not lead men straight to virtue by the will, it gradually draws them in that direction by their habits. If the principle of interest rightly understood were to sway the whole moral world, extraordinary virtues would doubtless be more rare, but I think that gross depravity would then also be less common. The principle of interest rightly understood perhaps prevents men from rising far above the level of mankind, but a great number of other men, who were falling far below it, are caught and restrained by it. Observe some few individuals, they are lowered by it; survey mankind, they are raised.

I am not afraid to say that the principle of self-interest rightly understood appears to me the best suited of all philosophical theories to the wants of the men of our time, and that I regard it as their chief remaining security against themselves. Towards it, therefore, the minds of the moralists of our age should turn; even should they judge it to be incomplete, it must nevertheless be adopted as necessary.

I do not think, on the whole, that there is more selfishness among us than in America; the only difference is that there it is enlightened, here it is not. Each American knows when to sacrifice some of his private interests to save the rest; we want to save everything, and often we lose it all. Everybody I see about me seems bent on teaching his contemporaries, by precept and example, that what is useful is never wrong. Will nobody undertake to make them understand how what is right may be useful?

No power on earth can prevent the increasing equality of conditions from inclining the human mind to seek out what is useful or from leading every member of the community to be wrapped up in himself. It must therefore be expected that personal interest will become more than ever the principal if not the sole spring of men's actions; but it remains to be seen how each man will understand his personal interest. If the members of the community, as they become more equal, become more ignorant and coarse, it is difficult to foresee to what pitch of stupid excesses their selfishness may lead them; and no one can foretell into what disgrace and wretchedness they would plunge themselves lest they should have to sacrifice something of their own well-being to the prosperity of their fellow creatures.

I do not think that the system of self-interest as it is professed in America is in all its parts self-evident, but it contains a great number of truths so evident that men, if they are only educated, cannot fail to see them. Educate, then, at any rate, for the age of implicit self-sacrifice and instinctive virtues is already flitting far away from us, and the time is fast approaching when freedom, public peace, and social order itself will not be able to exist without education.

Chapter IX

THAT THE AMERICANS APPLY THE PRINCIPLE OF SELF-INTEREST RIGHTLY UNDERSTOOD TO RELIGIOUS MATTERS

If the principle of self-interest rightly understood had nothing but the present world in view, it would be very insufficient, for there are many sacrifices that can find their recompense only in another; and whatever ingenuity may be put forth to demonstrate the utility of virtue, it will never be an easy task to make that man live aright who has no thought of dying.

It is therefore necessary to ascertain whether the principle of self-interest rightly understood can be easily reconciled with religious belief. The philosophers who inculcate this system of morals tell men that to be happy in this life they must watch their own passions and steadily control their excess; that lasting happiness can be secured only by renouncing a thousand transient gratifications; and that a man must perpetually triumph over himself in order to secure his own advantage. The founders of almost all religions have held to the same language. The track they point out to man is the same, only the goal is more remote; instead of placing in this world the reward of the sacrifices they impose, they transport it to another.

Nevertheless, I cannot believe that all those who practice virtue from religious motives are actuated only by the hope of a recompense. I have known zealous Christians who constantly forgot themselves to work with greater ardor for the happiness of their fellow men, and I have heard them declare that all they did was only to earn the blessings of a future state. I cannot but think that they deceive themselves; I respect them too much to believe them.

Christianity, indeed, teaches that a man must prefer his neighbor to himself in order to gain eternal life; but Christianity also teaches that men ought to benefit their fellow creatures for the love of God! A sublime expression! Man searches by his intellect into the divine conception and sees that order is the purpose of God; he freely gives his own efforts to aid in prosecuting this great design, and, while he sacrifices his personal interests to this consummate order of all created things, expects no other recompense than the pleasure of contemplating it.

I do not believe that self-interest is the sole motive of religious men, but I believe that self-interest is the principal means that religions themselves employ to govern men, and I do not question that in this way they strike the multitude and become popular. I do not see clearly why the principle of interest rightly understood should undermine the religious opinions of men; it seems to me more easy to show why it should strengthen them. Let it be supposed that in order to attain happiness in this world, a man combats his instincts on all occasions and deliberately calculates every action of his life; that instead of yielding blindly to the impetuosity of first desires, he has learned the art of resisting them, and that he has accustomed himself to sacrifice without an effort the pleasure of a moment to the lasting interest of his whole life. If such a man believes in the religion that he professes, it will cost him but little to submit to the restrictions it may impose. Reason herself counsels him to obey, and habit has prepared him to endure these limitations. If he should have conceived any doubts as to the object of his hopes, still he will not easily allow himself to be stopped by them; and he will decide that it is wise to risk some of the advantages of this world in order to preserve his rights to the great inheritance promised him in another. "To be mistaken in believing that the Christian religion is true," says Pascal, "is no great loss to anyone; but how dreadful to be mistaken in believing it to be false!"

Chapter X

OF THE TASTE FOR PHYSICAL WELL-BEING IN AMERICA

In America the passion for physical well-being is not always exclusive, but it is general; and if all do not feel it in the same manner, yet it is felt by all. The effort to satisfy even the least wants of the body and to provide the little conveniences of life is uppermost in every mind. Something of an analogous character is more and more apparent in Europe. Among the causes that produce these similar consequences in both hemispheres, several are so connected with my subject as to deserve notice.

When riches are hereditarily fixed in families, a great number of men enjoy the comforts of life without feeling an exclusive taste for those comforts. The heart of man is not so much caught by the undisturbed possession of anything valuable as by the desire, as yet imperfectly satisfied, of possessing it and by the incessant dread of losing it. In aristocratic communities the wealthy, never having experienced a condition different from their own, entertain no fear of changing it; the existence of such conditions hardly occurs to them. The comforts of life are not to them the end of life, but simply a way of living; they regard them as existence itself, enjoyed but scarcely thought of. As the natural and instinctive taste that all men feel for being well off is thus satisfied without trouble and without apprehension, their faculties are turned elsewhere and applied to more arduous and lofty undertakings, which excite and engross their minds.

Hence it is that in the very midst of physical gratifications the members of an aristocracy often display a haughty contempt of these very enjoyments and exhibit singular powers of endurance under the privation of them. All the revolutions which have ever shaken or destroyed aristocracies have shown how easily men accustomed to superfluous luxuries can do without the necessaries of life; whereas men who have toiled to acquire a competency can hardly live after they have lost it.

If I turn my observation from the upper to the lower classes, I find analogous effects produced by opposite causes. Among a nation where aristocracy predominates in society and keeps it stationary, the people in the end get as much accustomed to poverty as the rich to their opulence. The latter bestow no anxiety on their physical comforts because they enjoy them without an effort; the former do not think of things which they despair of obtaining and which they hardly know enough of to desire. In communities of this kind the imagination of the poor is driven to seek another world; the miseries of real life enclose it, but it escapes from their control and flies to seek its pleasures far beyond.

When, on the contrary, the distinctions of ranks are obliterated and privileges are destroyed, when hereditary property is subdivided and education and freedom are widely diffused, the desire of acquiring the comforts of the world haunts the imagination of the poor, and the dread of losing them that of the rich. Many scanty fortunes spring up; those who possess them have a sufficient share of physical gratifications to conceive a taste for these pleasures, not enough to satisfy it. They never procure them without exertion, and they never indulge in them without apprehension. They are therefore always straining to pursue or to retain gratifications so delightful, so imperfect, so fugitive.

If I were to inquire what passion is most natural to men who are stimulated and circumscribed by the obscurity of their birth or the mediocrity of their fortune, I could discover none more peculiarly appropriate to their condition than this love of physical prosperity. The passion for physical comforts is essentially a passion of the middle classes; with those classes it grows and spreads, with them it is preponderant. From them it mounts into the higher orders of society and descends into the mass of the people.

I never met in America any citizen so poor as not to cast a glance of hope and envy on the enjoyments of the rich or whose imagination did not possess itself by anticipation of those good things that fate still obstinately withheld from him.

On the other hand, I never perceived among the wealthier inhabitants of the United States that proud contempt of physical gratifications which is sometimes to be met with even in the most opulent and dissolute aristocracies. Most of these wealthy persons were once poor; they have felt the sting of want; they were long a prey to adverse fortunes; and now that the victory is won, the passions which accompanied the contest have survived it; their minds are, as it were, intoxicated by the small enjoyments which they have pursued for forty years.

Not but that in the United States, as elsewhere, there is a certain number of wealthy persons who, having come into their property by inheritance, possess without exertion an opulence they have not earned. But even these men are not less devotedly attached to the pleasures of material life. The love of well-being has now become the predominant taste of the nation; the great current of human passions runs in that channel and sweeps everything along in its course.

Chapter XI

PECULIAR EFFECTS OF THE LOVE
OF PHYSICAL GRATIFICATIONS
IN DEMOCRATIC TIMES

It may be supposed, from what has just been said, that the love of physical gratifications must constantly urge the Americans to irregularities in morals, disturb the peace of families, and threaten the security of society at large. But it is not so: the passion for physical gratifications produces in democracies effects very different from those which it occasions in aristocratic nations.

It sometimes happens that, wearied from public affairs and sated with opulence, amid the ruin of religious belief and the decline of the state, the heart of an aristocracy may by degrees be seduced to the pursuit of sensual enjoyments alone. At other times the power of the monarch or the weakness of the people, without stripping the nobility of their fortune, compels them to stand aloof from the administration of affairs and, while the road to mighty enterprise is closed, abandons them to the disquietude of their own desires; they then fall back heavily upon themselves and seek in the pleasures of the body oblivion of their former greatness.

When the members of an aristocratic body are thus exclusively devoted to the pursuit of physical gratifications, they commonly turn in that direction all the energy which they derive from their long experience of power. Such men are not satisfied with the pursuit of comfort; they require sumptuous depravity and splendid corruption. The worship they pay the senses is a gorgeous one, and they seem to vie with one another in the art of degrading their own natures. The stronger, the more famous, and the more free an aristocracy has been, the more depraved will it then become; and however brilliant may have been the luster of its virtues, I dare predict that they will always be surpassed by the splendor of its vices.

The taste for physical gratifications leads a democratic people into no such excesses. The love of well-being is there displayed as a tenacious, exclusive, universal passion, but its range is confined. To build enormous palaces, to conquer or to mimic nature, to ransack the world in order to gratify the passions of a man, is not thought of, but to add a few yards of land to your field, to plant an orchard, to enlarge a dwelling, to be always making life more comfortable and convenient, to avoid trouble, and to satisfy the smallest wants without effort and almost without cost. These are small objects, but the soul clings to them; it dwells upon them closely and day by day, till they at last shut out the rest of the world and sometimes intervene between itself and heaven.

. . .

The special taste that the men of democratic times entertain for physical enjoyments is not naturally opposed to the principles of public order; nay, it often stands in need of order that it may be gratified. Nor is it adverse to regularity of morals, for good morals contribute to public tranquillity and are favorable to industry. It may even be frequently combined with a species of religious morality; men wish to be as well off as they can in this world without forgoing their chance of another. Some physical gratifications cannot be indulged in without crime; from such they strictly abstain.

The reproach I address to the principle of equality is not that it leads men away in the pursuit of forbidden enjoyments, but that it absorbs them wholly in quest of those which are allowed. By these means a kind of virtuous materialism may ultimately be established in the world, which would not corrupt, but enervate, the soul and noiselessly unbend its springs of action.

Chapter XII

WHY SOME AMERICANS MANIFEST A SORT OF FANATICAL SPIRITUALISM

Although the desire of acquiring the good things of this world is the prevailing passion of the American people, certain momentary outbreaks occur when their souls seem suddenly to burst the bonds of matter by which they are restrained and to soar impetuously towards heaven. In all the states of the Union, but especially in the half-peopled country of the Far West, itinerant preachers may be met with who hawk about the word of God from place to place. Whole families, old men, women, and children, cross rough passes and untrodden wilds, coming from a great distance, to join a camp-meeting, where, in listening to these discourses, they totally forget for several days and nights the cares of business and even the most urgent wants of the body.

Here and there in the midst of American society you meet with men full of a fanatical and almost wild spiritualism, which hardly exists in Europe. From time to time strange sects arise which endeavor to strike out extraordinary paths to eternal happiness. Religious insanity is very common in the United States.

. . .

The soul has wants which must be satisfied; and whatever pains are taken to divert it from itself, it soon grows weary, restless, and disquieted amid the enjoyments of sense. If ever the faculties of the great majority of mankind were exclusively bent upon the pursuit of material objects, it might be anticipated that an amazing reaction would take place in the souls of some men. They would drift at large in the world of spirits, for fear of remaining shackled by the close bondage of the body.

It is not, then, wonderful if in the midst of a community whose thoughts tend earthward a small number of individuals are to be found who turn their looks to heaven. I should be surprised if mysticism did not soon make some advance among a people solely engaged in promoting their own worldly welfare.

Chapter XIII

WHY THE AMERICANS ARE SO RESTLESS IN THE MIDST OF THEIR PROSPERITY

In certain remote corners of the Old World you may still sometimes stumble upon a small district that seems to have been forgotten amid the general tumult, and to have remained stationary while everything around it was in motion. The inhabitants, for the most part, are extremely ignorant and poor; they take no part in the business of the country and are frequently oppressed by the government, yet their countenances are generally placid and their spirits light.

In America I saw the freest and most enlightened men placed in the happiest circumstances that the world affords; it seemed to me as if a cloud habitually hung upon their brow, and I thought them serious and almost sad, even in their pleasures.

The chief reason for this contrast is that the former do not think of the ills they endure, while the latter are forever brooding over advantages they do not possess. It is strange to see with what feverish ardor the Americans pursue their own welfare, and to watch the vague dread that constantly torments them lest they should not have chosen the shortest path which may lead to it.

A native of the United States clings to this world's goods as if he were certain never to die; and he is so hasty in grasping at all within his reach that one would suppose he was constantly afraid of not living long enough to enjoy them. He clutches everything, he holds nothing fast, but soon loosens his grasp to pursue fresh gratifications.

In the United States a man builds a house in which to spend his old age, and he sells it before the roof is on; he plants a garden and lets [rents] it just as the trees are coming into bearing; he brings a field into tillage and leaves other men to gather the crops; he embraces a profession and gives it up; he settles in a place, which he soon afterwards leaves to carry his changeable longings elsewhere. If his private affairs leave him any leisure, he instantly plunges into the vortex of politics; and if at the end of a year of unremitting labor he finds he has a few days' vacation, his eager curiosity whirls him over the vast extent of the United States, and he will travel fifteen hundred miles in a few days to shake off his happiness. Death at length overtakes him, but it is before he is weary of his bootless chase of that complete felicity which forever escapes him.

At first sight there is something surprising in this strange unrest of so many happy men, restless in the midst of abundance. The spectacle itself, however, is as old as the world; the novelty is to see a whole people furnish an exemplification of it.

Their taste for physical gratifications must be regarded as the original source of that secret disquietude which the actions of the Americans betray and of that inconstancy of which they daily afford fresh examples. He who has set his heart exclusively upon the pursuit of worldly welfare is always in a hurry, for he has but a limited time at his disposal to reach, to grasp, and to enjoy it. The recollection of the shortness of life is a constant spur to him. Besides the good things that he possesses, he every instant fancies a thousand others that death will prevent him from trying if he does not try them soon. This thought fills him with anxiety, fear, and regret and keeps his mind in ceaseless trepidation, which leads him perpetually to change his plans and his abode.

If in addition to the taste for physical well-being a social condition be added in which neither laws nor customs retain any person in his place, there is a great additional stimulant to this restlessness of temper. Men will then be seen continually to change their track for fear of missing the shortest cut to happiness.

It may readily be conceived that if men passionately bent upon physical gratifications desire eagerly, they are also easily discouraged; as their ultimate object is to enjoy, the means to reach that object must be prompt and easy or the trouble of acquiring the gratification would be greater than the gratification itself. Their prevailing frame of mind, then, is at once ardent and relaxed, violent and enervated. Death is often less dreaded by them than perseverance in continuous efforts to one end.

The equality of conditions leads by a still straighter road to several of the effects that I have here described. When all the privileges of birth and fortune are abolished, when all professions are accessible to all, and a man's own energies may place him at the top of any one of them, an easy and unbounded career seems open to his ambition and he will readily persuade himself that he is born to no common destinies. But this is an erroneous notion, which is corrected by daily experience. The same equality that allows every citizen to conceive these lofty hopes renders all the citizens less able to realize them; it circumscribes their powers on every side, while it gives freer scope to their desires. Not only are they themselves powerless, but they are met at every step by immense obstacles, which they did not at first perceive. They have swept away the privileges of some of their fellow creatures which stood in their way, but they have opened the door to universal competition; the barrier has changed its shape rather than its position. When men are nearly alike and all follow the same track, it is very difficult for any one individual to walk quickly and cleave a way through the dense throng that surrounds and presses on him. This constant strife between the inclination springing from the equality of condition and the means it supplies to satisfy them harasses and wearies the mind.

It is possible to conceive of men arrived at a degree of freedom that should completely content them; they would then enjoy their independence without anxiety and without impatience. But men will never establish any equality with which they can be contented.

. . .

When inequality of conditions is the common law of society, the most marked inequalities do not strike the eye; when everything is nearly on the same level, the slightest are marked enough to hurt it. Hence the desire of equality always becomes more insatiable in proportion as equality is more complete.

Among democratic nations, men easily attain a certain equality of condition, but they can never attain as much as they desire. It perpetually retires from before them, yet without hiding itself from their sight, and in retiring draws them on. At every moment they think they are about to grasp it; it escapes at every moment from their hold. They are near enough to see its charms, but too far off to enjoy them; and before they have fully tasted its delights, they die.

To these causes must be attributed that strange melancholy which often haunts the inhabitants of democratic countries in the midst of their abundance, and that disgust at life which sometimes seizes upon them in the midst of calm and easy circumstances. Complaints are made in France that the number of suicides increases; in America suicide is rare, but insanity is said to be more common there than anywhere else. These are all different symptoms of the same disease. The Americans do not put an end to their lives, however disquieted they may be, because their religion forbids it; and among them materialism may be said hardly to exist, notwithstanding the general passion for physical gratification. The will resists, but reason frequently gives way.

In democratic times enjoyments are more intense than in the ages of aristocracy, and the number of those who partake in them is vastly larger: but, on the other hand, it must be admitted that man's hopes and desires are oftener blasted, the soul is more stricken and perturbed, and care itself more keen.

Chapter XIV

HOW THE TASTE FOR PHYSICAL GRATIFICATIONS IS UNITED IN AMERICA TO LOVE OF FREEDOM AND ATTENTION TO PUBLIC AFFAIRS

When a democratic state turns to absolute monarchy, the activity that was before directed to public and to private affairs is all at once centered on the latter. The immediate consequence is, for some time, great physical prosperity, but this impulse soon slackens and the amount of productive industry is checked. I do not know if a single trading or manufacturing people can be cited, from the Tyrians down to the Florentines and the English, who were not a free people also. There is therefore a close bond and necessary relation between these two elements, freedom and productive industry.

This proposition is generally true of all nations, but especially of democratic nations. I have already shown that men who live in ages of equality have a continual need of forming associations in order to procure the things they desire; and, on the other hand, I have shown how great political freedom improves and diffuses the art of association. Freedom in these ages is therefore especially favorable to the production of wealth; nor is it difficult to perceive that despotism is especially adverse to the same result.

The nature of despotic power in democratic ages is not to be fierce or cruel, but minute and meddling. Despotism of this kind, though it does not trample on humanity, is directly opposed to the genius of commerce and the pursuits of industry.

Thus the men of democratic times require to be free in order to procure more readily those physical enjoyments for which they are always longing. It sometimes happens, however, that the excessive taste they conceive for these same enjoyments makes them surrender to the first master who appears. The passion for worldly welfare then defeats itself and, without their perceiving it, throws the object of their desires to a greater distance.

There is, indeed, a most dangerous passage in the history of a democratic people. When the taste for physical gratifications among them has grown more rapidly than their education and their experience of free institutions, the time will come when men are carried away and lose all self-restraint at the sight of the new possessions they are about to obtain. In their intense and exclusive anxiety to make a fortune they lose sight of the close connection that exists between the private fortune of each and the prosperity of all. It is not necessary to do violence to such a people in order to strip them of the rights they enjoy; they themselves willingly loosen their hold. The discharge of political duties appears to them to be a troublesome impediment which diverts them from their occupations and business. If they are required to elect representatives, to support the government by personal service, to meet on public business, they think they have no time, they cannot waste their precious hours in useless engagements; such idle amusements are unsuited to serious men who are engaged with the more important interests of life. These people think they are following the principle of self-interest, but the idea they entertain of that principle is a very crude one; and the better to look after what they call their own business, they neglect their chief business, which is to remain their own masters.

As the citizens who labor do not care to attend to public

affairs, and as the class which might devote its leisure to these duties has ceased to exist, the place of the government is, as it were, unfilled. If at that critical moment some able and ambitious man grasps the supreme power, he will find the road to every kind of usurpation open before him. If he attends for some time only to the material prosperity of the country, no more will be demanded of him. Above all, he must ensure public tranquillity: men who are possessed by the passion for physical gratification generally find out that the turmoil of freedom disturbs their welfare before they discover how freedom itself serves to promote it. If the slightest rumor of public commotion intrudes into the petty pleasures of private life, they are aroused and alarmed by it. The fear of anarchy perpetually haunts them, and they are always ready to fling away their freedom at the first disturbance.

I readily admit that public tranquillity is a great good, but at the same time I cannot forget that all nations have been enslaved by being kept in good order. Certainly it is not to be inferred that nations ought to despise public tranquillity, but that state ought not to content them. A nation that asks nothing of its government but the maintenance of order is already a slave at heart, the slave of its own well-being, awaiting only the hand that will bind it.

By such a nation the despotism of faction is not less to be dreaded than the despotism of an individual. When the bulk of the community are engrossed by private concerns, the smallest parties need not despair of getting the upper hand in public affairs. At such times it is not rare to see on the great stage of the world, as we see in our theaters, a multitude represented by a few players, who alone speak in the name of an absent or inattentive crowd: they alone are in action, while all others are stationary; they regulate everything by their own caprice; they change the laws and tyrannize at will over the manners of the country; and then men wonder to see into how small a number of weak and worthless hands a great people may fall.

Hitherto the Americans have fortunately escaped all the perils that I have just pointed out, and in this respect they are really deserving of admiration. Perhaps there is no country in the world where fewer idle men are to be *met* with than in America, or where all who work are more eager to promote their own welfare. But if the passion of the Americans for physical gratifications is vehement, at least it is not indiscriminate; and reason, though unable to restrain it, still directs its course.

An American attends to his private concerns as if he were alone in the world, and the next minute he gives himself up to the common welfare as if he had forgotten them. At one time he seems animated by the most selfish cupidity; at another, by the most lively patriotism. The human heart cannot be thus divided. The inhabitants of the United States alternately display so strong and so similar a passion for their own welfare and for their freedom that it may be supposed that these passions are united and mingled in some part of their character. And indeed the Americans believe their freedom to be the best instrument and surest safeguard of their welfare; they are attached to the one by the other. They by no means think that they are not called upon to take a part in public affairs; they believe, on the contrary, that their chief business is to secure for themselves a government which will allow them to acquire the things they covet and which will not debar them from the peaceful enjoyment of those possessions which they have already acquired.

Chapter XV

HOW RELIGIOUS BELIEF SOMETIMES TURNS THE THOUGHTS OF AMERICANS TO IMMATERIAL PLEASURES

In the United States on the seventh day of the week the trading and working life of the nations seems suspended; all noises cease; a deep tranquillity, say rather the solemn calm of meditation, succeeds the turmoil of the week, and the soul resumes possession and contemplation of itself. On this day the marts of traffic are deserted; every member of the community, accompanied by his children, goes to church, where he listens to strange language which would seem unsuited to his ear. He is told of the countless evils caused by pride and covetousness; he is reminded of the necessity of checking his desires, of the finer pleasures that belong to virtue alone, and of the true happiness that attends it. On his return home he does not turn to the ledgers of his business, but he opens the book of Holy Scripture; there he meets with sublime and affecting descriptions of the greatness and goodness of the Creator, of the infinite magnificence of the handiwork of God, and of the lofty destinies of man, his duties, and his immortal privileges.

Thus it is that the American at times steals an hour from himself, and, laying aside for a while the petty passions which agitate his life, and the ephemeral interests which engross it, he strays at once into an ideal world, where all is great, eternal, and pure.

I have endeavored to point out, in another part of this

work, the causes to which the maintenance of the political institutions of the Americans is attributable, and religion appeared to be one of the most prominent among them. I am now treating of the Americans in an individual capacity, and I again observe that religion is not less useful to each citizen than to the whole state. The Americans show by their practice that they feel the high necessity of imparting morality to democratic communities by means of religion.

· · ·

If it be easy to see that it is more particularly important in democratic ages that spiritual opinions should prevail, it is not easy to say by what means those who govern democratic nations may make them predominate. I am no believer in the prosperity any more than in the durability of official philosophies; and as to state religions, I have always held that if they be sometimes of momentary service to the interests of political power, they always sooner or later become fatal to the church. Nor do I agree with those who think that, to raise religion in the eyes of the people and to make them do honor to her spiritual doctrines, it is desirable indirectly to give her ministers a political influence which the laws deny them. I am so much alive to the almost inevitable dangers which beset religious belief whenever the clergy take part in public affairs, and I am so convinced that Christianity must be maintained at any cost in the bosom of modern democracies, that I had rather shut up the priesthood within the sanctuary than allow them to step beyond it.

What means then remain in the hands of constituted authorities to bring men back to spiritual opinions or to hold them fast to the religion by which those opinions are suggested?

My answer will do me harm in the eyes of politicians. I believe that the sole effectual means which governments can employ in order to have the doctrine of the immortality of the soul duly respected is always to act as if they believed in it themselves; and I think that it is only by scrupulous conformity to religious morality in great affairs that they can hope to teach the community at large to know, to love, and to observe it in the lesser concerns of life.

Chapter XVI

HOW EXCESSIVE CARE FOR WORLDLY WELFARE MAY IMPAIR THAT WELFARE

There is a closer tie than is commonly supposed between the improvement of the soul and the amelioration of what belongs to the body. Man may leave these two things apart and consider each of them alternately, but he cannot sever them entirely without at last losing sight of both.

. . .

Whatever elevates, enlarges, and expands the soul renders it more capable of succeeding in those very undertakings which do not concern it. Whatever, on the other hand, enervates or lowers it weakens it for all purposes, the chief as well as the least, and threatens to render it almost equally impotent for both. Hence the soul must remain great and strong, though it were only to devote its strength and greatness from time to time to the service of the body. If men were ever to content themselves with material objects, it is probable that they would lose by degrees the art of producing them; and they would enjoy them in the end, like the brutes, without discernment and without improvement.

Chapter XVII

HOW, WHEN CONDITIONS ARE EQUAL AND SKEPTICISM IS RIFE, IT IS IMPORTANT TO DIRECT HUMAN ACTIONS TO DISTANT OBJECTS

In ages of faith the final aim of life is placed beyond life. The men of those ages, therefore, naturally almost involuntarily accustom themselves to fix their gaze for many years on some immovable object towards which they are constantly tending, and they learn by insensible degrees to repress a multitude of petty passing desires in order to be the better able to content that great and lasting desire which possesses them. When these same men engage in the affairs of this world, the same habits may be traced in their conduct. They are apt to set up some general and certain aim and end to their actions here below, towards which all their efforts are directed; they do not turn from day to day to chase some novel object of desire; but they have settled designs which they are never weary of pursuing.

This explains why religious nations have so often achieved such lasting results; for while they were thinking only of the other world, they had found out the great secret of success in this. Religions give men a general habit of conducting themselves with a view to eternity; in this respect they are not less useful to happiness in this life than to felicity hereafter, and this is one of their chief political characteristics.

But in proportion as the light of faith grows dim, the range of man's sight is circumscribed, as if the end and aim of human actions appeared every day to be more within his reach. When men have once allowed themselves to think no more of what is to befall them after life, they readily lapse into that complete and brutal indifference to futurity which is but too conformable to some propensities of mankind. As soon as they have lost the habit of placing their chief hopes upon remote events, they naturally seek to gratify without delay their smallest desires; and no sooner do they despair of living forever, than they are disposed to act as if they were to exist but for a single day. In skeptical ages it is always to be feared, therefore, that men may perpetually give way to their daily casual desires, and that, wholly renouncing whatever cannot be acquired without protracted effort, they may establish nothing great, permanent, and calm.

If the social condition of a people, under these circumstances, becomes democratic, the danger which I here point out is thereby increased. When everyone is constantly striving to change his position, when an immense field for competition is thrown open to all, when wealth is amassed or dissipated in the shortest possible space of time amid the turmoil of democracy, visions of sudden and easy fortunes, of great possessions easily won and lost, of chance under all its forms haunt the mind. The instability of society itself fosters the natural instability of man's desires. In the midst of these perpetual fluctuations of his lot, the present looms large upon his mind; it hides the future, which becomes indistinct, and men seek only to think about tomorrow.

Chapter XVIII

WHY AMONG THE AMERICANS ALL HONEST CALLINGS ARE CONSIDERED HONORABLE

Among a democratic people, where there is no hereditary wealth, every man works to earn a living, or has worked, or is born of parents who have worked. The notion of labor is therefore presented in the mind, on every side, as the necessary, natural, and honest condition of human existence. Not only is labor not dishonorable among such a people, but it is held in honor; the prejudice is not against it, but in its favor. In the United States a wealthy man thinks that he owes it to public opinion to devote his leisure to some kind of industrial or commercial pursuit or to public business. He would think himself in bad repute if he employed his life solely in living. It is for the purpose of escaping this obligation to work that so many rich Americans come to Europe, where they find some scattered remains of aristocratic society, among whom idleness is still held in honor.

Equality of conditions not only ennobles the notion of labor, but raises the notion of labor as a source of profit.

In aristocracies it is not exactly labor that is despised, but labor with a view to profit. Labor is honorable in itself when it is undertaken at the bidding of ambition or virtue. Yet in aristocratic society it constantly happens that he who works for honor is not insensible to the attractions of profit. But these two desires intermingle only in the depths of his soul; he carefully hides from every eye the point at which they join; he would gladly conceal it from himself. In aristocratic

445

countries there are few public officers who do not affect to serve their country without interested motives. Their salary is an incident of which they think but little and of which they always affect not to think at all. Thus the notion of profit is kept distinct from that of labor; however they may be united in point of fact, they are not thought of together.

In democratic communities these two notions are, on the contrary, always palpably united. As the desire of well-being is universal, as fortunes are slender or fluctuating, as everyone wants either to increase his own resources or to provide fresh ones for his progeny, men clearly see that it is profit that, if not wholly, at least partially leads them to work. Even those who are principally actuated by the love of fame are necessarily made familiar with the thought that they are not exclusively actuated by that motive; and they discover that the desire of getting a living is mingled in their minds with the desire of making life illustrious.

. . .

Chapter XIX

WHAT CAUSES ALMOST ALL AMERICANS TO FOLLOW INDUSTRIAL CALLINGS

Agriculture is perhaps, of all the useful arts, that which improves most slowly among democratic nations. Frequently, indeed, it would seem to be stationary, because other arts are making rapid strides towards perfection. On the other hand, almost all the tastes and habits that the equality of condition produces naturally lead men to commercial and industrial occupations.

Suppose an active, enlightened, and free man, enjoying a competency, but full of desires; he is too poor to live in idleness, he is rich enough to feel himself protected from the immediate fear of want, and he thinks how he can better his condition. This man has conceived a taste for physical gratifications, which thousands of his fellow men around him indulge in; he has himself begun to enjoy these pleasures, and he is eager to increase his means of satisfying these tastes more completely. But life is slipping away, time is urgent; to what is he to turn? The cultivation of the ground promises an almost certain result to his exertions, but a slow one; men are not enriched by it without patience and toil. Agriculture is therefore only suited to those who already have great superfluous wealth or to those whose penury bids them seek only a bare subsistence. The choice of such a man as we have supposed is soon made; he sells his plot of ground, leaves his dwelling, and embarks on some hazardous but lucrative calling.

Democratic communities abound in men of this kind; and in proportion as the equality of conditions becomes greater, their multitude increases. Thus, democracy not only swells the number of working-men, but leads men to prefer one kind of labor to another; and while it diverts them from agriculture, it encourages their tastes for commerce and manufactures.

. . .

The United States of America has only been emancipated for half a century from the state of colonial dependence in which it stood to Great Britain; the number of large fortunes there is small and capital is still scarce. Yet no people in the world have made such rapid progress in trade and manufactures as the Americans; they constitute at the present day the second maritime nation in the world, and although their manufactures have to struggle with almost insurmountable natural impediments, they are not prevented from making great and daily advances.

In the United States the greatest undertakings and speculations are executed without difficulty, because the whole population are engaged in productive industry, and because the poorest as well as the most opulent members of the commonwealth are ready to combine their efforts for these purposes. The consequence is that a stranger is constantly amazed by the immense public works executed by a nation which contains, so to speak, no rich men. The Americans arrived but as yesterday on the territory which they inhabit, and they have already changed the whole order of nature for their own advantage. They have joined the Hudson to the Mississippi and made the Atlantic Ocean communicate with the Gulf of Mexico, across a continent of more than five hundred leagues in extent which separates the two seas. The longest railroads that have been constructed up to the present time are in America.

But what most astonishes me of the United States is not so much the marvelous grandeur of some undertakings as the innumerable multitude of small ones. Almost all the farmers of the United States combine some trade with agriculture; most of them make agriculture itself a trade. It seldom happens that an American farmer settles for good upon the land which he occupies; especially in the districts of the Far West, he brings land into tillage in order to sell it again, and not to farm it; he builds a farmhouse on the speculation that, as the state of the country will soon be changed by the increase of population, a good price may be obtained for it.

Every year a swarm of people from the North arrive in the Southern states and settle in the parts where the cotton plant and the suger-cane grow. These men cultivate the soil in order to make it produce in a few years enough to enrich them; and they already look forward to the time when they may return home to enjoy the competency thus acquired. Thus the Americans carry their businesslike qualities into agriculture, and their trading passions are displayed in that as in their other pursuits.

. . .

Chapter XX

HOW AN ARISTOCRACY MAY BE CREATED BY MANUFACTURES

I have shown how democracy favors the growth of manufactures and increases without limit the numbers of the manufacturing classes; we shall now see by what side-road manufacturers may possibly, in their turn, bring men back to aristocracy.

It is acknowledged that when a workman is engaged every day upon the same details, the whole commodity is produced with greater ease, speed, and economy. It is likewise acknowledged that the cost of production of manufactured goods is diminished by the extent of the establishment in which they are made and by the amount of capital employed or of credit. These truths had long been imperfectly discerned, but in our time they have been demonstrated. They have been already applied to many very important kinds of manufactures, and the humblest will gradually be governed by them. I know of nothing in politics that deserves to fix the attention of the legislator more closely than these two new axioms of the science of manufactures.

When a workman is unceasingly and exclusively engaged in the fabrication of one thing, he ultimately does his work with singular dexterity; but at the same time he loses the general faculty of applying his mind to the direction of the work. He every day becomes more adroit and less industrious; so that it may be said of him that in proportion as the workman improves, the man is degraded. What can be expected of a man who has spent twenty years of his life in making heads for pins? And to what can that mighty human intelligence which has so often stirred the world be applied in him except it be to investigate the best method of making pins' heads? When a workman has spent a considerable portion of his existence in this manner, his thoughts are forever set upon the object of his daily toil; his body has contracted certain fixed habits, which it can never shake off; in a word, he no longer belongs to himself, but to the calling that he has chosen. It is in vain that laws and manners have been at pains to level all the barriers round such a man and to open to him on every side a thousand different paths to fortune; a theory of manufactures more powerful than customs and laws binds him to a craft, and frequently to a spot, which he cannot leave; it assigns to him a certain place in society, beyond which he cannot go; in the midst of universal movement it has rendered him stationary.

In proportion as the principle of the division of labor is more extensively applied, the workman becomes more weak, more narrow-minded, and more dependent. The art advances, the artisan recedes. On the other hand, in proportion as it becomes more manifest that the productions of manufactures are by so much the cheaper and better as the manufacture is larger and the amount of capital employed more considerable, wealthy and educated men come forward to embark in manufactures, which were heretofore abandoned to poor or ignorant handicraftsmen. The magnitude of the efforts required and the importance of the results to be obtained attract them. Thus at the very time at which the science of manufactures lowers the class of workmen, it raises the class of masters.

While the workman concentrates his faculties more and more upon the study of a single detail, the master surveys an extensive whole, and the mind of the latter is enlarged in proportion as that of the former is narrowed. In a short time the one will require nothing but physical strength without intelligence; the other stands in need of science, and almost of genius, to ensure success. This man resembles more and more the administrator of a vast empire; that man, a brute.

The master and the workman have then here no similarity, and their differences increase every day. They are connected only like the two rings at the extremities of a long chain. Each of them fills the station which is made for him, and which he does not leave; the one is continually, closely, and necessarily dependent upon the other and seems as much born to obey as that other is to command. What is this but aristocracy?

As the conditions of men constituting the nation become more and more equal, the demand for manufactured commodities becomes more general and extensive, and the cheapness that places these objects within the reach of slender fortunes becomes a great element of success. Hence there are every day more men of great opulence and education who devote their wealth and knowledge to manufactures and who seek, by opening large establishments and by a strict division of labor, to meet the fresh demands which are made on all sides. Thus, in proportion as the mass of the nation turns to democracy, that particular class which is engaged in manufactures becomes more aristocratic. Men grow more alike in the one, more different in the other; and inequality increases in the less numerous class in the same ratio in which it decreases in the community. Hence it would appear, on searching to the bottom, that aristocracy should naturally spring out of the bosom of democracy.

But this kind of aristocracy by no means resembles those kinds which preceded it. It will be observed at once that, as it applies exclusively to manufactures and to some manufacturing callings, it is a monstrous exception in the general aspect of society. The small aristocratic societies that are formed by some manufacturers in the midst of the immense democracy of our age contain, like the great aristocratic societies of former ages, some men who are very opulent and a multitude who are wretchedly poor. The poor have few means of escaping from their condition and becoming rich, but the rich are constantly becoming poor, or they give up business when they have realized a fortune. Thus the elements of which the class of the poor is composed are fixed, but the elements of which the class of the rich is composed are not so. To tell the truth, though there are rich men, the class of rich men does not exist; for these rich individuals have no feelings or purposes, no traditions or hopes, in common; there are individuals, therefore, but no definite class.

Not only are the rich not compactly united among themselves, but there is no real bond between them and the poor. Their relative position is not a permanent one; they are constantly drawn together or separated by their interests. The workman is generally dependent on the master, but not on any particular master; these two men meet in the factory, but do not know each other elsewhere; and while they come into contact on one point, they stand very far apart on all others. The manufacturer asks nothing of the workman but his labor; the workman expects nothing from him but his wages. The one contracts no obligation to protect nor the other to defend, and they are not permanently connected either by habit or by duty. The aristocracy created by business rarely settles in the midst of the manufacturing population which it directs; the object is not to govern that population, but to use it. An aristocracy thus constituted can have no great hold upon those whom it employs, and even if it succeeds in retaining them at one moment, they escape the next; it knows not how to will, and it cannot act.

The territorial aristocracy of former ages was either bound by law, or thought itself bound by usage, to come to the relief of its serving-men and to relieve their distresses. But the manufacturing aristocracy of our age first impoverishes and debases the men who serve it and then abandons them to be supported by the charity of the public. This is a natural consequence of what has been said before. Between the workman and the master there are frequent relations, but no real association.

I am of the opinion, on the whole, that the manufacturing aristocracy which is growing up under our eyes is one of the harshest that ever existed in the world; but at the same time it is one of the most confined and least dangerous. Nevertheless, the friends of democracy should keep their eyes anxiously fixed in this direction; for if ever a permanent inequality of conditions and aristocracy again penetrates into the world, it may be predicted that this is the gate by which they will enter.

THIRD BOOK

INFLUENCE OF DEMOCRACY ON MANNERS PROPERLY SO CALLED

Chapter I

HOW CUSTOMS ARE SOFTENED AS SOCIAL CONDITIONS BECOME MORE EQUAL

We perceive that for several centuries social conditions have tended to equality, and we discover that at the same time the customs of society have been softened. Are these two things merely contemporaneous or does any secret link exist between them so that the one cannot advance without the other? Several causes may concur to render the customs of a people less rude, but of all these causes the most powerful appears to me to be the equality of conditions. Equality of conditions and greater mildness in customs are, then, in my eyes, not only contemporaneous occurrences, but correlative facts.

.   .

When all men are irrevocably marshaled in an aristocratic community according to their professions, their property, and their birth, the members of each class, considering themselves as children of the same family, cherish a constant and lively sympathy towards one another, which can never be felt in an equal degree by the citizens of a democracy. But the same feeling does not exist between the several classes towards each other.

.   .   .

Although the serf had no natural interest in the fate of the nobles, he did not the less think himself obliged to devote his person to the service of that noble who happened to be his lord; and although the noble held himself to be a different nature from that of his serfs, he nevertheless held that his duty and his honor required him to defend, at the risk of his own life, those who dwelt upon his domains.

It is evident that these mutual obligations did not originate in the law of nature, but in the law of society; and that the claim of social duty was more stringent than that of mere humanity. These services were not supposed to be due from man to man, but to the vassal or to the lord. Feudal institutions awakened a lively sympathy for the sufferings of certain men, but none at all for the miseries of mankind. They infused generosity rather than mildness into the customs of the time; and although they prompted men to great acts of self-devotion, they created no real sympathies, for real sympathies can exist only between those who are alike, and in aristocratic ages men acknowledge none but the members of their own caste to be like themselves.

.   .   .

When all the ranks of a community are nearly equal, as all men think and feel in nearly the same manner, each of them may judge in a moment of the sensations of all the others; he casts a rapid glance upon himself, and that is enough. There is no wretchedness into which he cannot readily enter, and a secret instinct reveals to him its extent. It signifies not that strangers or foes are the sufferers; imagination puts him in their place; something like a personal feeling is mingled with his pity and makes himself suffer while the body of his fellow creature is in torture.

In democratic ages men rarely sacrifice themselves for one another, but they display general compassion for the members of the human race. They inflict no useless ills, and they are happy to relieve the griefs of others when they can do so without much hurting themselves; they are not disinterested, but they are humane.

Chapter II

HOW DEMOCRACY RENDERS THE HABITUAL INTERCOURSE OF THE AMERICANS SIMPLE AND EASY

Democracy does not attach men strongly to one another, but it places their habitual intercourse on an easier footing.

. . .

When it is birth alone, independent of wealth, that classes men in society, everyone knows exactly what his own position is in the social scale; he does not seek to rise, he does not fear to sink. In a community thus organized men of different castes communicate very little with one another; but if accident brings them together, they are ready to converse without hoping or fearing to lose their own position. Their intercourse is not on a footing of equality, but it is not constrained.

When a moneyed aristocracy succeeds to an aristocracy of birth, the case is altered. The privileges of some are still extremely great, but the possibility of acquiring those privileges is open to all; whence it follows that those who possess them are constantly haunted by the apprehension of losing them or of other men's sharing them; those who do not yet enjoy them long to possess them at any cost or, if they fail, to appear at least to possess them, this being not impossible. As the social importance of men is no longer ostensibly and permanently fixed by blood and is infinitely varied by wealth, ranks still exist, but it is not easy clearly to distinguish at a glance those who respectively belong to them. Secret hostilities then arise in the community; one set of men endeavor by innumerable artifices to penetrate, or to appear to penetrate, among those who are above them; another set are constantly in arms against these usurpers of their rights; or, rather, the same individual does both at once, and while he seeks to raise himself into a higher circle, he is always on the defensive against the intrusion of those below him.

. . .

In America, where the privileges of birth never existed and where riches confer no peculiar rights on their possessors, men unacquainted with one another are very ready to frequent the same places and find neither peril nor advantage in the free interchange of their thoughts. If they meet by accident, they neither seek nor avoid intercourse; their manner is therefore natural, frank, and open; it is easy to see that they hardly expect or learn anything from one another, and that they do not care to display any more than to conceal their position in the world. If their demeanor is often cold and serious, it is never haughty or constrained; and if they do not converse, it is because they are not in a humor to talk, not because they think it their interest to be silent.

. . .

Chapter III

WHY THE AMERICANS SHOW SO LITTLE SENSITIVENESS IN THEIR OWN COUNTRY AND ARE SO SENSITIVE IN EUROPE

The temper of the Americans is vindictive, like that of all serious and reflecting nations. They hardly ever forget an offense, but it is not easy to offend them, and their resentment is as slow to kindle as it is to abate.

In aristocratic communities, where a small number of persons manage everything, the outward intercourse of men is subject to settled conventional rules. Everyone then thinks he knows exactly what marks of respect or of condescension he ought to display, and none are presumed to be ignorant of the science of etiquette. These usages of the first class in society afterwards serve as a model to all the others; besides this, each of the latter lays down a code of its own, to which all its members are bound to conform. Thus the rules of politeness form a complex system of legislation, which it is difficult to be perfectly master of, but from which it is dangerous for anyone to deviate; so that men are constantly exposed involuntarily to inflict or to receive bitter affronts.

But as the distinctions of rank are obliterated, as men differing in education and in birth meet and mingle in the same places of resort, it is almost impossible to agree upon the rules of good breeding. As its laws are uncertain, to disobey them is not a crime, even in the eyes of those who know what they are; men attach more importance to intentions than to forms, and they grow less civil, but at the same time less quarrelsome.

There are many little attentions that an American does not care about; he thinks they are not due to him, or he presumes that they are not known to be due. He therefore either does not perceive a rudeness or he forgives it; his manners become less courteous, and his character more plain and masculine.

The mutual indulgence that the Americans display and the manly confidence with which they treat one another also result from another deeper and more general cause, which I have already referred to in the preceding chapter. In the United States the distinctions of rank in civil society are slight, in political society they are nil; an American, therefore, does not think himself bound to pay particular attentions to any of his fellow citizens, nor does he require such attentions from them towards himself. As he does not see that it is his interest eagerly to seek the company of any of his countrymen, he is slow to fancy that his own company is declined. Despising no one on account of his station, he does not imagine that anyone can despise him for that cause, and until he has clearly perceived an insult, he does not suppose that an affront was intended. The social condition of the Americans naturally accustoms them not to take offense in small matters, and, on the other hand, the democratic freedom which they enjoy transfuses this same mildness of temper into the character of the nation.

The political institutions of the United States constantly bring citizens of all ranks into contact and compel them to pursue great undertakings in concert. People thus engaged have scarcely time to attend to the details of etiquette, and they are besides too strongly interested in living harmoniously for them to stick at such things. They therefore soon acquire a habit of considering the feelings and opinions of those whom they meet more than their manners, and they do not allow themselves to be annoyed by trifles.

. . .

At first sight it appears surprising that the same man, transported to Europe, suddenly becomes so sensitive and captious that I often find it as difficult to avoid offending him here as it was there to put him out of countenance. These two opposite effects proceed from the same cause. Democratic institutions generally give men a lofty notion of their country and of themselves. An American leaves his country with a heart swollen with pride; on arriving in Europe, he at once finds out that we are not so engrossed by the United States and the great people who inhabit it as he had supposed, and this begins to annoy him. He has been informed that the conditions of society are not equal in our part of the globe, and he observes that among the nations of Europe the traces of rank are not wholly obliterated, that wealth and birth still retain some indeterminate privileges, which force themselves upon his notice while they elude definition. He is therefore profoundly ignorant of the place that he ought to occupy in this half-ruined scale of classes, which are sufficiently alike for him to be always confounding them. He is afraid of ranking himself too high; still more is he afraid of being ranked too low. This twofold peril keeps his mind constantly on the stretch and embarrasses all he says and does.

. . .

But this is not all: here is yet another queer twist of the human heart. An American is forever talking of the admirable equality that prevails in the United States; aloud he makes it the boast of his country, but in secret he deplores it for himself, and he aspires to show that, for his part, he is an exception to the general state of things which he vaunts.

There is hardly an American to be met with who does not claim some remote kindred with the first founders of the colonies; and as for the scions of the noble families of England, America seemed to me to be covered with them. When an opulent American arrives in Europe, his first care is to surround himself with all the luxuries of wealth; he is so afraid of being taken for the plain citizen of a democracy that he adopts a hundred distorted ways of bringing some new instance of his wealth before you every day. His house will be in the most fashionable part of the town; he will always be surrounded by a host of servants. I have heard an American complain that in the best houses of Paris the society was rather mixed; the taste which prevails there was not pure enough for him, and he ventured to hint that, in his opinion, there was a want of elegance of manner; he could not accustom himself to see wit concealed under such unpretending forms.

. . .

Chapter IV

CONSEQUENCES OF THE THREE PRECEDING CHAPTERS

When men feel a natural compassion for the sufferings of one another, when they are brought together by easy and frequent intercourse, and no sensitive feelings keep them asunder, it may readily be supposed that they will lend assistance to one another whenever it is needed. When an American asks for the co-operation of his fellow citizens, it is seldom refused; and I have often seen it afforded spontaneously, and with great goodwill. If an accident happens on the highway, everybody hastens to help the sufferer; if some great and sudden calamity befalls a family, the purses of a thousand strangers are at once willingly opened and small but numerous donations pour in to relieve their distress.

. . .

All this is not in contradiction to what I have said before on the subject of individualism. The two things are so far from combating each other that I can see how they agree. Equality of condition, while it makes men feel their independence, shows them their own weakness: they are free, but exposed to a thousand accidents; and experience soon teaches them that although they do not habitually require the assistance of others, a time almost always comes when they cannot do without it.

Chapter V

HOW DEMOCRACY AFFECTS THE RELATIONS OF MASTERS AND SERVANTS

An American who had traveled for a long time in Europe once said to me: "The English treat their servants with a stiffness and imperiousness of manner which surprise us; but, on the other hand, the French sometimes treat their attendants with a degree of familiarity or of politeness which we cannot understand. It looks as if they were afraid to give orders; the relative position of the superior and the inferior is poorly maintained." The remark was a just one, and I have often made it myself. I have always considered England as the country of all the world where in our time the bond of domestic service is drawn most tightly, and France as the country where it is most relaxed. Nowhere have I seen masters stand so high or so low as in these two countries. Between these two extremes the Americans are to be placed. Such is the fact as it appears upon the surface of things; to discover the causes of that fact, it is necessary to search the matter thoroughly.

No communities have ever yet existed in which social conditions have been so equal that there were neither rich nor poor, and, consequently, neither masters nor servants. Democracy does not prevent the existence of these two classes, but it changes their dispositions and modifies their mutual relations.

Among aristocratic nations servants form a distinct class, not more variously composed than that of their masters. A settled order is soon established; in the former as well as in the latter class a scale is formed, with numerous distinctions or marked gradations of rank, and generations succeed one another thus, without any change of position. These two communities are superposed one above the other, always distinct, but regulated by analogous principles. This aristocratic constitution does not exert a less powerful influence on the notions and manners of servants than on those of masters; and although the effects are different, the same cause may easily be traced.

. . .

The permanent inequality of conditions not only gives servants certain peculiar virtues and vices, but places them in a peculiar relation with respect to their masters. Among aristocratic nations the poor man is familiarized from his childhood with the notion of being commanded; to whichever side he turns his eyes, the graduated structure of society and the aspect of obedience meet his view. Hence in those countries the master readily obtains prompt, complete, respectful, and easy obedience from his servants, because they revere in him not only their master, but the class of masters. He weighs down their will by the whole weight of the aristocracy. He orders their actions; to a certain extent, he even directs their thoughts. In aristocracies the master often exercises, even without being aware of it, an amazing sway over the opinions, the habits, and the manners of those who obey him, and his influence extends even further than his authority.

. . .

Equality of conditions turns servants and masters into new beings, and places them in new relative positions. When social conditions are nearly equal, men are constantly changing their situations in life; there is still a class of menials and a class of masters, but these classes are not always composed of the same individuals, still less of the same families; and those who command are not more secure of perpetuity than those who obey. As servants do not form a separate class, they have no habits, prejudices, or manners peculiar to themselves; they are not remarkable for any particular turn of mind or moods of feeling. They know no vices or virtues of their condition, but they partake of the education, the opinions, the feelings, the virtues, and the vices of their contemporaries; and they are honest men or scoundrels in the same way as their masters are.

The conditions of servants are not less equal than those of masters. As no marked ranks or fixed subordination are to be found among them, they will not display either the meanness or the greatness that characterize the aristocracy of menials, as well as all other aristocracies.

. . .

In democracies servants are not only equal among themselves, but it may be said that they are, in some sort, the equals of their masters. This requires explanation in order to be rightly understood. At any moment a servant may become a master, and he aspires to rise to that condition; the servant is therefore not a different man from the master. Why, then, has the former a right to command, and what compels the latter to obey except the free and temporary consent of both their wills? Neither of them is by nature inferior to the other; they only become so for a time, by covenant. Within the terms of this covenant the one is a servant, the other a master; beyond it they are two citizens of the commonwealth, two men.

I beg the reader particularly to observe that this is not only the notion which servants themselves entertain of their own condition; domestic service is looked upon by masters in the same light, and the precise limits of authority and obedience are as clearly settled in the mind of the one as in that of the other.

When the greater part of the community have long attained a condition nearly alike and when equality is an old and acknowledged fact, the public mind, which is never affected by exceptions, assigns certain general limits to the value of man, above or below which no man can long remain placed. It is in vain that wealth and poverty, authority and obedience, accidentally interpose great distances between two men; public opinion, founded upon the usual order of things, draws them to a common level and creates a species of imaginary equality between them, in spite of the real inequality of their conditions. This all-powerful opinion penetrates at length even into the hearts of those whose interest might arm them to resist it; it affects their judgment while it subdues their will.

In their inmost convictions the master and the servant no longer perceive any deep-seated difference between them, and they neither hope nor fear to meet with either at any time. They are therefore subject neither to disdain nor to anger, and they discern in each other neither humility nor pride. The master holds the contract of service to be the only source of his power, and the servant regards it be as the only cause of his obedience. They do not quarrel about their reciprocal situations, but each knows his own and keeps it.

It would be preposterous to suppose that those warm and deep-seated affections which are sometimes kindled in the domestic service of aristocracy will ever spring up between these two men, or that they will exhibit strong instances of self-sacrifice. In aristocracies masters and servants live apart, and frequently their only intercourse is through a third person; yet they commonly stand firmly by one another. In democratic countries the master and the servant are close together: they are in daily personal contact, but their minds do not intermingle; they have common occupations, hardly ever common interests.

.   .

In all that precedes I wish that I could depend upon the example of the Americans as a whole; but I cannot do this without drawing careful distinctions regarding persons and places. In the South of the Union slavery exists; all that I have just said is consequently inapplicable there. In the North the majority of servants are either freedmen or the children of freedmen; these persons occupy an uncertain position in the public estimation; by the laws they are brought up to the level of their masters; by the manners of the country they are firmly kept below it. They do not themselves clearly know their proper place and are almost always either insolent or craven.

But in the Northern states, especially in New England, there are a certain number of whites who agree, for wages, to yield a temporary obedience to the will of their fellow citizens. I have heard that these servants commonly perform the duties of their situations with punctuality and intelligence and that, without thinking themselves naturally inferior to the person who orders them, they submit without reluctance to obey him. They appeared to me to carry into service some of those manly habits which independence and equality create. Having once selected a hard way of life, they do not seek to escape from it by indirect means; and they have sufficient respect for themselves not to refuse to their masters that obedience which they have freely promised. On their part, masters require nothing of their servants but the faithful and rigorous performance of the covenant: they do not ask for marks of respect, they do not claim their love or devoted attachment; it is enough that, as servants, they are exact and honest.

It would not, then, be true to assert that in democratic society the relation of servants and masters is disorganized; it is organized on another footing, the rule is different, but there is a rule.

Chapter VI

HOW DEMOCRATIC INSTITUTIONS AND MANNERS TEND TO RAISE RENTS AND SHORTEN THE TERMS OF LEASES

What has been said of servants and masters is applicable to a certain extent to landowners and farming tenants, but this subject deserves to be considered by itself.

In America there are, properly speaking, no farming tenants; every man owns the ground he tills. It must be admitted that democratic laws tend greatly to increase the number of landowners and to diminish that of farming tenants. Yet what takes place in the United States is much less attributable to the institutions of the country than to the country itself. In America land is cheap and anyone may easily become a landowner; its returns are small and its produce cannot well be divided between a landowner and a farmer. America therefore stands alone in this respect, as well as in many others, and it would be a mistake to take it as an example.

I believe that in democratic as well as in aristocratic countries there will be landowners and tenants, but the connection existing between them will be of a different kind. In aristocracies the hire of a farm is paid to the landlord, not only in rent, but in respect, regard, and duty; in democracies the whole is paid in cash. When estates are divided and passed from hand to hand, and the permanent connection that existed between families and the soil is dissolved, the landowner and the tenant are only casually brought into contact. They meet for a moment to settle the conditions of the agreement and then lose sight of each other; they are two strangers brought together by a common interest, who keenly talk over a matter of business, the sole object of which is to make money.

. . .

An aristocracy does not expire, like a man, in a single day; the aristocratic principle is slowly undermined in men's opinion before it is attacked in their laws. Long before open war is declared against it, the tie that had hitherto united the higher classes to the lower may be seen to be gradually relaxed. Indifference and contempt are betrayed by one class, jealousy and hatred by the others. The intercourse between rich and poor becomes less frequent and less kind, and rents are raised. This is not the consequence of a democratic revolution, but its certain harbinger; for an aristocracy that has lost the affections of the people once and forever is like a tree dead at the root, which is the more easily torn up by the winds the higher its branches have spread.

. . .

There is yet another sign by which it is easy to know that a great democratic revolution is going on or approaching. In the Middle Ages almost all lands were leased for lives or for very long terms; the domestic economy of that period shows that leases for ninety-nine years were more frequent then than leases for twelve years are now. Men then believed that families were immortal; men's conditions seemed settled forever, and the whole of society appeared to be so fixed that it was not supposed anything would ever be stirred or shaken in its structure. In ages of equality the human mind takes a different bent: the prevailing notion is that nothing abides, and man is haunted by the thought of mutability. Under this impression the landowner and the tenant himself are instinctively averse to protracted terms of obligation;

they are afraid of being tied up tomorrow by the contract that benefits them today. They do not trust themselves; they are afraid that, their standards changing, they may have trouble in ridding themselves of the thing which had been the object of their longing. And they are right to fear this, for in democratic times what is most unstable, in the midst of the instability of everything, is the heart of man.

Chapter VII

INFLUENCE OF DEMOCRACY
ON WAGES

Most of the remarks that I have already made in speaking of masters and servants may be applied to masters and workmen. As the gradations of the social scale come to be less observed, while the great sink and the humble rise and poverty as well as opulence ceases to be hereditary, the distance, both in reality and in opinion, which heretofore separated the workman from the master is lessened every day. The workman conceives a more lofty opinion of his rights, of his future, of himself; he is filled with new ambition and new desires, he is harassed by new wants. Every instant he views with longing eyes the profits of his employer; and in order to share them he strives to dispose of his labor at a higher rate, and he generally succeeds at length in the attempt.

In democratic countries as well as elsewhere most of the branches of productive industry are carried on at a small cost by men little removed by their wealth or education above the level of those whom they employ. These manufacturing speculators are extremely numerous; their interests differ; they cannot therefore easily concert or combine their exertions. On the other hand, the workmen have always some sure resources which enable them to refuse to work when they cannot get what they conceive to be the fair price of their labor. In the constant struggle for wages that is going on between these two classes, their strength is divided and success alternates from one to the other.

It is even probable that in the end the interest of the

working class will prevail, for the high wages which they have already obtained make them every day less dependent on their masters, and as they grow more independent, they have greater facilities for obtaining a further increase of wages.

. . .

I think that, on the whole, it may be asserted that a slow and gradual rise of wages is one of the general laws of democratic communities. In proportion as social conditions become more equal, wages rise; and as wages are higher, social conditions become more equal.

But a great and gloomy exception occurs in our own time. I have shown, in a preceding chapter, that aristocracy, expelled from political society, has taken refuge in certain departments of productive industry and has established its sway there under another form; this powerfully affects the rate of wages.

As a large capital is required to embark in the great manufacturing speculations to which I allude, the number of persons who enter upon them is exceedingly limited; as their number is small, they can easily concert together and fix the rate of wages as they please.

Their workmen, on the contrary, are exceedingly numerous, and the number of them is always increasing; for from time to time an extraordinary run of business takes place during which wages are inordinately high, and they attract the surrounding population to the factories. But when men have once embraced that line of life, we have already seen that they cannot quit it again, because they soon contract habits of body and mind which unfit them for any other sort of toil. These men have generally but little education and industry, with but few resources; they stand, therefore, almost at the mercy of the master.

When competition or some other fortuitous circumstance lessens his profits, he can reduce the wages of his workmen almost at pleasure and make from them what he loses by the chances of business. Should the workmen strike, the master, who is a rich man, can very well wait, without being ruined, until necessity brings them back to him; but they must work day by day or they die, for their only property is in their hands. They have long been impoverished by oppression, and the poorer they become, the more easily they may be oppressed; they can never escape from this fatal circle of cause and consequence.

It is not surprising, then, that wages, after having sometimes suddenly risen, are permanently lowered in this branch of industry; whereas in other callings the price of labor, which generally increases but little, is nevertheless constantly augmented.

This state of dependence and wretchedness in which a part of the manufacturing population of our time live forms an exception to the general rule, contrary to the state of all the rest of the community; but for this very reason no circumstance is more important or more deserving of the legislator; for when the whole of society is in motion, it is difficult to keep any one class stationary, and when the greater number of men are opening new paths to fortune, it is no less difficult to make the few support in peace their wants and their desires.

Chapter VIII

INFLUENCE OF DEMOCRACY
ON THE FAMILY

I have just examined the changes which the equality of conditions produces in the mutual relations of the several members of the community among democratic nations, and among the Americans in particular. I would now go deeper and inquire into the closer ties of family; my object here is not to seek for new truths, but to show in what manner facts already known are connected with my subject.

It has been universally remarked that in our time the several members of a family stand upon an entirely new footing towards each other; that the distance which formerly separated a father from his sons has been lessened; and that paternal authority, if not destroyed, is at least impaired.

Something analogous to this, but even more striking, may be observed in the United States. In America the family, in the Roman and aristocratic signification of the word, does not exist. All that remains of it are a few vestiges in the first years of childhood, when the father exercises, without opposition, that absolute domestic authority which the feebleness of his children renders necessary and which their interest, as well as his own incontestable superiority, warrants. But as soon as the young American approaches manhood, the ties of filial obedience are relaxed day by day; master of his thoughts, he is soon master of his conduct. In America there is, strictly speaking, no adolescence; at the close of boyhood the man appears and begins to trace out his own path.

It would be an error to suppose that this is preceded by a

domestic struggle in which the son has obtained by a sort of moral violence the liberty that his father refused him. The same habits, the same principles, which impel the one to assert his independence predispose the other to consider the use of that independence as an incontestable right. The former does not exhibit any of those rancorous or irregular passions which disturb men long after they have shaken off an established authority; the latter feels none of that bitter and angry regret which is apt to survive a bygone power. The father foresees the limits of his authority long beforehand, and when the time arrives, he surrenders it without a struggle; the son looks forward to the exact period at which he will be his own master, and he enters upon his freedom without precipitation and without effort, as a possession which is his own and which no one seeks to wrest from him.

It may perhaps be useful to show how these changes which take place in family relations are closely connected with the social and political revolution that is approaching its consummation under our own eyes.

There are certain great social principles that a people either introduces everywhere or tolerates nowhere. In countries which are aristocratically constituted with all the gradations of rank, the government never makes a direct appeal to the mass of the governed; as men are united together, it is enough to lead the foremost; the rest will follow. This is applicable to the family as well as to all aristocracies that have a head. Among aristocratic nations social institutions recognize, in truth, no one in the family but the father; children are received by society at his hands; society governs him, he governs them. Thus the parent not only has a natural right but acquires a political right to command them; he is the author and the support of his family, but he is also its constituted ruler.

In democracies, where the government picks out every individual singly from the mass to make him subservient to the general laws of the community, no such intermediate person is required; a father is there, in the eye of the law, only a member of the community, older and richer than his sons.

When most of the conditions of life are extremely unequal and the inequality of these conditions is permanent, the notion of a superior grows upon the imaginations of men; if the law invested him with no privileges, custom and public opinion would concede them. When, on the contrary, men differ but little from each other and do not always remain in dissimilar conditions of life, the general notion of a superior becomes weaker and less distinct; it is vain for legislation to strive to place him who obeys very much beneath him who commands; the manners of the time bring the two men nearer to one another and draw them daily towards the same level.

Although the legislation of an aristocratic people grants no peculiar privileges to the heads of families, I shall not be the less convinced that their power is more respected and more extensive than in a democracy; for I know that, whatever the laws may be, superiors always appear higher and inferiors lower in aristocracies than among democratic nations.

When men live more for the remembrance of what has been than for the care of what is, and when they are more given to attend to what their ancestors thought than to think themselves, the father is the natural and necessary tie between the past and the present, the link by which the ends of these two chains are connected. In aristocracies, then, the father is not only the civil head of the family, but the organ of its traditions, the expounder of its customs, the arbiter of its manners. He is listened to with deference, he is addressed with respect, and the love that is felt for him is always tempered with fear.

When the condition of society becomes democratic and men adopt as their general principle that it is good and lawful to judge of all things for oneself, using former points of belief not as a rule of faith, but simply as a means of information, the power which the opinions of a father exercise over those of his sons diminishes as well as his legal power.

Perhaps the subdivision of estates that democracy brings about contributes more than anything else to change the relations existing between a father and his children. When the property of the father of a family is scanty, his son and himself constantly live in the same place and share the same occupations; habit and necessity bring them together and force them to hold constant communication. The inevitable consequence is a sort of familiar intimacy, which renders authority less absolute and which can ill be reconciled with the external forms of respect.

Now, in democratic countries the class of those who are possessed of small fortunes is precisely that which gives strength to the notions and a particular direction to the manners of the community. That class makes its opinions preponderate as universally as its will, and even those who are most inclined to resist its commands are carried away in the end by its example. I have known eager opponents of democracy who allowed their children to address them with perfect colloquial equality.

Thus at the same time that the power of aristocracy is declining, the austere, the conventional, and the legal part of parental authority vanishes and a species of equality prevails around the domestic hearth. I do not know, on the whole, whether society loses by the change, but I am inclined to believe that man individually is a gainer by it. I think that in proportion as manners and laws become more democratic, the relation of father and son becomes more intimate and more affectionate; rules and authority are less talked of, confidence and tenderness are often increased, and it would seem that the natural bond is drawn closer in proportion as the social bond is loosened.

In a democratic family the father exercises no other power than that which is granted to the affection and the experience of age; his orders would perhaps be disobeyed, but his advice is for the most part authoritative. Though he is not hedged in with ceremonial respect, his sons at least accost him with confidence; they have no settled form of addressing him, but they speak to him constantly and are ready to consult him every day. The master and the constituted ruler have vanished; the father remains.

Nothing more is needed in order to judge of the difference between the two states of society in this respect than to peruse the family correspondence of aristocratic ages. The style is always correct, ceremonious, stiff, and so cold that the natural warmth of the heart can hardly be felt in the language. In democratic countries, on the contrary, the language addressed by a son to his father is always marked by mingled freedom, familiarity, and affection, which at once show that new relations have sprung up in the bosom of the family.

A similar revolution takes place in the mutual relations of children. In aristocratic families, as well as in aristocratic society, every place is marked out beforehand. Not only does the father occupy a separate rank, in which he enjoys extensive privileges, but even the children are not equal among themselves. The age and sex of each irrevocably determine his rank and secure to him certain privileges. Most of these distinctions are abolished or diminished by democracy.

In aristocratic families the eldest son, inheriting the greater part of the property and almost all the rights of the family, becomes the chief and to a certain extent the master of his brothers. Greatness and power are for him; for them, mediocrity and dependence. But it would be wrong to suppose that among aristocratic nations the privileges of the eldest son are advantageous to himself alone, or that they excite nothing but envy and hatred around him. The eldest son commonly endeavors to procure wealth and power for his brothers, because the general splendor of the house is reflected back on him who represents it; the younger sons seek to back the elder brother in all his undertakings, because the greatness and power of the head of the family better enable him to provide for all its branches. The different members of an aristocratic family are therefore very closely bound together; their interests are connected, their minds agree, but their hearts are seldom in harmony.

Democracy also binds brothers to each other, but by very different means. Under democratic laws all the children are perfectly equal and consequently independent; nothing brings them forcibly together, but nothing keeps them apart; and as they have the same origin, as they are trained under the same roof, as they are treated with the same care, and as no peculiar privilege distinguishes or divides them, the affectionate and frank intimacy of early years easily springs up between them. Scarcely anything can occur to break the tie thus formed at the outset of life, for brotherhood brings them daily together without embarrassing them. It is not, then, by interest, but by common associations and by the free sympathy of opinion and of taste that democracy unites brothers to each other. It divides their inheritance, but allows their hearts and minds to unite.

Such is the charm of these democratic manners that even the partisans of aristocracy are attracted by it; and after having experienced it for some time, they are by no means tempted to revert to the respectful and frigid observances of aristocratic families. They would be glad to retain the domestic habits of democracy if they might throw off its social conditions and its laws; but these elements are indissolubly united, and it is impossible to enjoy the former without enduring the latter.

The remarks I have made on filial love and fraternal affection are applicable to all the passions that emanate spontaneously from human nature itself.

If a certain mode of thought or feeling is the result of some peculiar condition of life, when that condition is altered nothing whatever remains of the thought or feeling. Thus a law may bind two members of the community very closely to each other; but that law being abolished, they stand asunder. Nothing was more strict than the tie that united the vassal to the lord under the feudal system; at the present day the two men do not know each other; the fear, the gratitude, and the affection that formerly connected them have vanished and not a vestige of the tie remains.

Such, however, is not the case with those feelings which are natural to mankind. Whenever a law attempts to tutor these feelings in any particular manner, it seldom fails to weaken them; by attempting to add to their intensity it robs them of some of their elements, for they are never stronger than when left to themselves.

Democracy, which destroys or obscures almost all the old conventional rules of society and which prevents men from readily assenting to new ones, entirely effaces most of the feelings to which these conventional rules have given rise; but it only modifies some others, and frequently imparts to them a degree of energy and sweetness unknown before.

Perhaps it is not impossible to condense into a single proposition the whole purport of this chapter, and of several others that preceded it. Democracy loosens social ties, but tightens natural ones; it brings kindred more closely together, while it throws citizens more apart.

Chapter IX

EDUCATION OF YOUNG WOMEN
IN THE UNITED STATES

No free communities ever existed without morals, and as I observed in the former part of this work, morals are the work of woman. Consequently, whatever affects the condition of women, their habits and their opinions, has great political importance in my eyes.

Among almost all Protestant nations young women are far more the mistresses of their own actions than they are in Catholic countries. This independence is still greater in Protestant countries like England, which have retained or acquired the right of self-government; freedom is then infused into the domestic circle by political habits and by religious opinions. In the United States the doctrines of Protestantism are combined with great political liberty and a most democratic state of society, and nowhere are young women surrendered so early or so completely to their own guidance.

Long before an American girl arrives at the marriageable age, her emancipation from maternal control begins; she has scarcely ceased to be a child when she already thinks for herself, speaks with freedom, and acts on her own impulse. The great scene of the world is constantly open to her view; far from seeking to conceal it from her, it is every day disclosed more completely and she is taught to survey it with a firm and calm gaze. Thus the vices and dangers of society are early revealed to her; as she sees them clearly, she views them without illusion and braves them without fear, for she is full of reliance on her own strength, and her confidence seems to be shared by all around her.

An American girl scarcely ever displays that virginal softness in the midst of young desires or that innocent and ingenuous grace which usually attend the European woman in the transition from girlhood to youth. It is rare that an American woman, at any age, displays childish timidity or ignorance. Like the young women of Europe she seeks to please, but she knows precisely the cost of pleasing. If she does not abandon herself to evil, at least she knows that it exists; and she is remarkable rather for purity of manners than for chastity of mind.

I have been frequently surprised and almost frightened at the singular address and happy boldness with which young women in America contrive to manage their thoughts and their language amid all the difficulties of free conversation; a philosopher would have stumbled at every step along the narrow path which they trod without accident and without effort. It is easy, indeed, to perceive that even amid the independence of early youth an American woman is always mistress of herself; she indulges in all permitted pleasures without yielding herself up to any of them, and her reason never allows the reins of self-guidance to drop, though it often seems to hold them loosely.

In France, where traditions of every age are still so strangely mingled in the opinions and tastes of the people, women commonly receive a reserved, retired, and almost conventual education, as they did in aristocratic times; and then they are suddenly abandoned without a guide and without assistance in the midst of all the irregularities inseparable from democratic society.

The Americans are more consistent. They have found out that in a democracy the independence of individuals cannot fail to be very great, youth premature, tastes ill-restrained, customs fleeting, public opinion often unsettled and power-less, paternal authority weak, and marital authority con-tested. Under these circumstances, believing that they had little chance of repressing in woman the most vehement passions of the human heart, they held that the surer way was to teach her the art of combating those passions for herself. As they could not prevent her virtue from being exposed to frequent danger, they determined that she should know how best to defend it, and more reliance was placed on the free vigor of her will than on safeguards which have been shaken or overthrown. Instead, then, of inculcating mistrust of herself, they constantly seek to enhance her confidence in her own strength of character. As it is neither possible nor desirable to keep a young woman in perpetual and complete ignorance, they hasten to give her a precocious knowledge on all subjects. Far from hiding the corruptions of the world from her, they prefer that she should see them at once and train herself to shun them, and they hold it of more importance to protect her conduct than to be over-scrupu-lous of the innocence of her thoughts.

Although the Americans are a very religious people, they do not rely on relgion alone to defend the virtue of woman; they seek to arm her reason also. In this respect they have followed the same method as in several others: they first make vigorous efforts to cause individual independence to control itself, and they do not call in the aid of religion until they have reached the utmost limits of human strength.

I am aware that an education of this kind is not without danger; I am sensible that it tends to invigorate the judgment at the expense of the imagination and to make cold and virtuous women instead of affectionate wives and agreeable companions to man. Society may be more tranquil and better regulated, but domestic life has often fewer charms. These, however, are secondary evils, which may be braved for the sake of higher interests. At the stage at which we are now arrived, the choice is no longer left to us; a democratic education is indispensable to protect women from the dangers with which democratic institutions and manners surround them.

Chapter X

THE YOUNG WOMAN IN THE
CHARACTER OF A WIFE

In America the independence of woman is irrecoverably lost in the bonds of matrimony. If an unmarried woman is less constrained there than elsewhere, a wife is subjected to stricter obligations. The former makes her father's house an abode of freedom and of pleasure; the latter lives in the home of her husband as if it were a cloister. Yet these two different conditions of life are perhaps not so contrary as may be supposed, and it is natural that the American women should pass through the one to arrive at the other.

Religious communities and trading nations entertain peculiarly serious notions of marriage: the former consider the regularity of woman's life as the best pledge and most certain sign of the purity of her morals; the latter regard it as the highest security for the order and prosperity of the household. The Americans are at the same time a puritanical people and a commercial nation; their religious opinions as well as their trading habits consequently lead them to require much abnegation on the part of woman and a constant sacrifice of her pleasures to her duties, which is seldom demanded of her in Europe. Thus in the United States the inexorable opinion of the public carefully circumscribes woman within the narrow circle of domestic interests and duties and forbids her to step beyond it.

Upon her entrance into the world a young American woman finds these notions firmly established; she sees the rules that are derived from them; she is not slow to perceive that she cannot depart for an instant from the established usages of her contemporaries without putting in jeopardy her peace of mind, her honor, nay, even her social existence; and she finds the energy required for such an act of submission in the firmness of her understanding and in the virile habits which her education has given her. It may be said that she has learned by the use of her independence to surrender it without a struggle and without a murmur when the time comes for making the sacrifice.

But no American woman falls into the toils of matrimony as into a snare held out to her simplicity and ignorance. She has been taught beforehand what is expected of her and voluntarily and freely enters upon this engagement. She supports her new condition with courage because she chose it. As in America paternal discipline is very relaxed and the conjugal tie very strict, a young woman does not contract the latter without considerable circumspection and apprehension. Precocious marriages are rare. American women do not marry until their understandings are exercised and ripened, whereas in other countries most women generally begin to exercise and ripen their understandings only after marriage.

I by no means suppose, however, that the great change which takes place in all the habits of women in the United States as soon as they are married ought solely to be attributed to the constraint of public opinion; it is frequently imposed upon themselves by the sole effort of their own will. When the time for choosing a husband arrives, that cold and stern reasoning power which has been educated and invigorated by the free observation of the world teaches an American woman that a spirit of levity and independence in the bonds of marriage is a constant subject of annoyance, not of pleasure; it tells her that the amusements of the girl cannot become the recreations of the wife, and that the sources of a married woman's happiness are in the home of her husband. As she clearly discerns beforehand the only road that can lead to domestic happiness, she enters upon it at once and follows it to the end without seeking to turn back.

The same strength of purpose which the young wives of America display in bending themselves at once and without repining to the austere duties of their new condition is no less manifest in all the great trials of their lives. In no country in the world are private fortunes more precarious than in the United States. It is not uncommon for the same man in the course of his life to rise and sink again through all the grades that lead from opulence to poverty. American women support these vicissitudes with calm and unquenchable energy; it would seem that their desires contract as easily as they expand with their fortunes.

The greater part of the adventurers who migrate every year to people the Western wilds belong, as I observed in the former part of this work, to the old Anglo-American race of the Northern states. Many of these men, who rush so boldly onwards in pursuit of wealth, were already in the enjoyment of a competency in their own part of the country. They take their wives along with them and make them share the countless perils and privations that always attend the commencement of these expeditions. I have often met, even on the verge of the wilderness, with young women who, after having been brought up amid all the comforts of the large towns of New England, had passed, almost without any intermediate stage, from the wealthy abode of their parents to a comfortless hovel in a forest. Fever, solitude, and a tedious life had not broken the springs of their courage. Their features were impaired and faded, but their looks were firm; they appeared to be at once sad and resolute. I do not doubt that these young American women had amassed, in the education of their early years, that inward strength which they displayed under these circumstances. The early culture of the girl may still, therefore, be traced, in the United States, under the aspect of marriage; her part is changed, her habits are different, but her character is the same.

Chapter XI

HOW EQUALITY OF CONDITION
CONTRIBUTES TO MAINTAIN
GOOD MORALS IN AMERICA

Some philosophers and historians have said or hinted that the strictness of female morality was increased or diminished simply by the distance of a country from the equator. This solution of the difficulty was an easy one, and nothing was required but a globe and a pair of compasses to settle in an instant one of the most difficult problems in the condition of mankind. But I am not sure that this principle of the materialists is supported by facts. The same nations have been chaste or dissolute at different periods of their history; the strictness or the laxity of their morals depended, therefore, on some variable cause and not alone on the natural qualities of their country, which were invariable. I do not deny that in certain climates the passions which are occasioned by the mutual attraction of the sexes are peculiarly intense, but I believe that this natural intensity may always be excited or restrained by the condition of society and by political institutions.

Although the travelers who have visited North America differ on many points, they all agree in remarking that morals are far more strict there than elsewhere. It is evident that on this point the Americans are very superior to their progenitors, the English. A superficial glance at the two nations will establish the fact.

In England, as in all other countries of Europe, public malice is constantly attacking the frailties of women. Philosophers and statesmen are heard to deplore that morals are not sufficiently strict, and the literary productions of the country constantly lead one to suppose so. In America all books, novels not excepted, suppose women to be chaste, and no one thinks of relating affairs of gallantry.

No doubt this great regularity of American morals is due in part to qualities of country, race, and religion, but all these causes, which operate elsewhere, do not suffice to account for it; recourse must be had to some special reason. This reason appears to me to be the principle of equality and the institutions derived from it. Equality of condition does not of itself produce regularity of morals, but it unquestionably facilitates and increases it.

Among aristocratic nations birth and fortune frequently make two such different beings of man and woman that they can never be united to each other. Their passions draw them together, but the condition of society and the notions suggested by it prevent them from contracting a permanent and ostensible tie. The necessary consequence is a great number of transient and clandestine connections. Nature secretly avenges herself for the constraint imposed upon her by the laws of man.

This is not so much the case when the equality of conditions has swept away all the imaginary or the real barriers that separated man from woman. No girl then believes that she cannot become the wife of the man who loves her, and this renders all breaches of morality before marriage very uncommon; for, whatever be the credulity of the passions, a woman will hardly be able to persuade herself that she is beloved when her lover is perfectly free to marry her and does not.

The same cause operates, though more indirectly, on married life. Nothing better serves to justify an illicit passion, either to the minds of those who have conceived it or to the world which looks on, than marriages made by compulsion or chance.

In a country in which a woman is always free to exercise her choice and where education has prepared her to choose rightly, public opinion is inexorable to her faults. The rigor of the Americans arises in part from this cause. They consider marriage as a covenant which is often onerous, but every condition of which the parties are strictly bound to fulfill because they knew all those conditions beforehand and were perfectly free not to have contracted them.

The very circumstances that render matrimonial fidelity more obligatory also render it more easy.

· · ·

The equality of conditions cannot, it is true, ever succeed in making men chaste, but it may impart a less dangerous character to their breaches of morality. As no one has then either sufficient time or opportunity to assail a virtue armed in self-defense, there will be at the same time a great number of courtesans and a great number of virtuous women. This state of things causes lamentable cases of individual hardship, but it does not prevent the body of society from being strong and alert; it does not destroy family ties or enervate the morals of the nation. Society is endangered, not by the great profligacy of a few, but by laxity of morals among all. In the eyes of a legislator prostitution is less to be dreaded than intrigue.

The tumultuous and constantly harassed life that equality makes men lead not only distracts them from the passion of love by denying them time to indulge it, but diverts them from it by another more secret but more certain road. All men who live in democratic times more or less contract the ways of thinking of the manufacturing and trading classes; their minds take a serious, deliberate, and positive turn; they are apt to relinquish the ideal in order to pursue some visible and proximate object which appears to be the natural and necessary aim of their desires. Thus the principle of equality does not destroy the imagination, but lowers its flight to the level of the earth.

No men are less addicted to reverie than the citizens of a democracy, and few of them are ever known to give way to those idle and solitary meditations which commonly precede and produce the great emotions of the heart. It is true they attach great importance to procuring for themselves that sort of deep, regular, and quiet affection which constitutes the charm and safeguard of life, but they are not apt to run after those violent and capricious sources of excitement which disturb and abridge it.

I am aware that all this is applicable in its full extent only to America and cannot at present be extended to Europe. In the course of the last half-century, while laws and customs have impelled several European nations with unexampled force towards democracy, we have not had occasion to observe that the relations of man and woman have become more orderly or more chaste. In some places the very reverse may be detected: some classes are more strict; the general morality of the people appears to be more lax. I do not hesitate to make the remark, for I am as little disposed to flatter my contemporaries as to malign them.

This fact must distress, but it ought not to surprise us. The propitious influence that a democratic state of society may exercise upon orderly habits is one of those tendencies which can be discovered only after a time. If equality of condition is favorable to purity of morals, the social commotion by which conditions are rendered equal is adverse to it. In the last fifty years, during which France has been undergoing this transformation, it has rarely had freedom, always disturbance. Amid this universal confusion of notions and this general stir of opinions, amid this incoherent mixture of the just and the unjust, of truth and falsehood, of right and might, public virtue has become doubtful and private morality wavering. But all revolutions, whatever may have been their object or their agents, have at first produced similar consequences; even those which have in the end drawn tighter the bonds of morality began by loosening them.

Chapter XII

HOW THE AMERICANS UNDERSTAND
THE EQUALITY OF THE SEXES

I have shown how democracy destroys or modifies the different inequalities that originate in society; but is this all, or does it not ultimately affect that great inequality of man and woman which has seemed, up to the present day, to be eternally based in human nature? I believe that the social changes that bring nearer to the same level the father and son, the master and servant, and, in general, superiors and inferiors will raise woman and make her more and more the equal of man. But here, more than ever, I feel the necessity of making myself clearly understood; for there is no subject on which the coarse and lawless fancies of our age have taken a freer range.

There are people in Europe who, confounding together the different characteristics of the sexes, would make man and woman into beings not only equal but alike. They would give to both the same functions, impose on both the same duties, and grant to both the same rights; they would mix them in all things—their occupations, their pleasures, their business. It may readily be conceived that by thus attempting to make one sex equal to the other, both are degraded, and from so preposterous a medley of the works of nature nothing could ever result but weak men and disorderly women.

It is not thus that the Americans understand that species of democratic equality which may be established between the sexes. They admit that as nature has appointed such wide differences between the physical and moral constitution of man and woman, her manifest design was to give a distinct employment to their various faculties; and they hold that improvement does not consist in making beings so dissimilar do pretty nearly the same things, but in causing each of them to fulfill their respective tasks in the best possible manner. The Americans have applied to the sexes the great principle of political economy which governs the manufacturers of our age, by carefully dividing the duties of man from those of woman in order that the great work of society may be the better carried on.

In no country has such constant care been taken as in America to trace two clearly distinct lines of action for the two sexes and to make them keep pace one with the other, but in two pathways that are always different. American women never manage the outward concerns of the family or conduct a business or take a part in political life; nor are they, on the other hand, ever compelled to perform the rough labor of the fields or to make any of those laborious efforts which demand the exertion of physical strength. No families are so poor as to form an exception to this rule. If, on the one hand, an American woman cannot escape from the quiet circle of domestic employments, she is never forced, on the other, to go beyond it. Hence it is that the women of America, who often exhibit a masculine strength of understanding and a manly energy, generally preserve great delicacy of personal appearance and always retain the manners of women although they sometimes show that they have the hearts and minds of men.

Nor have the Americans ever supposed that one consequence of democratic principles is the subversion of marital power or the confusion of the natural authorities in families. They hold that every association must have a head in order to accomplish its object, and that the natural head of the conjugal association is man. They do not therefore deny him the right of directing his partner, and they maintain that in the smaller association of husband and wife as well as in the great social community the object of democracy is to regulate and legalize the powers that are necessary, and not to subvert all power.

This opinion is not peculiar to one sex and contested by the other; I never observed that the women of America consider conjugal authority as a fortunate usurpation of their rights, or that they thought themselves degraded by submitting to it. It appeared to me, on the contrary, that they attach a sort of pride to the voluntary surrender of their own will and make it their boast to bend themselves to the yoke, not to shake it off. Such, at least, is the feeling expressed by the most virtuous of their sex; the others are silent; and in the United States it is not the practice for a guilty wife to clamor for the rights of women while she is trampling on her own holiest duties.

It has often been remarked that in Europe a certain degree of contempt lurks even in the flattery which men lavish upon women; although a European frequently affects to be the slave of woman, it may be seen that he never sincerely thinks her his equal. In the United States men seldom compliment women, but they daily show how much they esteem them. They constantly display an entire confidence in the understanding of a wife and a profound respect for her freedom; they have decided that her mind is just as fitted as that of man to discover the plain truth, and her heart as firm to embrace it; and they have never sought to place her virtue, any more than his, under the shelter of prejudice, ignorance, and fear.

It would seem in Europe, where man so easily submits to the despotic sway of women, that they are nevertheless deprived of some of the greatest attributes of the human species and considered as seductive but imperfect beings, and (what may well provoke astonishment) women ultimately look upon themselves in the same light and almost consider it as a privilege that they are entitled to show themselves futile, feeble, and timid. The women of America claim no such privileges.

Again, it may be said that in our morals we have reserved strange immunities to man, so that there is, as it were, one virtue for his use and another for the guidance of his partner, and that, according to the opinion of the public, the very same act may be punished alternately as a crime or only as a fault. The Americans do not know this iniquitous division of duties and rights; among them the seducer is as much dishonored as his victim.

It is true that the Americans rarely lavish upon women those eager attentions which are commonly paid them in Europe, but their conduct to women always implies that they suppose them to be virtuous and refined; and such is the respect entertained for the moral freedom of the sex that in the presence of a woman the most guarded language is used lest her ear should be offended by an expression. In America a young unmarried woman may alone and without fear undertake a long journey.

The legislators of the United States, who have mitigated almost all the penalties of criminal law, still make rape a capital offense, and no crime is visited with more inexorable severity by public opinion. This may be accounted for; as the Americans can conceive nothing more precious than a woman's honor and nothing which ought so much to be respected as her independence, they hold that no punishment is too severe for the man who deprives her of them against her will. In France, where the same offense is visited with far milder penalties, it is frequently difficult to get a verdict from a jury against the prisoner. Is this a consequence of contempt of decency or contempt of women? I cannot but believe that it is a contempt of both.

Thus the Americans do not think that man and woman have either the duty or the right to perform the same offices, but they show an equal regard for both their respective parts; and though their lot is different, they consider both of them as beings of equal value. They do not give to the courage of woman the same form or the same direction as to that of man, but they never doubt her courage; and if they hold that man and his partner ought not always to exercise their intellect and understanding in the same manner, they at least believe the understanding of the one to be as sound as that of the other, and her intellect to be as clear. Thus, then, while they have allowed the social inferiority of woman to continue, they have done all they could to raise her morally and intellectually to the level of man; and in this respect they appear to me to have excellently understood the true principle of democratic improvement.

As for myself, I do not hesitate to avow that although the women of the United States are confined within the narrow circle of domestic life, and their situation is in some respects one of extreme dependence, I have nowhere seen woman occupying a loftier position; and if I were asked, now that I am drawing to the close of this work, in which I have spoken of so many important things done by the Americans, to what the singular prosperity and growing strength of that people ought mainly to be attributed, I should reply: To the superiority of their women.

Chapter XIII

HOW THE PRINCIPLE OF EQUALITY NATURALLY DIVIDES THE AMERICANS INTO A MULTITUDE OF SMALL PRIVATE CIRCLES

It might be supposed that the final and necessary effect of democratic institutions would be to identify all the members of the community in private as well as in public life and to compel them all to live alike, but this would be to ascribe a very coarse and oppressive form to the equality which originates in democracy. No state of society or laws can render men so much alike but that education, fortune, and tastes will interpose some differences between them; and though different men may sometimes find it their interest to combine for the same purposes, they will never make it their pleasure. They will therefore always tend to evade the provisions of law, whatever they may be; and escaping in some respect from the circle in which the legislator sought to confine them, they will set up, close by the great political community, small private societies, united together by similitude of conditions, habits, and customs.

In the United States the citizens have no sort of pre-eminence over one another; they owe each other no mutual obedience or respect; they all meet for the administration of justice, for the government of the state, and, in general, to treat of the affairs that concern their common welfare; but I never heard that attempts have been made to bring them all to follow the same diversions or to amuse themselves promiscuously in the same places of recreation.

The Americans, who mingle so readily in their political assemblies and courts of justice, are wont carefully to separate into small distinct circles in order to indulge by themselves in the enjoyments of private life. Each of them willingly acknowledges all his fellow citizens as his equals, but will only receive a very limited number of them as his friends or his guests. This appears to me to be very natural. In proportion as the circle of public society is extended, it may be anticipated that the sphere of private intercourse will be contracted; far from supposing that the members of modern society will ultimately live in common, I am afraid they will end by forming only small coteries.

* * *

Chapter XIV

SOME REFLECTIONS ON AMERICAN MANNERS

Nothing seems at first sight less important than the outward form of human actions, yet there is nothing upon which men set more store; they grow used to everything except to living in a society which has not their own manners. The influence of the social and political state of a country upon manners is therefore deserving of its serious examination.

Manners are generally the product of the very basis of character, but they are also sometimes the result of an arbitrary convention between certain men. Thus they are at once natural and acquired.

When some men perceive that they are the foremost persons in society, without contest and without effort, when they are constantly engaged on large objects, leaving the more minute details to others, and when they live in the enjoyment of wealth which they did not amass and do not fear to lose, it may be supposed that they feel a kind of haughty disdain of the petty interests and practical cares of life and that their thoughts assume a natural greatness which their language and their manners denote. In democratic countries manners are generally devoid of dignity because private life is there extremely petty in its character; and they are frequently low because the mind has few opportunities of rising above the engrossing cares of domestic interests.

True dignity in manners consists in always taking one's proper station, neither too high nor too low, and this is as much within the reach of a peasant as of a prince. In democracies all stations appear doubtful; hence it is that the manners of democracies, though often full of arrogance, are commonly wanting in dignity, and, moreover, they are never either well trained or accomplished.

The men who live in democracies are too fluctuating for a certain number of them ever to succeed in laying down a code of good breeding and in forcing people to follow it. Every man therefore behaves after his own fashion, and there is always a certain incoherence in the manners of such times, because they are molded upon the feelings and notions of each individual rather than upon an ideal model proposed for general imitation.

. . .

When the equality of conditions is long established and complete, as all men entertain nearly the same notions and do nearly the same things they do not require to agree, or to copy from one another, in order to speak or act in the same manner; their manners are constantly characterized by a number of lesser diversities, but not by any great differences. They are never perfectly alike because they do not copy from the same pattern; they are never very unlike because their social condition is the same. At first sight a traveler would say that the manners of all Americans are exactly similar; it is only upon close examination that the peculiarities in which they differ may be detected.

. . .

In aristocracies the rules of propriety impose the same demeanor on everyone; they make all the members of the same class appear alike in spite of their private inclinations; they adorn and they conceal the natural man. Among a democratic people manners are neither so tutored nor so uniform, but they are frequently more sincere. They form, as it were, a light and loosely woven veil through which the real feelings and private opinions of each individual are easily discernible. The form and the substance of human actions, therefore, often stand there in closer relation; and if the great picture of human life is less embellished, it is more true. Thus it may be said, in one sense, that the effect of democracy is not exactly to give men any particular manners, but to prevent them from having manners at all.

. . .

Chapter XV

OF THE GRAVITY OF THE AMERICANS, AND WHY IT DOES NOT PREVENT THEM FROM OFTEN DOING INCONSIDERATE THINGS

Men who live in democratic countries do not value the simple, turbulent, or coarse diversions in which the people in aristocratic communities indulge; such diversions are thought by them to be puerile or insipid. Nor have they a greater inclination for the intellectual and refined amusements of the aristocratic classes. They want something productive and substantial in their pleasures; they want to mix actual fruition with their joy.

In aristocratic communities the people readily give themselves up to bursts of tumultuous and boisterous gaiety, which shake off at once the recollection of their privations. The inhabitants of democracies are not fond of being thus violently broken in upon, and they never lose sight of themselves without regret. Instead of these frivolous delights they prefer those more serious and silent amusements which are like business and which do not drive business wholly out of their minds.

An American, instead of going in a leisure hour to dance merrily at some place of public resort, as the fellows of his class continue to do throughout the greater part of Europe, shuts himself up at home to drink. He thus enjoys two pleasures; he can go on thinking of his business and can get drunk decently by his own fireside.

I thought that the English constituted the most serious nation on the face of the earth, but I have since seen the Americans and have changed my opinion. I do not mean to say that temperament has not a great deal to do with the character of the inhabitants of the United States, but I think that their political institutions are a still more influential cause.

I believe the seriousness of the Americans arises partly from their pride. In democratic countries even poor men entertain a lofty notion of their personal importance; they look upon themselves with complacency and are apt to suppose that others are looking at them too. With this disposition, they watch their language and their actions with care and do not lay themselves open so as to betray their deficiencies; to preserve their dignity, they think it necessary to retain their gravity.

But I detect another more deep-seated and powerful cause which instinctively produces among the Americans this astonishing gravity. Under a despotism communities give way at times to bursts of vehement joy, but they are generally gloomy and moody because they are afraid. Under absolute monarchies tempered by the customs and manners of the country, their spirits are often cheerful and even, because, as they have some freedom and a good deal of security, they are exempted from the most important cares of life; but all free nations are serious because their minds are habitually absorbed by the contemplation of some dangerous or difficult purpose. This is more especially the case among those free nations which form democratic communities. Then there is, in all classes, a large number of men constantly occupied with the serious affairs of the government; and those whose thoughts are not engaged in the matters of the commonwealth are wholly engrossed by the acquisition of a private fortune. Among such a people a serious demeanor ceases to be peculiar to certain men and becomes a habit of the nation.

. . .

But it must not be supposed that in the midst of all their toils the people who live in democracies think themselves to be pitied; the contrary is noticed to be the case. No men are fonder of their own condition. Life would have no relish for them if they were delivered from the anxieties which harass them, and they show more attachment to their cares than aristocratic nations to their pleasures.

. . .

Chapter XVI

WHY THE NATIONAL VANITY OF THE AMERICANS IS MORE RESTLESS AND CAPTIOUS THAN THAT OF THE ENGLISH

All free nations are vainglorious, but national pride is not displayed by all in the same manner. The Americans, in their intercourse with strangers, appear impatient of the small censure and insatiable of praise. The most slender eulogy is acceptable to them, the most exalted seldom contents them; they unceasingly harass you to extort praise, and if you resist their entreaties, they fall to praising themselves. It would seem as if, doubting their own merit, they wished to have it constantly exhibited before their eyes. Their vanity is not only greedy, but restless and jealous; it will grant nothing, while it demands everything, but is ready to beg and to quarrel at the same time.

If I say to an American that the country he lives in is a fine one, "Ay," he replies, "there is not its equal in the world." If I applaud the freedom that its inhabitants enjoy, he answers: "Freedom is a fine thing, but few nations are worthy to enjoy it." If I remark on the purity of morals that distinguishes the United States, "I can imagine," says he, "that a stranger, who has witnessed the corruption that prevails in other nations, would be astonished at the difference." At length I leave him to the contemplation of himself; but he returns to the charge and does not desist till he has got me to repeat all I had just been saying. It is impossible to conceive a more troublesome or more garrulous patriotism; it wearies even those who are disposed to respect it.

Such is not the case with the English. An Englishman calmly enjoys the real or imaginary advantages which, in his opinion, his country possesses. If he grants nothing to other nations, neither does he solicit anything for his own. The censure of foreigners does not affect him, and their praise hardly flatters him; his position with regard to the rest of the world is one of disdainful and ignorant reserve: his pride requires no sustenance; it nourishes itself. It is remarkable that two nations so recently sprung from the same stock should be so opposite to each other in their manner of feeling and conversing.

In aristocratic countries the great possess immense privileges, upon which their pride rests without seeking to rely upon the lesser advantages that accrue to them. As these privileges came to them by inheritance, they regard them in some sort as a portion of themselves, or at least as a natural right inherent in their own persons. They therefore entertain a calm sense of their own superiority; they do not dream of vaunting privileges which everyone perceives and no one contests, and these things are not sufficiently new to be made topics of conversation. They stand unmoved in their solitary greatness, well assured that they are seen by all the world without any effort to show themselves off, and that no one will attempt to drive them from that position. When an aristocracy carries on the public affairs, its national pride naturally assumes this reserved, indifferent, and haughty form, which is imitated by all the other classes of the nation.

When, on the contrary, social conditions differ but little, the slightest privileges are of some importance; as every man sees around himself a million people enjoying precisely similar or analogous advantages, his pride becomes craving and jealous, he clings to mere trifles and doggedly defends them. In democracies, as the conditions of life are very fluctuating, men have almost always recently acquired the advantages which they possess; the consequence is that they feel extreme pleasure in exhibiting them, to show others and convince themselves that they really enjoy them. As at any instant these same advantages may be lost, their possessors are constantly on the alert and make a point of showing that they still retain them. Men living in democracies love their country just as they love themselves, and they transfer the habits of their private vanity to their vanity as a nation.

The restless and insatiable vanity of a democratic people originates so entirely in the equality and precariousness of their social condition that the members of the haughtiest nobility display the very same passion in those lesser portions of their existence in which there is anything fluctuating or contested. An aristocratic class always differs greatly from the other classes of the nation, by the extent and perpetuity of its privileges; but it often happens that the only differences between the members who belong to it consist in small, transient advantages, which may any day be lost or acquired. The members of a powerful aristocracy, collected in a capital or a court, have been known to contest with virulence those frivolous privileges which depend on the caprice of fashion or the will of their master. These persons then displayed towards each other precisely the same puerile jealousies that animate the men of democracies, the same eagerness to snatch the smallest advantages which their equals contested, and the same desire to parade ostentatiously those of which they were in possession.

If national pride ever entered into the minds of courtiers, I do not question that they would display it in the same manner as the members of a democratic community.

Chapter XVII

HOW THE ASPECT OF SOCIETY IN THE UNITED STATES IS AT ONCE EXCITED AND MONOTONOUS

It would seem that nothing could be more adapted to stimulate and to feed curiosity than the aspect of the United States. Fortunes, opinions, and laws are there in ceaseless variation; it is as if immutable Nature herself were mutable, such are the changes worked upon her by the hand of man. Yet in the end the spectacle of this excited community becomes monotonous, and after having watched the moving pageant for a time, the spectator is tired of it.

Among aristocratic nations every man is pretty nearly stationary in his own sphere, but men are astonishingly unlike each other; their passions, their notions, their habits, and their tastes are essentially different: nothing changes, but everything differs. In democracies, on the contrary, all men are alike and do things pretty nearly alike. It is true that they are subject to great and frequent vicissitudes, but as the same events of good or adverse fortune are continually recurring, only the name of the actors is changed, the piece is always the same. The aspect of American society is animated because men and things are always changing, but it is monotonous because all these changes are alike.

Men living in democratic times have many passions, but most of their passions either end in the love of riches or proceed from it. The cause of this is not that their souls are narrower, but that the importance of money is really greater at such times. When all the members of a community are independent of or indifferent to each other, the co-operation of each of them can be obtained only by paying for it: this infinitely multiplies the purposes to which wealth may be applied and increases its value. When the reverence that belonged to what is old has vanished, birth, condition, and profession no longer distinguish men, or scarcely distinguish them; hardly anything but money remains to create strongly marked differences between them and to raise some of them above the common level. The distinction originating in wealth is increased by the disappearance or diminution of all other distinctions. Among aristocratic nations money reaches only to a few points on the vast circle of man's desires; in democracies it seems to lead to all.

The love of wealth is therefore to be traced, as either a principal or an accessory motive, at the bottom of all that the Americans do; this gives to all their passions a sort of family likeness and soon renders the survey of them exceedingly wearisome. This perpetual recurrence of the same passion is monotonous; the peculiar methods by which this passion seeks its own gratification are no less so.

· · ·

Chapter XVIII

OF HONOR IN THE UNITED STATES
AND IN DEMOCRATIC COMMUNITIES

．　．　．

Honor is simply that peculiar rule founded upon a peculiar state of society, by the application of which a people or a class allot praise or blame. Nothing is more unproductive to the mind than an abstract idea; I therefore hasten to call in the aid of facts and examples to illustrate my meaning.

I select the most extraordinary kind of honor which has ever been known in the world, and that which we are best acquainted with: namely, aristocratic honor springing out of feudal society. I shall explain it by means of the principle already laid down and explain the principle by means of this illustration.

．　．

The first thing that strikes me is that in the feudal world actions were not always praised or blamed with reference to their intrinsic worth, but were sometimes appreciated exclusively with reference to the person who was the actor or the object of them, which is repugnant to the general conscience of mankind. Thus some of the actions which were indifferent on the part of a man in humble life dishonored a noble; others changed their whole character according as the person aggrieved by them belonged or did not belong to the aristocracy.

When these different notions first arose, the nobility formed a distinct body amid the people, which it command-ed from the inaccessible heights where it was ensconced. To maintain this peculiar position, which constituted its strength, not only did it require political privileges, but it required a standard of right and wrong for its own special use.

That some particular virtue or vice belonged to the nobility rather than to the humble classes, that certain actions were guiltless when they affected the villein which were criminal when they touched the noble, these were often arbitrary matters; but that honor or shame should be attached to a man's actions according to his condition was a result of the internal constitution of an aristocratic community. This has been actually the case in all the countries which have had an aristocracy; as long as a trace of the principle remains, these peculiarities will still exist. To debauch a woman of color scarcely injures the reputation of an American; to marry her dishonors him.

In some cases feudal honor enjoined revenge and stigmatized the forgiveness of insults; in others it imperiously commanded men to conquer their own passions and required forgetfulness of self. It did not make humanity or kindness its law, but it extolled generosity; it set more store on liberality than on benevolence; it allowed men to enrich themselves by gambling or by war, but not by labor; it preferred great crimes to small earnings; cupidity was less distasteful to it than avarice; violence it often sanctioned, but cunning and treachery it invariably reprobated as contemptible.

. . .

Thus it was true, to a certain extent, that the laws of honor were capricious; but these caprices of honor were always confined within certain necessary limits. The peculiar rule which was called honor by our forefathers is so far from being an arbitrary law in my eyes that I would readily engage to ascribe its most incoherent and fantastic injunctions to a small number of fixed and invariable wants inherent in feudal society.

If I were to trace the notion of feudal honor into the domain of politics, I should not find it more difficult to explain its dictates. The state of society and the political institutions of the Middle Ages were such that the supreme power of the nation never governed the community directly. That power did not exist in the eyes of the people: every man looked up to a certain individual whom he was bound to obey; by that intermediate personage he was connected with all the others. Thus, in feudal society, the whole system of the commonwealth rested upon the sentiment of fidelity to the person of the lord; to destroy that sentiment was to fall into anarchy. Fidelity to a political superior was, moreover, a sentiment of which all the members of the aristocracy had constant opportunities of estimating the importance; for every one of them was a vassal as well as a lord and had to command as well as to obey. To remain faithful to the lord, to sacrifice oneself for him if called upon, to share his good or evil fortunes, to stand by him in his undertakings, whatever they might be, such were the first injunctions of feudal honor in relation to the political institutions of those times. The treachery of a vassal was branded with extraordinary severity by public opinion, and a name of peculiar infamy was invented for the offense; it was called *felony*.

On the contrary, few traces are to be found in the Middle Ages of the passion that constituted the life of the nations of antiquity; I mean patriotism. The word itself is not of very ancient date in the language. Feudal institutions concealed the country at large from men's sight and rendered the love of it less necessary. The nation was forgotten in the passions that attached men to persons. Hence it was no part of the strict law of feudal honor to remain faithful to one's country Not indeed that the love of their country did not exist in the hearts of our forefathers, but it constituted a dim and feeble instinct, which has grown more clear and strong in proportion as aristocratic classes have been abolished and the supreme power of the nation centralized.

. . .

Some loose notions of the old aristocratic honor of Europe are still to be found scattered among the opinions of the Americans, but these traditional opinions are few in number, they have but little root in the country and but little power. They are like a religion which has still some temples left standing, though men have ceased to believe in it. But amid these half-obliterated notions of exotic honor some new opinions have sprung up which constitute what may be termed in our days American honor.

I have shown how the Americans are constantly driven to engage in commerce and industry. Their origin, their social condition, their political institutions, and even the region they inhabit urge them irresistibly in this direction. Their present condition, then, is that of an almost exclusively manufacturing and commercial association, placed in the midst of a new and boundless country, which their principal object is to explore for purposes of profit. This is the characteristic that most distinguishes the American people from all others at the present time.

All those quiet virtues that tend to give a regular movement to the community and to encourage business will therefore be held in peculiar honor by that people, and to neglect those virtues will be to incur public contempt. All the more turbulent virtues, which often dazzle, but more frequently disturb society, will, on the contrary, occupy a subordinate rank in the estimation of this same people; they may be neglected without forfeiting the esteem of the community; to acquire them would perhaps be to run a risk of losing it.

The Americans make a no less arbitrary classification of men's vices. There are certain propensities which appear censurable to the general reason and the universal conscience of mankind, but which happen to agree with the peculiar and temporary wants of the American community: these propensities are lightly reproved, sometimes even encouraged; for instance, the love of wealth and the secondary propensities connected with it may be more particularly cited. To clear, to till, and to transform the vast uninhabited continent which is his domain, the American requires the daily support of an energetic passion; that passion can only be the love of wealth; the passion for wealth is therefore not reprobated in America, and, provided it does not go beyond the bounds assigned to it for public security, it is held in honor. The American lauds as a noble and praiseworthy ambition what our own forefathers in the Middle Ages stigmatized as severe cupidity, just as he treats as a blind and barbarous frenzy that ardor of conquest and martial temper which bore them to battle.

In the United States fortunes are lost and regained without difficulty; the country is boundless and its resources inexhaustible. The people have all the wants and cravings of a growing creature; and, whatever be their efforts, they are always surrounded by more than they can appropriate. It is not the ruin of a few individuals, which may be soon repaired, but the inactivity and sloth of the community at large that would be fatal to such a people. Boldness of enterprise is the foremost cause of its rapid progress, its strength, and its greatness. Commercial business is there like a vast lottery, by which a small number of men continually lose, but the state is always a gainer; such a people ought therefore to encourage and do honor to boldness in commercial speculations. But any bold speculation risks the fortune of the speculator and of all those who put their trust in him. The Americans, who make a virtue of commercial temerity, have no right in any case to brand with disgrace those who practice it. Hence arises the strange indulgence that is shown to bankrupts in the United States; their honor does not suffer by such an accident. In this respect the Americans differ, not only from the nations of Europe, but from all the commercial nations of our time; and accordingly they resemble none of them in their position or their wants.

In America all those vices that tend to impair the purity of morals and to destroy the conjugal tie are treated with a degree of severity unknown in the rest of the world. At first sight this seems strangely at variance with the tolerance shown there on other subjects, and one is surprised to meet with a morality so relaxed and also so austere among the selfsame people. But these things are less incoherent than they seem to be. Public opinion in the United States very gently represses that love of wealth which promotes the commercial greatness and the prosperity of the nation, and it especially condemns that laxity of morals which diverts the human mind from the pursuit of well-being and disturbs the internal order of domestic life which is so necessary to success in business. To earn the esteem of their countrymen, the Americans are therefore forced to adapt themselves to orderly habits; and it may be said in this sense that they make it a matter of honor to live chastely.

On one point American honor accords with the notions of honor acknowledged in Europe; it places courage as the highest virtue and treats it as the greatest of the moral necessities of man; but the notion of courage itself assumes a different aspect. In the United States martial valor is but little prized; the courage which is best known and most esteemed is that which emboldens men to brave the dangers of the ocean in order to arrive earlier in port, to support the privations of the wilderness without complaint, and solitude more cruel than privations, the courage which renders them almost insensible to the loss of a fortune laboriously acquired and instantly prompts to fresh exertions to make another. Courage of this kind is peculiarly necessary to the maintenance and prosperity of the American communities, and it is held by them in particular honor and estimation; to betray a want of it is to incur certain disgrace.

I have yet another characteristic point which may serve to place the idea of this chapter in stronger relief. In a democratic society like that of the United States, where fortunes are scanty and insecure, everybody works, and work opens a way to everything; this has changed the point of honor quite around and has turned it against idleness. I have sometimes met in America with young men of wealth, personally disinclined to all laborious exertion, but who had been compelled to embrace a profession. Their disposition and their fortune allowed them to remain without employment; public opinion forbade it, too imperiously to be disobeyed. In the European countries, on the contrary, where aristocracy is still struggling with the flood which overwhelms it, I have often seen men, constantly spurred on by their wants and desires, remain in idleness in order not to lose the esteem of their equals; and I have known them to submit to ennui and privations rather than to work. No one can fail to perceive that these opposite obligations are two different rules of conduct, both nevertheless originating in the notion of honor.

What our forefathers designated as honor absolutely was in reality only one of its forms; they gave a generic name to what was only a species. Honor, therefore, is to be found in democratic as well as in aristocratic ages, but it will not be difficult to show that it assumes a different aspect in the former. Not only are its injunctions different, but we shall shortly see that they are less numerous, less precise, and that its dictates are less rigorously obeyed

The rules of honor will always be less numerous among a people not divided into castes than among any other. If ever any nations are constituted in which it may even be difficult to find any peculiar classes of society, the notion of honor will be confined to a small number of precepts, which will be more and more in accordance with the moral laws adopted by the mass of mankind.

Thus the laws of honor will be less peculiar and less multifarious among a democratic people than in an aristocray. They will also be more obscure, and this is a necessary consequence of what goes before; for as the distinguishing marks of honor are less numerous and less peculiar, it must often be difficult to distinguish them. To this other reasons may be added. Among the aristocratic nations of the Middle Ages generation succeeded generation in vain; each family was like a never dying, ever stationary man, and the state of opinions was hardly more changeable than that of conditions. Everyone then had the same objects always before his eyes, which he contemplated from the same point; his eyes gradually detected the smallest details, and his discernment could not fail to become in the end clear and accurate. Thus not only had the men of feudal times very extraordinary opinions in matters of honor, but each of those opinions was present to their minds under a clear and precise form.

This can never be the case in America, where all men are in constant motion and where society, transformed daily by its own operations, changes its opinions together with its wants. In such a country men have glimpses of the rules of honor, but they seldom have time to fix attention upon them.

. . .

As honor among democratic nations is imperfectly defined, its influence is of course less powerful; for it is difficult to apply with certainty and firmness a law that is not distinctly known. Public opinion, the natural and supreme interpreter of the laws of honor, not clearly discerning to which side censure or approval ought to lean, can only pronounce a hesitating judgment. Sometimes the opinion of the public may contradict itself; more frequently it does not act and lets things pass.

The weakness of the sense of honor in democracies also arises from several other causes. In aristocratic countries the same notions of honor are always entertained by only a few persons, always limited in number, often separated from the rest of their fellow citizens. Honor is easily mingled and identified in their minds with the idea of all that distinguishes their own position; it appears to them as the chief characteristic of their own rank; they apply its different rules with all the warmth of personal interest, and they feel (if I may use the expression) a passion for complying with its dictates.

This truth is extremely obvious in the old black-letter lawbooks on the subject of trial by battle. The nobles in their disputes were bound to use the lance and sword, whereas the illeins among themselves used only sticks, "inasmuch as," to use the words of the old books, "villeins have no honor." This did not mean, as it may be imagined at the present day, that these people were contemptible, but simply that their actions were not to be judged by the same rules that were applied to the actions of the aristocracy.

It is surprising, at first sight, that when the sense of honor is most predominant, its injunctions are usually most strange; so that the further it is removed from common reason, the better it is obeyed; whence it has sometimes been inferred that the laws of honor were strengthened by their own extravagance. The two things, indeed, originate from the same source, but the one is not derived from the other. Honor becomes fantastic in proportion to the peculiarity of the wants that it denotes and the paucity of the men by whom those wants are felt; and it is because it denotes wants of this kind that its influence is great. Thus the notion of honor is not the stronger for being fantastic, but it is fantastic and strong from the selfsame cause.

Further, among aristocratic nations each rank is different, but all ranks are fixed. Every man occupies a place in his own sphere which he cannot relinquish, and he lives there among other men who are bound by the same ties. Among these nations no man can either hope or fear to escape being seen; no man is placed so low but that he has a stage of his own, and none can avoid censure or applause by his obscurity.

In democratic states, on the contrary, where all the members of the community are mingled in the same crowd and in constant agitation, public opinion has no hold on men; they disappear at every instant and elude its power. Consequently the dictates of honor will be there less imperious and less stringent, for honor acts solely for the public eye, differing in this respect from mere virtue, which lives upon itself, contented with its own approval.

. . .

Chapter XIX

WHY SO MANY AMBITIOUS MEN AND SO LITTLE LOFTY AMBITION ARE TO BE FOUND IN THE UNITED STATES

The first thing that strikes a traveler in the United States is the innumerable multitude of those who seek to emerge from their original condition; and the second is the rarity of lofty ambition to be observed in the midst of the universally ambitious stir of society. No Americans are devoid of a yearning desire to rise, but hardly any appear to entertain hopes of great magnitude or to pursue very lofty aims. All are constantly seeking to acquire property, power, and reputation; few contemplate these things upon a great scale; and this is the more surprising as nothing is to be discerned in the manners or laws of America to limit desire or to prevent it from spreading its impulses in every direction. It seems difficult to attribute this singular state of things to the equality of social conditions, for as soon as that same equality was established in France, the flight of ambition became unbounded. Nevertheless, I think that we may find the principal cause of this fact in the social condition and democratic manners of the Americans.

All revolutions enlarge the ambition of men. This is more peculiarly true of those revolutions which overthrow an aristocracy. When the former barriers that kept back the multitude from fame and power are suddenly thrown down, a violent and universal movement takes place towards that eminence so long coveted and at length to be enjoyed. In this first burst of triumph nothing seems impossible to anyone: not only are desires boundless, but the power of satisfying them seems almost boundless too. Amid the general and sudden change of laws and customs, in this vast confusion of all men and all ordinances, the various members of the community rise and sink again with excessive rapidity, and power passes so quickly from hand to hand that none need despair of catching it in turn.

It must be recollected, moreover, that the people who destroy an aristocracy have lived under its laws; they have witnessed its splendor, and they have unconsciously imbibed the feelings and notions which it entertained. Thus, at the moment when an aristocracy is dissolved, its spirit still pervades the mass of the community, and its tendencies are retained long after it has been defeated. Ambition is therefore always extremely great as long as a democratic revolution lasts, and it will remain so for some time after the revolution is consummated.

The recollection of the extraordinary events which men have witnessed is not obliterated from their memory in a day. The passions that a revolution has roused do not disappear at its close. A sense of instability remains in the midst of re-established order; a notion of easy success survives the strange vicissitudes which gave it birth; desires still remain extremely enlarged, while the means of satisfying them are diminished day by day. The taste for large fortunes persists, though large fortunes are rare; and on every side we trace the ravages of inordinate and unsuccessful ambition kindled in hearts which it consumes in secret and in vain.

At length, however, the last vestiges of the struggle are effaced; the remains of aristocracy completely disappear; the great events by which its fall was attended are forgotten; peace succeeds to war, and the sway of order is restored in the new realm; desires are again adapted to the means by which they may be fulfilled; the wants, the opinions, and the feelings of men cohere once more; the level of the community is permanently determined; and democratic society established.

A democratic nation, arrived at this permanent and regular state of things, will present a very different spectacle from that which I have just described, and we may readily conclude that if ambition becomes great while the conditions of society are growing equal, it loses that quality when they have grown so.

As wealth is subdivided and knowledge diffused, no one is entirely destitute of education or of property; the privileges and disqualifications of caste being abolished, and men having shattered the bonds that once held them fixed, the notion of advancement suggests itself to every mind, the desire to rise swells in every heart, and all men want to mount above their station; ambition is the universal feeling.

But if the equality of conditions gives some resources to all the members of the community, it also prevents any of them from having resources of great extent, which necessarily circumscribes their desires within somewhat narrow limits. Thus, among democratic nations, ambition is ardent and continual, but its aim is not habitually lofty; and life is generally spent in eagerly coveting small objects that are within reach.

What chiefly diverts the men of democracies from lofty ambitions is not the scantiness of their fortunes, but the vehemence of the exertions they daily make to improve them. They strain their faculties to the utmost to achieve paltry results, and this cannot fail speedily to limit their range of view and to circumscribe their powers. They might be much poorer and still be greater.

. . .

In a democratic society, as well as elsewhere, there is only a certain number of great fortunes to be made; and as the paths that lead to them are indiscriminately open to all, the progress of all must necessarily be slackened. As the candidates appear to be nearly alike, and as it is difficult to make a selection without infringing the principle of equality, which is the supreme law of democratic societies, the first idea which suggests itself is to make them all advance at the same rate and submit to the same trials. Thus, in proportion as men become more alike and the principle of equality is more peaceably and deeply infused into the institutions and manners of the country, the rules for advancement become more inflexible, advancement itself slower, the difficulty of arriving quickly at a certain height far greater. From hatred of privilege and from the embarrassment of choosing, all men are at last forced, whatever may be their standard, to pass the same ordeal; all are indiscriminately subjected to a multitude of petty preliminary exercises, in which their youth is wasted and their imagination quenched, so that they despair of ever fully attaining what is held out to them; and when at length they are in a condition to perform any extraordinary acts, the taste for such things has forsaken them.

. .

Men living in democracies ultimately discover these things; they find out at last that the laws of their country open a boundless field of action before them, but that no one can hope to hasten across it. Between them and the final object of their desires they perceive a multitude of small intermediate impediments, which must be slowly surmounted; this prospect wearies and discourages their ambition at once. They therefore give up hopes so doubtful and remote, to search nearer to themselves for less lofty and more easy enjoyments. Their horizon is not bounded by the laws, but narrowed by themselves.

I believe that ambitious men in democracies are less engrossed than any others with the interests and the judgment of posterity; the present moment alone engages and absorbs them. They are more apt to complete a number of undertakings with rapidity than to raise lasting monuments of their achievements, and they care much more for success than for fame. What they most ask of men is obedience, what they most covet is empire. Their manners, in almost all cases, have remained below their station; the consequence is that they frequently carry very low tastes into their extraordinary fortunes and that they seem to have acquired the supreme power only to minister to their coarse or paltry pleasures.

I think that in our time it is very necessary to purify, to regulate, and to proportion the feeling of ambition, but that it would be extremely dangerous to seek to impoverish and to repress it overmuch. We should attempt to lay down certain extreme limits which it should never be allowed to outstep; but its range within those established limits should not be too much checked.

I confess that I apprehend much less for democratic society from the boldness than from the mediocrity of desires. What appears to me most to be dreaded is that in the midst of the small, incessant occupations of private life, ambition should lose its vigor and its greatness; that the passions of man should abate, but at the same time be lowered; so that the march of society should every day become more tranquil and less aspiring.

. .

Chapter XX

THE TRADE OF PLACE-HUNTING IN CERTAIN DEMOCRATIC COUNTRIES

In the United States, as soon as a man has acquired some education and pecuniary resources, either he endeavors to get rich by commerce or industry, or he buys land in the uncleared country and turns pioneer. All that he asks of the state is not to be disturbed in his toil and to be secure in his earnings. Among most European nations, when a man begins to feel his strength and to extend his desires, the first thing that occurs to him is to get some public employment. These opposite effects, originating in the same cause, deserve our passing notice.

When public employments are few in number, ill-paid, and precarious, while the different kinds of business are numerous and lucrative, it is to business and not to official duties that the new and eager desires created by the principle of equality turn from every side. But if, while the ranks of society are becoming more equal, the education of the people remains incomplete or their spirit the reverse of bold, if commerce and industry, checked in their growth, afford only slow and arduous means of making a fortune, the various members of the community, despairing of ameliorating their own condition, rush to the head of the state and demand its assistance. To relieve their own necessities at the cost of the public treasury appears to them the easiest and most open, if not the only way of rising above a condition which no longer contents them; place-hunting becomes the most generally followed of all trades.

This must especially be the case in those great centralized

monarchies in which the number of paid offices is immense and the tenure of them tolerably secure, so that no one despairs of obtaining a place and of enjoying it as undisturbedly as a hereditary fortune.

I shall not remark that the universal and inordinate desire for place is a great social evil; that it destroys the spirit of independence in the citizen and diffuses a venal and servile humor throughout the frame of society; that it stifles the manlier virtues; nor shall I be at the pains to demonstrate that this kind of traffic creates only an unproductive activity, which agitates the country without adding to its resources. All these things are obvious. But I would observe that a government that encourages this tendency risks its own tranquillity and places its very existence in great jeopardy.

I am aware that at a time like our own, when the love and respect which formerly clung to authority are seen gradually to decline, it may appear necessary for those in power to lay a closer hold on every man by his own interest, and it may seem convenient to use his own passions to keep him in order and in silence; but this cannot long be so, and what may appear to be a source of strength for a certain time will assuredly become, in the end, a great cause of embarrassment and weakness.

Among democratic nations, as well as elsewhere, the number of official appointments has, in the end, some limits; but among those nations the number of aspirants is unlimited. It perpetually increases, with a gradual and irresistible rise, in proportion as social conditions become more equal, and is checked only by the limits of the population.

Thus, when public employments afford the only outlet for ambition, the government necessarily meets with a permanent opposition at last; for it is tasked to satisfy with limited means unlimited desires. It is very certain that, of all people in the world, the most difficult to restrain and to manage are a people of office-hunters. Whatever endeavors are made by rulers, such a people can never be contented; and it is always to be apprehended that they will ultimately overturn the constitution of the country and change the aspect of the state for the sole purpose of cleaning out the present office-holders.

The sovereigns of the present age, who strive to fix upon themselves alone all those novel desires which are aroused by equality and to satisfy them, will repent in the end, if I am not mistaken, that ever they embarked on this policy. They will one day discover that they have hazarded their own power by making it so necessary, and that the more safe and honest course would have been to teach their subjects the art of providing for themselves.

Chapter XXI

WHY GREAT REVOLUTIONS WILL
BECOME MORE RARE

. . .

Does the equality of social conditions habitually and permanently lead men to revolution? Does that state of society contain some perturbing principle which prevents the community from ever subsiding into calm and disposes the citizens to alter incessantly their laws, their principles, and their manners? I do not believe it; and as the subject is important, I beg for the reader's close attention.

Almost all the revolutions that have changed the aspect of nations have been made to consolidate or to destroy social inequality. Remove the secondary causes that have produced the great convulsions of the world and you will almost always find the principle of inequality at the bottom. Either the poor have attempted to plunder the rich, or the rich to enslave the poor. If, then, a state of society can ever be founded in which every man shall have something to keep and little to take from others, much will have been done for the peace of the world.

I am aware that among a great democratic people there will always be some members of the community in great poverty and others in great opulence; but the poor, instead of forming the immense majority of the nation, as is always the case in aristocratic communities, are comparatively few in number, and the laws do not bind them together by the ties of irremediable and hereditary penury.

The wealthy, on their side, are few and powerless; they

have no privileges that attract public observation; even their wealth, as it is no longer incorporated and bound up with the soil, is impalpable and, as it were, invisible. As there is no longer a race of poor men, so there is no longer a race of rich men; the latter spring up daily from the multitude and relapse into it again. Hence they do not form a distinct class which may be easily marked out and plundered; and, moreover, as they are connected with the mass of their fellow citizens by a thousand secret ties, the people cannot assail them without inflicting an injury upon themselves.

Between these two extremes of democratic communities stands an innumerable multitude of men almost alike, who, without being exactly either rich or poor, possess sufficient property to desire the maintenance of order, yet not enough to excite envy. Such men are the natural enemies of violent commotions; their lack of agitation keeps all beneath them and above them still and secures the balance of the fabric of society.

Not, indeed, that even these men are contented with what they have got or that they feel a natural abhorrence for a revolution in which they might share the spoil without sharing the calamity; on the contrary, they desire, with unexampled ardor, to get rich, but the difficulty is to know from whom riches can be taken. The same state of society that constantly prompts desires, restrains these desires within necessary limits; it gives men more liberty of changing, and less interest in change.

Not only are the men of democracies not naturally desirous of revolutions, but they are afraid of them. All revolutions more or less threaten the tenure of property; but most of those who live in democratic countries are possessed of property; not only do they possess property, but they live in the condition where men set the greatest store upon their property.

If we attentively consider each of the classes of which

society is composed, it is easy to see that the passions created by property are keenest and most tenacious among the middle classes. The poor often care but little for what they possess, because they suffer much more from the want of what they have not than they enjoy the little they have. The rich have many other passions besides that of riches to satisfy; and, besides, the long and arduous enjoyment of a great fortune sometimes makes them in the end insensible to its charms. But the men who have a competency, alike removed from opulence and from penury, attach an enormous value to their possessions. As they are still almost within the reach of poverty, they see its privations near at hand and dread them; between poverty and themselves there is nothing but a scanty fortune, upon which they immediately fix their apprehensions and their hopes. Every day increases the interest they take in it, by the constant cares which it occasions; and they are the more attached to it by their continual exertions to increase the amount. The notion of surrendering the smallest part of it is insupportable to them, and they consider its total loss as the worst of misfortunes.

Now, these eager and apprehensive men of small property constitute the class that is constantly increased by the equality of conditions. Hence in democratic communities the majority of the people do not clearly see what they have to gain by a revolution, but they continually and in a thousand ways feel that they might lose by one.

I have shown, in another part of this work, that the equality of conditions naturally urges men to embark on commercial and industrial pursuits, and that it tends to increase and to distribute real property; I have also pointed out the means by which it inspires every man with an eager and constant desire to increase his welfare. Nothing is more opposed to revolutionary passions than these things. It may happen that the final result of a revolution is favorable to commerce and manufactures; but its first consequence will almost always be the ruin of manufactures and mercantile men, because it must always change at once the general principles of consumption and temporarily upset the existing proportion between supply and demand.

I know of nothing more opposite to revolutionary attitudes than commercial ones. Commerce is naturally adverse to all the violent passions; it loves to temporize, takes delight in compromise, and studiously avoids irritation. It is patient, insinuating, flexible, and never has recourse to extreme measures until obliged by the most absolute necessity. Commerce renders men independent of one another, gives them a lofty notion of their personal importance, leads them to seek to conduct their own affairs, and teaches how to conduct them well; it therefore prepares men for freedom, but preserves them from revolutions.

In a revolution the owners of personal property have more to fear than all others; for, on one hand, their property is often easy to seize, and, on the other, it may totally disappear at any moment—a subject of alarm to which the owners of real property are less exposed, since, although they may lose the income of their estates, they may hope to preserve the land itself through the greatest vicissitudes. Hence the former are much more alarmed at the symptoms of revolutionary commotion than the latter. Thus nations are less disposed to make revolutions in proportion as personal property is augmented and distributed among them and as the number of those possessing it is increased.

Moreover, whatever profession men may embrace and whatever species of property they may possess, one characteristic is common to them all. No one is fully contented with his present fortune; all are perpetually striving, in a thousand ways, to improve it. Consider any one of them at any period of his life and he will be found engaged with some new project for the purpose of increasing what he has. Do not talk to him of the interests and the rights of mankind; this small domestic concern absorbs for the time all his thoughts and inclines him to defer political agitations to some other season. This not only prevents men from making revolutions, but deters men from desiring them. Violent political passions have but little hold on those who have devoted all their faculties to the pursuit of their well-being. The ardor that they display in small matters calms their zeal for momentous undertakings.

From time to time, indeed, enterprising and ambitious men will arise in democratic communities whose unbounded aspirations cannot be contented by following the beaten track. Such men like revolutions and hail their approach; but they have great difficulty in bringing them about unless extraordinary events come to their assistance. No man can struggle with advantage against the spirit of his age and country; and however powerful he may be supposed to be, he will find it difficult to make his contemporaries share in feelings and opinions that are repugnant to all their feelings and desires.

It is a mistake to believe that, when once equality of condition has become the old and uncontested state of society and has imparted its characteristics to the manners of a nation, men will easily allow themselves to be thrust into perilous risks by an imprudent leader or a bold innovator. Not indeed that they will resist him openly, by well-contrived schemes, or even by a premeditated plan of resistance. They will not struggle energetically against him, sometimes they will even applaud him; but they do not follow him. To his vehemence they secretly oppose their inertia, to his revolutionary tendencies their conservative interests, their homely tastes to his adventurous passions, their good sense to the flights of his genius, to his poetry their prose. With immense exertion he raises them for an instant, but they speedily escape from him and fall back, as it were, by their own weight. He strains himself to rouse the indifferent and distracted multitude and finds at last that he is reduced to impotence, not because he is conquered, but because he is alone.

I do not assert that men living in democratic communities are naturally stationary; I think, on the contrary, that a perpetual stir prevails in the bosom of those societies, and that rest is unknown there; but I think that men bestir themselves within certain limits, beyond which they hardly ever go. They are forever varying, altering, and restoring secondary matters; but they carefully abstain from touching what is fundamental. They love change, but they dread revolutions.

Although the Americans are constantly modifying or abrogating some of their laws, they by no means display revolutionary passions. It may be easily seen from the promptitude with which they check and calm themselves when public excitement begins to grow alarming, and at the very moment when passions seem most roused, that they dread a revolution as the worst of misfortunes and that every one of them is inwardly resolved to make great sacrifices to avoid such a catastrophe. In no country in the world is the love of property more active and more anxious than in the United States; nowhere does the majority display less inclination for those principles which threaten to alter, in whatever manner, the laws of property.

I have often remarked, that theories which are of a revolutionary nature, since they cannot be put in practice without a complete and sometimes a sudden change in the state of property and persons, are much less favorably viewed in the United States than in the great monarchical countries of Europe; if some men profess them, the bulk of the people reject them with instinctive abhorrence. I do not hesitate to say that most of the maxims commonly called democratic in France would be proscribed by the democracy of the United States. This may easily be understood: in America men have the opinions and passions of democracy; in Europe we have still the passions and opinions of revolution.

If ever America undergoes great revolutions, they will be brought about by the presence of the black race on the soil of the United States; that is to say, they will owe their origin, not to the equality, but to the inequality of condition.

When social conditions are equal, every man is apt to live apart, centered in himself and forgetful of the public. If the rules of democratic nations were either to neglect to correct this fatal tendency or to encourage it from a notion that it weans men from political passions and thus wards off revolutions, they might eventually produce the evil they seek to avoid, and a time might come when the inordinate passions of a few men, aided by the unintelligent selfishness or the pusillanimity of the greater number, would ultimately compel society to pass through strange vicissitudes. In democratic communities revolutions are seldom desired except by a minority, but a minority may sometimes effect them.

I do not assert that democratic nations are secure from revolutions; I merely say that the state of society in those nations does not lead to revolutions, but rather wards them off. A democratic people left to itself will not easily embark in great hazards; it is only led to revolutions unawares; it may sometimes undergo them, but it does not make them.

. . .

Amid the ruins which surround me shall I dare to say that revolutions are not what I most fear for coming generations? If men continue to shut themselves more closely within the narrow circle of domestic interests and to live on that kind of excitement, it is to be apprehended that they may ultimately become inaccessible to those great and powerful public emotions which perturb nations, but which develop them and recruit them. When property becomes so fluctuating and the love of property so restless and so ardent, I cannot but fear that men may arrive at such a state as to regard every new theory as a peril, every innovation as an irksome toil, every social improvement as a stepping-stone to revolution, and so refuse to move altogether for fear of being moved too far. I dread, and I confess it, lest they should at last so entirely give way to a cowardly love of present enjoyment as to lose sight of the interests of their future selves and those of their descendants and prefer to glide along the easy current of life rather than to make, when it is necessary, a strong and sudden effort to a higher purpose.

It is believed by some that modern society will be always changing its aspect; for myself, I fear that it will ultimately be too invariably fixed in the same institutions, the same prejudices, the same manners, so that mankind will be stopped and circumscribed; that the mind will swing backwards and forwards forever without begetting fresh ideas; that man will waste his strength in bootless and solitary trifling, and, though in continual motion, that humanity will cease to advance.

Chapter XXII

WHY DEMOCRATIC NATIONS NATURALLY DESIRE PEACE, AND DEMOCRATIC ARMIES, WAR

The same interests, the same fears, the same passions that deter democratic nations from revolutions deter them also from war; the spirit of military glory and the spirit of revolution are weakened at the same time and by the same causes. The ever increasing numbers of men of property who are lovers of peace, the growth of personal wealth which war so rapidly consumes, the mildness of manners, the gentleness of heart, those tendencies to pity which are produced by the equality of conditions, that coolness of understanding which renders men comparatively insensible to the violent and poetical excitement of arms, all these causes concur to quench the military spirit. I think it may be admitted as a general and constant rule that among civilized nations the warlike passions will become more rare and less intense in proportion as social conditions are more equal.

War is nevertheless an occurrence to which all nations are subject, democratic nations as well as others. Whatever taste they may have for peace, they must hold themselves in readiness to repel aggression, or, in other words, they must have an army. Fortune, which has conferred so many peculiar benefits upon the inhabitants of the United States, has placed them in the midst of a wilderness, where they have, so to speak, no neighbors; a few thousand soldiers are sufficient for their wants. But this is peculiar to America, not to democracy.

The equality of conditions and the manners as well as the

institutions resulting from it do not exempt a democratic people from the necessity of standing armies, and their armies always exercise a powerful influence over their fate. It is therefore of singular importance to inquire what are the natural propensities of the men of whom these armies are composed.

Among aristocratic nations, especially among those in which birth is the only source of rank, the same inequality exists in the army as in the nation; the officer is noble, the soldier is a serf; the one is naturally called upon to command, the other to obey. In aristocratic armies the private soldier's ambition is therefore circumscribed within very narrow limits. Nor has the ambition of the officer an unlimited range. An aristocratic body not only forms a part of the scale of ranks in the nation, but contains a scale of ranks within itself; the members of whom it is composed are placed one above another in a particular and unvarying manner. Thus one man is born to command of a regiment, another to that of a company. When once they have reached the utmost object of their hopes, they stop of their own accord and remain contented with their lot.

. . .

In democratic armies all the soldiers may become officers, which makes the desire of promotion general and immeasurably extends the bounds of military ambition. The officer, on his part, sees nothing that naturally and necessarily stops him at one grade more than at another; and each grade has immense importance in his eyes because his rank in society almost always depends on his rank in the army. Among democratic nations it often happens that an officer has no property but his pay and no distinction but that of military honors; consequently, as often as his duties change, his fortune changes and he becomes, as it were, a new man. What was only an appendage to his position in aristocratic armies has thus become the main point, the basis of his whole condition.

.   .   .

In democratic armies the desire of advancement is almost universal: it is ardent, tenacious, perpetual; it is strengthened by all other desires and extinguished only with life itself. But it is easy to see that, of all armies in the world, those in which advancement must be slowest in time of peace are the armies of democratic countries. As the number of commissions is naturally limited while the number of competitors is almost unlimited, and as the strict law of equality is over all alike, none can make rapid progress; many can make no progress at all. Thus the desire of advancement is greater and the opportunities of advancement fewer there than elsewhere. All the ambitious spirits of a democratic army are consequently ardently desirous of war, because war makes vacancies and warrants the violation of that law of seniority which is the sole privilege natural to democracy.

.   .   .

Chapter XXIII

WHICH IS THE MOST WARLIKE AND MOST REVOLUTIONARY CLASS IN DEMOCRATIC ARMIES

It is of the essence of a democratic army to be very numerous in proportion to the people to which it belongs, as I shall hereafter show. On the other hand, men living in democratic times seldom choose a military life. Democratic nations are therefore soon led to give up the system of voluntary recruiting for that of compulsory enlistment. The necessity of their social condition compels them to resort to the latter means, and it may easily be foreseen that they will all eventually adopt it.

When military service is compulsory, the burden is indiscriminately and equally borne by the whole community. This is another necessary consequence of the social condition of these nations and of their notions. The government may do almost whatever it pleases, provided it appeals to the whole community at once; it is the unequal distribution of the weight, not the weight itself, that commonly occasions resistance. But as military service is common to all the citizens, the evident consequence is that each of them remains for only a few years on active duty. Thus it is in the nature of things that the soldier in democracies only passes through the army, while among most aristocratic nations the military profession is one which the solider adopts, or which is imposed upon him, for life

This has important consequences. Among the soldiers of a democratic army some acquire a taste for military life; but the majority, being enlisted against their will and ever ready to go back to their homes, do not consider themselves as seriously engaged in the military profession and are always thinking of quitting it. Such men do not contract the wants and only half partake in the passions which that mode of life engenders. They adapt themselves to their military duties, but their minds are still attached to the interests and the duties that engaged them in civil life. They do not therefore imbibe the spirit of the army, or rather they infuse the spirit of the community at large into the army and retain it there. Among democratic nations the private soldiers remain most like civilians; upon them the habits of the nation have the firmest hold and public opinion has most influence. It is through the private soldiers especially that it may be possible to infuse into a democratic army the love of freedom and the respect for rights, if these principles have once been successfully inculcated in the people at large. The reverse happens among aristocratic nations, where the soldiery have eventually nothing in common with their fellow citizens and where they live among them as strangers and often as enemies.

In aristocratic armies the officers are the conservative element, because the officers alone have retained a strict connection with civil society and never forgo their purpose of resuming their place in it sooner or later. In democratic armies the private soldiers stand in this position, and from the same cause.

It often happens, on the contrary, that in these same democratic armies the officers contract tastes and wants wholly distinct from those of the nation, a fact which may be thus accounted for: Among democratic nations the man who becomes an officer severs all the ties that bound him to civil life; he leaves it forever, and no interest urges him to return to it. His true country is the army, since he owes all he has to the rank he has attained in it; he therefore follows the fortunes of the army, rises or sinks with it, and henceforward directs all his hopes to that quarter only. As the wants of an officer are distinct from those of the country, he may, perhaps, ardently desire war, or labor to bring about a revolution, at the very moment when the nation is most desirous of stability and peace.

There are, nevertheless, some causes that allay this restless and warlike spirit. Though ambition is universal and continual among democratic nations, we have seen that it is seldom great. A man who, being born in the lower classes of the community, has risen from the ranks to be an officer has already taken a prodigious step. He has gained a footing in a sphere above that which he filled in civil life, and has acquired rights which most democratic nations will always consider as inalienable. He is willing to pause after so great an effort and to enjoy what he has won. The fear of risking what he has already obtained damps the desire of acquiring what he has not got. Having conquered the first and greatest impediment that opposed his advancement, he resigns himself with less impatience to the slowness of his progress. His ambition will be more and more cooled in proportion as the increasing distinction of his rank teaches him that he has more to put in jeopardy. If I am not mistaken, the least warlike and also the least revolutionary part of a democratic army will always be its chief commanders.

Chapter XXIV

CAUSES WHICH RENDER DEMOCRATIC ARMIES WEAKER THAN OTHER ARMIES AT THE OUTSET OF A CAMPAIGN, AND MORE FORMIDABLE IN PROTRACTED WARFARE

Any army is in danger of being conquered at the outset of a campaign, after a long peace; any army that has long been engaged in warfare has strong chances of victory: this truth is peculiarly applicable to democratic armies. In aristocracies the military profession, being a privileged career, is held in honor even in time of peace. Men of great talents, great attainments, and great ambition embrace it; the army is in all respects on a level with the nation, and frequently above it.

We have seen, on the contrary, that among a democratic people the choicer minds of the nation are gradually drawn away from the military profession, to seek by other paths distinction, power, and especially wealth. After a long peace, and in democratic times the periods of peace are long, the army is always inferior to the country itself. In this state it is called into active service, and until war has altered it, there is danger for the country as well as for the army.

. . .

I am therefore of the opinion that when a democratic people engages in a war after a long peace, it incurs much more risk of defeat than any other nation; but it ought not easily to be cast down by its reverses, for the chances of success for such an army are increased by the duration of the war. When a war has at length, by its long continuance, roused the whole community from their peaceful occupations and ruined their minor undertakings, the same passions that made them attach so much importance to the maintenance of peace will be turned to arms. War, after it has destroyed all modes of speculation, becomes itself the great and sole speculation, to which all the ardent and ambitious desires that equality engenders are exclusively directed. Hence it is that the selfsame democratic nations that are so reluctant to engage in hostilities sometimes perform prodigious achievements when once they have taken the field.

As the war attracts more and more of public attention and is seen to create high reputations and great fortunes in a short space of time, the choicest spirits of the nation enter the military profession; all the enterprising, proud, and martial minds, no longer solely of the aristocracy, but of the whole country, are drawn in this direction. As the number of competitors for military honors is immense, and war drives every man to his proper level, great generals are always sure to spring up. A long war produces upon a democratic army the same effects that a revolution produces upon a people; it breaks through regulations and allows extraordinary men to rise above the common level. Those officers whose bodies and minds have grown old in peace are removed or superannuated, or they die. In their stead a host of young men is pressing on, whose frames are already hardened, whose desires are extended and inflamed by active service. They are bent on advancement at all hazards, and perpetual advancement; they are followed by others with the same passions and desires, and after these are others, yet unlimited by aught but the size of the army. The principle of equality opens the door of ambition to all, and death provides chances for ambition. Death is constantly thinning the ranks, making vacancies, closing and opening the career of arms.

Moreover, there is a secret connection between the military character and the character of democracies, which war brings to light. The men of democracies naturally are passionately eager to acquire what they covet and to enjoy it on easy conditions. They for the most part worship chance and are much less afraid of death than of difficulty. This is the spirit that they bring to commerce and manufactures; and this same spirit, carried with them to the field of battle, induces them willingly to expose their lives in order to secure in a moment the rewards of victory. No kind of greatness is more pleasing to the imagination of a democratic people than military greatness, a greatness of vivid and sudden luster, obtained without toil, by nothing but the risk of life.

. . . .

Chapter XXV

OF DISCIPLINE IN DEMOCRATIC ARMIES

It is a very common opinion, especially in aristocratic countries, that the great social equality which prevails in democracies ultimately renders the private soldier independent of the officer and thus destroys the bond of discipline. This is a mistake, for there are two kinds of discipline, which it is important not to confuse.

When the officer is noble and the soldier a serf, one rich, the other poor, the one educated and strong, the other ignorant and weak, the strictest bond of obedience may easily be established between the two men. The soldier is broken in to military discipline, as it were, before he enters the army; or rather military discipline is nothing but an enhancement of social servitude. In aristocratic armies the soldier will soon become insensible to everything but the orders of his superior officers; he acts without reflection, triumphs without enthusiasm, and dies without complaint. In this state, he is no longer a man, but he is still a most formidable animal trained for war.

A democratic people must despair of ever obtaining from soldiers that blind, minute, submissive, and invariable obedience which an aristocratic people may impose on them without difficulty. The state of society does not prepare them for it, and the nation might be in danger of losing its natural advantages if it sought artificially to acquire advantages of this particular kind. Among democratic communities military discipline ought not to attempt to annihilate the free action of the faculties; all that can be done by discipline is to direct it. The obedience thus inculcated is less exact, but it is more eager and more intelligent. It has its root in the will of him who obeys; it rests not only on his instinct, but on his reason; and consequently it will often spontaneously become more strict as danger requires. The discipline of an aristocratic army is apt to be relaxed in war because that discipline is founded upon habits, and war disturbs those habits. The discipline of a democratic army, on the contrary, is strengthened in sight of the enemy, because every soldier then clearly perceives that he must be silent and obedient in order to conquer

. . .

Chapter XXVI

SOME CONSIDERATIONS ON WAR
IN DEMOCRATIC COMMUNITIES

When the principle of equality is spreading, not only among a single nation, but among several neighboring nations at the same time, as is now the case in Europe, the inhabitants of these different countries, notwithstanding the dissimilarity of language, of customs, and of laws, still resemble each other in their equal dread of war and their common love of peace.

As the spread of equality, taking place in several countries at once, simultaneously impels their various inhabitants to follow manufactures and commerce, not only do their tastes become similar, but their interests are so mixed and entangled with one another that no nation can inflict evils on other nations without those evils falling back upon itself; and all nations ultimately regard war as a calamity almost as severe to the conqueror as to the conquered.

Thus, on the one hand, it is extremely difficult in democratic times to draw nations into hostilities; but, on the other, it is almost impossible that any two of them should go to war without embroiling the rest. The interests of all are so interlaced, their opinions and their wants so much alike, that none can remain quiet when the others stir. Wars therefore become more rare, but when they break out, they spread over a larger field.

. . .

A great aristocratic people cannot either conquer its neighbors or be conquered by them without great difficulty. It cannot conquer them because all its forces can never be collected and held together for a considerable period; it cannot be conquered because an enemy meets at every step small centers of resistance, by which invasion is arrested. War against an aristocracy may be compared to war in a mountainous country; the defeated party has constant opportunities of rallying its forces to make a stand in a new position.

Exactly the reverse occurs among democratic nations: they easily bring their whole disposable force into the field, and when the nation is wealthy and populous it soon becomes victorious; but if it is ever conquered and its territory invaded, it has few resources at command; and if the enemy takes the capital, the nation is lost. This may very well be explained: as each member of the community is individually isolated and extremely powerless, no one of the whole body can either defend himself or present a rallying-point to others. Nothing is strong in a democratic country except the state; as the military strength of the state is destroyed by the destruction of the army, and its civil power paralyzed by the capture of the chief city, all that remains is only a multitude without strength or government, unable to resist the organized power by which it is assailed.

FOURTH BOOK

INFLUENCE OF DEMOCRATIC IDEAS AND FEELINGS ON POLITICAL SOCIETY

I should imperfectly fulfill the purpose of this book if, after having shown what ideas and feelings are suggested by the principle of equality, I did not point out, before I conclude, the general influence that these same ideas and feelings may exercise upon the government of human societies. To succeed in this object I shall frequently have to retrace my steps, but I trust the reader will not refuse to follow me through paths already known to him, which may lead to some new truth.

Chapter I

EQUALITY NATURALLY GIVES MEN A TASTE FOR FREE INSTITUTIONS

The principle of equality, which makes men independent of each other, gives them a habit and a taste for following in their private actions no other guide than their own will. This complete independence, which they constantly enjoy in regard to their equals and in the intercourse of private life, tends to make them look upon all authority with a jealous eye and speedily suggests to them the notion and the love of political freedom. Men living at such times have a natural bias towards free institutions. Take any one of them at a venture and search if you can his most deep-seated instincts, and you will find that, of all governments, he will soonest conceive and most highly value that government whose head he has himself elected and whose administration he may control.

Of all the political effects produced by the equality of conditions, this love of independence is the first to strike the observing and to alarm the timid; nor can it be said that their alarm is wholly misplaced, for anarchy has a more formidable aspect in democratic countries than elsewhere. As the citizens have no direct influence on each other, as soon as the supreme power of the nation fails, which kept them all in their several stations, it would seem that disorder must instantly reach its utmost pitch and that, every man drawing aside in a different direction, the fabric of society must at once crumble away.

I am convinced, however, that anarchy is not the principal evil that democratic ages have to fear, but the least. For the principle of equality begets two tendencies: the one leads men straight to independence and may suddenly drive them into anarchy; the other conducts them by a longer, more secret, but more certain road to servitude. Nations readily discern the former tendency and are prepared to resist it; they are led away by the latter, without perceiving its drift; hence it is peculiarly important to point it out.

Personally, far from finding fault with equality because it inspires a spirit of independence, I praise it primarily for that every reason. I admire it because it lodges in the very depths of each man's mind and heart that indefinable feeling, the instinctive inclination for political independence, and thus prepares the remedy for the ill which it engenders. It is precisely for this reason that I cling to it.

Chapter II

THAT THE OPINIONS OF DEMOCRATIC NATIONS ABOUT GOVERNMENT ARE NATURALLY FAVORABLE TO THE CONCENTRATION OF POWER

The notion of secondary powers placed between the sovereign and his subjects occurred naturally to the imagination of aristocratic nations, because those communities contained individuals or families raised above the common level and apparently destined to command by their birth, their education, and their wealth. This same notion is naturally wanting in the minds of men in democratic ages, for converse reasons; it can only be introduced artificially, it can only be kept there with difficulty, whereas they conceive, as it were without thinking about the subject, the notion of a single and central power which governs the whole community by its direct influence. Moreover, in politics as well as in philosophy and in religion the intellect of democratic nations is peculiarly open to simple and general notions. Complicated systems are repugnant to it, and its favorite conception is that of a great nation composed of citizens all formed upon one pattern and all governed by a single power.

The very next notion to that of a single and central power which presents itself to the minds of men in the ages of equality is the notion of uniformity of legislation. As every man sees that he differs but little from those about him, he cannot understand why a rule that is applicable to one man should not be equally applicable to all others. Hence the slightest privileges are repugnant to his reason; the faintest dissimilarities in the political institutions of the same people offend him, and uniformity of legislation appears to him to be the first condition of good government.

I find, on the contrary, that this notion of a uniform rule equally binding on all the members of the community was almost unknown to the human mind in aristocratic ages; either it was never broached, or it was rejected.

These contrary tendencies of opinion ultimately turn on both sides to such blind instincts and ungovernable habits that they still direct the actions of men, in spite of particular exceptions. Notwithstanding the immense variety of conditions in the Middle Ages, a certain number of persons existed at that period in precisely similar circumstances; but this did not prevent the laws then in force from assigning to each of them distinct duties and different rights. On the contrary, at the present time all the powers of government are exerted to impose the same customs and the same laws on populations which have as yet but few points of resemblance.

As the conditions of men become equal among a people, individuals seem of less and society of greater importance; or rather every citizen, being assimilated to all the rest, is lost in the crowd, and nothing stands conspicuous but the great and imposing image of the people at large. This naturally gives the men of democratic periods a lofty opinion of the privileges of society and a very humble notion of the rights of individuals; they are ready to admit that the interests of the former are everything and those of the latter nothing. They are willing to acknowledge that the power which represents the community has far more information and wisdom than any of the members of that community; and that it is the duty, as well as the right, of that power to guide as well as govern each private citizen.

The Americans hold that in every state the supreme power ought to emanate from the people; but when once that power is constituted, they can conceive, as it were, no limits to it, and they are ready to admit that it has the right to do whatever it pleases. They have not the slightest notion of peculiar privileges granted to cities, families, or persons; their minds appear never to have foreseen that it might be possible not to apply with strict uniformity the same laws to every part of the state and to all its inhabitants.

These same opinions are more and more diffused in Europe; they even insinuate themselves among those nations that most vehemently reject the principle of the sovereignty of the people.

. . .

They are produced by equality, and in turn they hasten the progress of equality.

In France, where the revolution of which I am speaking has gone further than in any other European country, these opinions have got complete hold of the public mind. If we listen attentively to the language of the various parties in France, we find that there is not one which has not adopted them. Most of these parties censure the conduct of the government, but they all hold that the government ought perpetually to act and interfere in everything that is done. Even those which are most at variance are nevertheless agreed on this head. The unity, the ubiquity, the omnipotence of the supreme power, and the uniformity of its rules constitute the principal characteristics of all the political systems that have been put forward in our age. They recur even in the wildest visions of political regeneration; the human mind pursues them in its dreams.

If these notions spontaneously arise in the minds of private individuals, they suggest themselves still more forcibly to the minds of princes. While the ancient fabric of

European society is altered and dissolved, sovereigns acquire new conceptions of their opportunities and their duties; they learn for the first time that the central power which they represent may and ought to administer, by its own agency and on a uniform plan, all the concerns of the whole community

. .

Our contemporaries are therefore much less divided than is commonly supposed: they are constantly disputing as to the hands in which supremacy is to be vested, but they readily agree upon the duties and the rights of that supremacy. The notion they all form of government is that of a sole, simple, providential, and creative power.

Chapter III

THAT THE SENTIMENTS OF DEMOCRATIC NATIONS ACCORD WITH THEIR OPINIONS IN LEADING THEM TO CONCENTRATE POLITICAL POWER

As the men who inhabit democratic countries have no superiors, no inferiors, and no habitual or necessary partners in their undertakings, they readily fall back upon themselves and consider themselves as beings apart. I had occasion to point this out at considerable length in treating of individualism. Hence such men can never, without an effort, tear themselves from their private affairs to engage in public business; their natural bias leads them to abandon the latter to the sole visible and permanent representative of the interests of the community; that is to say, to the state. Not only are they naturally wanting in a taste for public business, but they have frequently no time to attend to it. Private life in democratic times is so busy, so excited, so full of wishes and of work, that hardly any energy or leisure remains to each individual for public life. I am the last man to contend that these propensities are unconquerable, since my chief object in writing this book has been to combat them. I maintain only that at the present day a secret power is fostering them in the human heart, and that if they are not checked, they will wholly overgrow it.

I have also had occasion to show how the increasing love of well-being and the fluctuating character of property cause democratic nations to dread all violent disturbances. The love of public tranquillity is frequently the only passion which these nations retain, and it becomes more active and powerful among them in proportion as all other passions droop and die. This naturally disposes the members of the community constantly to give or to surrender additional rights to the central power, which alone seems to be interested in defending them by the same means that it uses to defend itself.

As in periods of equality no man is compelled to lend his assistance to his fellow men, and none has any right to expect much support from them, everyone is at once independent and powerless. These two conditions, which must never be either separately considered or confounded together, inspire the citizen of a democratic country with very contrary propensities. His independence fills him with self-reliance and pride among his equals; his debility makes him feel from time to time the want of some outward assistance, which he cannot expect from any of them, because they are all impotent and unsympathizing. In this predicament he naturally turns his eyes to that imposing power which alone rises above the level of universal depression. Of that power his wants and especially his desires continually remind him, until he ultimately views it as the sole and necessary support of his own weakness.

. . .

Every central power, which follows its natural tendencies, courts and encourages the principle of equality; for equality singularly facilitates, extends, and secures the influence of a central power.

In like manner it may be said that every central government worships uniformity; uniformity relieves it from inquiry into an infinity of details, which must be attended to if rules have to be adapted to different men, instead of indiscriminately subjecting all men to the same rule. Thus the government likes what the citizens like and naturally hates what they hate. These common sentiments, which in democratic nations constantly unite the sovereign and every member of the community in one and the same conviction, establish a secret and lasting sympathy between them. The faults of the government are pardoned for the sake of its inclinations; public confidence is only reluctantly withdrawn in the midst even of its excesses and its errors, and it is restored at the first call. Democratic nations often hate those in whose hands the central power is vested, but they always love that power itself.

Thus by two separate paths I have reached the same conclusion. I have shown that the principle of equality suggests to men the notion of a sole, uniform, and strong government; I have now shown that the principle of equality imparts to them a taste for it. To governments of this kind the nations of our age are therefore tending. They are drawn thither by the natural inclination of mind and heart; and in order to reach that result, it is enough that they do not check themselves in their course.

I am of the opinion that, in the democratic ages which are opening upon us, individual independence and local liberties will ever be the products of art; that centralization will be the natural government.

Chapter IV

OF CERTAIN PECULIAR AND ACCIDENTAL CAUSES WHICH EITHER LEAD A PEOPLE TO COMPLETE THE CENTRALIZATION OF GOVERNMENT OR DIVERT THEM FROM IT

If all democratic nations are instinctively led to the centralization of government, they tend to this result in an unequal manner. This depends on the particular circumstances which may promote or prevent the natural consequences of that state of society, circumstances which are exceedingly numerous, but of which I shall mention only a few.

Among men who have lived free long before they became equal, the tendencies derived from free institutions combat, to a certain extent, the propensities superinduced by the principle of equality; and although the central power may increase its privileges among such a people, the private members of such a community will never entirely forfeit their independence. But when equality of conditions grows up among a people who have never known or have long ceased to know what freedom is (and such is the case on the continent of Europe), as the former habits of the nation are suddenly combined, by some sort of natural attraction, with the new habits and principles engendered by the state of society, all powers seem spontaneously to rush to the center. These powers accumulate there with astonishing rapidity, and the state instantly attains the utmost limits of its

563

strength, while private persons allow themselves to sink as suddenly to the lowest degree of weakness.

The English who emigrated three hundred years ago to found a democratic commonwealth on the shores of the New World had all learned to take a part in public affairs in their mother country; they were conversant with trial by jury; they were accustomed to liberty of speech and of the press, to personal freedom, to the notion of rights and the practice of asserting them. They carried with them to America these free institutions and manly customs, and these institutions preserved them against the encroachments of the state. Thus among the Americans it is freedom that is old; equality is of comparatively modern date. The reverse is occurring in Europe, where equality, introduced by absolute power and under the rule of kings, was already infused into the habits of nations long before freedom had entered into their thoughts.

I have said that, among democratic nations the notion of government naturally presents itself to the mind under the form of a sole and central power, and that the notion of intermediate powers is not familiar to them. This is peculiarly applicable to the democratic nations which have witnessed the triumph of the principle of equality by means of a violent revolution. As the classes that managed local affairs have been suddenly swept away by the storm, and as the confused mass that remains has as yet neither the organization nor the habits which fit it to assume the administration of these affairs, the state alone seems capable of taking upon itself all the details of government, and centralization becomes, as it were, the unavoidable state of the country.

Napoleon deserves neither praise nor censure for having centered in his own hands almost all the administrative power of France; for after the abrupt disappearance of the nobility and the higher rank of the middle classes, these powers devolved on him of course: it would have been almost as difficult for him to reject as to assume them. But a similar necessity has never been felt by the Americans, who, having passed through no revolution, and having governed themselves from the first, never had to call upon the state to act for a time as their guardian. Thus the progress of centralization among a democratic people depends not only on the progress of equality, but on the manner in which this equality has been established.

At the commencement of a great democratic revolution, when hostilities have but just broken out between the different classes of society, the people endeavor to centralize the public administration in the hands of the government, in order to wrest the management of local affairs from the aristocracy. Towards the close of such a revolution, on the contrary, it is usually the conquered aristocracy that endeavors to make over the management of all affairs to the state, because such an aristocracy dreads the tyranny of a people that has become its equal and not infrequently its master. Thus it is not always the same class of the community that strives to increase the prerogative of the government; but as long as the democratic revolution lasts, there is always one class in the nation, powerful in numbers or in wealth, which is induced, by peculiar passions or interests, to centralize the public administration, independently of that hatred of being governed by one's neighbor which is a general and permanent feeling among democratic nations.

It may be remarked that at the present day the lower orders in England are striving with all their might to destroy local independence and to transfer the administration from all the points of the circumference to the center; whereas the higher classes are endeavoring to retain this adminstration within its ancient boundaries. I venture to predict that a time will come when the very reverse will happen.

These observations explain why the supreme power is

always stronger, and private individuals weaker, among a democratic people that has passed through a long and arduous struggle to reach a state of equality than among a democratic community in which the citizens have been equal from the first. The example of the Americans completely demonstrates the fact. The inhabitants of the United States were never divided by any privileges; they have never known the mutual relation of master and inferior; and as they neither dread nor hate each other, they have never known the necessity of calling in the supreme power to manage their affairs. The lot of the Americans is singular: they have derived from the aristocracy of England the notion of private rights and the taste for local freedom; and they have been able to retain both because they have had no aristocracy to combat.

If education enables men at all times to defend their independence, this is most especially true in democratic times. When all men are alike, it is easy to found a sole and all-powerful government by the aid of mere instinct. But men require much intelligence, knowledge, and art to organize and to maintain secondary powers under similar circumstances and to create, amid the independence and individual weakness of the citizens, such free associations as may be able to struggle against tyranny without destroying public order.

Hence the concentration of power and the subjection of individuals will increase among democratic nations, not only in the same proportion as their equality, but in the same proportion as their ignorance.

. . .

I think that extreme centralization of government ultimately enervates society and thus, after a length of time, weakens the government itself; but I do not deny that a centralized social power may be able to execute great undertakings with facility in a given time and on a particular point. This is more especially true of war, in which success depends much more on the means of transferring all the resources of a nation to one single point than on the extent of those resources. Hence it is chiefly in war that nations desire, and frequently need, to increase the powers of the central government. All men of military genius are fond of centralization, which increases their strength; and all men of centralizing genius are fond of war, which compels nations to combine all their powers in the hands of the government. Thus the democratic tendency that leads men unceasingly to multiply the privileges of the state and to circumscribe the rights of private persons is much more rapid and constant among those democratic nations that are exposed by their position to great and frequent wars than among all others.

I have shown how the dread of disturbance and the love of well-being insensibly lead democratic nations to increase the functions of central government as the only power which appears to be intrinsically sufficiently strong, enlightened, and secure to protest them from anarchy. would now add that all the particular circumstances which tend to make the state of a democratic community agitated and precarious enhance this general propensity and lead private persons more and more to sacrifice their rights to their tranquillity.

. . .

I have already examined several of the incidents that may concur to promote the centralization of power, but the principal cause still remains to be noticed. The foremost of the incidental causes which may draw the management of all affairs into the hands of the ruler in democratic countries is the origin of that ruler himself and his own propensities. Men who live in the ages of equality are naturally fond of central power and are willing to extend its privileges; but if it happens that this same power faithfully represents their own interests and exactly copies their own inclinations, the confidence they place in it knows no bounds, and they think that whatever they bestow upon it is bestowed upon themselves.

. . .

Chapter V

THAT AMONG THE EUROPEAN NATIONS OF OUR TIME THE SOVEREIGN POWER IS INCREASING, ALTHOUGH THE SOVEREIGNS ARE LESS STABLE

On reflecting upon what has already been said, the reader will be startled and alarmed to find that in Europe everything seems to conduce to the indefinite extension of the prerogatives of government and to render every day private independence more weak, more subordinate, and more precarious.

The democratic nations of Europe have all the general and permanent tendencies which urge the Americans to the centralization of government, and they are moreover exposed to a number of secondary and incidental causes with which the Americans are unacquainted. It would seem as if every step they make towards equality brings them nearer to despotism.

And, indeed, if we only look around, we shall be convinced that such is the fact. During the aristocratic ages that preceded the present time, the sovereigns of Europe had been deprived of, or had relinquished, many of the rights inherent in their power. Not a hundred years ago, among the greater part of European nations, numerous private persons and corporations were sufficiently independent to administer justice, to raise and maintain troops, to levy taxes, and frequently even to make or interpret the law. The state has everywhere resumed to itself alone these natural attributes of sovereign power; in all matters of government the state tolerates no intermediate agent between itself and the people, and it directs them by itself in general affairs. I am far from blaming this concentration of power, I simply point it out.

At the same period a great number of secondary powers existed in Europe, which represented local interests and administered local affairs. Most of these local authorities have already disappeared; all are speedily tending to disappear or to fall into the most complete dependence. From one end of Europe to the other the privileges of the nobility, the liberties of cities, and the powers of provincial bodies are either destroyed or are upon the verge of destruction.

In the course of the last half-century Europe has endured many revolutions and counter-revolutions, which have agitated it in opposite directions; but all these perturbations resemble each other in one respect: they have all shaken or destroyed the secondary powers of government. The local privileges which the French did not abolish in the countries they conquered have finally succumbed to the policy of the princes who conquered the French. Those princes rejected all the innovations of the French Revolution except centralization; that is the only principle they consented to receive from such a source.

My object is to remark that all these various rights which have been successively wrested, in our time, from classes, guilds, and individuals have not served to raise new secondary powers on a more democratic basis, but have uniformly been concentrated in the hands of the sovereign. Everywhere the state acquires more and more direct control over the humblest members of the community and a more exclusive power of governing each of them in his smallest concerns.

Almost all the charitable establishments of Europe were

formerly in the hands of private persons or of guilds; they are now almost all dependent on the supreme government, and in many countries are actually administered by that power. The state almost exclusively undertakes to supply bread to the hungry, assistance and shelter to the sick, work to the idle, and to act as the sole reliever of all kinds of misery.

Education, as well as charity, has become in most countries at the present day a national concern. The state receives, and often takes, the child from the arms of the mother to hand it over to official agents; the state undertakes to train the heart and to instruct the mind of each generation. Uniformity prevails in the courses of public instruction as in everything else; diversity as well as freedom is disappearing day by day.

Nor do I hesitate to affirm that among almost all the Christian nations of our days, Catholic as well as Protestant, religion is in danger of falling into the hands of the government. Not that rulers are over-jealous of the right of settling points of doctrine, but they get more and more hold upon the will of those by whom doctrines are expounded; they deprive the clergy of their property and pay them salaries; they divert to their own use the influence of the priesthood, they make them their own ministers, often their own servants, and by this alliance with religion they reach the inner depths of the soul of man.

But this is as yet only one side of the picture. The authority of government has not only spread, as we have just seen, throughout the sphere of all existing powers, till that sphere can no longer contain it, but it goes further and invades the domain heretofore reserved to private independence. A multitude of actions which were formerly entirely beyond the control of the public administration have been subjected to that control in our time, and the number of them is constantly increasing.

Among aristocratic nations the supreme government usually contented itself with managing and superintending the community in whatever directly and ostensibly concerned the national honor, but in all other respects the people were left to work out their own free will. Among these nations the government often seemed to forget that there is a point at which the faults and the sufferings of private persons involved the general prosperity, and that to prevent the ruin of a private individual must sometimes be a matter of public importance.

The democratic nations of our time lean to the opposite extreme It is evident that most of our rulers will not content themselves with governing the people collectively; it would seem as if they thought themselves responsible for the actions and private condition of their subjects, as if they had undertaken to guide and to instruct each of them in the various incidents of life and to secure their happiness quite independently of their own consent. On the other hand, private individuals grow more and more apt to look upon the supreme power in the same light; they invoke its assistance in all their necessities, and they fix their eyes upon the administration as their mentor or their guide.

I assert that there is no country in Europe in which the public administration has not become, not only more centralized, but more inquisitive and more minute; it everywhere interferes in private concerns more than it did; it regulates more undertakings, and undertakings of a lesser kind; and it gains a firmer footing every day about, above, and around all private persons, to assist, to advise, and to coerce them.

Formerly a sovereign lived upon the income of his lands or the revenue of his taxes; this is no longer the case now that his wants have increased as well as his power. Under the same circumstances that formerly compelled a prince to put on a new tax, he now has recourse to a loan. Thus the state gradually becomes the debtor of most of the wealthier members of the community and centralizes the largest amounts of capital in its own hands.

Small capital is drawn into its keeping by another method. As men are intermingled and conditions become more equal, the poor have more resources, more education, and more desires; they conceive the notion of bettering their condition, and this teaches them to save. These savings are daily producing an infinite number of small capitals, the slow and gradual produce of labor, which are always increasing. But the greater part of this money would be unproductive if it remained scattered in the hands of its owners. This circumstance has given rise to a philanthropic institution which will soon become, if I am not mistaken, one of our most important political institutions. Some charitable persons conceived the notion of collecting the savings of the poor and placing them out at interest. In some countries these benevolent associations are still completely distinct from the state; but in almost all they manifestly tend to identify themselves with the government; and in some of them, the government has superseded them, taking upon itself the enormous task of centralizing in one place, and putting out at interest, on its own responsibility, the daily savings of many millions of the working classes.

Thus the state draws to itself the wealth of the rich by loans and has the poor man's mite at its disposal in the savings banks. The wealth of the country is perpetually flowing around the government and passing through its hands; the accumulation increases in the same proportion as the equality of conditions; for in a democratic country the state alone inspires private individuals with confidence, because the state alone appears to be endowed with strength and durability.

Thus the sovereign does not confine himself to the management of the public treasury; he interferes in private money matters; he is the superior, and often the master, of all the members of the community; and in addition to this he assumes the part of their steward and paymaster.

The central power not only fulfills of itself the whole of the duties formerly discharged by various authorities, extending those duties, and surpassing those authorities, but it performs them with more alertness, strength, and independence than it displayed before. All the governments of Europe have, in our time, singularly improved the science of administration: they do more things, and they do everything with more order, more celerity, and at less expense; they seem to be constantly enriched by all the experience of which they have stripped private persons. From day to day, the princes of Europe hold their subordinate offices under stricter control and invent new methods for guiding them more closely and inspecting them with less trouble. Not content with managing everything by their agents, they undertake to manage the conduct of their agents in everything; so that the public administration not only depends upon one and the same power, but it is more and more confined to one spot and concentrated in the same hands. The government centralizes its agency while it increases its prerogative; hence a twofold increase of strength.

In examining the ancient constitution of the judicial power among most European nations, two things strike the mind: the independence of that power and the extent of its functions. Not only did the courts of justice decide almost all differences between private persons, but in very many cases they acted as arbiters between private persons and the state.

I do not here allude to the political and administrative functions that courts of judicature had usurped in some countries, but to the judicial duties common to them all. In most of the countries of Europe there were, and there still are, many private rights, connected for the most part with the general right of property, which stood under the protection of the courts of justice, and which the state could not violate without their sanction. It was this semi-political power that mainly distinguished the European courts of judicature from all others; for all nations have had judges, but all have not invested their judges with the same privileges.

Upon examining what is now occurring among the democratic nations of Europe that are called free, as well as among the others, it will be observed that new and more dependent courts are everywhere springing up by the side of the old ones, for the express purpose of deciding, by an extraordinary jurisdiction, such litigated matters as may rise between the government and private persons. The elder judicial power retains its independence, but its jurisdiction is narrowed; and there is a growing tendency to reduce it to be exclusively the arbiter between private interests.

The number of these special courts of justice is continually increasing, and their functions increase likewise. Thus the government is more and more absolved from the necessity of subjecting its policy and its rights to the sanction of another power. As judges cannot be dispensed with, at least the state is to select them and always to hold them under its control; so that between the government and private individuals they place the effigy of justice rather than justice itself. The state is not satisfied with drawing all concerns to itself, but it acquires an ever increasing power of deciding on them all, without restriction and without appeal.

There exists among the modern nations of Europe one great cause, independent of all those which have already been pointed out, which perpetually contributes to extend the agency or to strengthen the prerogative of the supreme power, though it has not been sufficiently attended to: I mean the growth of manufactures, which is fostered by the progress of social equality. Manufacturers generally collect a multitude of men on the same spot, among whom new and complex relations spring up. These men are exposed by their calling to great and sudden alternations of plenty and want, during which public tranquillity is endangered. It may also happen that these employments sacrifice the health and even the life of those who gain by them or of those who live by them. Thus, the manufacturing classes require more regulation, superintendence, and restraint than the other classes of society, and it is natural that the powers of government should increase in the same proportion as those classes.

This is a truth of general application; what follows more especially concerns the nations of Europe. In the centuries which preceded that in which we live, the aristocracy was in possession of the soil, and was competent to defend it; landed property was therefore surrounded by ample securities, and its possessors enjoyed great independence. This gave rise to laws and customs that have been perpetuated, notwithstanding the subdivision of lands and the ruin of the nobility; and at the present time landowners and agriculturists are still those among the community who most easily escape from the control of the supreme power.

In these same aristocratic ages, in which all the sources of our history are to be traced, personal property was of small importance and those who possessed it were despised and weak. The manufacturing class formed an exception in the midst of those aristocratic communities; as it had no certain patronage, it was not outwardly protected and was often unable to protect itself. Hence a habit sprang up of considering manufacturing property as something of a peculiar nature, not entitled to the same deference and not worthy of the same securities as property in general; and manufacturers were looked upon as a small class in the social hierarchy, whose independence was of small importance and who might with propriety be abandoned to the disciplinary passions of princes. On glancing over the codes of the Middle Ages, one is surprised to see, in those periods of personal independence, with what incessant royal regulations manufactures were hampered, even in their smallest details; on this point centralization was as active and as minute as it can ever be.

Since that time a great revolution has taken place in the world; manufacturing property, which was then only in the germ, has spread till it covers Europe: the manufacturing class has been multiplied and enriched by the remnants of all other ranks; it has grown and is still perpetually growing in number, in importance, in wealth. Almost all those who do not belong to it are connected with it at least on some one point; after having been an exception in society, it threatens to become the chief, if not the only class. Nevertheless, the notions and political habits created by it of old still continue. These notions and habits remain unchanged, because they are old, and also because they happen to be in perfect accordance with the new notions and general habits of our contemporaries.

Manufacturing property, then, does not extend its rights in the same ratio as its importance. The manufacturing classes do not become less dependent while they become more numerous, but, on the contrary, it would seem as if despotism lurked within them and naturally grew with their growth.

As a nation becomes more engaged in manufactures, the lack of roads, canals, harbors, and other works of a semipublic nature, which facilitate the acquisition of wealth, is more strongly felt; and as a nation becomes more democratic, private individuals are less able, and the state more able, to execute works of such magnitude. I do not hesitate to assert that the manifest tendency of all governments at the present time is to take upon themselves alone the execution of these undertakings, by which means they daily hold in closer dependence the population which they govern.

On the other hand, in proportion as the power of a state

increases and its necessities are augmented, the state consumption of manufactured produce is always growing larger; and these commodities are generally made in the arsenals or establishments of the government. Thus in every kingdom the ruler becomes the principal manufacturer: he collects and retains in his service a vast number of engineers, architects, mechanics, and handicraftsmen.

Not only is he the principal manufacturer, but he tends more and more to become the chief, or rather the master, of all other manufacturers. As private persons become powerless by becoming more equal, they can effect nothing in manufactures without combination; but the government naturally seeks to place these combinations under its own control.

It must be admitted that these collective beings, which are called companies, are stronger and more formidable than a private individual can ever be, and that they have less of the responsibility for their own actions; whence it seems reasonable that they should not be allowed to retain so great an independence of the supreme government as might be conceded to a private individual.

Rulers are the more apt to follow this line of policy as their own inclinations invite them to it. Among democratic nations it is only by association that the resistance of the people to the government can ever display itself; hence the latter always looks with ill favor on those associations which are not in its own power; and it is well worthy of remark that among democratic nations the people themselves often entertain against these very associations a secret feeling of fear and jealousy, which prevents the citizens from defending the institutions of which they stand so much in need. The power and the duration of these small private bodies in the midst of the weakness and instability of the whole community astonish and alarm the people, and the free use which each association makes of its natural powers is almost regarded as a dangerous privilege. All the associations that spring up in our age are, moreover, new corporate powers, whose rights have not been sanctioned by time; they come into existence at a time when the notion of private rights is weak and when the power of government is unbounded. Hence it is not surprising that they lose their freedom at their birth.

Among all European nations there are some kinds of associations or companies which cannot be formed until the state has examined their by-laws and authorized their existence. In several others attempts are made to extend this rule to all associations; the consequences of such a policy, if it were successful, may easily be foreseen.

If once the sovereign had a general right of authorizing associations of all kinds upon certain conditions, he would not be long without claiming the right of superintending and managing them, in order to prevent them from departing from the rules laid down by himself. In this manner the state, after having reduced all who are desirous of forming associations into dependence, would proceed to reduce into the same condition all who belong to associations already formed; that is to say, almost all the men who are now in existence.

Governments thus appropriate to themselves and convert to their own purposes the greater part of this new power which manufacturing interests have in our time brought into the world. Manufactures govern us, they govern manufactures.

I attach so much importance to all that I have just been saying that I am tormented by the fear of having impaired my meaning in seeking to render it more clear. If the reader thinks that the examples I have adduced to support my observations are insufficient or ill-chosen, if he imagines that I have anywhere exaggerated the encroachments of the supreme power, and, on the other hand, that I have underrated the extent of the sphere which still remains open to the exertions of individual independence, I entreat him to lay down the book for a moment and to turn his mind to reflect upon the subjects I have attempted to explain. Let him attentively examine what is taking place in France and in other countries, let him inquire of those about him, let him search himself, and I am much mistaken if he does not arrive, without my guidance, and by other paths, at the point to which I have sought to lead him.

He will perceive that, for the last half-century, centralization has everywhere increased in a thousand different ways. Wars, revolutions, conquests, have served to promote it; all men have labored to increase it. In the course of the same period, during which men have succeeded one another with singular rapidity at the head of affairs, their notions, interests, and passions have been infinitely diversified; but all have, by some means or other, sought to centralize. This instinctive centralization has been the only settled point amid the extreme mutability of their lives and their thoughts.

. . .

As long as the democratic revolution was glowing with heat, the men who were bent upon the destruction of old aristocratic powers hostile to that revolution displayed a strong spirit of independence; but as the victory of the principle of equality became more complete, they gradually surrendered themselves to the propensities natural to that condition of equality, and they strengthened and centralized their governments. They had sought to be free in order to make themselves equal; but in proportion as equality was more established by the aid of freedom, freedom itself was thereby rendered more difficult of attainment.

. . .

Chapter VI

WHAT SORT OF DESPOTISM DEMOCRATIC NATIONS HAVE TO FEAR

I had remarked during my stay in the United States that a democratic state of society, similar to that of the Americans, might offer singular facilities for the establishment of despotism; and I perceived, upon my return to Europe, how much use had already been made, by most of our rulers, of the notions, the sentiments, and the wants created by this same social condition, for the purpose of extending the circle of their power. This led me to think that the nations of Christendom would perhaps eventually undergo some oppression like that which hung over several of the nations of the ancient world.

A more accurate examination of the subject, and five years of further meditation, have not diminished my fears, but have changed their object.

No sovereign ever lived in former ages so absolute or so powerful as to undertake to administer by his own agency, and without the assistance of intermediate powers, all the parts of a great empire; none ever attempted to subject all his subjects indiscriminately to strict uniformity of regulation and personally to tutor and direct every member of the community. The notion of such an undertaking never occurred to the human mind; and if any man had conceived it, the want of information, the imperfection of the administrative system, and, above all, the natural obstacles caused by the inequality of conditions would speedily have checked the execution of so vast a design.

When the Roman emperors were at the height of their power, the different nations of the empire still preserved usages and customs of great diversity; although they were subject to the same monarch, most of the provinces were separately administered; they abounded in powerful and active municipalities; and although the whole government of the empire was centered in the hands of the Emperor alone and he always remained, in case of need, the supreme arbiter in all matters, yet the details of social life and private occupations lay for the most part beyond his control . The emperors possessed, it is true, an immense and unchecked power, which allowed them to gratify all their whimsical tastes and to employ for that purpose the whole strength of the state. They frequently abused that power arbitrarily to deprive their subjects of property or of life; their tyranny was extremely onerous to the few, but it did not reach the many; it was confined to some few main objects and neglected the rest; it was violent, but its range was limited.

It would seem that if despotism were to be established among the democratic nations of our days, it might assume a different character; it would be more extensive and more mild; it would degrade men without tormenting them. I do not question that, in an age of instruction and equality like our own, sovereigns might more easily succeed in collecting all political power into their own hands and might interfere more habitually and decidedly with the circle of private interests than any sovereign of antiquity could ever do. But this same principle of equality which facilitates despotism tempers its rigor. We have seen how the customs of society become more humane and gentle in proportion as men become more equal and alike. When no member of the community has much power or much wealth, tyranny is, as it were, without opportunities and a field of action. As all fortunes are scanty, the passions of men are naturally circumscribed, their imagination limited, their pleasures simple. This universal moderation moderates the sovereign himself and checks within certain limits the inordinate stretch of his desires.

Independently of these reasons, drawn from the nature of the state of society itself, I might add many others arising from causes beyond my subject; but I shall keep within the limits I have laid down.

Democratic governments may become violent and even cruel at certain periods of extreme effervescence or of great danger, but these crises will be rare and brief. When I consider the petty passions of our contemporaries, the mildness of their manners, the extent of their education, the purity of their religion, the gentleness of their morality, their regular and industrious habits, and the restraint which they almost all observe in their vices no less than in their virtues, I have no fear that they will meet with tyranny in their rules, but rather with guardians.

I think, then, that the species of oppression by which democratic nations are menaced is unlike anything that ever before existed in the world; our contemporaries will find no prototype of it in their memories. I seek in vain for an expression that will accurately convey the whole of the idea I have formed of it; the old words *despotism* and *tyranny* are inappropriate: the thing itself is new, and since I cannot name, I must attempt to define it.

I seek to trace the novel features under which despotism may appear in the world. The first thing that strikes the observation is an innumerable multitude of men, all equal and alike, incessantly endeavoring to procure the petty and paltry pleasures with which they glut their lives. Each of them, living apart, is as a stranger to the fate of all the rest; his children and his private friends constitute to him the whole of mankind. As for the rest of his fellow citizens, he is close to them, but does not see them; he touches them, but he does not feel them; he exists only in himself and for himself alone; and if his kindred still remain to him, he may be said at any rate to have lost his country.

Above this race of men stands an immense and tutelary power, which takes upon itself alone to secure their gratifications and to watch over their fate. That power is absolute, minute, regular, provident, and mild. It would be like the authority of a parent if, like that authority, its object was to prepare men for manhood; but it seeks, on the contrary, to keep them in perpetual childhood: it is well content that the people should rejoice, provided they think of nothing but rejoicing. For their happiness such a government willingly labors, but it chooses to be the sole agent and the only arbiter of that happiness; it provides for their security, foresees and supplies their necessities, facilitates their pleasures, manages their principal concerns, directs their industry, regulates the descent of property, and subdivides their inheritances: what remains, but to spare them all the care of thinking and all the trouble of living?

Thus it every day renders the exercise of the free agency of man less useful and less frequent; it circumscribes the will within a narrower range and gradually robs a man of all the uses of himself. The principle of equality has prepared men for these things; it has predisposed men to endure them and often to look on them as benefits.

After having thus successively taken each member of the community in its powerful grasp and fashioned him at will, the supreme power then extends its arm over the whole community. It covers the surface of society with a network of small complicated rules, minute and uniform, through which the most original minds and the most energetic characters cannot penetrate, to rise about the crowd. The will of man is not shattered, but softened, bent, and guided; men are seldom forced by it to act, but they are constantly restrained from acting. Such a power does not destroy, but it prevents existence; it does not tyrannize, but it compresses, enervates, extinguishes, and stupefies a people, till each nation is reduced to nothing better than a flock of timid and industrious animals, of which the government is the shepherd.

I have always thought that servitude of the regular, quiet, and gentle kind which I have just described might be combined more easily than is commonly believed with some of the outward forms of freedom, and that it might even establish itself under the wing of the sovereignty of the people.

Our contemporaries are constantly excited by two conflicting passions: they want to be led, and they wish to remain free. As they cannot destroy either the one or the other of these contrary propensities, they strive to satisfy them both at once. They devise a sole, tutelary, and all-powerful form of government, but elected by the people. They combine the principle of centralization and that of popular sovereignty; this gives them a respite: they console themselves for being in tutelage by the reflection that they have chosen their own guardians. Every man allows himself to be put in leading-strings, because he sees that it is not a person or a class of persons, but the people at large who hold the end of his chain.

By this system the people shake off their state of dependence just long enough to select their master and then relapse into it again. A great many persons at the present day are quite contented with this sort of compromise between administrative despotism and the sovereignty of the people; and they think they have done enough for the protection of individual freedom when they have surrendered it to the power of the nation at large. This does not satisfy me: the nature of him I am to obey signifies less to me than the fact of extorted obedience.

I do not deny, however, that a constitution of this kind appears to me to be infinitely preferable to one which, after having concentrated all the powers of government, should vest them in the hands of an irresponsible person or body of persons. Of all the forms that democratic despotism could assume, the latter would assuredly be the worst.

When the sovereign is elective, or narrowly watched by a legislature which is really elective and independent, the oppression that he exercises over individuals is sometimes greater, but it is always less degrading; because every man, when he is oppressed and disarmed, may still imagine that, while he yields obedience, it is to himself he yields it, and that it is to one of his own inclinations that all the rest give way. In like manner, I can understand that when the sovereign represents the nation and is dependent upon the people, the rights and the power of which every citizen is deprived serve not only the head of the state, but the state itself; and that private persons derive some return from the sacrifice of their independence which they have made to the public. To create a representation of the people in every centralized country is, therefore, to diminish the evil that extreme centralization may produce, but not to get rid of it.

I admit that, by this means, room is left for the intervention of individuals in the more important affairs; but it is not the less suppressed in the smaller and more private ones. It must not be forgotten that it is especially dangerous to enslave men in the minor details of life. For my own part, I should be inclined to think freedom less necessary in great things than in little ones, if it were possible to be secure of the one without possessing the other.

Subjection in minor affairs breaks out every day and is felt by the whole community indiscriminately. It does not drive men to resistance, but it crosses them at every turn, till they are led to surrender the exercise of their own will. Thus their spirit is gradually broken and their character enervated; whereas that obedience which is exacted on a few important but rare occasions only exhibits servitude at certain intervals and throws the burden of it upon a small number of men. It is in vain to summon a people who have been rendered so dependent on the central power to choose from time to time the representatives of that power; this rare and brief exercise of their free choice, however important it may be, will not prevent them from gradually losing the faculties of thinking, feeling, and acting for themselves, and thus gradually falling below the level of humanity.

I add that they will soon become incapable of exercising the great and only privilege which remains to them. The democratic nations that have introduced freedom into their political constitution at the very time when they were augmenting the despotism of their administrative constitution have been led into strange paradoxes. To manage those minor affairs in which good sense is all that is wanted, the people are held to be unequal to the task; but when the government of the country is at stake, the people are invested with immense powers; they are alternately made the playthings of their ruler, and his masters, more than kings and less than men. After having exhausted all the different modes of election without finding one to suit their purpose, they are still amazed and still bent on seeking further; as if the evil they notice did not originate in the constitution of the country far more than in that of the electoral body.

It is indeed difficult to conceive how men who have entirely given up the habit of self-government should succeed in making a proper choice of those by whom they are to be governed; and no one will ever believe that a liberal, wise, and energetic government can spring from the suffrages of a subservient people.

A constitution republican in its head and ultra-monarchical in all its other parts has always appeared to me to be a shortlived monster. The vices of rulers and the ineptitude of the people would speedily bring about its ruin; and the nation, weary of its representatives and of itself, would create freer institutions or soon return to stretch itself at the feet of a single master.

Chapter VII

CONTINUATION OF THE
PRECEDING CHAPTERS

I believe that it is easier to establish an absolute and despotic government among a people in which the conditions of society are equal than among any other; and I think that if such a government were once established among such a people, it not only would oppress men, but would eventually strip each of them of several of the highest qualities of humanity. Despotism, therefore, appears to me peculiarly to be dreaded in democratic times. I should have loved freedom, I believe, at all times, but in the time in which we live I am ready to worship it.

On the other hand, I am persuaded that all who attempt, in the ages upon which we are entering, to base freedom upon aristocratic privilege will fail; that all who attempt to draw and to retain authority within a single class will fail. At the present day no ruler is skillful or strong enough to found a despotism by re-establishing permanent distinctions of rank among his subjects; no legislator is wise or powerful enough to preserve free institutions if he does not take equality for his first principle and his watchword. All of our contemporaries who would establish or secure the independence and the dignity of their fellow men must show themselves the friends of equality; and the only worthy means of showing themselves as such is to be so: upon this depends the success of their holy enterprise. Thus the question is not how to reconstruct aristocratic society, but how to make liberty proceed out of that democratic state of society in which God has placed us.

These two truths appear to me simple, clear, and fertile in consequences; and they naturally lead me to consider what kind of free government can be established among a people in which social conditions are equal.

It results from the very constitution of democratic nations and from their necessities that the power of government among them must be more uniform, more centralized, more extensive, more searching, and more efficient than in other countries. Society at large is naturally stronger and more active, the individual more subordinate and weak; the former does more, the latter less; and this is inevitably the case.

It is not, therefore, to be expected that the range of private independence will ever be so extensive in democratic countries; nor is this to be desired; for among aristocratic nations the mass is often sacrificed to the individual, and the prosperity of the greater number to the greatness of the few. It is both necessary and desirable that the government of a democratic people should be active and powerful; and our object should not be to render it weak or indolent, but solely to prevent it from abusing its aptitude and its strength.

The circumstance which most contributed to secure the independence of private persons in aristocratic ages was that the supreme power did not affect to take upon itself alone the government and administration of the community. Those functions were necessarily partially left to the members of the aristocracy; so that, as the supreme power was always divided, it never weighed with its whole weight and in the same manner on each individual.

Not only did the government not perform everything by its immediate agency, but as most of the agents who discharged its duties derived their power, not from the state, but from the circumstance of their birth, they were not perpetually under its control. The government could not make or unmake them in an instant, at pleasure, or bend them in strict uniformity to its slightest caprice; this was an additional guarantee of private independence.

I readily admit that recourse cannot be had to the same means at the present time, but I discover certain democratic expedients that may be substituted for them. Instead of vesting in the government alone all the administrative powers of which guilds and nobles have been deprived, a portion of them may be entrusted to secondary public bodies temporarily composed of private citizens: thus the liberty of private persons will be more secure, and their equality will not be diminished.

The Americans, who care less for words than the French, still designate by the name of County the largest of their administrative districts; but the duties of the count or lord-lieutenant are in part performed by a provincial assembly.

At a period of equality like our own, it would be unjust and unreasonable to institute hereditary officers; but there is nothing to prevent us from substituting elective public officers to a certain extent. Election is a democratic expedient, which ensures the independence of the public officer in relation to the government as much as hereditary rank can ensure it among aristocratic nations, and even more so.

Aristocratic countries abound in wealthy and influential persons who are competent to provide for themselves and who cannot be easily or secretly oppressed; such persons restrain a government within general habits of moderation and reserve. I am well aware that democratic countries contain no such persons naturally, but something analogous to them may be created by artificial means. I firmly believe that an aristocracy cannot again be founded in the world, but I think that private citizens, by combining together, may constitute bodies of great wealth, influence, and strength, corresponding to the persons of an aristocracy. By this means many of the greatest political advantages of aristocracy would be obtained without its injustice or its dangers. An association for political, commercial, or manufacturing purposes, or even for those of science and literature, is a powerful and enlightened member of the community, which cannot be disposed of at pleasure or oppressed without remonstrance, and which, by defending its own rights against the encroachments of the government, saves the common liberties of the country.

In periods of aristocracy every man is always bound so closely to many of his fellow citizens that he cannot be assailed without their coming to his assistance. In ages of equality every man naturally stands alone; he has no hereditary friends whose co-operation he may demand, no class upon whose sympathy he may rely; he is easily got rid of, and he is trampled on with impunity. At the present time an oppressed member of the community has therefore only one method of self-defense: he may appeal to the whole nation, and if the whole nation is deaf to his complaint, he may appeal to mankind. The only means he has of making this appeal is by the press. Thus the liberty of the press is infinitely more valuable among democratic nations than among all others; it is the only cure for the evils that equality may produce. Equality sets men apart and weakens them; but the press places a powerful weapon within every man's reach, which the weakest and loneliest of them all may use. Equality deprives a man of the support of his connections, but the press enables him to summon all his fellow countrymen and all his fellow men to his assistance. Printing has accelerated the progress of equality, and it is also one of its best correctives.

I think that men living in aristocracies may, strictly speaking, do without the liberty of the press; but such is not the case with those who live in democratic countries. To protect their personal independence I do not trust to great political assemblies, to parliamentary privilege, or to the assertion of popular sovereignty. All these things may, to a certain extent, be reconciled with personal servitude. But that servitude cannot be complete if the press is free; the press is the chief democratic instrument of freedom.

Something analogous may be said of the judicial power. It is a part of the essence of judicial power to attend to private interests and to fix itself with predilection on minute objects submitted to its observation. Another essential quality of judicial power is never to volunteer its assistance to the oppressed, but always to be at the disposal of the humblest of those who solicit it; their complaint, however feeble they may themselves be, will force itself upon the ear of justice and claim redress, for this is inherent in the very constitution of courts of justice.

A power of this kind is therefore peculiarly adapted to the wants of freedom, at a time when the eye and finger of the government are constantly intruding into the minutest details of human actions, and when private persons are at once too weak to protect themselves and too much isolated for them to reckon upon the assistance of their fellows. The strength of the courts of law has always been the greatest security that can be offered to personal independence; but this is more especially the case in democratic ages. Private rights and interests are in constant danger if the judicial power does not grow more extensive and stronger to keep pace with the growing equality of conditions.

Equality awakens in men several propensities extremely dangerous to freedom, to which the attention of the legislator ought constantly be directed. I shall only remind the reader of the most important among them.

Men living in democratic ages do not readily comprehend the utility of forms: they feel an instinctive contempt for them, I have elsewhere shown for what reasons. Forms excite their contempt and often their hatred; as they commonly aspire to none but easy and present gratifications, they rush onwards to the object of their desires, and the slightest delay exasperates them. This same temper, carried with them into political life, renders them hostile to forms, which perpetually retard or arrest them in some of their projects.

Yet this objection which the men of democracies make to forms is the very thing which renders forms so useful to freedom; for their chief merit is to serve as a barrier between the strong and the weak, the ruler and the people, to retard the one and give the other time to look about him. Forms become more necessary in proportion as the government becomes more active and more powerful, while private persons are becoming more indolent and more feeble. Thus democratic nations naturally stand more in need of forms than other nations, and they naturally respect them less. This deserves most serious attention.

Nothing is more pitiful than the arrogant disdain of most of our contemporaries for questions of form, for the smallest questions of form have acquired in our time an importance which they never had before; many of the greatest interests of mankind depend upon them. I think that if the statesmen of aristocratic ages could sometimes despise forms with impunity and frequently rise above them, the statesmen to whom the government of nations is now confided ought to treat the very least among them with respect and not neglect them without imperious necessity. In aristocracies the observance of forms was superstitious; among us they ought to be kept up with a deliberate and enlightened deference.

Another tendency which is extremely natural to democratic nations and extremely dangerous is that which leads them to despise and undervalue the rights of private persons. The attachment that men feel to a right and the respect that they display for it are generally proportioned to its importance or to the length of time during which they have enjoyed it. The rights of private persons among democratic nations are commonly of small importance, of recent growth, and extremely precarious; the consequence is that they are often sacrificed without regret and almost always violated without remorse.

But it happens that, at the same period and among the same nations in which men conceive a natural contempt for the rights of private persons, the rights of society at large are naturally extended and consolidated; in other words, men become less attached to private rights just when it is most necessary to retain and defend what little remains of them. It is therefore most especially in the present democratic times, that the true friends of the liberty and the greatness of man ought constantly to be on the alert to prevent the power of government from lightly sacrificing the private rights of individuals to the general execution of its designs. At such times no citizen is so obscure that it is not very dangerous to allow him to be oppressed; no private rights are so unimportant that they can be surrendered with inpunity to the caprices of a government. The reason is plain: if the private right of an individual is violated at a time when the human mind is fully impressed with the importance and the sanctity of such rights, the injury done is confined to the individual whose right is infringed; but to violate such a right at the present day is deeply to corrupt the manners of the nation and to put the whole community in jeopardy, because the very notion of this kind of right constantly tends among us to be impaired and lost.

There are certain habits, certain notions, and certain vices which are peculiar to a state of revolution and which a protracted revolution cannot fail to create and to propagate, whatever, in other respects, are its character, its purpose, and the scene on which it takes place. When any nation has, within a short space of time, repeatedly varied its rulers, its opinions, and its laws, the men of whom it is composed eventually contract a taste for change and grow accustomed to see all changes effected by sudden violence. Thus they naturally conceive a contempt for forms which daily prove ineffectual; and they do not support without impatience the dominion of rules which they have so often seen infringed.

As the ordinary notions of equity and morality no longer suffice to explain and justify all the innovations daily begotten by a revolution, the principle of public utility is called in, the doctrine of political necessity is conjured up, and men accustom themselves to sacrifice private interests without scruple and to trample on the rights of individuals in order more speedily to accomplish any public purpose.

These habits and notions, which I shall call revolutionary because all revolutions produce them, occur in aristocracies just as much as among democratic nations; but among the former they are often less powerful and always less lasting, because there they meet with habits, notions, defects, and impediments that counteract them. They consequently disappear as soon as the revolution is terminated, and the nation reverts to its former political courses. This is not always the case in democratic countries, in which it is ever to be feared that revolutionary tendencies, becoming more gentle and more regular, without entirely disappearing from society, will be gradually transformed into habits of subjection to the administrative authority of the government. I know of no countries in which revolutions are more dangerous than in democratic countries, because, independently of the accidenta and transient evils that must always attend them, they may always create some evils that are permanent and unend ng.

I believe that there are such things as justifiable resistance and legitimate rebellion· I do not therefore assert as an absolute proposition tha the men of democratic ages ought never to make revolut ons; but I think that they have especial reason to hesitate before they embark on them and that it is far better to endure many grievances in their present condition than to have recourse to so perilous a remedy.

I shall conclude with one general idea, which comprises not only all the particular ideas that have been expressed in the present chapter, but also most of those of which it is the object of this book to treat. In the ages of aristocracy which preceded our own, there were private persons of great power and a social authority of extreme weakness. The outline of society itself was not easily discernible and was constantly confounded with the different powers by which the community was ruled. The principal efforts of the men of those times were required to strengthen, aggrandize, and secure the supreme power; and, on the other hand, to circumscribe individual independence within narrower limits and to subject private interests to the interests of the public. Other perils and other cares await the men of our age. Among the greater part of modern nations the government, whatever may be its origin, its constitution, or its name, has become almost omnipotent, and private persons are falling more and more into the lowest stage of weakness and dependence.

In olden society everything was different; unity and uniformity were nowhere to be met with. In modern society everything threatens to become so much alike that the peculiar characteristics of each individual will soon be entirely lost in the general aspect of the world. Our forefathers were always prone to make an improper use of the notion that private rights ought to be respected; and we are naturally prone, on the other hand, to exaggerate the idea that the interest of a private individual ought always to bend to the interest of the many.

The political world is metamorphosed; new remedies must henceforth be sought for new disorders. To lay down extensive but distinct and settled limits to the action of the government; to confer certain rights on private persons, and to secure to them the undisputed enjoyment of those rights; to enable individual man to maintain whatever independence, strength, and original power he still possesses; to raise him by the side of society at large, and uphold him in that position; these appear to me the main objects of legislators in the ages upon which we are now entering.

It would seem as if the rulers of our time sought only to use men in order to make things great; I wish that they would try a little more to make great men; that they would set less value on the work and more upon the workman; that they would never forget that a nation cannot long remain strong when every man belonging to it is individually weak; and that no form or combination of social polity has yet been devised to make an energetic people out of a community of pusillanimous and enfeebled citizens.

I trace among our contemporaries two contrary notions which are equally injurious. One set of men can perceive nothing in the principle of equality but the anarchical tendencies that it engenders; they dread their own free agency, they fear themselves. Other thinkers, less numerous but more enlightened, take a different view: beside that track which starts from the principle of equality to terminate in anarchy, they have at last discovered the road that seems to lead men to inevitable servitude. They shape their souls beforehand to this necessary condition; and, despairing of remaining free, they already do obeisance in their hearts to the master who is soon to appear. The former abandon freedom because they think it dangerous; the latter, because they hold it to be impossible.

If I had entertained the latter conviction, I should not have written this book, but I should have confined myself to deploring in secret the destiny of mankind. I have sought to point out the dangers to which the principle of equality exposes the independence of man, because I firmly believe that these dangers are the most formidable as well as the least foreseen of all those which futurity holds in store, but I do not think that they are insurmountable.

The men who live in the democratic ages upon which we are entering have naturally a taste for independence; they are naturally impatient of regulation, and they are wearied by the permanence even of the condition they themselves prefer. They are fond of power, but they are prone to despise and hate those who wield it, and they easily elude its grasp by their own mobility and insignificance.

These propensities will always manifest themselves, because they originate in the groundwork of society, which will undergo no change; for a long time they will prevent the establishment of any despotism, and they will furnish fresh weapons to each succeeding generation that struggles in favor of the liberty of mankind. Let us, then, look forward to the future with that salutary fear which makes men keep watch and ward for freedom, not with that faint and idle terror which depresses and enervates the heart.

Chapter VII'

GENERAL SURVEY OF THE SUBJECT

Before finally closing the subject that I have now discussed, I should like to take a parting survey of all the different characteristics of modern society and appreciate at last the general influence to be exercised by the principle of equality upon the fate of mankind; but I am stopped by the difficulty of the task, and, in presence of so great a theme, my sight is troubled and my reason fails.

The society of the modern world, which I have sought to delineate and which I seek to judge, has but just come into existence. Time has not yet shaped it into perfect form; the great revolution by which it has been created is not yet over; and amid the occurrences of our time it is almost impossible to discern what will pass away with the revolution itself and what will survive its close. The world that is rising into existence is still half encumbered by the remains of the world that is waning into decay; and amid the vast perplexity of human affairs none can say how much of ancient institutions and former customs will remain or how much will completely disappear.

Although the revolution that is taking place in the social condition, the laws, the opinions, and the feelings of men is still very far from being terminated, yet its results already admit of no comparison with anything that the world has ever before witnessed. I go back from age to age up to the remotest antiquity, but I find no parallel to what is occurring before my eyes; as the past has ceased to throw its light upon the future, the mind of man wanders in obscurity.

Nevertheless, in the midst of a prospect so wide, so novel, and so confused, some of the more prominent characteristics may already be discerned and pointed out. The good things and the evils of life are more equally distributed in the world: great wealth tends to disappear, the number of small fortunes to increase; desires and gratifications are multiplied, but extraordinary prosperity and irremediable penury are alike unknown. The sentiment of ambition is universal, but the scope of ambition is seldom vast. Each individual stands apart in solitary weakness, but society at large is active, provident, and powerful; the performances of private persons are insignificant, those of the state immense.

There is little energy of character, but customs are mild and laws humane. If there are few instances of exalted heroism or of virtues of the highest, brightest, and purest temper, men's habits are regular, violence is rare, and cruelty almost unknown. Human existence becomes longer and property more secure; life is not adorned with brilliant trophies, but it is extremely easy and tranquil. Few pleasures are either very refined or very coarse, and highly polished manners are as uncommon as great brutality of tastes. Neither men of great learning nor extremely ignorant communities are to be met with; genius becomes more rare, information more diffused. The human mind is impelled by the small efforts of all mankind combined together, not by the strenuous activity of a few men. There is less perfection, but more abundance, in all the productions of the arts. The ties of race, of rank, and of country are relaxed; the great bond of humanity is strengthened.

If I endeavor to find out the most general and most prominent of all these different characteristics, I perceive that what is taking place in men's fortunes manifests itself under a thousand other forms. Almost all extremes are softened or blunted: all that was most prominent is superseded by some middle term, at once less lofty and less low, less brilliant and less obscure, than what before existed in the world.

When I survey this countless multitude of beings, shaped in each other's likeness, amid whom nothing rises and nothing falls, the sight of such universal uniformity saddens and chills me and I am tempted to regret that state of society which has ceased to be. When the world was full of men of great importance and extreme insignificance, of great wealth and extreme poverty, of great learning and extreme ignorance, I turned aside from the latter to fix my observation on the former alone, who gratified my sympathies. But I admit that this gratification arose from my own weakness; it is because I am unable to see at once all that is around me that I am allowed thus to select and separate the objects of my predilection from among so many others. Such is not the case with that Almighty and Eternal Being whose gaze necessarily includes the whole of created things and who surveys distinctly, though all at once, mankind and man.

We may naturally believe that it is not the singular prosperity of the few, but the greater well-being of all that is most pleasing in the sight of the Creator and Preserver of men. What appears to me to be man's decline is, to His eye, advancement; what afflicts me is acceptable to Him. A state of equality is perhaps less elevated, but it is more just: and its justice constitutes its greatness and its beauty. I would strive, then, to raise myself to this point of the divine contemplation and thence to view and to judge the concerns of men.

No man on the earth can as yet affirm, absolutely and generally, that the new state of the world is better than its former one; but it is already easy to perceive that this state is different. Some vices and some virtues were so inherent in the constitution of an aristocratic nation and are so opposite to the character of a modern people that they can never be infused into it; some good tendencies and some bad propensities which were unknown to the former are natural to the latter; some ideas suggest themselves spontaneously to the imagination of the one which are utterly repugnant to the mind of the other. They are like two distinct orders of human beings, each of which has its own merits and defects, its own advantages and its own evils. Care must therefore be taken not to judge the state of society that is now coming into existence by notions derived from a state of society that no longer exists; for as these states of society are exceedingly different in their structure, they cannot be submitted to a just or fair comparison. It would be scarcely more reasonable to require of our contemporaries the peculiar virtues which originated in the social condition of their forefathers, since that social condition is itself fallen and has drawn into one promiscuous ruin the good and evil that belonged to it.

But as yet these things are imperfectly understood. I find that a great number of my contemporaries undertake to make a selection from among the institutions, the opinions, and the ideas that originated in the aristocratic constitution of society as it was; a portion of these elements they would willingly relinquish, but they would keep the remainder and transplant them into their new world. I fear that such men are wasting their time and their strength in virtuous but unprofitable efforts. The object is, not to retain the peculiar advantages which the inequality of conditions bestows upon mankind, but to secure the new benefits which equality may supply. We have not to seek to make ourselves like our progenitors but to strive to work out that species of greatness and happiness which is our own.

For myself, who now look back from this extreme limit of my task and discover from afar, but at once, the various objects which have attracted my more attentive investigation upon my way, I am full of apprehensions and of hopes. I perceive mighty dangers which it is possible to ward off, mighty evils which may be avoided or alleviated; and I cling with a firmer hold to the belief that for democratic nations to be virtuous and prosperous, they require but to will it.

I am aware that many of my contemporaries maintain that nations are never their own masters here below, and that they necessarily obey some insurmountable and unintelligent power, arising from anterior events, from their race, or from the soil and climate of their country. Such principles are false and cowardly; such principles can never produce aught but feeble men and pusillanimous nations. Providence has not created mankind entirely independent or entirely free. It is true that around every man a fatal circle is traced beyond which he cannot pass; but within the wide verge of that circle he is powerful and free; as it is with man, so with communities. The nations of our time cannot prevent the conditions of men from becoming equal, but it depends upon themselves whether the principle of equality is to lead them to servitude or freedom, to knowledge or barbarism, to prosperity or wretchedness.

MODERN LIBRARY COLLEGE EDITIONS